Understanding Those Who Create

2nd Edition

Jane Piirto, Ph.D.

Gifted Psychology Press, Inc.
1998

Understanding Those Who Create

Developmental Editor: Linda Senter
Cover Design/Layout: Jacob Lewis
Interior Layout Editor: Spring Winnette
Indexer: Joan Griffits

Published by
Gifted Psychology Press, Inc.
P.O. Box 5057
Scottsdale, AZ 85261

Formerly
Ohio Psychology Press
P.O. Box 90095
Dayton, OH 45490

Printed and bound in the United States of America.
03 02 01 00 99 98   6 5 4 3 2 1

Library of Congress Cataloging-in-Publication Data

Piirto, Jane, 1941-
      Understanding Those Who Create / Jane Piirto. -- 2nd ed.
            p.   cm.
      Includes bibliographical references and index.
      ISBN 0-910707-27-8 (pbk.)
      1. Creative ability. 2. Creative ability--Testing. 3. Creative
      ability--Case studies. 4. Creative ability in children.   I. Title.
BF408.P87   1998
153.3'5--dc21   98-11314
                                                          CIP

ISBN 0-910707-27-8

This book is dedicated to
Pearl Piirto
my creative mother
who taught us to love the arts
to use the public library
to walk in the woods
to value solitude
and to take a sauna whenever possible.

There have appeared, from time to time,
individuals who grew to maturity without losing
the full inventory of their innate, intuitive, and
spontaneously coordinate faculties. These unscathed
individuals inaugurated whole new eras of
physical environmental transformation so important
as, in due course, to affect the lives of all ensuing
humanity . . . such unscathed, comprehensively effective,
and largely unidentified articulators
are the artist-scientists of history.
—Buckminster Fuller

Books by Jane Piirto

mamamama (poetry chapbook)
1979, Sisu Press

Postcards from the Upper Peninsula (poetry chapbook)
1983, Pocasse Press

The Three-Week Trance Diet (novel)
1985, Carpenter Press

Understanding Those Who Create (nonfiction)
1992/1998, Gifted Psychology Press

Talented Children and Adults: Their Development and Education
(textbook) 1994/1999, Macmillan/Merrill

A Location in the Upper Peninsula (essays, poetry, stories)
1995, Sampo Publishers

Between the Memory and the Experience (poetry chapbook)
1996, Sisu Press

My Teeming Brain: Creativity in Creative Writers (nonfiction)
in preparation, Hampton Press

Table of Contents

Preface ....**xv**

  Acknowledgements...xvi

PART I. Definitions and Processes of Creativity.........................**1**

CHAPTER 1—Creativity and Talent Development..........................**5**

The Term *Creativity*...6

  American Usage of the Term "Creative"...8

  Philosophic, Psychoanalytic, and Religious Overtones....................8

Creativity and Psychology 9

  Divergent Production as a Factor of Intellect................................10

  The University of Chicago Studies..11

  Torrance's Tests..12

The Federal Definitions 12

  The Tangling of Giftedness and Creativity.....................................13

  A New School Definition of Giftedness..14

Psychological Research on Creativity 15

  Developmental Psychology..15

    Gruber's Darwin Study 16

    Feldman's Gambit 16

    Erikson's Stages 18

    Csikszentmihalyi's Big C and little c..18

  Social Psychology..18

    Simonton's **Greatness** 19

  Cognitive Psychology 20

    Gardner's Frames 20

    Sternberg's Triarchies and Hierarchies..21

  Educational Psychology 22

  Humanistic Psychology..22

    Dabrowski: Overexcitabilities and Developmental Levels 23

  Psychometric Psychology 25

Why Are We so Interested in Creativity, Anyway? 25

  Reasons of Quantity..25

  Quality as Creativity 26

  Creativity and Nationalism 28

  Creativity and Equity 28

Creativity and the Future 29
Creativity as Human Freedom 30
Can a Person Be Creative Without a Product? 31
Precocity as Predictive 31
Creativity of the Moment and for the Ages 32
Creativity Can Take Place without Mastery 33
The Existence and Development of Talent 34
The Pyramid of Talent Development Model 35
The Pyramid of Talent Development 36
1. The Emotional 36
2. The Cognitive 37
3. Talent in Domains 37
4. Environmental Suns 38
Talent Multipotentiality: Feeling the Call, or the "Thorn" 40
Creativity Is Natural 41
Summary 42
CHAPTER 2—The Creative Process 43
Traditional Theories of the Creative 44
The Visitation of the Muse 44
Common Descriptions of the Creative Process 46
Wallas' Four Stages 46
The Work of Brewster Ghiselin 46
Flow 49
The Importance of Rituals 53
Illuminations and Aha!s 53
Newer Theories of the Creative Process 54
Right/Left Brain and the Creative Process 55
Substances and the Creative Process 56
Natural Highs 58
The Need for Solitude 58
Visualization, Imagery, and New Age Creativity 61
Meditation 62
Creative Imagery and Athletics 64
Creativity as the Process of a Life 65
Transpersonal and Ecosychology: Creation of a New Earth
Peace 65
Improvisation and an Attitude of Playfulness 70
The Creative Process as Cognitive Science 70

Perkins' **The Mind's Best Work** 71
The Creative Problem Solving Process (CPS) 74
Summary 75

PART II. CreativityAssessment and Training 77
CHAPTER 3 —Creativity Testing 81
Testing for Creativity 87
   Two Schools of Thought...87
Validity 88
   Content/Construct Validity..88
   Criterion Validity...90
      Predictive Validity of Creativity Tests 90
   The Threshold Theory..91
   Concurrent Validity of Creativity Tests 91
Reliability...93
   Reliability in Administering Tests 94
   Reliability in Scoring 94
Studies of Significant Results..96
   A Flawed Study of Creative Adolescents....................................97
   Transfer 98
   The Normal Curve Assumption..98
Summary 99
CHAPTER 4—Questionnaires, Checklists, Promising Practices,
          and Creativity Training 101
Using Personality Questionnaires..101
   The Dabrowski Theory and the Overexcitabilities Questionnaire...102
      The Need for Qualitative Assessment 108
   The Myers-Briggs Type Indicator..108
   The Adjective Check List 109
   Cattell High School Personality Questionnaire (HSPQ) 111
Personality and Behavioral Checklists 113
   MMY Reviews of Williams CAP 113
   MMY Reviews of Renzulli-Hartman Scales 114
   GIFT, GIFFI, PRIDE...116
Promising Practices...117
   Performance Assessment 117
Creativity Training 119
   An Example of Divergent Production Training...........................119

Creativity Training in College Courses 121
 Creativity Studies Project...122
Creativity Training in the Schools...124
Creativity Training as Differentiation for the Talented 128
Creativity Training Is Fun...129
Teachers Get More Empathy with Creativity Training 129
Summary 130

PART III. Personality and Intellectual Characteristics of
    Creative People in Various Domains...........................131
Predictive Behaviors and Crystallizing Experiences............................134

CHAPTER 5—Visual Artists and Architects 135
Spatial Intelligence...136
Predictive Behaviors for Visual Arts Talent.....................................136
Problem-Finding and Visual Artists 138
 Characteristics of Arts Students...138
 Artists' Personalities 140
 Differences among Artists According to Specialty 142
 The Successful, High Achieving Artists.......................................142
 The Classic Experiment re Problem-Finding in Artists 144
 The Importance of Luck and Other Social Factors for Success....145
Other Studies of Visual Artists 148
 Roe's Findings...149
 Barron Finds Gentleman Pirates 149
 The MBTI Shows N and F 152
 Goertzel, Goertzel, Goertzel and 700 Famous People...................154
 Having a Supportive Husband Helps...155
 Sculptors Show Commitment 156
Recent Research...159
 Pablo Picasso Was Influenced by an Earthquake 159
 Gardner's Case Study of Picasso 160
 Cross-Fertilization and Cross-Cultural Influences among Artists.162
Architects 162
 Frank Lloyd Wright 166
Summary 170

CHAPTER 6—Creative Writers **171**
Themes under the Sun of *Home* 174
Themes under the Sun of *Community and Culture* 174
Themes under the Sun of *School* 175
Themes under the Sun of *Chance* 175
Themes under the Sun of *Gender* 175
Barron's and Other Studies of Creative Writers.................176
Creative Writers and Deviance 183
The Myers-Briggs and Writers 186
The Biographical Approaches 186
Midcentury Writers: The Academicians 189
Midcentury Writers: The Beats..191
Midcentury Writers: The Women 193
Writers and Depression...194
A Sense of Humor 200
Summary 202

CHAPTER 7—Creative Writers: Children with Extraordinary
               Writing Talent **203**
Qualities Found in the Writing of Children Who Display
   Extraordinary Talent 206
      Ripples of Liquid Caterpillars....................................207
      Star Poem 207
      Expression...208
      Sin-Eater...208
      Colorful Wildlife...209
Prose Talent..209
      The Dog Who Stayed with Me 210
      Philosophy...213
      Music...213
      Lyrics...213
      Bugs...214
Predictive Behaviors in Children with Writing Talent 214
Famous Writers as Children 217
      George Eliot 217
      Stephen Crane 217
      Jane Austen 218
      Sinclair Lewis 218
      Dylan Thomas..219

Thomas Wolfe 219
Virginia Woolf 219
Tennessee Williams 220
The Brontë Family 220
Harry Crews 220
John Updike and C.S. Lewis 221
Graham Greene 222
Summary 224

CHAPTER 8—Creative Scientists, Mathematicians, Inventors,
       and Entrepreneurs 225
Predictive Behaviors for Science and Mathematics 227
   Intelligence of Scientists and Mathematicians 230
   Gruber on Darwin 232
   Simonton's Historiometric Studies 235
Family and Educational Factors 238
The Influence of the Zeitgeist 242
Studies of Mathematicians 244
   Helson's Study of Creative Female Mathematicians 244
   The SMPY Studies and the Iowa Studies 247
   Insight in Mathematicians and Scientists 248
Inventors 250
Entrepreneurs 252
   J. Paul Getty, Warren Buffett, and Bill Gates 256
Summary 261

CHAPTER 9—Musicians, Conductors, and Composers 263
Predictive Behaviors for Musical Talent 264
   Standardized Tests 266
   Developmental Research 266
   Choosing a Career in Music 267
Personality Attributes of Musicians 268
   Personalities of Composers 271
      Shyness 271
   Attributes Necessary for Conductors 272
Intelligence of Musicians 276
Development of Talent in the Domain of Music 277
Sosniak's Study of Concert Pianists 277
   Stage One: The Early Years of Talent Development
      in Music 278

Stage Two: The Middle Years of Talent Development
in Music 279
Stage Three: The Musician as Adult 279
Biographical Studies 282
Simonton's Studies of Composers 283
Life at Juilliard 283
Folk and Popular Musicians 285
The Influence of African Americans on Contemporary Music.....286
Improvisation and Creativity 290
Why Are there so Few Women Composers? 294
Marilyn Shrude 295
Summary 300

CHAPTER 10—Physical Performers: Actors, Dancers, and Athletes..301
Performers 302
Predictive Behaviors for Acting 305
Actors on Acting 313
Laurence Olivier 313
Michael Redgrave 313
Stella Adler 314
Judith Malina 314
Peter Brook 315
Jeff Corey 317
Psychological and Biographical Studies of Actors 318
Dancers 320
The Aesthetics of Dance 321
Biographies and Memoirs of Dancers 323
Suzanne Farrell 324
Gelsey Kirkland 327
Alvin Ailey 329
Physical Repercussions 331
Personality Studies of Dancers and Athletes 333
Gifted and Tolerated 333
Androgyny in Athletes 334
Barron's Study of Dancers 335
Summary 337

Stage Two: The Middle Years of Talent Development
    in Music 279
Stage Three: The Musician as Adult 279
Biographical Studies 282
Simonton's Studies of Composers 283
Life at Juilliard...283
Folk and Popular Musicians 285
The Influence of African Americans on Contemporary Music.....286
Improvisation and Creativity 290
Why Are there so Few Women Composers?...........................294
Marilyn Shrude 295
Summary 300

CHAPTER 10—Physical Performers:Actors, Dancers, and Athletes..301
Performers..302
Predictive Behaviors for Acting 305
Actors on Acting...313
Laurence Olivier 313
Michael Redgrave 313
Stella Adler 314
Judith Malina...314
Peter Brook 315
Jeff Corey 317
Psychological and Biographical Studies of Actors 318
Dancers..320
The Aesthetics of Dance 321
Biographies and Memoirs of Dancers 323
Suzanne Farrell 324
Gelsey Kirkland 327
Alvin Ailey...329
Physical Repercussions 331
Personality Studies of Dancers and Athletes...............................333
Gifted and Tolerated 333
Androgyny in Athletes..334
Barron's Study of Dancers...335
Summary 337

PART IV. How to Enhance Creativity..**339**

**CHAPTER 11—Encouraging Creativity: Motivation
                    and Schooling**..**341**

What Creative Writers Said about Their Schooling..........................342
Motivating Creative Behavior 348
    Strong Emotion as a Motivator...348
    Close Your Eyes...350
    Escaping and Getting the Giggles...352
    Creativity as Spontaneous Adventures 353
Intrinsic Motivation for Creativity..354
    Rewards..355
Summary 356

**CHAPTER 12—How Parents and Teachers Can Enhance
                    Creativity in Children** **357**

1. Provide a Private Place for Creative Work To Be Done 357
2. Provide Materials (e.g., Musical Instruments, Sketchbooks)........359
3. Encourage and Display the Child's Creative Work, but Avoid
     Overly Evaluating It..361
4. Do Your Own Creative Work, and Let the Child See You
     Doing It 364
5. Set a Creative Tone 366
6. Value the Creative Work of Others 368
7. What Is Your Family Mythology? 369
8. Avoid Emphasizing Sex-role Stereotypes 371
9. Provide Private Lessons and Special Classes...............................373
10. If Hardship Comes into Your Life, Use It Positively to Teach
     the Child Expression Through Metaphor 376
11. Emphasize that Talent is Only a Small Part of Creative
     Production, and that Discipline and Practice Are Important 379
12. Allow the Child to be "Odd;" Avoid Emphasizing
     Socialization at the Expense of Creative Expression 381
13. Develop a Creative Style: Use Kind Humor and Get
     Creativity Training..383
        A Typical Creativity Course..385
Summary 386

APPENDIX A—Creativity Theory..387

APPENDIX B—Focus Questions for Teachers Who Use
                Understanding Those Who Create.......................395

References...403

About the Author...445

Figures and Tables
  FIGURE 1. The Pyramid of Talent Development 36
  TABLE 1. Overexcitability Questionnaire..104
  TABLE 2. An Exercise in Divergent Production..................................120
  TABLE 3. A Sampling of Creativity Training Programs 124
  TABLE 4. Poets & Writers with Depression or Manic-Depression 196
  TABLE 5. Myers-Briggs Type Indicator Preferences of
                Entrepreneurs and Managers 254
  TABLE 6. Kough's List of Characteristics of Dramatic Talent
                in Young Children...306

APPENDIX A.—Repertoire Theory 387

APPENDIX B.—Options/Actions for Teachers Who Are
Understanding Three Who Create 395

References 403

About the Author 415

Figures and Tables

Figure 1.   The Pyramid of Talent Development 60
Figure 2.   Overexcitability Questionnaire ....
Figure 3.   Exercise in Divergent Production 120
Figure 4.   A Sampling of Creativity Training Programs ....
Figure 5.   People Writers with Depression or Manic-Depression ....
Figure 6.   Myers-Briggs Type Indicator Preference of
            Entrepreneurs and Managers ....

Table 1a.   Rough Trait Characteristics of Dramatic Talent
            in Young Children ....

Preface to the Second Edition

The journey of this book began at Tony Packo's ribs restaurant in Toledo, Ohio, in 1990. Waiting in line for a table, I got to talking with Dr. James Webb, who had just purchased Ohio Psychology Press (now Gifted Psychology Press). "What you need," I told him, "is a good book on creativity. The field needs a new book."

"Hmm," he said. "Want to write it?"

He sent me the prospectus and I filled it out. For over a year I read and wrote and thought. The first edition of this book came out in April, 1992. I invited all my friends to a book party. Little did I know it would go into a second edition. But here it is. Perhaps I'll have another party.

My life has changed since the first edition came out. I have had a chance to talk about my work on creativity at many conferences and in many classrooms. Among my favorite places were the Art Quilters League meeting held in an old monastery, the trip to the Frank Lloyd Wright signature home in Iowa, and the opportunity to teach in Finland at the University of Tampere at Hameenlinna Summer University.

The first edition of *Understanding Those Who Create* has also led to many writing opportunities. The first of these was my textbook for Merrill/ Prentice Hall, *Talented Children and Adults: Their Development and Education*, published in 1994. After that, I explored my own creativity in an essay, part of a collection of my stories, poems and essays called *A Location In the Upper Peninsula*. As my search for inner truth grows, my poetry and fiction writing continue; I am expanding Chapter 6, which is about creative writers, into book length. Amazingly, the fountain sprung from the book you are about to read has not yet gone dry, and the muse continues to visit.

All this writing and reading has informed my thinking about this revision. The patterns, even archetypes, that I was surprised to uncover in the lives of creators in various domains have been affirmed and reaffirmed by hundreds of biographical studies done by my graduate and undergraduate students as assignments in creativity courses I teach. Now when I read a biography of a scientist, a writer, a visual artist, a rock musician, I am barely surprised at the turns their lives have taken, the paths that led them to enough eminence to be worthy of a biographical study. Tentative steps taken toward theorizing about these patterns in the first edition of this book have this time led me to be more sure-footed. As I added architects, entrepreneurs, and athletes to this edition,

I read more biographies and tried to relate them to each other in meaningful ways. Perhaps the patterns I have uncovered will lend those of us who work with children, and who parent children, some grace in helping them along the paths to their fulfillment, as we try to understand those who create.

New features in this edition include the following. In Chapter 1, I have focused on talent development and on my Pyramid of Talent Development. In Chapter 2, I have added more examples of what I call "non-linear" examples of the creative process. Chapters 3 and 4, on tests and assessment, have been reorganized to focus more on new ways of assessment and creativity training. In Chapter 5, a section about architects has been added, as well as new work on visual artists. Chapter 6, on creative writers, is much the same, but includes new work on the psychology of creative writing. Chapter 7, on young creative writers, is relatively unchanged, with some new biographies and student writings. In Chapter 8, on scientists and mathematicians, I have added information on inventors and entrepreneurs. Chapter 9 includes a discussion of popular, jazz, and African American musicians as well as conductors. Chapter 10 has refocused on physical performers, including actors, dancers, and athletes. Chapter 11 is much the same as it was in the first edition, still focusing on what writers said about school and the motivation for creativity. Chapter 12, which contains twelve suggestions for teachers and parents on how to enhance creativity in children, also contains suggestions for direct teaching gathered from my own teaching practice. Appendix B has been added. Since this book has been used in college classrooms, I have included the focus questions I use in my classes. Students engaging these questions have produced many spectacular stories over the years, and as their teacher I have taken great joy in discovering my students through their stories in answer to the questions.

Acknowledgements

Thanks to kind reviewers of the first edition—book editor George Myers of the Columbus (Ohio) *Dispatch*, who featured it on the Sunday Arts page—also Scott Hunsaker, Joan Smutney, and Russell Eisenman. Thanks to researchers who called me and wrote me and mentioned my work in their articles and books. Thanks to parents and teachers who wrote, called, and E-mailed me. For thoughts and long conversations on creativity, thanks to David Henry Feldman, Mark Runco, Bonnie Cramond, Jeannie Goertz, Ellen Fiedler, Diane Montgomery, Kari Uusikylä, Rena Subotnik, Barbara Kerr, Barry Grant, Geri Cassone, Michael Piechowski, and Susan Assouline.

Thanks to students in Ohio and Georgia who provided suggestions for revision. Thanks especially to my colleague F. Christopher Reynolds who, after teaching from the first edition, read the new pages and critiqued them with insight and power. Thanks to my editors Linda Senter and Spring Winnette, and, of course, my publisher, Gifted Psychology Press. Thanks to God, my sisters and their families, Steven and Denise (of course), Ralph, and our gift of a girl, Danielle.

Enjoy. And may your creativity walk into new dimensions.

Jane Piirto
Ashland University
Ashland, Ohio
44805

It was a convention for teachers of the talented. Katherine Miller had just been hired to teach in a pullout program for fourth, fifth, and sixth grade talented students. She was glad for the opportunity, for in her undergraduate years, during her student teaching experiences, she had always seemed to gravitate towards the bright students, the ones whom her cooperating teachers called "too big for his britches" or "too mouthy." Her new superintendent had received an announcement for the state convention for teachers of the talented, and had told Katherine that he would pay her way to go, so she could learn what she was supposed to teach.

There was no written curriculum to guide her in her first teaching job, and so in addition to learning how to teach exceptional students, Katherine had to develop her own curriculum. A further handicap for her was that, as is true in most states, Katherine was not required to have had any special training with talented students. But she had been hired, her superintendent had said, because she was bright and young, not jaded, and the school district could afford her because with no teaching experience she would come in on the lowest rung of the salary scale.

In fact, Katherine had not been taught anything about talented children in her education courses, though she had taken a whole course in the education of other special children, so she went to the library to read up before her interview. She memorized the categories of the talented children that the state served; among these were creative children. Although it was a word she'd used all her life, Katherine couldn't come up with a working definition of creativity. She was even less sure exactly who the creative children were—the ones who colored outside the lines? The ones who looked a little weird? She had gotten the job without ever figuring it out, and now, here she was at this convention. She stepped into the large hotel ballroom, took a cup of coffee, and nestled in for the keynote speaker, introduced by the conference organizer as an expert on creativity. "Finally!" Katherine thought.

As he started off with a joke or two, she noticed he was a little mussed, his hair caught into a fashionable ponytail. His cowboy boots and jeans contrasted with his blazer and striped tie. Through the microphone his voice boomed over the hotel ballroom. Katherine had not expected so many people to be here—almost a thousand! Were they all educators of the gifted and talented?

That ephemeral, invisible entity, creativity, bloomed onto transparency after transparency on the giant screen, transformed into diagrams, curves, *arrows, and dots, with cartoons from **Peanuts** to illustrate various points. There was a list of tests, also; Katherine found it difficult to believe she could administer tests to measure children's creativity, but she assumed he must know his subject.*

She scanned the day's schedule as he spoke, underlining all sessions on creativity, for if this keynote speaker of a conference on teaching talented students spoke nearly exclusively on creativity, then obviously as a teacher of talented children she was expected to focus on creativity. After his address, she collected the handouts of dots and diagrams and psychological words and hurried down the hallway to a small room.

There, with a pitcher of iced water and two glasses, behind a table with a podium and a microphone, a smaller screen, and another overhead projector, were two middle-aged women. Coordinators of programs for the gifted and talented in a faraway corner of the state, they were going to talk about how to enhance creativity in elementary school children. They also had many overheads, and they led the group in some games. It was fun, and everyone relaxed. But Katherine was getting anxious: the coordinators, very good speakers, used words like "fluency," "flexibility" and "elaboration," and they talked about creativity as if it were problem-solving.

Well, they must know, Katharine thought again, for they've been in this field a lot longer than I have. But in the back of her mind, she thought that creativity was a little bit more than fun and games and generating alternative solutions. Katherine followed her plan, attending all seven sessions where creativity was part of the title, and by Friday night she was exhausted. She had a briefcase full of stapled handouts, with dots and arrows and curves and diagrams and key words highlighted with graphic bullets. She had played games and had practiced techniques. She had packets of ideas for lessons. But she still didn't know what creativity was. Oh, well, she'd think about it next week.

On Saturday, she and her fiancé, Brad, a computer consultant who had been an infamous hacker during his high school and college years, were off to a weekend retreat at a camp in the woods some fifty miles away. There they would attend a workshop on transformational empowerment. Nature-loving Brad, seriously into preserving the environment, was intrigued by many New Age ideas, and he wanted Katherine to appreciate the mystery and beauty of inner contemplation. This was the third session they had been to.

Katherine had been reared in her family's traditional Methodist church, and her mother was not very pleased that she was attending these workshops. "I don't want you to be influenced by a cult," her mother said.

"Mother! We just meditate and visualize and relax as we probe our inner selves. Brad wants us to take our place in saving the earth, and in order to do that, we first have to understand our inner selves. Why don't you come sometime? I feel very creative when I visualize and meditate. You will, too. We do that and then we write for awhile, or draw, or share. We want to be the best that we can be. It's like when you went to that church retreat for a weekend and took that intensive journal workshop a few years ago. Remember?" Just then Katherine realized she'd used that word again: "creative."

All the way to the camp, she sat silently, thinking about the teachers' conference and about how wonderful she always felt when she and Brad sat with the group and meditated. Then she remembered her high school track coach, who had the girls visualize themselves running the track before they went into competition. Was this visualization "creativity" as much as the black-line lessons she'd collected to use with her children at her new job?

She had a lot to learn, she knew. But she felt good about it, despite her confusion, for she knew she would sort it all out sooner or later.

Chapter 1

Creativity and Talent Development

The secret at the heart of all creative activity has something to do with our desire to complete a work, to impose perfection upon it, so that, hammered out of profane materials, it becomes sacred: Which is to say, no longer merely personal.
—Joyce Carol Oates

A colleague in the art department gave workshops on creativity for art teachers. I asked him whether I could attend his Saturday workshop, and as we talked our conversation got around to the extreme difficulty educators in various disciplines have in discussing creativity. We all seem to have different definitions in mind. His primary purpose for offering the workshop, he said, was not to focus on definitions, but to help teachers help their students generate ideas for their projects, since even his undergraduate art majors often get stuck looking for ideas.

He said he wasn't going to use that "education and psychology baloney and gobbledygook that no one can even understand," but a book about lateral thinking by a man called de Bono. I reminded him de Bono is an educator, and pointed out that this creativity interest clearly crosses disciplinary boundaries. I inquired whether he was going to show his students how to brainstorm. He responded that, yes, brainstorming is a good way to generate new ideas.

I could tell that he, as an artist, like me, a writer, was struggling to make sense of creativity. That the practice of group brainstorming to enhance creativity would have moved from its beginnings in 1955 at the Buffalo, New York, Creative Problem-Solving Institute, to the art studio illustrates the wide impact of the work on creativity enhancement in the last fifty years. That this evolved term, "creativity"—literally, the making of something new—should come to mean so much to all sorts of people is a wonder.

One thing I have found: we all have a proprietary interest in creativity. Every discipline, every person, has a separate definition, and each believes in creativity as something that really exists. As I was beginning to write this book, I ran into an administrator friend who asked what I'd been doing lately. When I told him, he said he had just read in an airline's magazine a wonderful article on what is wrong with the schools, namely that schools don't allow children to be creative. We suppress their creativity.

health/medical viewpoint; philosophy, which studies creativity from a causal standpoint, especially through aesthetics, a branch of philosophy; the humanities, which studies creativity from the viewpoint of the artistic creator, in terms of biographical history or domain-specific phenomenological practice and insight (e.g. dance, literature, visual arts, theater, music, and the like); and business, which studies creativity with the goal of sparking corporate innovation and entrepreneurship. Psychology, too, has several threads of research into creativity.

Divergent Production as a Factor of Intellect

In 1950, J.P. Guilford, President of the American Psychological Association, gave a speech that marks the beginning of interest in creativity as a measurable phenomenon. Guilford developed the Structure of Intellect theory which proposes that there are 120 kinds of measurable intelligence factored across five operations, four contents, and six products. In his 1967 book, *The Nature of Human Intelligence*, Guilford proved that one can measure divergent production, which is the generation of ideas from given information with an emphasis on variety and quality of output from the same source. Divergent production is one of Guilford's five cognitive abilities, the others being cognition, memory, evaluation and convergent production. In his 1950 speech, Guilford called for research on two questions: (1) how to find the promise of creativity in our children; and (2) how to enhance the development of the creative personality. In this address, he called for the analysis of several factors of what is called *divergent production*. Here are Guilford's original definitions of the terms that have gained such currency in the creativity enhancement world:

1. **Fluency:** Guilford said, "It is rather that the person who is capable of producing a large number of ideas per unit of time, other things being equal, has a greater chance of having significant ideas."
2. **Novelty:** "The creative person has novel ideas."
3. **Flexibility:** " . . . the ease with which he changes set."
4. **Synthesizing ability:** The ability to put unlike ideas together.
5. **Analyzing ability:** "Much creative thinking requires the organizing of ideas into larger, more inclusive patterns . . . Symbolic structures must often be broken down before new ones can be built."
6. **Reorganization or redefinition of already existing ideas:** "Many inventions have been in the nature of a transformation of an existing object into one of different design, function, or use."

7. **Degree of complexity:** "How many interrelated ideas can the person manipulate at the same time?"
8. **Evaluation:** "Creative work that is to be realistic or accepted must be done under some degree of evaluative restraint."

An interesting point here, one not widely reported, is that in this address, Guilford specified that these factors are probably only characteristic of scientists or technologists, and that they probably do not describe those with creative planning abilities—political and military leaders and economists. Nor do they describe writers, graphic artists, or musical composers. However, today it is not uncommon to have programs in creativity training that emphasize fluency, flexibility, and novelty (or originality) for *all* students, not just future scientists or technologists. The problem is that divergent production has been confused with creativity. Divergent production can be measured easily, but is it creativity? Guilford himself demurred from going so far as to claim this.

Guilford differentiated between convergent and divergent intellect. Convergent intellect is a mode of cognition, a way of thinking, that emphasizes remembering what is known, being able to learn what exists, and being able to save that information in one's brain. Divergent intellect is a mode of cognition or way of thinking that emphasizes the revision of what is already known, of exploring what would be known, and of building new information. People who prefer the convergent mode of intellect supposedly tend to do what is expected of them, while those who prefer the divergent mode tend to take risks and to speculate.

The University of Chicago Studies

Among the most cited studies that took divergent and convergent intellect into account was that of Getzels and Jackson, who studied sixth through twelfth graders in a private school in Illinois. The Getzels and Jackson study was widely interpreted to imply that those with high creative potential need a certain *threshold* of intelligence, but not necessarily the highest intelligence.

Wallach and Kogan made another often-cited attempt to quantify creativity, replicating the Getzels and Jackson study with fifth graders. They found that an untimed, open-ended, nonthreatening testing atmosphere produces better responses on the divergent mode of intellect paper and pencil tests. By 1971, Wallach said that the most fruitful researches would probably be into the areas of creativity within domains:

> If we want to learn about the enhancement of creativity, we
> had better consider training arrangements that make a person
> more competent at creative attainments themselves—such as
> writing novels well, excellence in acting, skill as a musician,
> or quality of art work produced. In like manner, we have
> seen that learning about what covaries with creativity differ-
> ences requires us to consider correlates of creative attain-
> ments themselves.

These studies continue by researchers interested in the cognitive aspects of
creativity and whether or not students can be trained in them. Whether they
have any utility or application in schools is still debated, as the validity of
divergent production measures continues to be questioned.

Torrance's Tests

E.P. Torrance took Guilford seriously and set out to create and validate tests
that would identify creative potential. His Torrance Tests of Creative Thinking
(TTCT) began to be widely used in schools. These tests, similar to the
Guilford tests of divergent production, quantified or put numbers on fluency,
flexibility and the like. The higher the score, the more potentially creative the
child was. In attempting to show that paper and pencil testing of aspects of the
divergent mode of intellect can truly identify creative potential, Guilford,
Getzels and Jackson, Torrance, Wallach and Kogan, and others began a con-
troversial practice that still continues today. Mainstream educators still
attempt to identify creative potential by calling creativity a *separate* type of
giftedness, rather than a necessary aspect of all giftedness. Their reasons for
doing so have to do with a need to be inclusive. That is, those children who
have creative potential may not be found by other means, but they may
become included in programs by the use of paper and pencil vehicles such as
tests and checklists. This separation of creativity and intelligence has led to
much confusion in the practitioners' sector.

The Federal Definitions

Is general intelligence or IQ, as measured by an intelligence test such as the
Wechsler or the Stanford-Binet, different from, the same as, or even related to
creativity? "Well," said educators of the gifted, "yes and no." The struggle to
define giftedness went on. Current U.S. and Canadian definitions are varia-

tions of the 1972 Marland Report. According to Marland, giftedness takes six forms: superior cognitive ability, specific academic ability, creativity, leadership ability, visual and performing arts ability, and psychomotor ability. The research being done on divergent production was operationalized and carried into the public schools. In 1972, the federal government made the first bureaucratic mention that creativity is a *form* of giftedness.

The Tangling of Giftedness and Creativity

When Marland postulated that one of the forms of giftedness is creativity, schools were presented with a quandary. How would they find and serve people who have so-called *creative* giftedness? Taking the Chicago research on the threshold effect—that people who score highest on divergent production tests often have above average IQs—schools began to operationally define creativity. First the child had to score above average on an IQ test. Second, the child had to score high on some other test that purportedly measured creativity. Most popular of these were checklists and divergent production tests.

In 1978, Renzulli defined giftedness as the presence of three characteristics: above average intelligence, creativity, and task commitment. Renzulli is the only theorist whose work has been adopted by the public schools to any great degree who insists that the gifted person must have creativity, not simply a high IQ. Other theorists such as Sternberg and Feldman, who have also said creativity is a necessary aspect of giftedness, have not seen their theories receive much practical application in schools. Gardner's theory of multiple intelligences says that creativity is possible within each intelligence. But for schools to say that creative potential is measurably separate from academic ability or high academic achievement is the tough part. What does that mean?

Marland's definition also separated out the visual and performing arts and athletics as separate kinds of giftedness. Being gifted in painting, drawing, acting, music, dance, sculpture, and sports is identified by experts and professionals evaluating a person's performance by means of a portfolio or an audition. That visual and performing arts, athletics, and intellectual giftedness are different from creative giftedness is sometimes difficult to understand. Aren't brainy scientists creative? Aren't verbal writers creative? Aren't visual artists creative? Aren't actors creative? Aren't dancers creative? Aren't musicians creative? Aren't athletes creative?

The inclusion of creativity as a separate *type* of giftedness in Marland's definition, rather than *as* giftedness, has posed many problems for contemporary educators as they struggle to make distinctions between high IQ and creative potential, as they wrestle with thresholds of test scores and measures of ability, and as they try to meet demands of public accountability as defined in numerical outcomes.

Critics have attacked the Marland definition of giftedness as having aspects that are too difficult to identify and measure. Hoge in an article in 1988 said that educators have misused the tests: instead of being used to identify giftedness, the tests have become in themselves the definitions of giftedness.

A New School Definition of Giftedness

In 1991, an advisory panel to the Javits Act administrators in the U.S. Office of Educational Research and Improvement (U.S.O.E.R.I.) proposed a revised definition of gifted and talented children that was informed by new cognitive research and by concerns for the inequity in participation in programs for the intellectually gifted. The first report on the U.S.'s duty to educate the brightest since the Marland Report, the new report was called *National Excellence: A Case for Developing America's Talent*, published in November, 1992. The new definition proposed that giftedness—or talent—occurs in all groups across all cultures and is not necessarily shown in test scores but in a person's "high performance capability" in the intellectual, *creative*, and artistic realms. The word *gifted* was eliminated, the terms *outstanding talent* and *exceptional talent* embraced. The importance of environmental influence upon a person is apparent in this definition. Giftedness is said to connote "a mature power rather than a developing ability." Talent is to be found by "observing students at work in rich and varied educational settings." The best way to find talented children is by "providing opportunities and observing performance." Here is the 1992 definition:

> Children and youth with outstanding talent perform or show the potential for performing at remarkably high levels of accomplishment when compared with others of their age, experience, or environment.
>
> These children and youth exhibit high performance capability in intellectual, creative, and/or artistic areas, possess an unusual leadership capacity, or excel in specific academic fields. They require services or activities not ordinarily provided by the schools.

> Outstanding talents are present in children and youth from all cultural groups, across all economic strata, and in all areas of human endeavor.

Here, in this 1992 attempt to define the role of schools in nurturing talent, we see again that the intellectual, the creative, and the artistic are separated. This seems to imply that the intellectual is not creative, the creative is not intellectual, the artistic is not intellectual or creative. Common sense says that both the intellectually and the artistically talented are creative, and creative people can be both intellectual and artistic. How confusing such policy statements become when schools try to make programs based on these definitions!

Since these federal reports have the purpose of influencing and guiding educational policy in the states and then in the local school districts, the school people turn to the experts to help them define what is intellectual, what is creative, and what is artistic. They look to researchers, primarily researchers in psychology, to guide their practical applications. This is not to say that the psychological researchers have an interest in the education of talented children, but rather that the educators of talented children want to know what researchers are finding. An uneasy marriage has arisen between psychologists and educators.

Psychological Research on Creativity

Creativity has been researched by specialists in several branches of psychology: developmental, educational, cognitive, social, and humanistic psychology. And of course one must include the psychometric branch of educational psychology, the makers of divergent production tests.

Developmental Psychology

Developmental psychologists seek to understand the stages in the development of the creative person. Creativity is realized in the process of a lifetime in various stages, through a network of enterprises along a predictable developmental path. Stage theory assumes that one must pass through a lower stage in order to reach a higher stage, thus its view of creativity is hierarchical. One way to figure out what the stages are is to do a developmental case study.

behavior." These authors assert that Skinner's notions of behaviorism are not dead, only reframed.

Domain experts such as Pfeiffer have traced the evolutionary path of the arts and religions. Ornstein has traced the sources of human consciousness and thus human creativity through a synthesis of evolutionary theory and historical event. Studying creativity with a historical evolutionary view of the interaction of biology and culture yields insights that take into account the totality of human experience, according to Csikszentmihalyi in his 1993 work on evolution and creativity.

Erikson's Stages

Joan Erikson worked with her husband Erik, who described the psychosocial stages of life that every education major has memorized: 1. Trust vs. Mistrust; 2. Autonomy vs. Shame; 3. Initiative vs. Guilt; 4. Industry vs. Inferiority; 5. Identity vs. Role Diffusion; 6. Intimacy vs. Isolation; 7. Generativity vs. Stagnation; 8. Integrity vs. Despair. She described generativity and integrity in the final two stages as being enhanced by a person's creative working. Wisdom, wonder, awe, and reverence are gained through being creative.

Csikszentmihalyi's Big C and little c

Mihalyi Csikszentmihalyi's own developmental path as a psychologist has taken him from collaboration with Getzels in a study of visual artists, to a study of talented teenagers, to interviews of a hundred persons known for transforming their domains. He defines the Big "C" creative person as eminent, one whose work is well known by people within the field and domain. The little c creative person is not so known. Big "C" Creativity is that which leads to a domain being changed, while little "c" creativity is that by which human beings lead their everyday lives, figuring out ways to prevent raccoons from tipping over the garbage can or how to get to work faster. In his 1995 book *Creativity*, Csikszentmihalyi wrote, "Creativity is any act, idea, or product that changes an existing domain, or that transforms an existing domain into a new one."

Social Psychology

Creative people are intrinsically motivated and often aggressive in pursuing their creativity as they interact with the Zeitgeist or milieu. Such environmental influences on the creative person are studied by the social psychologist, who also examines such phenomena as motivation. A social psychological approach to creativity has been that of Albert, who focused on genius, continuing in the wake of Galton, Lombroso, Hollingworth, Terman, and Oden. Creative people begin creative production early and continue to be productive throughout life; they experienced parental warmth and closeness with at least one care giver. Another social psychologist, Amabile, has contributed significantly with her experiments utilizing practicing artists. Amabile's Venn diagram, similar to Renzulli's, defines creativity as occurring when intrinsic motivation intersects with the skills required to master the domain and with the skills of creative production.

Simonton's *Greatness*

Following upon the work of Albert and the Goertzels, the social psychologist Dean Keith Simonton, in his 1995 *Greatness*, showed also that creativity is the result of the work of a life, and that this lifetime must encompass certain aspects of environment, depending on the type of product being created. In a 1991 address, Simonton said that he considers only "first-rate geniuses" in his studies of the social factors impinging on the genius from birth to grave. Simonton has built upon the 1960 work of Campbell, who said that creativity is the measure of a total number of variations an individual can produce. Combining a consideration of rates of information processing, age at career onset, developmental antecedents, and other phenomena such as lifetime productivity, the sheer quantity of output as compared to the quality of output and what Simonton calls "the swan-song phenomenon"—an odd but notable increase in the quality and nature of a creator's output five years before death—Simonton has employed a statistical technique called historiometry. His deductions from statistics on attributes and characteristics show features of the lives of geniuses presented throughout this book. Simonton viewed creativity as a form of leadership in that the creator is a persuader. Creativity has often been viewed through the lens of process, product, or person, but chance intervenes to make the true creator a persuader. There are two types of genius, the intuitive and the analytical. Both are characterized by extreme productivity. The more works, the more the chance of influencing the domain and of assuming leadership in the domain.

Cognitive Psychology

The cognitive psychologist seeks to find out what happens in the mind while a person is creating. Creativity is insight, intuition, a process of selection, and the ability to adapt to novelty. Creative people who are successful find problems that enhance the domain. In their 1976 ground-breaking study of problem-finding in visual artists, Getzels and Csikszentmihalyi thought that creativity was an attempt to reduce tension that may or may not be perceived consciously. The way artists did this was to simultaneously seek problems that could be symbolically solved through human imagination. When an artist works, the conflict that the artist feels is changed within himself into a problem. The artist "finds" a problem that will lead to a work of art which is the symbolic solution to that problem. This happens over and over again as the artist works. This study will be discussed in detail in Chapter 5.

Csikszentmihalyi, Rathunde, and Whaley have conducted several other studies investigating the notion of flow, a sense of timelessness while creating, by using beepers on talented teenagers, interrupting them to ask what they are doing and when they create. The book, *Talented Teens* (1993), describes this study. They have also interviewed creative producers in the arts and the sciences, inquiring about their creative processes. Csikszentmihalyi's 1995 book, *Creativity*, details the latter studies.

Gardner's Frames

Howard Gardner, in his 1983 *Frames of Mind*, said there are seven different intelligences: linguistic, musical, logical-mathematical, spatial, bodily-kinesthetic, interpersonal, and intrapersonal. In late 1996 (Hoerr, 1996) Gardner added another intelligence, that of the naturalist (such as John James Audubon and Charles Darwin). According to Gardner's theory, creativity is an aspect of each of these intelligences as they are perfected and developed, not a separate intelligence or ability. In 1988, Gardner asserted that creativity cannot take place without the *asynchrony*—the odd interaction—of place, time, talent, and morality. In creativity there is tautness or strain "between intellectual and personality styles, and by a striking lack of fit between personality and domain, intelligence and field, and biological constitution and choice of career." He said that this pressure may be the impetus that causes a person to go off and make something new and creative

Gardner has been exploring these intelligences domain by domain. In 1993 he published *Creating Minds,* seven case studies of geniuses in each of the seven intelligences. In 1995 he considered the intelligences of leaders and politicians in *Leading Minds*. In 1997, he formulated principles leading to the development of extraordinariness in *Extraordinary Minds*. Every one of his books has the word *mind* in the title, emphasizing that this cognitive psychologist is speaking of the cognitive. His theories have had great impact on educators in the mid-1990s, and many schools now call themselves MI (Multiple Intelligence) schools. His definition of creativity is that a creative person "solves problems, fashions products, or poses new questions within a domain in a way that is initially considered to be unusual but is eventually accepted within at least one cultural group."

Sternberg's Triarchies and Hierarchies

Another contemporary cognitive scientist, Robert Sternberg, in his 1985 *The Triarchic Mind*, named three types of giftedness, one of which is creative giftedness, the ability to adapt to that which is novel, or the ability to make something new. In a 1988 essay Sternberg wrote, "Those gifted individuals who make the greatest long-range contributions to society are probably those whose gifts involve coping with novelty—specifically, in the area of insight." He called his theory triarchic, insisting that each intelligent act incorporates creativity in insight, planning, and research in accomplishing the act. Like many contemporary psychologists and educators, Sternberg suggested that a high IQ is not the main requirement for a successful life, but that other components are necessary. Again we see an idea evolving: that creativity is necessary in the development of talent. In a 1991 address Sternberg focused on the everyday creativity that is exhibited when one leads an intelligent life. The six facets of creativity are (1) having creative intelligence, (2) having specific knowledge within the domain, (3) having a certain style of mind and (4) certain aspects of personality, (5) having motivation, and (6) having a nurturing environment. None of these is earth-shaking or new, and by 1991, consensus had been reached in the psychological field that these were necessary. By 1995 Sternberg and his colleague Lubart had published several variations of a theory of creativity called the investment theory, which Lubart elaborated on at a 1996 international conference in Vienna. Using the somewhat cute metaphor of the stock market, these two psychologists stated that the truly creative risk taker tries to buy low and sell high; in other words, "creatively insightful people need to invest themselves in their projects to yield the value added to the initial idea."

Educational Psychology

For educational psychologists, successful creators have similar patterns of education and familial influence, depending on the domain in which the creativity is practiced. Studies done by Bloom and his colleagues at the University of Chicago explored the patterns in the lives of research neurologists, pianists, sculptors, mathematicians, and tennis players. These studies will be discussed in more detail in Part III. Likewise, in a multitude of studies done at the Study for Mathematically Precocious Youth (SMPY), Benbow, Brody, and Stanley have examined the paths that lead to high mathematical creativity and its cousin, scientific creativity.

These studies of creative people within domains of achievement have led to some of the best evidence of which behaviors and situations can predict the likelihood of creative productivity in adulthood. I have called these *predictive behaviors* of creative performance throughout childhood to adulthood. One focus of my research has been specifically about the paths in the lives of creative writers. Subotnik has interviewed masters in the sciences, mathematics, medicine, music, chess, theater, biology and the like. She noted, "The masters . . . devoted years of creative energy and disciplined practice to the perfection of their skills and productive ideas." Educational psychology researchers such as these have devoted their research efforts to studying persons by domain of achievement rather than by general creativity aptitude, with a view to how their life paths can inform the educational process.

Humanistic Psychology

The humanistic psychologists have had their influence. Maslow, in discussing creativity, said that he had to revise his whole definition of it when he considered the lives of truly self-actualized people. He found that self-actualized (SA) creativeness "stresses first the personality rather than its achievements," and may even be "synonymous with health itself." Maslow also differentiated between big-picture creativity and everyday creativity.

In addition to Maslow, humanistic psychologists Carl Rogers, Clark Moustakas and Rollo May also contributed to confusion about creativity when they insisted that no product of creativity is necessary but the product of a healthy life. Do several small c acts of creativity amount to a Large C Creative Life? Such discussions verge on the spiritual, which brings us back to the original meaning of creativity as a connection with the divine: "God created the Heaven and the Earth." Psychologist Kazmierz Dabrowski and his translator and co-researcher, counseling psychologist Michael Piechowski, studied creative producers and found they possessed high overexcitabilities in the emotional, intellectual, and imaginational areas.

Dabrowski: Overexcitabilities and Developmental Levels

The Dabrowski theory, recently generating much interest in the field of creativity studies and gifted education, identifies five levels of emotional development, each level mediated by intensities or overexcitabilities. Dabrowski, a Polish psychologist, wrote of the existence of an intense "inner psychic milieu" in "a sensitive, capable, introverted child" who is often pushed to the margins by schooling and by childhood and early adult experiences of rejection, misunderstanding and devaluing by the rest of the world. Such individuals may come to resemble people with mental illness, but they are not mentally ill as they undergo a multi-level transformation from the primitive to the transcendent. Only a very few reach the highest levels, levels IV and V, whom Piechowski described as "characterized by deliberate, self-directed inner growth guided by the highest ideals." One's path is hierarchical; through a process of "positive disintegration," that is, a breaking down of lower functions in order to reorganize at a higher level, the individual restructures the psyche. In a 1975 monograph, Piechowski said, "If there is no restructuring, there is no development."

In the Dabrowski theory, and also among adherents to the New Age spiritual movement arising out of humanistic psychology, one's *life* is the creative product as a person labors to become a vibrant, alive, transcendent being as the ultimate in creativity. That is why I place Dabrowski's theory in the humanistic, as opposed to the developmental, realm of psychology, although Dabrowski's work fits into both. One grows from level to level through conflict, and one's propensity for growth is termed "developmental potential." The levels are not fixed in time; that is, they do not occur at certain ages, but they may occur simultaneously as a person is in a conflict of growth and development. Piechowski said, "There are periods of great intensity and disequilibrium (psychoneuroses, depression, creative process), and there are periods of equilibrium . . . but the more development is advanced . . . the less possible it is for it to slacken off and cease to carry on the process of intrapsychic transformation." The transition occurs and the higher level dominates.

At Level I, Primary Integration, the motivation to act is based on main primitive drives. At Level II, Unilevel Disintegration, one experiences multi-

Creativity and Nationalism

Others have said we should develop our children's creativity for nationalistic reasons. In the late 1950s and throughout the Cold War, a nationalistic spirit prevailed in the U.S., especially after the Russians put Sputnik into orbit. Creativity was deemed necessary to keep the U.S. ahead of Russia. Mid-century psychologists saw creativity as necessary for combating the Soviet threat. In recent years, a twist on this nationalistic argument has emerged, in particular with reference to competition with the Japanese and Europeans. A common assertion among patriotic educators is that the U.S. still leads the world in patent applications, and that U.S. inventors actually design, while the Japanese and Germans only improve on the basic designs. These patriotic people then go on to repeat the call for an emphasis on creativity training in the schools.

Creativity and Equity

A fourth reason for emphasizing certain kinds of creativity is implicitly racist and classist. This rationale begins with the assertion that people in the middle and upper socioeconomic classes score better on IQ and achievement tests than people in the lower classes, no matter what the ethnicity, and that poor people don't score particularly well on IQ tests. But we do know that poor African Americans have invented American popular music, rhythm and blues, and jazz and have revolutionized all sports they have been exposed to; as a result, African Americans have been stereotyped as having musical creativity and superior physical giftedness. Latinos have also had great influence on popular dance and music—tango, cha-cha, lambada. Therefore, the current thinking goes, these particular aspects of performance and creativity should be nurtured in the schools in order to identify for talent development education programs those who might not score so well on IQ tests. The goal seems to be to identify as having creative potential, and to include in special programs, students from lower socioeconomic classes who would not be in the programs if only IQ and achievement were criteria.

Thus, by implication, poor people are creatively gifted and not intellectually gifted. Alternative high schools such as the La Guardia High School for the Performing Arts in New York City attract more poor and minority students than do the academic high schools, Stuyvesant, Hunter, or the Bronx High School of Science. All of these tuition-free, alternative high schools admit students from all five boroughs of New York City by competitive standards. Stuyvesant, Hunter, and the Bronx High Schools advertise themselves as serving academically talented students, and although great efforts are made to enroll students of Hispanic and black ethnicity, the majority of the students are white and Asian. In 1997 a group of African American and Hispanic parents both protested the admission standards and, in order to help their children meet them, began a special summer school for the study of mathematics.

Although creativity, as argued here, is a valuable asset in any domain, it is often associated most with the visual and performing arts. Cutoff scores on tests that emphasize scholastic achievement and IQ are used for the academic high schools, and their graduates often go on to elite colleges in greater numbers and thus have tickets to join the establishment when they enter professions. Since the students supposedly have different potentials, they attend different special high schools. The academic high schools struggle to attract poor students, with schemes such as special nominations by local superintendents, but the test score on the admission test is often the deciding factor. At La Guardia, the "Fame" school, the specialties of vocal music and theater attract more poor minority students than do the specialties of instrumental music and dance, for one does not need special lessons in vocal music and theater in order to be picked out as talented in the competitive auditions.

The grave disparity in numbers of participants of certain ethnic minorities and children of the lower socioeconomic classes has led to a concerted effort by the U.S. Office of Education. Since the early 1990s, millions of dollars in Javits Grants were awarded to people seeking ways to identify and serve disadvantaged, culturally different, or handicapped children who are talented. The grants have been used throughout the nation to develop portfolios, multiple intelligences, case studies, and other means to bypass standardized IQ tests in order to find talent potential among the poor.

Creativity and the Future

Perhaps another reason that we want to identify creativity is to increase it in specific ways. The justification for special programs for the academically talented has often been that certain children have special talents that can be used creatively to save the world from itself. We want our outstandingly talented students to be creative leaders. Here the implication is that intelligence and creativity are meshed and not separate.

This idea is promoted among educators of the talented, who say that talented children will save the world as our future leaders, and that with their creativity they will help the world solve its problems. A popular nationwide program called Future Problem Solving, where teams of children solve current problems such as overpopulation or acid rain, is an illustration of this. One of its goals is to enhance the creativity of children in having them solve real dilemmas.

Most educators of the talented take for granted that creativity can be enhanced, and they believe there is a need for more creative production, as well for higher quality creative production. In all the educational literature on creativity, no one questions these premises. The corollary premise is that creative promise, or creative potential, as it is often called, can be identified by the means available to school personnel. This premise is a shaky one, as we shall see.

Creativity as Human Freedom

To summarize, why all this theorizing about creativity and the creative process? Another look at the philosophical point of view provides an answer. There is so much interest in unmasking the mystery of creativity precisely because it is so unexplainable. We write so much and think so much about creativity because we simply want to explain the creative achievement, to find out the truth about what makes a creative product. However, once we think we've discovered the process, it eludes us.

The philosopher's reason for studying creativity is that creativity implies a kind of freedom. The existentialist philosophers, especially, were concerned with freedom, and thinkers such as Wittgenstein and Sartre said that human beings have the freedom to create themselves. Despite what Calvinists and astrologers may assert, a life is not pre-determined, and a person demonstrates creativity in how she makes her life productive. This philosophy is a very popular one today, as shall be seen in Chapter 2's description of the creative process.

On the other hand, the psychologist's reason for studying creativity is very practical. The psychologists have set out to identify the creative personality, as opposed to the non-creative personality, if such a thing exists. They are also interested in what happens in the mind while a person is being creative. They set out to make up tests and design experiments that ferret out the people who will be able to produce creatively. They write about the process which people go through in order to create products. This fascination with these three—personality, process, and product—continues.

Domain specialists—creative people such as artists, writers, mathematicians and dancers—are not very interested in what happens in the mind while a person creates, or about what the personalities of various creators show. Practitioners of the various creative disciplines are more interested in the products that the creator makes. Is it new? Is it valuable? Does it extend the field?

Can a Person Be Creative without a Product?

A major concern of the creativity theorists is whether one can be creative without a created product. Logic suggests that without a created product, we cannot conclude that a person is creative; in other words, in order to be judged creative, one must have created *something*. But in fact such a non-product assessment of creativity is essentially what is done in talent development education when creativity is defined as creative potential and is considered an inherent type of giftedness. Often children are identified as creative or as having creative potential without any reference whatsoever to products they have produced or will produce. And indeed, if the creative product is a person's life, then no concrete thing is necessary—no music, no poem, no pot, no theorem.

Psychologists who developed cognitive tests such as the divergent production tests of Guilford have highly influenced the schools by giving the impression that a young child who scores well on such paper and pencil tests will become an adult who produces a creative product. But is this impression valid?

Precocity as Predictive

A related concern is how to objectively judge whether or not a product is creative, that is, a valuable novelty. Recent practices have emphasized the development of portfolios for an assessment of authentic work rather than abstract test scores. We have begun to look at creativity in children as demonstrated by what they do. Some may object, saying that in young children the creative product is still in the tadpole stage, and who knows what the future products will be like? Runco in 1997 cautioned against looking at student products as indicators of giftedness, though he admitted that creative people should produce products.

Others note that there are developmental paths in each talent domain, and that experts who know these paths can tell which children are exceptional.

The Pyramid of Talent Development

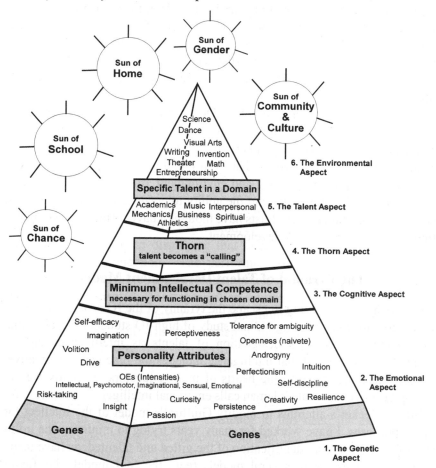

FIGURE 1. Piirto Pyramid of Talent Development. (Revised 10/97). From the Prentice Hall/ Macmillan/ Merrill College Text. *Talented Children and Adults. Their Development and Education.* (1994). By Jane Piirto, Ph.D.

1. The Emotional

Many studies have emphasized that successful creators in all domains have certain *personality attributes* in common. These attributes, making up the base of the model and resting on the foundation of genes, are the affective or emotional intelligences that one needs in order to succeed. These rest on the foundation of *genes.* Among these are *androgyny, creativity, imagination, insight, intuition, naiveté or openness to experience, overexcitabilities, passion for work in a domain, perceptiveness, persistence, preference for complexity, resilience, risk-taking capabilities, self-discipline, self-efficacy, tolerance for ambiguity, and volition or will.*[1]

Talented adults who achieve success possess many of these attributes. Although this list is by no means discrete or complete, it does indicate that the varied research into the personalities of creative people converges to show that creative adults achieve effectiveness partially by force of personality. Such personality attributes help the person to tap into his or her own special creative process and to continue the work over the period of time necessary to acquire the necessary mastery, even in adverse circumstances. These aspects of personality are present in some way in highly creative people. These attributes may be innate, but they can also be developed or even directly taught.

2. The Cognitive

The *cognitive* dimension as measured by the IQ score has been over-emphasized. When it was seen that the intelligence test often served only to obfuscate our efforts at talent identification, the IQ was designated as a *minimum* criterion, mortar and paste, with a certain level of intellectual ability considered necessary for functioning in the world, but studies by researchers such as Baird have repeatedly shown that a high IQ is not necessary for the realization of most talents. If there were no IQ tests, we would still be able to find and help talented children. Rather, graduation from college seems to be a strong indicator of creative success (except for professional basketball players, actors, and entertainers), and most college graduates have above average, but not stratospheric, IQs.

3. Talent in Domains

The *talent* itself—inborn, innate, mysterious—which must be developed. Each school or community has experts in most of the talent domains that students will enter, such as *mathematics, visual arts, music, theater, sciences, writing and lit-*

---

[1] Here is research support for the personality attributes: *androgyny* (Barron 1968; Csikszentmihalyi, Rathunde, and Whalen 1993; Piirto and Fraas, 1995); *creativity* (Renzulli, 1978; Tannenbaum 1983); *imagination* (Dewey, 1934; Langer, 1957; Plato; Santayana, 1896); *insight* (Sternberg and Davidson, 1985; Davidson 1992); *intuition* (Myers and McCaulley 1985); *naiveté or openness to experience* (Ghiselin, 1952; Cattell, 1971); the presence of *overexcitabilities*, called OEs (Dabrowski, 1964;1967;1972; Dabrowski & Piechowski, 1977; Piechowski 1979; Silverman, 1993; *passion for work in a domain* (Benbow, 1992; Bloom, 1985; Piirto, 1994); *perceptiveness* (Myers and McCaulley 1985); *perfectionism* (Silverman, 1993); *persistence* (Renzulli, 1978); *preference for complexity* (Barron, 1968; 1995); *resilience* (Jenkins-Friedman 1992; Block & Kremen, 1996); *risk-taking* (MacKinnon 1978; Torrance 1987); *self-discipline* (Renzulli 1978); *self-efficacy* (Zimmerman, Bandura and Martinez-Pons 1992; Sternberg and Lubart 1992); *tolerance for ambiguity* (Barron, 1968; 1995); and *volition, or will.* (Corno and Kanfer, 1993).

erature, business, entrepreneurship and economics, athletics, dance, the spiritual and theological, philosophy, psychology, and the interpersonal. They are all quite well-defined academically, and people can go to school to study in any of them. Education, or pedagogy, is a domain as well. When a child can draw so well she is designated the class artist, when he can throw a ball 85 miles an hour, or when a student is accused of cheating on her short story assignment because it sounds so adult, talent is present.

Most talents are recognized through what I have called certain *predictive behaviors*, for example voracious reading for linguistically talented students, and preferring to be class treasurer for mathematically talented students. These talents are demonstrated within domains that are socially recognized and valued within the society, and thus may differ from society to society. Hunting talent—acuity of eye combined with a honed instinct for shooting and a knowledge of animal habitat—is not as valued in western society as is verbal ability, a sensitivity to words and their nuances as expressed through grammatical and idiomatic constructions on paper, but in the past, hunting talent was valued much more than verbal talent. The hunting talent is still born in certain children, no matter how much urbanites divorced from nature and its cruelties deny that it exists.

4. Environmental Suns

These three levels of what Picchowski has called the "Piirto **Pii**ramid" could theoretically be called the individual person. In addition, everyone is influenced by five suns, which may be likened to certain factors in the environment. Many teachers feel that they are merely putting their finger into the dike because the students have so many outside-of-school influences that bear upon their school performance, and even upon whether or not the students can be taught.

There are three major suns. The first is the *sun of home.* This refers to a child's being in a positive and nurturing *home* environment. Second is the *sun of community and culture.* This refers to a child being in a community and culture that conveys values compatible with the educational institution and that provides support for the home and the school. Third is the *sun of school.* The *school* is a key factor, especially for those children whose other suns may have clouds in front of them.

Other smaller suns are also environmentally influential. Fourth is the influence of *gender*, for there have been found few gender differences in personality attributes in adult creative producers; but still great gender differences in achievement of creative potential exists. Fifth is the *sun of chance*. The presence or absence of all or several of these make the difference between whether a talent develops into mature expression or whether it atrophies.

Unfortunately, it could be said that when a student emerges into adulthood with his or her talent nurtured and developed, it is a miracle, because there are so many influences that encroach on talent development. We all know of outstandingly talented people who were not able to use or develop their talent due to negative circumstances within one or more of these suns. A student whose home life is traumatized by poverty or severe family strife may be so overwhelmed by that trauma that his talent cannot flower. In the absence of home stability and parental talent development (e.g., lessons, an encouraging atmosphere), the role of the school and the teacher or coach becomes to recognize the talent and to encourage lessons, mentors or special experiences. In other words, often the school must do what parents cannot, when metaphorically the suns of a child's life are hidden by clouds; in such cases, the school is especially key to the child's development.

As another example, a person of a certain race, class, or culture may be treated differently in different environments. In a racist society, his talents may be unfairly dealt with or ignored. Once again the *school*, in addition to the *community and culture,* must uniquely provide for his development to offset society's general opinion of his background. Retired General Colin Powell has said that he entered the army because he saw the military as the only place in a racist society where he would be treated fairly, where, as an African American, his genetic inheritance would not be discriminated against, where he could develop his talents fully.

The sun of *gender* is considered environmental, which may seem curious at first. Even though many gender differences are genetic and innate, the influence of one's gender on talent development is environmental. Boys in general are surely not born with more talent than girls. At the starting gate of birth surely both sexes are more or less equal, but something happens along the way to adulthood in the nurture, manifestation and societal recognition of the talent of boys and girls. Mentally and attitudinally, creative boys and girls are very similar: few personality attributes are significantly common to one sex over the other, except for thinking and feeling on the Myers-Briggs Type Indicator (MBTI) and Tough Poise on the 16 Personality Factors Inventory (l6 PF). Furthermore, few intelligence test scores show significant gender differences, though boys consistently score higher in spatial ability and in mathematics. Hence if men outpace women in the mature, creative expression of talent, we should look at environmental influences on the development of talent according to gender. Gender differences according to creative domain of talent will be discussed along the way.

The importance of *chance* or luck cannot be overemphasized. As the principal of a school in New York City, I received many calls from casting agents and producers wanting to look at our bright children for possible roles in movies, television, and theater. These children had the luck of being born in and living in a center for theatrical activity. I'll warrant few school principals in Kansas City or Seattle get the weekly or even daily calls I got from casting agents.

The influence of chance comes when a person happens to meet someone who can connect her to another person who can help or influence the first person's opportunities to interact with the field or domain. A play was even written about this phenomenon, John Guare's *Six Degrees of Separation*. The sun of chance has clouds over it when a talented adolescent does not get the counseling needed to make a college choice that will enhance a career. For example, in consulting with overseas schools, I noticed that most of the counselors recommended colleges in the East and in West. One counselor began recommending his own alma mater, a state university in the Midwest, and was subsequently asked to leave, as too many of the high school students began to apply to this university for their Eastern-establishment parents' comfort. The chance of college choice was expected to be enhanced by a counselor who knew the Ivy League. Chance can be improved by manipulating oneself so that one can indeed be in the right place at the right time.

Talent Multipotentiality: Feeling the Call, or the "Thorn"

However, although absolutely necessary, the presence of talent is not sufficient. Many people have more than one talent, and wonder what to do with them. What is the impetus, what is the reason, for one talent taking over and capturing the passion and commitment of the person who has the talent? A useful explanation comes from Socrates, who described the inspiration of the Muse (Plato, *Ion*). Carl Jung (1965) described the passion that engrosses; Csikszentmihalyi (1991) described the process of flow, and depth psychologist James Hillman (1996), described the presence of the *daimon* in creative lives. All these give clue to what talent a person will choose to develop.

Hillman described the talents in a way similar to Plato's and Jung's: "The talent is only a piece of the image; many are born with musical, mathematical, and mechanical talent, but only when the talent serves the fuller image and is carried by its character do we recognize exceptionality." Hillman's idea is similar to the notion of *vocation* or *call*. I would call it inspiration or passion for the domain. Philosophers would call it *soul*. Thus I have put an asterick, or "thorn," on the pyramid to exemplify that talent is not enough for the realization of a life commitment. Without going into the classical topics of Desire, Emotion, Art, Poetry, Beauty, Wisdom, or Soul (Adler, 1952), suffice it to say that the entire picture of talent development ensures when a person is pierced or bothered by a thorn, the *daimon*, that leads to commitment.

Feldman was close when he described the *crystallizing experience* (Feldman, 1982), but the thorn is more than crystallizing; it is fortifying. As mentioned above, one of the definitions of *gift* comes from Old French for *poison* (See OED) and this is what the talent that bothers may be come to a person if the person doesn't pay attention to it. As well as a joy it is a burden. As well as a pleasure it is a pain. However, the person who possesses the talent also must possess the will and fortitude to pursue the talent down whatever labyrinth it may lead. Feldman in a speech in Little Rock, Arkansas in 1997 said that the purpose of talent development education should be to "keep my players in the game until the fourth quarter so they have a chance to win" by providing them the situations which enhance the development of potential for excellence in their chosen domain. He urged students to follow their hearts and to move that way.

Creativity Is Natural

So, dear reader, listen up. Here is what I have come to think after all my reading and talking and dreaming: *Creativity is in the personality, the process, and the product within a domain in interaction with genetic influences and with optimal environmental influences of home, school, community and culture, gender, and chance. Creativity is a basic human instinct to make that which is new.* While creativity is the natural propensity of human being-ness, creativity can be either enhanced or stifled. The creative personality can be either developed or thwarted.

Creativity takes certain habits of mind. Creativity is not separate from intelligence or artistry, but part of the whole. What is unnatural is for it to be repressed, suppressed, and stymied through the process of growing up and being educated. What happens to most of us is that somewhere along the way, and often necessarily, we begin to distrust our creative self. Survival dictates

Traditional Theories of the Creative Process

For centuries people have tried to explain what happens when a person creates. Our interest in the creative process has stemmed from our deepest, most unconscious being and our most ancient mythologies. From the visitation of the muse to Wallas's four steps in the process; from Ghiselin's anthology of how creators have worked to *Aha!*s and *Eureka*s; from magical dreams to mysterious coincidences; from ritualistic obsessions to hypnotic trances, the creative process is intriguing, fascinating, and frustrating.

The Visitation of the Muse

A popularly held conception of the creative process, originating centuries ago and common to many cultures, was that the creating person was in a sort of trance caused by the visitation of the Muse. In fact, in Greek mythology there were nine Muses, all daughters of Memory (Mnemosyne) and Jupiter. Each had her own province in music, literature, art, and science, according to Bulfinch in his 1855 *Mythology*. The muse of epic poetry was Calliope; the muse of history, Clio; the muse of lyric poetry, Euterpe; the muse of tragedy, Melpomene; the muse of choral dance and song, Terpsichore. Erato was the muse of love poetry, and Polyhymnia was the muse of sacred poetry. Urania was the muse of astronomy, and Thalia the muse of comedy.

The Muses came to symbolize the feminine principle, while the masculine principle was symbolized by the Seven Spheres. Thus The Music of the Spheres symbolized the union of the male and female principles, the male being the animus, the female the anima. The male creator unites with his anima, or female side, and the female creator unites with her animus, her male side, according to Jungian thought. Dante had his Beatrice, Lancelot his Guinevere, Tristan his Isolde, Ilmarainen his Maid Of North Farm. At the beginning of Homer's *Iliad*, the blind poet invokes the muses in order to help him tell his story. For our purposes here, though, suffice it to say that the muses were inspirations to creative men.

Do creative women have muses? "Yes," said Carolyn Kizer in an essay called, appropriately, "A Muse." This particular muse was her mother, but women's muses need not always be their mothers. Creative women, as well as creative men, often have desired sexual partners as muses. Inspiration comes in response to a feeling for someone, quite possibly a sexual feeling, certainly an emotional identification. Everyone has written a secret love poem to a love, requited or unrequited. Getzels and Csikszentmihalyi, in *The Creative*

Vision, suggested that another primary reason artists make art, poets write poems, musicians compose music, is the erotic reason. They called it the "libidinous" reason, the longing for sexual connection.

For example, the painter Magritte said that seeing a catalogue of Futurist paintings in 1919 changed the course of his art explorations, as he realized that "one pure and powerful emotion, eroticism, kept me from falling at that time into a more traditional search for formal perfection." The contemporary homoerotic works of Eric Fischl, David Hockney, Robert Mapplethorpe, and Judy Chicago come to mind, as do the heterosexual paintings of Andrew Wyeth, the longing lyrics of the Brownings, and the romantic balletic creations of Balanchine. The place of erotic desire and longing for sexual union cannot be underestimated in considering the products of any artist. Poets write love poems. Choreographers make ballets. Visual artists paint nudes. Many of these works are efforts to express eroticism within the boundaries of the medium within which the artists are working. Several poet friends of mine have experienced whole new surges of poetic energy when they fell in love later on in life, after they thought that sexual love was lost to them, and they wrote what they considered the best poems of their careers, poems that combined mature skill with innocent longing.

Muses are virginal, pure and faithful. The artist longs for the Muse, and in the process of longing creates a song, a play, a poem, a theorem. Many creative people, especially poets, still speak about their work in muselike terms. Poems "come" to them. "I got this poem," a friend of mine said. "I'm waiting for poems," another said.

When the creative person is being visited by the Muse, he often feels possessed as he enters another world, a world of reverie, of be*mus*ed silence. This state can be likened to how a person feels when driving alone for a long time on a boring interstate highway, deep in thought. Many people tell me they get their best ideas while driving. Suddenly a car crosses the median and you slam on the brakes. The adrenalin flows. Alertness. A beating heart. You have awakened from the creative, meditational, half-awake yet alert state, and are thrust suddenly back to an awareness of daily life.

In relation to the mystique of the muse, some novelists describe their characters as having lives of their own. Others can't believe they wrote what they did; they thought they were incapable of it. They feel as if they were go-betweens, mediums. Abell quoted the composer Brahms: "I have to be in a semitrance condition to get such results—a condition when the conscious mind is in temporary abeyance, and the subconscious mind is in control."

Common Descriptions of the Creative Process

Several basic old chestnuts appear and reappear when one is reading about the creative process. For example, Graham Wallas's list of steps in the creative process; Kekule's dream of snakes coiling, providing the clue to the benzene ring; Poincaré's trust in the unconscious to solve his mathematical problems; Albert Einstein's vivid visualization, without words, of his thoughts; Coleridge's use of opium when he wrote "Kubla Khan;" or A.E. Housman's meditative walks after lunch and a pint of beer. Though old, these stories are instructive.

Wallas's Four Stages

Here is Wallas's oft-quoted summary of the process, written about in his 1926 book, *The Art of Thought*. Wallas was one of the pioneers in critical thinking, working out of the tradition established by John Dewey and Horace Mann. He said that there are four stages in the creative process: (1) preparation; (2) incubation; (3) illumination; and (4) verification. In the first stage, the person does both formal and informal work—she readies herself for the act of creation by studying, thinking, searching for answers, asking people. In the second stage, the process rests in gestation; the creator is pregnant with the creative product as the unconscious works on the problem. In the third stage, a solution arises, a light is thrown on the problem. The most famous example of this in the creativity literature is the vision of Archimedes rising from his bathtub and running naked down the streets, shouting "Eureka!" when he grasped the concept of the displacement of water. After this moment of illumination, the creative person has to prove the theory, literally or metaphorically, through the created product. This is the fourth stage.

The Work of Brewster Ghiselin

Brewster Ghiselin, a fine poet, became better known for editing an anthology of essays, *The Creative Process*, in 1952, than for his poetry. His own essay, the introduction to the book, summarized and explained what creative people have said about the process. Often there is a feeling of oceanic consciousness preceding the almost automatic producing of the work. High emotion is felt and is expressed as the creator exercises intense concentration in her field of talent.

Oceanic Consciousness. The creative process may begin with a state that Ghiselin called "primitive, a condition of complete indecision." He likened this "yielding to oceanic consciousness," in some people, to an intense or vague religious experience, the surrender of the self to some internal necessity, a call that seems greater than the self, greater than the puny ego. It may be a yearning or a hunch, but it is usually preverbal, vague, an "intimation of approaching or potential resolution."

What is to be invented then appears partially and spontaneously, "sometimes in the form of a mere glimpse serving as a clue, or like a germ to be developed; sometimes a fragment of the whole, whether rudimentary and requiring to be worked into shape or already in its final form."

Automaticity. The work then is done with some automaticity. This automaticity, already highly developed in the creator, has arisen as he has acquired the necessary tools within the domain of creative activity. Ghiselin pointed out that the part of the creative process most often underplayed is the enormous preparation that creators have to do within their fields. The viewer sees the finished work and forgets the "sweat and litter of the workroom." He said, "The impression it gives of unlabored force is not to be trusted." Indeed, we rarely appreciate or realize the time and effort put into creative works. One estimate is that the average person in an art museum spends about 1½ seconds per painting, a very short time to apprehend the effort of the painter and to make judgment on the work of art. Our instant culture may lead us to expect creative output from ourselves or from others instantaneously, but Bloom, in *Developing Talent in Young People*, and Bamberger, in an essay about the development of musical talent, highlighted the need for the creative person to methodically or even laboriously learn the field before expression or execution of the necessary skills can be automatic.

Restlessness. The creative process is characterized also by restlessness, and creative people often move on to other projects just when the rest of the world is beginning to catch on to what they have done. The word "movement" as in "Romantic Movement," "Neoclassical Movement," "Abstract Expressionist Movement" illustrates this restlessness. It was said of Picasso that he was not in any movements; he started them (see Chapter 5). Ghiselin pointed out that the creator casts himself loose from the "ties of security," which requires courage and a willingness to work alone, counter to the popular taste, and with a fair amount of uncertainty. A person who is too formalistic in following current rules will probably create nothing. This is perhaps why the inventors and entrepreneurs who are not employed by large companies are often the most innovative.

A sense of the beauty of the creator's field. Ghiselin noted that whatever the creator's field, the creator feels great emotion—a feeling for the aesthetics, for the beauty unique to the field. Mathematicians admire the elegant proof. Scientists marvel at the beauty of cells and theories, musicians' eyes well up when they hear complex music. Artists notice unique patterns in the visual world. Poets write about ordinary details that no one else notices. Actors study humans in action and speech and reproduce this to the amazement of audiences. Dancers and athletes tone and tune their bodies to be able to leap and lunge. The creator is drawn toward activity in a specific domain, and expresses this appetite by a passion for the aesthetics of the field. As a writer, I agonize over and adore subtleties of punctuation; I even love semicolons!

Organic unconsciousness. However, Ghiselin pointed out that the unconscious work in any field of creativity is done organically, and is not "canny calculation governed by wish, will, and expediency." This is not to say that the creative mind is undisciplined, for it needs to be managed in order to discover what needs to be done next, and to assure that movement towards the end product is economical and certain. Much of the work is imitation, especially in young creators, but the creator must go on, "for only on the fringes of consciousness and in the deeper backgrounds into which they fade away is freedom attainable."

Trancelike state. Ghiselin then described the physical manifestations of the creative process, the *massive concentration* that the creator exhibits. One could say that the person is in kind of a trance, concentrating so much that he seems to be hypnotized or sleepwalking. But this state differs from hypnotism or trance, for the person is collected, autonomous, and watchful. Ghiselin said that this trancelike state is common to all creative activity, but it is an indirect result that comes from the creator's passion for the particular domain, not as a direct intention: "In short, the creative discipline when successful may generate a trancelike state, but one does not throw oneself into a trance in order to create."

In an interview for the *Paris Review* "Writers At Work" series, John Hersey, the writer who changed the world with his portrait of Hiroshima's devastation, described his creative dreamlike state: "When the writing is really working, I think there is something like dreaming going on. I don't know how to draw the line between the conscious management of what you're doing and this state." Hersey said that this dreamlike mood happens during the first stages, the drafts of his work, and he thought it was similar to daydreaming. He said, "When I feel really engaged with a passage, I become so lost in it that I'm unaware of my real surroundings, totally involved in the pictures and sounds that that passage evokes." He went on to say that this mysterious feeling may be one of the things that attract those of us who write.

Flow

What Hersey and many other creative people describe is now called *flow*. In 1990 psychologist Mihalyi Csikszentmihalyi coined the word and wrote a book about his research with it. The flow feeling occurs "when a person's body or mind is stretched to its limits in a voluntary effort to accomplish something difficult and worthwhile." Csikszentmihalyi's 1995 book, *Creativity: Flow and the Psychology of Discovery and Invention*, described the results of interviews with 91 eminent creators in the sciences, business, government, and the arts. An example of the type of question asked by Csikszentmihalyi is this: "How important is rationality versus intuition in your work?"

The researchers noted nine elements that made up flow:

- (1) There are clear goals every step of the way.
- (2) There is immediate feedback to one's actions.
- (3) There is a balance between challenges and skills.
- (4) Actions and awareness are merged.
- (5) Distractions are excluded from consciousness.
- (6) There is no worry of failure.
- (7) Self-consciousness disappears.
- (8) The sense of time becomes distorted.
- (9) The activity becomes an end in itself, or autotelic.

Some people may say that flow resembles happiness, but Csikszentmihalyi pointed out that while one is in the middle of doing something creative, he doesn't think about *being* happy; it is only afterwards that he realizes that he *was* happy.

When I begin to write, I just know whether an emotional experience will come out as a poem or a story. I experience a vague itchiness to jot a few rough lines before the sensation is lost, and I often put the idea in my notebook or draw it in my sketchbook so I won't lose it. When I begin to work on it, I often lose hours of consciousness about time. In creating poetry I work, revise, envision, revise, envision, revise, pace, think, pace; then I look up and it's several hours later. In fiction I get lost in the characters' lives.

An artist friend reported the same phenomenon. She begins in the morning, only to discover it's dusk; she's been concentrating so much she's lost track of time. She said that's why she gave up painting. When her kids came home from school, she'd look up, surprised to realize she had done no house-home from school, she'd look up, surprised to realize she had done no house-work, run no errands. Her angry husband and children did not understand her passion for her work. Many creative women have experienced shame and guilt and conflict about their work, to the point of giving it up.

The Will and Organic Form. In the creative process, a willingness to sit down and concentrate is not enough. Though the will to create is important, alone it is not sufficient, for "will belongs to the conscious life only," Ghiselin noted. Will can keep a person at her desk or help her organize a project, but it can also stultify and inhibit the development of what is truly new. Virginia Woolf wrote that she had planned and organized the structure of her novel, *Mrs. Dalloway,* but had to abandon that organization when it didn't work. She then proceeded blindly, without a plan. Clearly, the previous plan had not been what she needed in order to express her impulse in writing the book. Therefore, for a plan to work, it must be organic.

Julian Green spoke about teaching fiction writing at Goucher College. His students expected that he would give them a recipe for writing a novel, but Green told them, "I know of no other rule for writing a novel than sitting down at a table and starting off with Chapter One." On the other hand, John Irving in an interview with D. Stanton said that he preferred to "not only know the end of the novel before the end of the novel, but the end of the chapter before I begin the chapter, the end of the scene before I begin the scene."

Most writers proceed organically rather than in the organized manner that Irving noted, with the exception of a few such as the novelist Norman Mailer. When he was learning how to write as a student at Harvard, Mailer vowed to write three thousand words a day, every day. His first wife, Bea, said of his writing habits a few years later: "There was never a question of waiting for the muse to descend." He worked through the whole outlines of the books he was writing: how many chapters, how each chapter would move the plot forward. He had three-by-five-inch cards on which he kept track of plot structure and the personalities of the characters and would shuffle these to make sure he was on track. He wrote about 25 pages a week on the first draft of the 750-page manuscript. In his memoir, Gore Vidal noted that Mailer majored in engineering and said:

> I have a theory that the mind of an engineer, though well suited for many things, is ill suited for either literature or politics. For the engineer everything must connect; while the natural writer or politician knows, instinctively, that nothing ever really connects except in what we imagine science to

be. Literature, like the politics of a Franklin Roosevelt, requires a divergent mind. Engineering (Mailer and Solzhenitsyn) requires a convergent mind. Compare Roosevelt's inspired patternless arabesques as a politician, artfully dodging this way and that, to the painstaking engineer Jimmy Carter, doggedly trying to make it all add up, and failing.

Not only engineers and novelists, but poets and prose writers work differently. The poet Louis Simpson commented about how prose writers just don't understand how a poet works. "Descriptions of poetry by men who are not poets is usually ridiculous, for they describe rational thought processes." In one novel, George Orwell described a poet at work. Simpson said, "This is completely false; prose may be written in this way, but not poetry. A poet begins by losing control; he does not choose his thoughts; they seem to be choosing him." Rhythms come from the unconscious, and the poet hears the poem much as a composer of music does.

The need for hard work. Organic needs must also dictate the subject of the creative project, for choosing a subject the creator is not inclined to and forcing his mind to elaborate on it is not productive. Finally, this inspiration must be realized by good hard work.

After the work is completed, the process is not finished, for the creator must determine whether or not she has created something new, fresh, and useful. Often she will find that the value of the work has been in its intrinsic benefit to her development. When she submits it to critical review, it may be found wanting. Then she may work on it some more, or reject it and begin again. Shelley, for example, left behind many parts of poems because he didn't like to revise.

The Concentration of a Life. Ghiselin said that ultimate achievement through the creative process demands not only concentration while doing the project, but "the concentration of a life." And even concentrating one's life upon the field may not be enough if the talent isn't there, if the chance and milieu aren't there. Concentrating one's life on the field means viewing the world in fresh, new ways. The creative person must remain open to eccentricity and deviation. Ghiselin said that if a person is afraid of deviation, he may not be capable of inventing, because everything that is new "is liable to seem eccentric and perhaps dangerous." Creative people are obligated to pay attention to the odd, the strange, the eccentric: "We must practice to some extent an imaginative surrender to every novelty that has even the most tenuous credentials." Ghiselin called this "imaginative surrender;" Getzels and Csikszentmihalyi, in observing creative visual artists, described something akin to it and called it naiveté. Julian Green went so far as to say that this naiveté is a component of what we call talent:

> One of the secrets of real talent is to see everything for the first time, to look at a leaf as though one had never seen one before, for then only can it appear to us in all its newness. The power of marveling makes up the genius of childhood, so quickly blunted by habit and education, and no one will ever be able to fit words together in an acceptable order unless he knows a little how to see creation through Adam's eyes. In art, truth lies in surprising. When one looks at a stone as though it were a miniature mountain, one begins to see it as it really is.

Ferrucci, in *Inevitable Grace*, said that the true artistic person shows himself through his attitude toward the "ugly and banal." He said,

> Neither repulsion nor judgment is present, nor, on the other hand, morbid pleasure; rather, we find an attitude of universality—the ability to love and appreciate even the most unlikely subject—as in the "old women's throats" to which Leonardo devoted hours of attention and observation for several of his drawings; or even in cigarette butts, in which the Russian painter Wassily Kandinsky claimed he could see the "secret soul" of things.

Ferrucci quoted a letter of Van Gogh's in which the great artist said that he saw "drawings and pictures in the poorest huts, in the dirtiest corner. And my mind is drawn toward these things by an irresistible force." This is a basic personality characteristic of creative people, the attitude of naiveté, the attitude of openness, the acceptance of, and curiosity about the odd or strange.

Ghiselin's "Introduction" still remains among the best summaries of what happens during the creative process. Over the years, I have developed several teaching activities on the organic side of the creative process. These are described in Chapter 12.

The Importance of Rituals

The creative process often has ritualistic aspects. For example, some creators like to work in the morning, some at night. Some can work anywhere, but most have a place to work, a studio, a workshop, an office. Some find that their minds get excited with certain stimuli, such as music heard in solitude, chemical agents, certain company, reading or exercise. Like athletes who put their uniforms on in a certain order before the big game, creative people often instinctively follow certain rituals before and while working.

Illuminations and Aha!s

Much has been written on the illumination phase, for that is the most dramatic. A very entertaining book by Madigan and Elwood, *Brainstorms & Thunderbolts: How Creative Genius Works*, described the *Aha!*s of many creative people. The illuminations or inspirations come from the following types of experiences:

1. **Triggers and flashes:** For example, a sunset and a poem by Goethe inspired Tesla's design for an alternating current motor.
2. **Obvious connections:** Buckminster Fuller discovered the stability of the triangle, the basis for his famous geodesic dome, in kindergarten while building structures from toothpicks and dried peas. Frank Lloyd Wright's mother gave him Froebel's wooden blocks when he was in kindergarten; he later said that he began to think about being an architect while building with them.
3. **Visions and voices:** While she was in church, Harriet Beecher Stowe saw the image of Uncle Tom on the ice chunk trying to escape. This vision inspired her writing of the serialized novel instrumental in the cause of abolition.
4. **Dreams and drugs:** Mary Shelley dreamed the idea for her book about Frankenstein after several days at a retreat with other writers trying to make up the most scary ghost story. Isaac Singer first dreamed the solution to the sewing machine problem—that the needle had to have its eye in its point. In fact, much has been written about the place of dreaming in the creative process, and creative people often keep journals of their dreams, hoping they'll give both insight and material, which dreams often do. Psychologist David Feldman wrote a 1988 essay on what insights into creativity two dreams had given him.

5. **Reflections on death:** The death of Selman Waksman's sister from diphtheria greatly influenced his developing streptomycin, for which he later won the Nobel Prize. Alfred Lord Tennyson wrote an elegy for his dear friend, Hallam, that became the poem for which he became most famous, "In Memoriam."

6. **Being in love:** The Taj Mahal was built in Agra, India, as a tribute to the wife of Shah Jehan, Mumtaz Mahal. Although the Shah did not design it, he was inspired to create it by his wife; many, many poems and stories are inspired by the yearning for a loved one.

7. **Following trains of thought:** Rorschach, inventor of the ink blot test, belonged to a poet's group who wrote on topics suggested to them by ink blots. An artist who had attended art school before turning to medical studies, Rorschach developed his psychological test as a result of this chain of interests.

8. **Debates and suggestions:** Janov's Primal Therapy was suggested by a comedy act one of his clients had seen.

9. **Plain old creative thievery:** Velcro, invented by the Swiss inventor George de Mestral, was suggested by burrs sticking to hunting clothes; the idea for the process to make it came from the principle of barber's thinning shears. Vaseline petroleum jelly, refined by the chemist George Chesebrough in 1870, was an idea cribbed from oil-men who complained about the rod wax that clogged oil pumps.

10. **Fakes, mistakes, and accidents:** Ivory soap, the soap that floats, was supposedly discovered when a worker accidentally left his whipping vat on while he went to lunch and too much air was whipped into the batch. Afraid of a reprimand, he poured the substance into the frames anyway, and Ivory soap was born.

These amusing accounts of the beginnings of startling products and ideas illustrate the strange, wonderful processes, intentional or otherwise of creativity. The purpose of creativity training, say some experts, is to make the accidental seem intentional by creating the proper atmosphere for creative flourish.

Newer Theories of the Creative Process

Writing about and interest in creativity has recently burgeoned, with many writers on the subject focusing on the creative process. Brain research has been popularized, and simplistic theories of right and left brain thinking have evolved. The outgrowth of the 1960s Vietnam War and the civil rights movement led to the "me" generation in the 1980s, with people trying to make themselves the manifestation of creativity. This thinking has continued into the 1990s, with creativity often used in connection with spirituality and the divine as people seek inner growth. Research on the influence of substances on the creative process has been done. Techniques for enhancing creativity have included meditation and exercise. Psychologists and psychoanalysts have begun to consider creativity as the work of a lifetime, not of the moment. Cognitive scientists have sought to isolate what happens when the creator is creating. All of this has led to some interesting postulation.

Right/Left Brain and the Creative Process

One popular cultural myth has been that creativity is the province of the right brain, while noncreativity is of the left. A favorite pastime is for people to identify themselves as right- or left-brained. Speakers go from company to company, school to school, giving pop psychology tests that purportedly show the test-taker's side-of-brain dominance, and people can be overheard saying, "Well, I'm right-brained, and my husband is left-brained, so that's why we don't get along. He's so organized, and I'm so disorganized." Right-brained people are supposedly creative though spacey, while the left-brained are supposedly methodical, mathematical, sequential. Many books and articles have been written on the subject, many researchers have joined in to prove or disprove, and many interesting workshops have helped people tap into their right brains.

Betty Edwards's popular 1979 book, *Drawing on the Right Side of the Brain*, taught how to draw more accurately by activating the right side of the brain, using reversals and upside-down techniques to keep verbal codes from interfering with seeing what is actually there. Gabriele Rico taught how to write this "natural" way in her book, subtitled *Using Right Brain Techniques To Release Your Expressive Powers.*

I took workshops from both Edwards and Rico. Edwards had all of us draw our best drawing. We laboriously reproduced, from our left-brain memories, that first-grade house with a sun, that second-grade snowman with a dog, that fourth-grade horse that mother had kept framed on the wall for all these years. Edwards pointed out that we had all stopped drawing with these early efforts: because we couldn't draw well enough to suit our own standards, we fell into reproducing codes and symbols, censoring our right brains with our left brains. Rico had us write after webbing our ideas, going back in our associational memories to early childhood. The remembrance was so powerful for one man that he let out a sob, later commenting that he hadn't thought of that experience for years.

I have also used a similar technique in workshops—a reminding chain or memory probe. Holding up, for instance, a Granny Smith apple, I remind participants that this apple first came to the United States from New Zealand, on the other side of the world, and then I tell a story about its voyage, talking about how it is winter here but summer down there, and eventually I turn my listeners' perceptions topsy-turvy. Then I ask them to complete this line: "The Granny Smith apple reminds me of . . ." Someone might write, ". . . of a green spring day," then continue, ". . . a green spring day reminds me of . . ." I guide them through the first few lines, then leave them to write, asking them to use concrete images from their associational memories and not abstractions like love, peace, happiness or sadness. I play soft music, baroque or New Age. People have said that my simple associational exercise unleashed memories they'd long forgotten. Many are able to associate all the way back to very early emotional experiences.

Rico, after landing her book contract, was stuck in the writing of it. Finally she decided to take her own advice and put butcher paper all over the kitchen floor and, using associational thinking, outlined—webbed—the book that has gained such popularity. Whether one side of her brain or the other was dominant as she forced this breakthrough, the point is that her creativity was enhanced by webbing on the butcher paper, just as the creative process is also enhanced by paying attention, in Edwards' workshop, to edges and contours, and in Rico's workshop, to associations brought on by other associations. We now know we use our whole brain unless we have had a brain injury, and the right-left brain fad has passed, with phrases *right brain* and *left brain* becoming codes for "more creative" or "flakey," and "less creative" or "dull and logical."

Substances and the Creative Process

Many people have used chemical substances to enhance the creative process, to put themselves into that semi-trance state of creative production. Jack Kerouac supposedly wrote *On The Road* nonstop while on amphetamines and alcohol, typing typing typing on a roll of butcher paper. Aldous Huxley experimented with mescaline in the late 1920s and wrote *The Doors of Perception*. Carlos Castaneda used mushrooms to enhance his journey to spiritual awareness. Heroin was used by many musicians and writers, including Charlie Parker and William S. Burroughs. Alcohol is the drug of choice for many performers, writers, and creative writers; absinthe, popular at the turn of the century, is returning as a favored substance. A list of the clients at the Betty Ford Clinic, as reported by *People* magazine every week or so, includes many of the most respected talents in the arts. The tragic deaths of John Belushi, Janis Joplin, Jimi Hendrix and Kurt Cobain—to mention just a few—all point to the attraction of drugs for creative people.

Alan Bold edited an anthology of prose inspired by alcohol, *Drink To Me Only*, in 1982. In his introduction, he wrote that the association of creative people, especially creative men, with alcohol has been going on for a long time, and the word "drunken" has become "the essential epithet of the poet," with many believing in a "close relationship between booze and the muse. The artistic temperament is indissolubly associated with drunkenness and we expect musicians to perform outrageously and painters to make exhibitions of themselves."

A Jungian analyst, Clarissa Pinkola Estés, in *Women Who Run With The Wolves,* theorizes that creative women's addiction to substances may be a result of loss of soul, loss of the essential creative self through conformity and suppression in order to "be good." "No play, no creative life. Be good, no creative life. Sit still, no creative life. Speak, think, act only demurely, little creative juice." She uses the example of Janis Joplin, "instinct-injured by spirit-crushing forces." A good student and talented visual artist, Joplin was "vilified by her teachers and many of those who surrounded her in the 'good-girl' white Southern Baptist community." She liked to climb rocks and sing jazz. When she grew up and escaped, "she was so starved she could no longer tell when enough was enough. She had no limits around sex, liquor, or drugs." Estés also mentions Bessie Smith, Anne Sexton, Edith Piaf, Marilyn Monroe, and Judy Garland in this context of being starved and vilified until they became addicted, intemperate, unable to quit.

Another Jungian analyst, Linda Leonard, in *Witness To The Fire: Creativity And The Evil of Addiction,* asserts that creative people often use substances such as cocaine or alcohol to artificially achieve states where they feel they can be creative, but then they stand risk of becoming addicted to the substances. But, she noted, addiction and creativity are parallel processes, not causal, for addiction does not necessarily lead to creativity. She noted that both addicts and artists "descend into chaos, into the unknown underworld of the unconscious. Both are fascinated by what they find there. Both encounter death, pain, suffering." But there is a difference, for the addict is pulled, whereas the creative person chooses to plummet into inner depths. Even though some people can continue to create masterfully while under the influence or as addicts, many others eventually lose their creative edge to addiction.

Meditation

Some have said the past decade and the next are marked by a spiritual need for communion with the self and with others. Some religious fundamentalists fear that New Age concepts constitute a dangerous new religion; however, the 1990 census indicated that most people continue with their traditional religions, and fewer than one percent of the United States people identified their religious preference as "New Age."

As an ongoing curiosity about Eastern religions continues from the 1960s, an astonishing number of poets, artists, musicians, and writers have embraced Buddhism. One suspects this is because of the attention paid to meditation, solitude, and going within of that religious faith. Many creators — even scientists—with backgrounds in Christianity and Judaism seem to reject the dogma and traditions of the religion of their childhood and study Eastern faiths. A partial list of such creators includes Allen Ginsberg, Robert Bly, W. S. Merwin, Anselm Hollo, Anne Waldman, Gary Snyder, Jane Augustine, John Cage, William Heyen, Lucien Stryk, and Philip Whalen. Others have embraced the contemplative life of the Christian monastery, for example poets Kathleen Norris and Daniel Berrigan. In an interview, poet Sarah Wood spoke about what attracts her to Buddhism:

> Creativity seems to get activated by meditation (my teacher quotes T.S. Eliot, a "frog voice" seeking to be born, something like that). On sesshins (meditation retreats) poems sometimes come flooding up. A potter friend says pottery designs do for him. Or ideas like that . . . There is a dynamic source that meditation brings us closer to, and that energy surges up through us. So, it may be not that poets went to Eastern religions, but that religions like Buddhism with meditation and other such practices, created the poets. First they were Buddhists and then they were poets. For me, my poetry had died out except for a ragged scrap of a poem every year or two when I was really upset or dreamy. But with the Buddhism, my poetry came back.

Some vehicles deemed useful in discovering one's inner self are breath control, meditational techniques, visualization and imagery. Several workshops I attended were remarkably similar. The leaders took us through exercises where we progressively relaxed our toes, our feet, our legs, and the rest of our bodies, breathing deeply. Then we were mentally placed in a setting, often a beach with the waves crashing, or a forest with birds singing and leaves rustling, or the ramparts of a castle looking over the purple plain. Soft synthesizer music or tinkly bells played on a tape recorder as we visualized ourselves in these places. In 1997, along with 500 other people, I attended a workshop in New York City led by Daniel Goleman, whose best-selling book *Emotional Intelligence* has taken the world by storm, even in places like Taiwan, where it is the best selling book ever. Before he described his work in school systems throughout the world, his wife, a psychotherapist, took us through a meditation on being mindful by having us contemplate and slowly taste a raisin. This illustrates how meditational techniques have even permeated the lives of hard-bitten editors for the *New York Times* such as Goleman.

These group relaxation and visualization techniques help us contemplate our inner selves, discover our inner truths, quiet us to the point where we pay attention to what is going on inside, and calm and release us from the pressures of the hustle bustle. Of course, these workshops and techniques are based on truths that creative and spiritual people have known for ages. Artists, writers, mystics and ascetics of all religions have known for all time that calming inner solitude is essential for true knowledge of self, and in fact, altered states of consciousness are common to all religions, from whirling dervishes to fasting Christians. Christ fasted in the wilderness for forty days before he led his followers into Jerusalem. Various creeds within the Christian faith refer to God speaking through the prophets, and the stories of prophets from all religions who received their inspirations and knowledge from dreams and visions would fill volumes.

The connection of the spiritual with therapy is implicit, with therapists often viewed as priests or gurus. This investiture of psychology with religious import was evident with the advent of psychoanalysis. The novelist Dan Wakefield said that for his generation of young, creative people in the 1950s, psychotherapy replaced God: "I entered psychoanalysis with the high seriousness of purpose and commitment of any acolyte taking his vows to a rigorous religious order. Like many in my generation, I had already made the intellectual substitution of Freud for God." Wakefield conducted a workshop on spiritual autobiography which I attended. He conducts many such workshops, also workshops on the creative process, and has a large mailing list to announce where he will be speaking. In his book on New York in the 1950s, he told how his group of young writers used to disdain the Beats, led by Allen Ginsberg and Jack Kerouac, yet now, like many Beats of the fifties, he has given up alcohol and has turned to meditation, yoga, and other spiritually-based practices to enhance his and others' creativity.

By the 1970s and 1980s, connections between spirituality and creativity were made explicit. One of the most popular authors and speakers about this process, Shakti Gawain, in her 1986 best-selling book, *Living in the Light*, said that creative visualization aids in creating the self, for creative visualization is not just a technique but ultimately is a state of consciousness in which we deeply realize that we are the continuous creators of our universe, and we take responsibility for that fact at all moments. There is no separation between people and God; we are divine expressions of the creative principle on this level of existence. Gawain likened living to art: "I like to think of myself as an artist, and my life is my greatest work of art." She called her life (not her creative products) "a magnificent art form." Now, toward the end of the millennium, computer companies have meditation rooms for their inventive employees, and businessmen read books like *The Zen of Selling*.

Creative Imagery and Athletics

Another expanded definition of the creative process has been in the use of meditation, visualization and imaging in athletics. Athletes imagine their performances before they do them; they visualize the ski run, for example, or the football play, or the course for the marathon, and imagine themselves on every part of the course. The adoption by athletes of such methods has given their use respectability and cachet; books such as *The Inner Game of Tennis* specifically teach how to let go of the mind and reach flow in playing. Athletes often meditate and put on their "game faces" before athletic games and events.

However, people in all sections of the U.S. fear that these methods, now in common use by coaches and teachers, involve hypnotism or even Satanism. Some further assert that these practices constitute a new, anti-Christian religion, pro-Hindu and Buddhist. That emotional assessment is too simplistic, even though essentially the impulse behind the New Age movement has been a spiritual impulse intertwined with a creative impulse. Upon trying relaxation and visualization techniques as a means of enhancing children's creativity or preparing them for standardized testing, teachers have been closely questioned by parents. When this happens, teachers often refer parents to the coaches, because athletes use visualization extensively nowadays.

But there is research evidence, beyond the enthusiastic chanting of mantras and the progressive relaxations of toes and knees, that altered consciousness does aid people not only in divergent thinking but in capturing internal essence. Cowger and Torrance trained students in either meditation or relaxation; according to results of pre- and post-tests using the Torrance Tests of Creative Thinking, the meditators had significant gains in heightened consciousness of problems, perceived change, invention, sensory experience, expression of emotion and feeling, synthesis, unusual visualization, internal visualization, humor and fantasy. Those trained in relaxation had drops in verbal fluency and originality as well as in figural fluency and originality, but had gains in synthesis and unusual visualization. This use of a standardized divergent production test to measure changes in internal processes is one way of showing that meditation and relaxation do have some relationship to perceived processes of creativity, at least in their effect on paper and pencil measures. For divergent production testing, see Chapter 3.

In a 1987 study, Gondola found that even one session of aerobic dancing enhanced students' creative thinking. In her experiment, Gondola first administered creative thinking measures, then had students participate in a twenty-minute aerobic dance class before testing them again. Analysis of the posttest showed significant differences in all three aspects of creative thinking.

Creativity as the Process of a Life

The influence of the New Age definition of creativity not as the making of works of art or thought but as the power to create oneself can be seen in any chain bookstore at the mall, where shelves are filled with books by many authors—most of whom are fond of the term *creativity*—on channeling, out-of-body experiences, reincarnation and meditation. Preferred over such traditional creative works as poetry or novels, these New Age books rival the amazingly popular self-help books in sales. A poet friend marketed her book as New Age, thinking people would be more likely to buy it. She was right.

Transpersonal and Ecopsychology: Creation of a New Earth Peace

In psychology, New Age thinking is related to what came to be called the Human Potential Movement, which has evolved into a field called transpersonal psychology. Researchers study higher states of awareness—including that required for the giving and receiving of information in ways other than the ordinary—as they seek to understand how inspiration, insight, intuition, imagination, and creativity operate. Experiments in the effects of mind-altering drugs during the 1960s influenced the beginning of the transpersonal philosophy: these drugs, before becoming available, albeit illegally, as recreational drugs, were researched for their potential to induce or improve creativity and awareness.

The experience of attaining a sense of unity with all the universe is also a part of transpersonal psychology, and devotees speak of using their creativity in enhancing a global consciousness. The earth is personified into a female creature called Gaia, and we are all charged with not harming our Mother Earth by burning forests in the Amazon or by polluting blue coral in Japan.

Similar in its elevation of earth-consciousness is another new field of psychology, ecopsychology, led by Theodore Roszak and others. In an anthology of essays edited by Roszak, depth psychologist Stephen Aizenstat writes, "Underpinning the creative process of human invention are the archetypal patterns of the natural world." Proponents claim that people should realize and recover their deep connection with the earth: "Imagine a world in which carpenter knows beaver, lawyer knows eagle, philosopher knows the silence of the deep night." According to ecopsychology's tenets, when people re-establish this essential connection, they will be "compelled to make the journey back to the source in nature that inspires their work."

For many, the desired result of visualization, imagery, and solitary or group meditation is to be a functioning part of the ultimate creative product: a peaceful world order, a universal consciousness. Harman and Rheingold called it "higher creativity." The sought-after product is not any single painting, poem, or mathematical theorem, but many such, made for the purposes of achieving a global unity. People who are thus consciously creating themselves and their lives view creativity and creative processes as producing life art that transcends the narrow and personal in its universal affirmation of the human spirit. President Bush called it "a thousand points of light."

One of the most amazing of these works was the First Earth Run, in 1986, where teams of runners circled the globe carrying a torch that symbolized earth, beginning and ending at the United Nations. Hundreds of thousands of people participated. Dictators such as the leader of Bangladesh even wrote poems as the teams came through their countries bearing the torch. The organizers of the First Earth Run, David Gershon and Gail Straub, said that they could not call it a "First Peace Run," because peace is to many a warlike word, but everyone can unite about the concept of saving the earth.

Here we see creativity directly tied to its earliest root meaning, the creation (i.e., of God, or earth itself) and the process of creativity as recapturing the ancient unity of all creatures, including humans, with all life. Roszak, in *Voice of the Earth*, notes the great influence of the philosopher Henri Bergson, who believed that an essential fluid (*elan vital*) exists which shapes a soul of the world (*anima mundi*), whose highest creative level is the creation of human intelligence. "The mind that mattered was that of the artist and saint, the mind gifted with intuition. Below that level, consciousness is flawed in ways that produce suffering and carnage." Roszak noted that most philosophies say that the creative and spiritual capabilities represent the highest form of evolution.

Others have also viewed the creative process not merely as an altered consciousness, an immense concentration, or an attainment of solitude. Through biography, we can see how an adult creative producer lives his life. Gruber, in *Darwin On Man*, looked at Darwin's life from the psychological perspective, to see how lifelong creativity unfolded and developed. Simonton has done much work on this also, with a method called historiometry, working with published biographies of creative persons.

Storr noted three periods in the process of the creative life. The first is the imitative stage, when the young creative person learns what has been already done and spends a lot of time imitating. During the second period, the creative person dispenses with what has already been done and enters upon an assured and masterful period of production in which the need to communicate with a wide public is clear. In the third period, the creative person pulls back from the need to communicate and may turn to unconventional forms without rhetoric or posing, and continue an exploration of areas that are not intrapersonal but perhaps spiritual or universal.

Similarly, LeoNora Cohen proposed a developmental theory, stating that creativity evolves on a continuum of "adaptive creative behaviors" from infancy to adulthood. She said there may be six levels of development: (1) Learning something new; universal novelty; (2) Making connections that are rare compared to those of peers; (3) Demonstrating talents; (4) Producing information; (5) Creating by extending the field; (6) Creating by revolutionizing the field.

Mary Catherine Bateson, in *Composing A Life*, adopted a slightly different focus, at least in creative women's lives, noting a sense of making it up as one goes along. Although creative development may follow general stages, the paths of women often show sudden changes. She studied five prominent women and in each of their lives found a requisite willingness to drop everything and change plans, often subordinating their creative work to the needs of their husbands and growing families. These women spoke of the implications and repercussions of small choices, and of a constant sense of conflict between their creative work and their family's needs.

Dabrowski and Piechowski in their 1977 book spoke to lifelong development, of life as a process and not a series of stages. Higher forms of development are achieved once a person has moved beyond primitive drives, selfishness and feelings of inferiority toward others, to transcendence, self-determination and "sustained creativity and lucidity of the mind in spite of infirmity of the body." In the Dabrowski theory of emotional development, with reference to the creative person, creativity is manifested in the person's overexcitability, or "enhanced and intensified mental activity distinguished by characteristic forms of expression which are above common and average."

Creative people, artists at least, have emotional sensitivity and intensity, a great range of feeling, as well as high imaginational overexcitability, "spontaneous activity of a mind that freely makes unexpected associations, reaches into invented realms, takes any form as a stimulus to perceive other forms, including nonvisual ones," according to Piechowski, Silverman, and Falk.

It has been said that most people live with the radio on, but creative people have satellite dishes. These are their amplified overexcitabilities. Dabrowski, in an introduction to a 1975 monograph by Piechowski, said he witnessed, throughout his life, "geniuses of mankind and saints" who showed psychological disturbances but who "create the highest and the most lasting values." These disturbances came because of "great creative and developmental richness" in trying to reach the highest levels of development.

The Dabrowski theory describes several levels of development, Levels I through V, which can support creative production. An example is the writer Antoine de St. Exupery, whom Piechowski in a 1978 monograph described as having reached Level IV, a level which is similar to Maslow's concept of self-actualization, almost the highest level of human development. Eleanor Roosevelt was described as having reached Level V—the highest level, reached by very few people according to Piechowski and Tyska in 1982. Piechowski, in a 1990 essay called "Emotional Giftedness," asserts that Level V encompasses "incomprehensible freedom found in total selflessness, in love truly unconditional, expecting nothing in return, love that accurately perceives the divine spark even in the most darkened soul." In 1997 he said that this emotional giftedness is an elaborate form of Gardner's description of "intrapersonal intelligence."

Certainly, creativity can be present in any of these levels, but the process of a life can also be viewed as creativity. The notions that creativity is not momentary but lifelong, that creativity has a universal purpose, and that creativity evolves developmentally seem to be the most logical definitions of creativity.

Another theory of the creative process is proposed by archetypal psychologist James Hillman. In 1996's *The Soul's Code*, he propounds his acorn theory: "Each life is formed by its unique image, an image that is the essence of that life and calls it to a destiny." The person's image is a guide, a "daimon," reminding the person of the call. The daimon is perceived through intuition or gut feelings as to which path to take. The notion of a call, or vocation, in response to prodding by the daimon is included in my Pyramid of Talent Development (See Chapter 1).

The acorn theory is similar to Feldman's idea of the crystallizing experience that grabs a person and sets her on her path. It also mirrors my observation that certain predictive behaviors are common to each domain of talent, for Hillman's explanation of how a person gets to be what he gets to be is to cite many telling incidents gleaned from biographies. Saying that the acorn theory is neither fatalistic (for a person can refuse the intuition and the insight) nor deterministic (for a person's destiny is not preformed), Hillman argues that human creativity follows a certain developmental path. His concept of the daimon as a sort of scout leader, setting one on her path up the mountain to the campsite at the top where she can behold the wonders of the self, takes into account the five *I*s essential to the realization of creativity: *imagery, intuition, imagination, inspiration,* and *insight.*

In 1997, commenting on the theory of the acorn, Reynolds said the daimon can be discerned in the life of an individual by considering the etymological difference between the words *talented* and *gifted* (See Chapter 1.) A *talent* is like a valuable to be used at the convenience of the owner. There are many people who have a talent for music but who feel free to take it or leave it. However, the root of the Germanic word *gift* includes the concept of poison. Someone gifted is blessed and poisoned all at once. The gift is inhuman and uses the individual, for in using the gift one experiences oceanic consciousness, loses track of time, becomes so involved in the frenzied doing of the creative passion that time, food, sleep, and place don't matter. The gift is all-consuming, dazzling; the person loves doing it, and when he's not doing it he's thinking about it, and if he doesn't do it, he becomes ill.

Through a car crash, therapy, or a life-altering experience one may discover that she should have been a writer, a musician, a scientist. According to

Reynolds, this is the daimon interceding to return the individual to her gift, where the mind is appropriately on fire, full of light and din. When he teaches his Creativity, Inc., course to high school and college students, Reynolds assists the students in finding where their gift has been at work in their lives. This might be in where they have been wounded, or where they have spent much time as children but have forgotten what caught their hearts. Reynolds asks his students to bring their favorite book from preschool to his classes, and to recapture the images that engaged them then.

Improvisation and an Attitude of Playfulness

The jazz musician Nachmanovitch, in *Free Play,* also spoke of the creative life as improvisation and risky business: "To follow your own course, not patterned on parents, peers, or institutions, involves a delicate balance of tradition and personal freedom, a delicate balance of sticking to your guns and remaining open to change."

The importance of improvisation and an attitude of playfulness cannot be understated. To play your musical instrument without music in front of you is frightening to some who have learned to trust in their reading ability and not in their intuition and musical memory. The "play" is a necessity. Think of children making up the game as they go along, lost in imagination, forming teams and sides in a fluid all-day motion generated by the discourse of the moment. This fluidity, this improvisational forming and re-forming, is long lost to most adults. Games of charades, Pictionary, and other improvisational toys often capture that delicious feeling of glee, joy, and bawdy humor that lends itself to creative expression.

Theater games, scat singing, doodling and word rivers are techniques I use in teaching improvisation. Fantasy games with role-playing also encourage improvisation, a trust that one will land on one's feet when sent out into the jungle.

The Creative Process as Cognitive Science

Cognitive science uses the computer and scientific analysis to answer questions that have long troubled philosophers. It is an interdisciplinary field, combining philosophy, neuroscience, anthropology, psychology and artificial intelligence. Howard Gardner, in his 1985 history of cognitive science, *The Mind's New Science*, proposes that the questions cognitive scientists answer should "provide a cogent scientific account of how human beings achieve their most remarkable symbolic products: how we come to compose symphonies, write poems, invent machines (including computers), or construct theories (including cognitive-scientific ones)." That Deep Blue finally beat Kazmarov at chess is a triumph for the cognitive scientists who are artificial intelligence researchers. The complaint that Kazmarov was not allowed to see the chess games programmed into the computer makes one wonder what would have happened if this creative chess player had had that opportunity.

Perkins's *The Mind's Best Work*

The cognitive psychologist and philosopher David Perkins in 1981 tested many of the creative process postulations that have been described in this chapter. His book, *The Mind's Best Work*, is one of the most interesting cognitive-psychology creativity books in the literature. Perkins makes what he calls propositions based on the prevailing thought about the creative process, then examines the evidence and refutes or modifies the propositions, calling them "revised propositions." In generating the revisions he primarily used results of psychological experiments in how creative people form schemata, how creative people recognize patterns, and how creative people solve problems, to name a few. Among the techniques he used was the observation of working poets and artists, interrupting them while they were painting or writing and asking them what they were thinking. Here are some of his propositions and their revisions.

The Expert Witness Proposition. Many accounts have been written by creative persons about what was happening when they were creating. Some believe that people like Coleridge and Poe were trustworthy witnesses of their own creative processes. Perkins, however, asserts that people writing about their own creativity don't give valid accounts, because we can't tell whether or not they are telling the truth, or whether they correctly remembered what happened. Thus autobiographical accounts of what happens during the creative process are quite unreliable and shouldn't be taken seriously.

The Notebooks Proposition. Some people believe that one can psychoanalyze what happens in the creative process by painstakingly reading the scribbles, doodles, and other notes left by creative people. Perkins says such physical evidence seldom or never shows "the judgments, aims, and alternatives making up the process and the ways these emerge in the mind of the maker."

Much has been written about great mental leaps that creative people make when they receive the illumination. Here are three propositions commonly made about mental leaps, and Perkins' responses:

Mental Leap Proposition 1: That mental leaps occur very rapidly and are characterized by no conscious thought. They solve problems that a person has been stuck on, and help achieve insight into problems or situations that seemed impossible. Perkins pointed out that a mental leap may seem a quick unitary event, but there are some steps that can be discerned. These steps are progressive, even though the mental leap seems to skip a few logical steps in producing the insight more quickly than if logical thought had been used.

Mental Leap Proposition 2: That mental leaps are the result of long unconscious processing that suddenly come to the consciousness of the person. Perkins writes, "Extended unconscious thinking does not occur." Such strategies as "deferring a troublesome problem and returning to it later" work sometimes, but this has nothing to do with what is going on in the unconscious.

Mental Leap Proposition 3: That mental leaps are faster, compressing much thought into a short time. Perkins showed that the processes of "recognizing and realizing" account for mental leaps to a much greater degree than has been suspected. We may call it a mental leap if such recognizing and realizing help us organize material that we were unable to organize before.

The Discovery Proposition: In past views of the creative process, the word *discovery* was often used. For example, who discovered penicillin? Who discovered America? Who discovered the light bulb? In this sense, to discover means to be the first to find out, to realize. Some people believe that the processes that help in discovery are special, but Perkins shows that a person makes discoveries when he wants to discover. Memory, paying attention or noticing, forming metaphors and analogies, and combining unlike things are helpful in making discoveries, but the *intention* to discover is most important. Many accounts of the creative process emphasize that the person who is doing the creating, especially in the arts, is in a state of heightened emotion, but that the creation cannot take place without using the rational processes of mind.

Perkins, in insisting that emotionality and rationality are parts of the whole, disagrees with those who believe that affect (feeling) and cognition (knowing) "enter distinctively and essentially into creating." He writes, "Cognition and affect are not distinct aspects of creative experience." Emotions (affect) are ways of cognition (knowing).

Ultimately, according to Perkins, the creative process is one of selection, and there's not much mystery about it. The backbone of his theory of creativity is Perkins's list of ten ways that the creative person selects in order to come up with the creative product. During the creative process, the creative person does the following:

1. Notices opportunities.
2. Notices flaws.
3. Directs the memory to pertinent information.
4. Notices the critical reactions of others and of herself while the work is in progress and forms judgments based on those reactions.
5. Looks at the work in progress with certain criteria in mind.
6. Sets the work aside for awhile and comes back to it.
7. Makes long searches for options during the process, generating and rejecting solutions until a sound option is found.
8. Figuratively climbs a hill during the process, as each option is tried out, with a step up the hill being a narrowing down and a step back down the hill an opening up for new options.
9. Is familiar with the schemata of the field.
10. Can find new and challenging creative problems to work on.

Perkins might say that there is no such thing in the creative process as genuine surprise, even though many people have had such surprises. Such a position implies that a genuine surprise only comes to the person who is prepared to recognize the implications of that surprise.

You may think that Perkins has taken the mystery out of the creative process, has deflated its connection with the spiritual and with the search for truth. But demystification is the job of cognitive science, since *cognitive* refers, after all, to that which happens in the mind. Edward Wilson, in his forward to Findlay and Lumsden's 1988 book, *The Creative Mind*, calls the creative process the "grandmother of problems in the human sciences." The creative process is intractable. The creative process is "the gale of destruction that destabilizes the study of human evolution, reduces much of the social sciences to hermeneutics, and threatens to maintain the chasm separating the sciences from the humanities." Thus the work of demystification, like that of Perkins and the other cognitive scientists, is important in understanding the human process called creativity, even though many of us would like to retain the mystery.

8. Contemporary psychological and religious thought have emphasized that the creative process has universal implications.
9. So-called right-brain thinking, visualization, metaphorization, and imagery seem to help people in the creative process.
10. The creative process is a concern of scientists as well as humanists. Scientific experimentation has resulted in the demystifying of many popular creative process beliefs.
11. The repertoires of school people, who often use only the CPS process in enhancing creativity, should be expanded.

PART II

Creativity Assessment and Training

Several months have passed since Katherine Miller attended the state con-ference. She has been so busy she hasn't had time to think about what cre-ativity and the creative process are. She has sixty fourth, fifth, and sixth graders who come to her for five hours per week. She has obtained several levels of the basic textbooks, and the superhighway between her school and the regional office that serves her school district has grooves from her car wheels as she goes back and forth with materials from the media center. She has coached a team for the Odyssey of the Mind Competitions, and her stu-dents have joined Math Olympiad and Academic Challenge teams. These kids are really something!

Even though she spends every weekend preparing for the week ahead and hardly sees Brad at all, she feels on fire. She's working with kids who really want to learn. One morning she has a note in her mailbox from the regional coordinator, who also serves 79 other schools. It's time to begin selection of kids for the fourth grade class of next year. Has she given the creativity test and checklist to the third grade teachers yet?

"What test? What checklist?" Katherine wonders out loud.

The principal overhears her as he passes on his way to the coffee pot. "You have to identify kids for next year. Just call the regional office and ask how to do it. It has something to do with special tests. But don't ask me what. Testing was never my strong point."

Katherine makes the call. The regional coordinator is out. They play phone tag for several days. Then there's another note. "What test are you planning to use? Half the districts are using the Renzulli and half are using the Torrance. Let me know, and I'll drop them off for you."

"Don't counselors give tests? Isn't that what they do?" Katherine asks the principal.

"Our elementary counselor serves seven buildings, and we need her for the kids at the other end of the potential continuum. Just read the directions and give the test—or the checklist if you prefer. What did you learn at that workshop? Didn't you say you attended a lot of sessions on creativity? What did they teach you?"

Katherine goes back to her handouts and notes from the convention. She hasn't had time to do much with them. There, among her handouts of dots, arrows, and charts, are her notes from one of the sessions, "How To Choose A Creativity Test—If You Really Must."

"Why can't I just look at what the child does?" Katherine asked everyone. "I guess I can tell whether or not something is creative, can't I?"

"Oh, really?" an art teacher asked. "Do you know when a child is truly creative in art?"

"Well, maybe not," Katherine answered. "But if I'm in doubt, I can just ask you, can't I?" But then she thought, "Well, that's art talent, the potential to be creative in art, and not just being creative. And isn't it my responsibility simply to find those kids who are just plain creative, not necessarily creative in something?"

You may be tempted to skip this section, especially if you have a fear of numbers or testing, but try not to skip it. What Katherine is about to learn is important, especially since testing is now a major part of every child's life, and especially since important decisions about children are made as the result of their taking tests.

Chapter 3

Creativity Testing

If creative behavior were determined by heredity, there would be little that parents could do to increase it. There is compelling evidence that this is not true. How a young child's creative behavior is treated by parents and other important people in his life seems to make all the difference.
—E. Paul Torrance

The complexity of creativity and the effects of innumerable personal, familial, and environmental factors do not permit the development of a comprehensive, highly valid Creativity Quotient test that can make long-range predictions of outstanding creative achievement.
—Gary Davis

Mrs. Larson, third grade teacher, gets a test from the specialist in talent development education, Katherine Miller. It is a paper and pencil test, and the directions are simple. Mrs. Larson makes sure all her third graders have sharpened pencils and scratch paper, that they can hear her, and that she can see them all. "All right, boys and girls. Today we are going to test your creativity. Listen carefully. I'll read you some directions, and you will do some tasks according to my directions. Are you all listening?"

Bobby, the class clown, who brings Calvin and Hobbes cartoons each day to share with her, is restless. He can't seem to sit still. Bobby, like Hobbes, also has an imaginary playmate, only his is a boy, just his age. Bobby, an only child, is lonesome at home because his mother and father are divorced. He carries his key on a string around his neck and must spend two hours locked in his house after he returns home from school, until his mother comes home from her job at the telephone company.

"Boys and girls, listen now. Here are a group of squiggles. We are going to do some drawing." Mrs. Larson follows the directions and points to the squiggles on the page, making sure all the children have their eyes on her. "Bobby, are you watching? Bobby, I want your eyes on me," she says kindly, walking over to him and putting down the pencil clutched in his hand as he makes doodles on the squiggles already. "Bobby, you have to wait until I say

'Begin.' " She instructs the children to make the squiggles into whatever they want, anything is okay, and then tells them to begin.

Bobby, having lost interest in making each squiggle into something different, proceeds to make all of them into letters of the alphabet, some cursive, some printed. In the first box, he begins to sketch his imaginary playmate, but soon time is up and Mrs. Larson goes on to the next part. "Now you are going to write a story about one of these boxes. The story must begin with the words 'Let's pretend.' "

All the children dutifully write, laboriously forming the letters into slow cursive shapes, proud of their writing. They have studied the Writing Process, and Mrs. Larson is pleased with their daily work. But this is a test. This is different. Bobby begins to write about a television show he saw last night, when his mother was passed out from the marijuana she had smoked with her boyfriend. He began, "Let's pretend I got high on marijuana." He has trouble spelling *marijuana*, crosses it out, writes *grass*. Then he realizes this is not right, and crosses out the whole story except for the first two required words. Bobby has a whole notebook of stories at home; he writes while watching soap operas and quiz shows. In one of his stories a third-grade boy on a quiz show wows them all by throwing a tomato at the face of a bigger boy. The third-grade boy becomes known as Ketchup to millions of adoring fans, and he begins a whole new way of dealing with bullies.

In another story Bobby and his imaginary playmate, Tony, sneak into a neighbor's basement to spy on him, because the neighbor looks like a spy from a foreign land. The neighbor carries a cane and wears a pointed beard and sunglasses; Bobby and Tony believe that he carries secret maps rolled up in the cane. Bobby wonders whether he can write any of those stories, but it's too late.

"Time," Mrs. Larson says. She is reading from the manual Katherin Miller gave her. "Now, let's see how creative you can be with numbers." She instructs them to turn to a page with many numbers on it, and she reads the directions for the sample question: "How many ways can you think of to get to 43?" These directions are confusing to the students—should they add or subtract? Just as Bobby is figuring out that 43 is made up of no prime numbers, Mrs. Larson says "Time." Bobby's father is an engineer and sometimes, when he's not yelling about what a horrible person Bobby's mother is, he does math with Bobby. Bobby's father taught him about prime numbers last week.

Bobby looks over at the girl next to him, and the boy across from him, and sees that they have both filled out all the blanks with numbers such as 42 + 1 and 44 - 1. All the blanks! In fact, all the squiggles are made into interesting drawings on the boy's paper, and all the lines for the story are filled up with neat penmanship on the girl's. All Bobby has done is get confused, and just when he gets an idea, Mrs. Larson calls time.

This scenario illustrates some of the difficulties with creativity testing. The test will probably be scored according to set scoring rules in which the test scorer has been trained. The first score that Bobby will get will be in fluency, meaning "how many." Bobby will score all right in fluency on the first test because he did use all the squiggles to make letters of the alphabet. On the second test, however, Bobby's slow motor skills hampered him, and even though the test is normed with other third grade boys who have similar motor developmental problems, perhaps Bobby's slowness has to do with a sense of quality as well as speed. On the third, Bobby's fluency score will be low, because he took too much time thinking of the problem and didn't write down the easy answers that his two friends did. No matter that Bobby's thoughts were about prime numbers, there is no way that the creativity test can judge that, or these types of tests the fluent always win.

These tests also measure flexibility, or the variety of different ideas the test taker had. In the first test, Bobby had only two ideas, even though he used all the squiggles. Letters of the alphabet is one idea, and drawing his imaginary friend is another. On the second test, Bobby's hesitancy about what to write was his downfall, and he will stand with a fluency score of 0 or 2, depending on whether the manual allows points for the "Let's pretend" stem. He gets no points for what he crosses out, and again, he scores nothing on the numbers test.

While Bobby is probably too young to even be tested with a creativity test, such tests are in wide use in the schools, and for good reasons: they are practical and seem to be objective. That is, they don't discriminate against Bobby because he lives in a single parent home and has a mother who smokes marijuana. But Bobby didn't do very well on the test.

Katherine Miller wants to be sure that youngsters like Bobby aren't missed, and so she gives the teachers a checklist as well. She has chosen the checklist recommended by the State Department of Education—clearly, then, the best choice. She has even done her homework and looked it up in the latest *Mental Measurements Yearbook*, where its reviewer calls it the best creativity checklist available. Using a Likert Scale, the teacher must consider the child as she knows him and check *sometimes, always,* or *never* to such questions as *Does he exhibit curiosity? Does he have a sense of humor? Does he ask questions?*

The checklist doesn't ask specifically whether he can write, sing, dance, draw, do science experiments, or think of new mathematical ideas; this checklist asks abstract questions about personality characteristcs that may lead to being a creative adult. Doesn't it seem strange that the checklist doesn't ask about self-generated, potentially creative activities? The checklist does not allow teachers to assess overt creative behavior in established domains because experts have led educators to believe that creativity exists separately and on its own, separate from the ability to dance, sing, write, or draw. Experts have led educators to believe that *creative potential* exists and can be uncovered by filling out a checklist such as this. Bobby can be talented in *creative thinking* he does not need to be able to dance, sing, write, act, draw, make up science experiments or conceive of mathematical ideas.

At first, Mrs. Larson didn't consider assessing Bobby using the checklist because his school ability index (falsely called an IQ by many school people), extrapolated from the Iowa Test of Basic Skills taken when the students were in second grade, came out at 113. The rules for the talent development education program state that those students who are identified by a creativity checklist must have IQs of ll8 minus the standard error of measurement, and Bobby is one point below the minimum.

But Bobby perhaps indicates creative potential in that he takes unusual books out of the school library. Last week it was *Moby Dick*. The amazed librarian told Mrs. Larson, who then asked Bobby why he was interested in a book she's never been able to get through. "Isn't it just a little hard for you?"

"Well, I like whales!"

"Let me know when you finish it then!" When Mrs. Larson shared this story in the teachers' lounge, they all had a good laugh, but the teacher wondered.

She told Katherine Miller about Bobby's interest in difficult literature. In addition to strongly recommending that Bobby be given the checklist, Katherine called the regional coordinator of the programs for the talented.

"Sorry, Katherine, but my hands are tied. We've got parents insisting we put their kids in the program for the gifted and talented—all the kids have IQs of over 130, based on last year's Iowa, and we can't do a thing because we've got no more room. Bobby's IQ just isn't high enough, and where's the proof that a kid who wants to read *Moby Dick* is outstandingly talented in creative thinking? Have you heard from his mother?"

No one—neither the coordinator, the teacher of the special program for the talented, nor the classroom teacher—ever thought to give Bobby's mom a checklist. She had been evidently too busy to come to parent-teacher conferences last Wednesday night. Maybe she didn't care all that much.

Bobby had brought the Open House announcement home, and the invitation from the principal arrived by mail, but she had so much to do at work, selling that new line, that when she gets home at 7:00 P.M. she just wants to relax, not go out again to the school. Besides, if something was wrong, the school would let her know, wouldn't they?

She adores Bobby. He is her only child so he gets lonely, she's sure, but he never complains. He just does his own thing all afternoon, and his notebook is so great, especially now that he does sketches along with his stories. They have to set a place for his imaginary friend Tony, right along with them, when they get to eat supper together. Of course, they rarely eat together because of their schedules. She brings home some hamburgers or stops for a pizza, and when she had to work so late last Wednesday, Bobby zapped some canned Chef Boyardee in the microwave and ate that.

The school never gave Bobby's father a checklist either. Bobby's dad both wrote and called to ask when the parent's night was, but he's still not on the mailing list, even though the school says that both parents of the child of divorce should be involved. He gets a little angry and calls the principal. How the heck can he get involved if he doesn't get the announcement, he wants to know. And when he calls Bobby's mother, they just get into the old recriminations about the custody battle. Bobby's father had wanted joint custody, but Bobby's mother pulled out that little indiscretion he'd had, the cause of their divorce. Now Bobby doesn't even want to visit him every other weekend anymore, since his dad started living with his new girlfriend. This time it's going to last, Bobby's father hopes, and Bobby will have a stepmother and everything can get back to normal.

Bobby feels pulled between his parents and wants to please them both. He does like school, though. School is fun. Last week he even told a joke and the rest of the kids laughed. It was when Mrs. Larson had her back turned, writing the day's schedule on the board. Bobby rolled his eyes up and sat back, his heels hitting the floor, and said, "Oh, my God! She's got a tail!" and everyone laughed, so he started writing more jokes in his notebook. Maybe he'll send a couple to Rosie O'Donnell . . .

Back in high school, Bobby's mother used to sing with a rock 'n' roll band, and everybody said she had a good voice. She has a great collection of tapes and CDs, which Bobby sometimes plays while he is waiting for her to get home from work. He asked her for music lessons, and she said she'd think about it. He wants to learn to play the guitar, or maybe the drums. She buys him a keyboard and a book of chords, and surprisingly, he finds the notes are easy to learn. He has learned the B flat scale. The music teacher notices that he has a good ear and gives him a small solo in the Halloween program. Bobby asks his mother to come, but she forgets.

Mrs. Larson's only hope for getting Bobby into any special program is this checklist that Katherine wants her to fill out for him. It's common knowledge among teachers that to get a marginal student into the program, they have to give maximum points—four—on every item on the checklist. Mrs. Larson needs to spend a little more time on Bobby's checklist, but she sails right through the one for Christine, the adorable girl who starred in last year's *Nutcracker* and who has the most cunning little smile and the most devilish speed as she climbs to the top of the jungle gym. Christine's mother is active on the advisory committee for the program for the academically talented and has helped in the classroom with birthdays. Mrs. Larson gives the girl all fours, even though Christine is already in the program for the gifted and talented, qualifying according to the *academically talented in specific ability* guideline. The girl is a fantastic reader and even better in the writing process.

Does Mrs. Larson know enough about Bobby's secret life to fill out the checklist? Well, it's October, and she's only known him since September, and while he's certainly a sweet boy, she notices he comes to school with a strange smell on him, sort of like tobacco, a stale smell. Often his hair isn't combed, his clothes are rumpled, and he seems to have only one pair of jeans. The flaps on his shoes are always loose, and he has an annoying habit of zipping the Velcro back and forth while she is reading to the students aloud. He gets so involved in the story, he doesn't know he's doing it. Finally, last week, she told him to take his shoes off during story time.

Bobby's reading level is fine, but he's not in the top group because he has no patience for prefixes. He tries, but he's a whole-word reader, not a phonics reader. Mrs. Larson, while she believes in the Whole Language approach and has attended several workshops on it, is still a firm believer that phonics is the way to teach reading. New fads come and go, but Mrs. Larson knows that phonics teaching is the best way. No one can change her on that.

Is Bobby outstandingly talented in creative thinking? The first test didn't indicate this, and we'll see about the creativity checklist. His behavior at home is the predictor, but who knows about that? His mother doesn't even know the full extent of his creative activities. His slowness and lack of flexibility worked against him in timed testing. Perhaps his tumultuous home life and retreat into secret notebooks, sketch books, music, and isolated thought operate for him. But even if Bobby had done well on the timed creativity test, *could* the test predict that he would be a creatively productive adult?

Testing for Creativity

Why assess or measure creativity, if indeed such a thing can even be done? Donald Treffinger, in a 1987 article, gave seven reasons that the schools attempt to do so: (1) to recognize individual strengths; (2) to go beyond IQ and achievement testing; (3) to give schools, charged with practical concerns, some basic data so they can compare their students with norms; (4) to include creativity information in the basic profiles of students; (5) to help teachers discover their own creative talents; (6) to advance the research about nurturing and developing behavior that is creative; (7) to take away the mystery from the consideration of creativity.

Two Schools of Thought

Two vying schools of thought exist on the value of testing for creativity—or, more accurately, testing for the ability to do divergent production. The aspects of divergent production, defined by Guilford and described in Chapter 1, include fluency, flexibility, elaboration and the like. On the one hand, Isaksen (1987) asserts, "There is mounting evidence that creativity can be assessed systematically and scientifically." Cramond and Meeker believe that using such divergent production tests as the Torrance Tests of Creative Thinking (TTCT) and the Structure of Intellect Creativity Test (SOI) is better than not testing at all for divergent production. In fact, the practice of testing for divergent production cognition has continued out of a concern for inclusiveness: if IQ doesn't get some kids in, what will? In 1994 Bonnie Cramond defended the use of divergent production tests: "Why not use any and all methods available to ascertain where children's strengths lie?"

On the other hand, some cognitive psychologists insist that creativity testing has little value. Robert Sternberg of Yale, in 1988, noted, "Such tests [psychometric tests of creativity] capture at best only the most trivial aspects of creativity." Howard Gardner of Harvard, in 1982, commented, "The measures on which they have relied in their studies have almost all been brief tasks—learning word lists, mastery of a maze—which can be surmounted in a matter of minutes (and which are even more rapidly forgotten)." James Borland of Columbia Teacher's College wrote, "There are reasons to consider the basic issue as to the extent of the realm of divergent production," noting that the Educational Testing Service had dropped tests for spontaneous flexibility and originality from their battery called Factor-Referenced Cognitive Tests.

The discussion lines are thus drawn, between one group who has spent the last forty or fifty years trying to develop tests that have validity and relia-bility, and another group who insists that creativity is a process that is explain-able by observing how creative people think. Among the latter is Perkins, who in 1988 called for the inclusion of motivation in the assessment of creativity. After all, what are people creating for? Why does the writer write, the painter paint, the inventor invent, the scientist experiment? He said that the creativi-ty testing people may be off base: "Whereas testing for creativity typically emphasizes flexibility, fluency, and similar indices, values and patterns of deployment seem to offer the best predictors of creativity." That is, Bobby has motivation to do creative activities, on his own, at home. His mother values his creativity. He does many types of activities, none of which were repre-sented when he was tested for flexibility and fluency.

Amidst all this controversy is the bewildered professional responsible for educating the outstandingly talented and whose state department may, as departments in Ohio, Georgia and others states do, require that students with creative thinking potential be identified through creativity tests or checklists as well as authentic portfolios. The busy educator often does not have the time or the propensity to wade through the research evidence, and the research itself is often done by the people who can benefit most from showing that their own tests and checklists have validity and reliability.

Validity

Validity is best described as the test's truthfulness. That is, does the test mea-sure what it says it will measure? There are three kinds of validity: (1) con-tent/construct validity; (2) criterion validity; and (3) concurrent validity.

Content/Construct Validity

Content or construct validity is necessary in order to determine whether the test has measured what it says it measured. To determine whether a creativity test is valid, one must look at what it measures. Divergent production is not creativity, nor is creativity exclusively divergent production. Creativity is called a *construct*, an unobservable phenomenon that helps to explain a per-son's behavior. Csikszentmihalyi in 1994 wrote that creativity is a *domain* in itself, which means that it is *a symbolic system that has a set of rules for rep-resenting thought and action.*

It's clear that confusion abounds concerning construct, domain and definitions. The lack of a universal definition for creativity and the complexity of creativity are major problems in developing valid tests or measures. Some researchers use one aspect of creativity—for example, divergent production of figural units or free drawing within circles and squares—and then conclude that people who were pre- and post-tested on that one test were improved in creativity. That is certainly not so. This is where consideration of the content of what is measured comes in. Creativity is too complex to be measured by a simple five-minute test, or even an hour-long test.

People using anything called a creativity test should look carefully at its content. Is filling in blanks or drawing within boxes true creativity? Even if the tests are divergent production tests, does divergent production, by implication, translate itself to creativity, as is assumed in state guidelines requiring that a divergent production test be given in order to assess creative potential?

Treffinger also said that construct validity should be concerned with creativity testing as a total field, not as an individual test: "Construct validity refers . . . to the total pattern of research evidence that supports an instrument." He concluded, "Although there are still many isolated, fragmented studies, then, there have also been some promising signs of progress in validating several specific creativity assessment procedures." Those who disagree might say that no battery, no matter how widely it is conceived, can measure the creativity construct.

The subject is a difficult one, and the practitioner must trust in the authorities, for wading through the contradictory evidence is a mammoth task. Most districts do not have a testing or measurement person, and even if they do, this person might be swayed by the charming personalities of those who go from conference to conference, propounding one system of creativity assessment over another.

Another issue having to do with construct validity is whether or not creativity stands separately from intelligence. Davis in 1997 asserted that having high intelligence certainly enhances one's creativity, because the intelligent person's mind is so full that there are many options that surface when he is called on to be divergent. However, while a high IQ is a benefit in functioning in the world, it is not absolutely necessary for creativity. Since creativity is realized in fields and domains, developed talent in a specific domain is necessary. Divergent production researchers continue to look at the threshold, trying to define that magic number below which a person is not creative. Thus we can see that content/construct validity presents many problems when considering whether a test can measure creativity—or even the aspect of creativity called divergent production.

Criterion Validity

Criterion validity is how much the test scores can predict one's performance in other areas, especially one's performance later on in life. For example, does a high score on a creativity test given in elementary school predict that a person will be a true creative achiever when she is an adult, or even when she is in high school?

Predictive Validity of Creativity Tests

Why even test students on such instruments if the tests don't show something about how the person is going to be as an adult? Test developers such as Torrance have spent a lifetime testing students, following them up, trying to find out whether their scores on such tests have predictive validity. Unfortunately, the answers are mixed.

Optimally, predictive validity studies would be independently done. Instead, the test-maker must take the responsibility for proving predictive validity, which often takes many years. The researcher must keep up with, or find, people who took the test in early years, and must control for other life variables as well as provide a comparison group who did not take the test. The issue of bias towards the instrument being validated is a real one, for who wants to spend a lifetime working on a test and doing studies on its validity, and then report that the results were not what were planned? Partners in validation studies are often graduate students seeking degrees, beholden to the professor whose test they are trying to validate. While independent reviewers and researchers do some validation work, much of it is done by the test-makers, who may design studies that reflect their drive to prove by any means that their test works.

Here is an example of one of the Torrance studies, written up in an article in 1993: Torrance, testing the predictive validity of his tests, did a follow up thirty years after students had taken the test as high school seniors. He described two of the students who had scored moderately high as "Beyonders." Both had made substantial creative accomplishments, one in medicine, the other in anthropology. Torrance concluded that there were several critically important forces operating in these two successfully creative lives: "Forces such as love of one's work, persistence, purpose in life, love of challenge, diversity of experience, high energy level, a sense of mission . . . are dominating over creative ability, intelligence, and high school achievement." Perhaps, then, it is not possible to validate such instruments for predictability.

Milgram and Hong assessed the predictive validity of the Tel-Aviv Creativity Test, a measure of ideational fluency. In a 1993 article they said that the creative thinking scores of high school seniors were related to the number of adult leisure activities seventeen years later. A fluency and flexibility score combined into an index can predict how many leisure activities an adult will have. One must ask whether *more* activities are necessarily better. They also said that a checklist about extracurricular activities given to these seniors was related to their adult vocations seventeen years later. They suggested that identification procedures should also include some indications of what the students do in their leisure time.

The Threshold Theory

Runco and Albert in 1986 said that the threshold theory—that one needs above-average intelligence in order to be creative—is incorrect. Certainly, the "savant syndrome" of exceptional skill in otherwise mentally retarded persons brings the threshold theory at least somewhat into question (Miller, 1994). Many studies have looked for a relation between IQ and various measures of creativity, with several finding a moderate relation in groups having below-average IQ, but essentially no relation between creativity and intelligence once IQ is 120 or higher. Some studies of creativity and its relationship to intelligence used IQs derived from ability tests such as the Stanford-Binet. Other studies used IQs derived from achievement tests, such as the California Achievement Test. These two tests—and the types they represent—do not measure the same things, however. In other cases, the measures of creativity chosen by researchers were ones that virtually required intelligence or achievement as measured by such tests.

Thus, statements that one must have above-average intelligence in order to show a good score on a creativity test are questionable. Runco and Albert said, "For now, it appears that the traditional view of the threshold of intelligence necessary for creativity is at least partly a psychometric artifact." By psychometric artifact they mean the results were due to characteristics of the test being used, rather than to real differences among people.

Concurrent Validity of Creativity Tests

Concurrent validity establishes whether the test measures what real people in the field supposedly being measured really do. Morse and Khatena published a study in 1989 showing how the Something About Myself and the What Kind Of Person Are You? inventories were related to an index of life accomplishments. Here is a brief description of the study. The creative adults who filled out this biographical inventory were conference leaders attending the annual Creative Problem Solving Institute. The creative productivity of the adults was determined by a point system over eight categories: (1) job/vocation; (2) interests; (3) leadership; (4) membership in the Creative Education Foundation; (5) artistic endeavors and accomplishments in an artistic field; (6) musical accomplishment; (7) miscellaneous accomplishment, or accomplishment in any field of the performing arts other than visual arts or music; and (8) creative production, or products other than visual arts, music, or performing arts.

Only the last four of these categories, for one point each, had anything to do with creative production. One could score up to three points on the first three indicators, which asked about the number of different positions the person had held, the number of subgroups within the Creative Education Foundation that the person belonged to, and the managerial positions the person had held. Yet a writer who had published many well-reviewed novels would get only one point, in one category (8). Likewise a ground-breaking scientist or mathematician would receive only one point. But someone who had joined many special interest groups, an activity creative people are not known for, would receive three points.

The results were that the adult creative producers studied here had accomplishments higher than the norm of the 1976 Khatena and Torrance technical manual, and that the Something About Myself Questionnaire items were related moderately to biographical information. The authors concluded, rather weakly, that "Some evidence for the validity of self-report measures such as the Khatena Torrance Creative Performance Index can be mustered." They concluded that "such measures can and do have validity as indicators of creative potential." This is an illustration of an attempt to establish concurrent validity.

Confused? Don't be shy about admitting it. These experiments demonstrate the complexity of research into creativity testing. Many eminent researchers are spending their professional lives trying to help us make sense of things. Many smart people are trying to figure out how to make tests that sample the domain being tested so that there are no gender differences, ethnic differences, or socioeconomic differences shown in the results. They try to validate the tests with large, representative samples of people who resemble those who will take the tests. They try to determine which items to include and which to throw out in order to make the test more fair. This very expensive process is not always done well. Many test-makers release their tests for commercial adoption without the validation studies necessary for the consumer to be able to trust in the results.

The trouble is that the schools make decisions based on contradictory research. School leaders choose the research that seems to support their already-held points of view, and justify decisions by describing them as "research based." There is a long-standing cry in the education profession for the research to be translated to solid practice, and maybe someday it will be, but for now, two carriage horses called inertia and practicality are the main pullers of practice.

In summary, the validity studies of divergent production tests have been weak to mixed. However, Mark Runco, the editor of the *Creativity Research Journal*, in the 1990 book *Divergent Production* has shed much light on these studies, and the reader should consult his extensive and expert evaluations. In a 1993 article he stated that the tests have been changing to reflect real world problems that the students experience rather than such artificial ones as naming all the uses one can think of for a brick.

Reliability

Three interrelated types of reliability must be considered by the person using creativity testing: (1) stability, (2) equivalence, and (3) internal consistency. Is the test stable? If a person takes the test once in the morning and then again later in the day, will the results be relatively the same? The best way to assure stability is to administer equivalent, alternate forms of the test; that is why most standardized tests have Form A and Form B, two equivalent tests. The assumption is that one's score on Form A will be repeated on Form B, thus assuring that the final assessment is stable and consistent.

However, in the field of creativity testing this reliability is difficult to establish, due to the nature of what is being measured. One reason is that in an open-ended format with no right answers, it is very difficult to make items equivalent. Is asking a person to list unusual uses for a ball equivalent to asking a person to list unusual uses for a bat?

Another way to establish equivalence is to split the test in half, and see whether the scores from each half are about the same, using odds and evens or other ways of splitting the test. Does the test have internal consistency? This is called split-half reliability. Again this is difficult in testing for creativity.

Reliability of tests can be increased by administering the tests in a standardized way, by using objective scoring measures, by having item difficulties that are equal (is listing unusual uses for a ball easier than listing unusual uses for a bat?), by having the test measure only one aspect of creativity, and by increasing the number of items on the test. But administering the tests in a standardized way and scoring them objectively is particularly difficult for divergent production tests. Mrs. Larson followed the directions printed on her direction sheet, as she should have done, even though her standardized administering of the test left Bobby confused and behind.

Reliability in Administering Tests

Lissitz and Willhoft found that the Torrance Tests were highly sensitive to how the directions were given: "The degree to which test takers feel restricted or encouraged may well have a critical effect on their performance." In administering a test to four sets of students, they used the standard procedure with one group; the second was told to be practical and reasonable; the third was told to list as many ideas as possible; the fourth was told to include unusual, weird, or illogical ideas. After finding that such differences in giving directions changed the results, they cautioned other researchers that "studies using the Torrance Tests should be viewed with extreme caution." More importantly, schools should remember they are using the tests for making decisions about students' lives and educational futures, since children receive differential treatment because of their scores on tests.

Runco, in two articles in 1986 and 1987, similarly wrote that telling two groups of students, one with high IQs and another with moderate IQs, to be original with their answers increased their fluency (i.e., the number of responses they gave), but that telling high IQ students to be original did not. Since fluency is always a large proportion of the total scores given in such divergent production tests, increasing the fluency raises the child's test scores. But if some test givers tell the students to be original, and some do not, test scores will not be comparable.

Reliability in Scoring

Scoring is also a problem, for it's not as easy as grading a multiple choice test. The responses, as varied as the people taking the test, have been codified into classes so that the trained scorer can recognize certain patterns. For example, a response is called *original* if it occurs once or twice in a group of 30 people. The scorer must remember who has said what and how many times the response has occurred. I have received and given extensive training in one particular form of divergent production testing and have scored thousands of divergent production tests, yet there is still an inconsistency in my scoring, especially for humor or the macabre. My mood and hence my receptivity may be different from day to day.

In assessing student writing for a divergent production test once, I discovered a high percentage of stories ending with a moral. According to the directions for scoring the test, a story ending with a moral received a higher score. Had I unearthed a whole group of gifted students? Not necessarily. In class, the students had been writing fables for two weeks. Tested one month earlier or one month later, most of the students would not have ended their stories with morals, their scores would not have been as high, and decisions ultimately made on the basis of those scores would have been different.

Because decisions based on testing do have far-reaching effects, it is good to have several people, or interraters, score the same tests independently. If they come up with similar scores, the scoring is said to have high interrater reliability. Another way to score such difficult tests is holistically: several interraters' scores on a student's test are averaged, with highest and lowest scores ignored. The Advanced Placement essay test and other composition tests are scored this way.

However, interrater scoring of tests also presents difficulties, in overrating and underrating the test information as well as in giving the same student high scores but for substantially different reasons. Independent researchers such as Baer, DeMers, Graybeal, the Halpins, Rosenthal, Stilwell, Wakefield and Zins have found these scoring disparities to occur. This means that even if scorers are highly trained, there still will be differences that affect the final scores.

Sending tests to be hand-scored by the publisher is supposedly the best idea, both for relative accuracy of scores and cost. A school district trying to save money by having local people score the tests should factor in the dollar value of the local scorers' time and the cost of properly training local people. Often the district will find that sending the tests to be scored will save money. Many new revisions of standardized tests use essays now, scored by hired readers. But even this method is flawed: a part-time scorer of essay tests was urged to rate an average of 300 essays in 4 hours—that's one minute and fifteen seconds per essay. Or per life, depending on the use of the score. Worse still, the company, a major testing firm, had only one person score each essay. "Oh, the exposé I could write about the new testing practices if I hadn't signed a waiver swearing confidentiality," this person reported. Just because the testing company is large and famous does not mean it uses ethical scoring practices.

Concerning divergent production testing, Heausler and Thompson noted that when the same set of responses is scored several different ways, with the scorers looking for different aspects of divergent production during each scoring, there is too much relatedness in the scoring. They recommend that people who use the Torrance Tests should be cautious in thinking that the subscales derived from the scoring "provide meaningfully different information." All divergent production tests I know of are scored by looking at the same material several different ways. That the reliability is thus made questionable is a caution to take note of.

Studies of Significant Results

Beyond the concern of whether tests are valid and reliable comes the consideration of whether or not there are significant results. If the results are truly significant, people in the schools pay attention. But significance is the play territory of college professors of statistics. The level of significance is shown like this: (1) $p < .05$, which means that the results are due to nonchance factors 95% of the time; (2) $p < .01$, which means that the results would occur one percent of the time, or less, by chance; and (3) $p < .001$, which means that the results would occur less than one time out of a thousand, by chance.

Many of the studies of creativity testing are correlational. They compare one test with another to see whether the tests are related. If the tests are related, more than would be expected by chance, the results are significant. But few researchers question whether the tests are in fact measuring creativity and have construct validity. Other studies try to isolate the factors being measured on the tests; if the researchers find that the factors are indeed separate and isolatable, the results are considered significant. These studies are theoretical and necessary—but not very helpful to the practitioner. And if the study is not correlational or factorial, but experimental, and the results are significant, what does that really mean? For example, Torrance, in 1987, reviewed 142 studies that investigated methods used to teach students to think creatively. For 103 of those studies significance was determined by using the Torrance Tests of Creative Thinking as an indicator. If the determiner of significant correlation has questionable validity, what does that mean for the findings? He said that he would "strongly favor" using "more real-life criteria," but that those who used his test were using the best measure available.

A Flawed Study of Creative Adolescents

I did a study of creative adolescents who attended a summer institute for fifteen intensive days, where they wrote and performed operas and participated in creative writing and printmaking. When the students arrived, I pretested them with the SOI Test of Creative Thinking (Meeker and Meeker, 1975), a test derived from the Guilford Tests. I administered DFU, Divergent Production of Figural Units, and also DMU, Divergent Production of Semantic Units.

The day the creative adolescents left, I post-tested them with the same two tests; each testing session took ten minutes. When I scored the DMU and DFU and applied tests of significance to the results, I found that the students had improved to a significant degree in fluency. The significance was $p < .001$ for the girls—about as significant as you can get—though that does not mean that the results are meaningful; it merely means that the results are not due to chance. The students who made transformational drawings on the pretest did so on the posttest, and no other students did so. The two weeks of intensive creative work did nothing for their transformational ability on the test.

But what do those results really mean? The faculty and the boys also improved in fluency to the significance of $p < .05$, or a 95% likelihood that the results were not by chance. Can I measure what the summer institute meant to fifty teenagers who wrote, thought, created, made, composed music, performed, and talked until four A.M., driving their resident assistants crazy with their creativity and humor, by giving them ten minutes of two divergent production tests? What does a significant difference in fluency mean? That these students became more creative? That the faculty became more creative as a group? One would certainly hope so, for the state had granted us $40,000, but one would also have trouble believing that putting down a few more items on a five-minute test would actually prove it.

My small research study doesn't show much at all, even though when I presented the results at the state talent development education conference, people were impressed that I had found statistically significant changes. About two-thirds of the students did indeed attend a one-hour class daily where fluency, flexibility, elaboration, and originality were taught separately from the process through which they were going, but there were no differences between those who participated in this formal creativity training and those who did not take the class. The ones who did not take creativity training still improved in flexibility, fluency, and originality as much as those who took creativity training.

But I didn't have a real control group of teens not involved in any creativity exercises at all. Without a control group, how can I say that these adolescents truly became more fluent? And even more to the point, did they *need* to become more fluent? Since the divergent production test measured fluency, I measured fluency. That's all. I didn't compare them with a randomly chosen matched group of adolescents who were doing what adolescents usually do in August. If I had tested a matched group of adolescents and teachers, perhaps they would have become as fluent as my experimental group of adolescents during that fifteen-day period, without going to a summer institute.

So my significant results aren't significant at all, and even if they were, my question is, so what? So what if there was an increase in fluency, flexibility, or originality? Should we be impressed?

Transfer

The real question is, what was the *transfer* of fluency, flexibility, and originality, and then, if it transferred, how do we measure it? Transfer means what one learns is applicable to real life or to another field. For example, what is the transfer of algebra? Some people would say there is no transfer. Therefore, they would say it is useless to study algebra. Others would say that algebra teaches one to think logically. Transfer is the main problem in discussions of both creative and critical thinking. Say a person practices separate skills, for example, fluency and flexibility: in what situations can the student draw on those skills? If one learns to add and subtract, those skills transfer when the person balances a checkbook. If a student learns to put down more answers in a short amount of time, where does that skill transfer? What did the people who underwent creativity training gain? What should they gain? Transfer is the purpose of all education.

The Normal Curve Assumption

Another issue with testing is the assumption that the scores obtained fall on a normal curve, with 68 percent in the middle and sixteen percent on either end. Though one can derive a normal curve for any test, the underlying assumption that there is a naturally-occurring normal curve of creativity—or to put it another way, the underlying assumption that some people have a fuller cup of creativity than other people—has not been proven. This is an important issue in creativity testing, for it is assumed that the person with the higher score has more creativity, whereas a lower score indicates less creativity. This is nonsense. We do not know enough about creativity to measure "amounts," and thus cannot assert that one has more creativity than someone else based on some hypothetical normal curve.

Hence we may not be qualified based on test scores to say that someone has *more* creativity or *less* creativity. But if you use a paper and pencil test and obtain a score, you'll be tempted to label, and admit to the program, the highest scorers as those with more creative potential. To establish a cutoff score below which no one gets into the creative thinking program is what many school districts do. The assumption that people fall on a normal curve of creative thinking is operational here. People fall on a normal curve on *any* test, and the normal curve is just an indication of how people did on *that test*, and the question becomes whether or not the test is a true measure of the domain of creative thinking.

Often the person who is most fluent, or gives the most answers, will get a high score. If the test is measuring writing fluency, the person who spews out a lot of words will get a higher score than the careful, reticent, accurate poet who writes a few well-taken words. In fact, in divergent production testing, the fluent always seem to win. However, even with these concerns, some educational psychologists who are experts in creativity seem to think that the tests should still be given. Davis in his 1997 article wrote that creativity testing is all right: "Creativity tests and inventories are useful when scores are combined with other information—perhaps scores on a second test or teachers' ratings—in order to make reliable judgments." I would use the tests only to include, never to exclude.

The next chapter will continue this discussion of creativity assessment. When Katherine Miller was hired to teach outstandingly talented students, she had no idea she would be asked to give creativity tests, nor did she have a suitable background for deciding what tests to give, why she should give them, and how to interpret the scores once she obtained them. Chapter 4 will discuss how creativity checklists and personality inventories are used and how creativity training has mushroomed in the past few years. You are now halfway through the most difficult section of this book. Congratulations!

Summary

1. Teachers are often not well-trained in administering creativity tests and checklists.
2. School districts should understand the research base that went into the checklist or creativity test.

3. Sometimes the research is confusing, since validity and reliability can be expressed in different ways. What kind of validity? What kind of reliability? should be considered.
4. Predictive validity—of creativity tests, of creativity training, and of creativity checklists—is most difficult to establish because the tasks on the tests have little relationship to real life creativity.
5. Scoring is also difficult on creativity tests because scoring requires subjective judgment and scorers must be trained.
6. When reading the results of studies that say the treatment made the group more creative, see whether or not that meant more fluent, flexible, etc., and judge the results accordingly.
7. There is no reason to assume a normal curve of creativity.
8. Transfer is the purpose of all education.

Chapter 4

Questionnaires, Checklists, Promising Practices and Creativity Training

If one turns to the literature of creativity research and asks the simple questions—what is being measured? what is creativity?—one soon realizes that the entire research enterprise moves on very thin ice.
—Mihalyi Csikszentmihalyi

The challenge I see before us in the study of creativity . . . must be to find a coordinating simplicity. This means using our data differently, making connections among sciences and points of view, finding a common language, advancing to more comprehensive theories. Quite realistically, at least $100 million have gone into research on creativity.
—Frank Barron

Chapter 3 dealt with creativity testing and its difficulties. This chapter continues along the same lines. Creativity checklists and personality questionnaires will also be discussed.

Using Personality Questionnaires

Personality assessment is not a part of divergent production tests, but Hocevar noticed that "many researchers who purport to study the creative personality choose tests of divergent thinking as their criterion" instead of measures of how people achieve creatively in the real world. Milgram and Hong also said that "intelligence test scores did not predict adult life accomplishment" and "grades in school were unrelated to any accomplishments in adult life beyond the academic area." They suggested that both personality and leisure activities inventories are more predictive of adult vocational and creative accomplishment than standardized tests and grades.

The Dabrowski Theory and the Overexcitabilities Questionnaire

Other research we conducted, into personality attributes during our summer institutes seems more promising than our finding significant changes in fluency and flexibility. Based on new questions about giftedness and creativity posed by Piechowski and his colleagues working with Dabrowski's theory, we wanted to do some exploring with our creative adolescents in an attempt to understand what creative adolescents are all about. We were interested in the intriguing possibility that creative people have certain patterns of overexcitabilities. Piechowski, Silverman, and Falk defined an overexcitability as "enhanced and intensified mental activity distinguished by characteristic forms of expression which are above common and average." These forms of expression are psychomotor, sensual, intellectual, imaginational, and emotional. Creative individuals often have temperaments with a predisposition to emotional, imaginational, and intellectual intensity or overexcitability.

According to Piechowski, **emotional overexcitability** might show itself as intense feeling, inhibition, fear, anxiety, depressive moods, memory of emotions, empathy, self-judgment, feelings of inadequacy and inferiority, and attachments to places, people, and animals. **Imaginational overexcitability** manifests itself in inventiveness, vivid visualization, dream recall, use of metaphor, an interest in fairy tales and magical tales, poetry, drama, and having imaginary playmates. **Intellectual overexcitability** shows itself as curiosity, thirst for knowledge and analysis, a preoccupation with logic, the ability to intuitively integrate and synthesize seemingly unlike and disparate ideas, and the capacity for sustained intellectual effort. **Sensual overexcitability** shows itself in a love of physical comfort, in tasting, seeing, smelling, touching, hearing, in overeating, sexual indulgence, buying sprees, and sartorial pleasures. **Psychomotor overexcitability** shows itself in a surplus of physical energy, rapid speech, acting out, compulsive talking, workaholism, needing always to be moving, and nervous habits such as nailbiting.

Laurence Nixon in 1996 said that creative people are similar to mystics in the possession of these overexcitabilities. Four environmental factors that predispose people to be creative are encouragement in childhood, training or modeling of creativity in childhood, having access to formal training in adolescence or early adulthood, and experiencing stress or loss in childhood. The experience of stress and loss leads to a sense of insecurity which the creative students experience extremely intensely. Nixon said, "Creative persons may seek to compensate for their losses and fulfill their needs by engaging in projects which have as their result an idea, a service, or a product that is valued by society."

Using the Dabrowski Overexcitability Questionnaire (OEQ), each student required a minimum of about an hour and a half to answer the questions. Coding the information was more difficult than counting fluency and flexibility on a divergent production questionnaire. It is necessary to attend a Dabrowski Coding Training session for a few days to learn to score to at least a ninety percent interrater agreement. All questionnaires are coded by at least two trained raters, and if there is a disagreement, a third person codes and a discussion ensues.

We found that artistic teenagers who came to study musical theater, creative writing, and visual arts had higher imaginational overexcitability than academically talented students who did not attend such a summer program. This would be expected. These results are similar to those that Piechowski and Cunningham found in adult creative artists, except they also found that the creative people were also higher than others in emotional overexcitability. We found no differences; both groups were high in emotional overexcitability.

The creative artists thought with vivid imagery and associations and had a great capacity for metaphorical and animistic thinking. They also had great depth and intensity in their emotional lives and were able to perceive subtleties in emotional experience. Piechowski and Cunningham also found that the artists were quite similar to the intellectually gifted in intellectual overexcitability, which is characterized by curiosity and a thirst for knowledge.

Our studies with adolescents and the Overexcitabilities Questionnaire continue. My colleagues Geri Cassone, John Fraas, and I have been writing up the data. Summer by summer we collect more OEQs from the students, trying to build up a large data base of responses from talented adolescents. Our comparisons of these students with others (for example, with Cheryl Ackerman's Canadian group) are tending to show that the intellectual and emotional overexcitabilities are indeed higher in students who are creative and in students who have high IQs, and that those who are interested in domains of the arts also seem to have higher imaginational overexcitability, but we cannot make any conclusive statements yet.

What the Overexcitability Questionnaire does yield, besides the labor-intensive inter-rating of the questionnaires (each question is scored for each overexcitability by at least two and sometimes three coders) is some *qualitative* insight into the young people's thoughts about themselves, about their lives.

Here is the overexcitability questionnaire. I have included sample answers from 21 of the adolescents who studied musical theater, art, or writing. (Used with the permission of Michael Piechowski.)

TABLE 1. Overexcitability Questionnaire

1. **Do you ever feel really high, ecstatic, or incredibly happy? Describe your feelings.** *When I'm talking to someone who really understands and relates to me because many people cannot do that. I like to talk when I get to talk about **real** things: life, feelings, and **writing**. I become very hyper and talkative and I can really just feel the words and thoughts rushing out of my gut and I feel like I'm really here, and really attached to the world. Also, when I write something and I really like it, and am praised by someone I really respect about it. It makes me feel really accomplished and that I want to work harder.* Female, age 15. MBTI Type: INFP.

2. **What has been your experience of the most intense pleasure?** *Hearing Mozart's Symphony No. 38 for the first time.* Male, age 16. MBTI Type: INTP.

3. **What are your special daydreams and fantasies?** *I sometimes like to dream about a world in which we can truly be ourselves. There is no hate, there is no rejection. We can be who we really are. Then reality whops me in the face and I realize what a fantasy a world like that would be.* Male, age 17. MBTI type: INFP.

4. **What kinds of things get your mind going?** *Sad things get my mind turning because I start looking for a way to make it better. I like to discover new things. I like to know everything about everything. I can't stand not knowing about anything. I love to find answers to everything. Sometimes I might look at a simple thing and think of a hundred questions. I can think up 50 questions about a rock that I just kind of wait to discover the answer. I LOVE ANSWERS. I could live on an encyclopedia. Most of the time I do read them. I wonder about everything.* Female, age 15. MBTI type: ISFJ

5. **When do you feel the most energy, and what do you do with it?** *I feel the most energy when I'm in a good mood, usually at night. I get a tremendous second wind and practically bounce off the walls. Sometimes I use it to draw, but I like to use it with contemporary or abstract painting more. I use a lot of it by going out or partying at home or just talking to my friends who know me well.* Female, age 15. MBTI type: ENTP.

6. **In what manner do you observe and analyze others?** *I ignore what is visible and concentrate on what is hidden inside. I also try to observe what their analysis of me is.* Male, age 16. MBTI type: INTP

TABLE 1. Overexcitability Questionnaire

7. **How do you act when you get excited?**   *A panorama of positive ideas fills my mind. Sometimes I feel faint.* Male, age 16. MBTI type: INTJ

8. **How precisely can you visualize events, real or imaginary?**   *I can do it great! I see everything as clearly as a window that has just been cleaned.* Female, age 15. MBTI type: INFP.

9. **What do you like to concentrate on the most?**   *What do you mean? I'm the most confusing person in the world and I don't understand half your questions. You need to be more specific; many words have more than one meaning, like "dreams." Thinking, I concentrate on everything. Writing, I concentrate on everything. Academically, English and speech. Physically, creating a better body.* Female, age 16. MBTI type: INTP.

10. **What kind of physical activity (or inactivity) gives you the most satisfaction?**   *Running because it is a solitary sport and I can clear my mind.* Female, age 16. MBTI type: INTP.

11. **Is tasting something very special to you? Describe in what way it is special.**   *Tasting as in feeling. Tasting the moment (I'm not trying to keep going off on tangents like this; it sounds really stupid but this is what I'm thinking of first). I wrote a poem once about licking the sides of someone's word and another about someone drinking up me. I like that image because that is what it is and many times I'm tasting depression and indifference like now.* Female, age 15. MBTI type: ENFP.

12. **Do you ever catch yourself seeing, hearing, or imagining things that aren't really there? Give examples.**   *I often think I hear someone call my name—sometimes when I'm alone, or sometimes when I'm with others.* Female, age 16. MBTI type: INFP.

13. **Do you ever think about your own thinking? Describe.**   *Yes, in my journal I write all of the time about how strange it is for me to ask all of these questions of myself such as why I do things, etc. Most people, it seems, don't do that (or just don't show it and I'm not sure that I show it either). I sometimes think life would be easier if I just accepted things and didn't worry about it or question it.* Female, age 16. MBTI type: INTP.

14. **When do you feel the greatest urge to do something? Explain.**   *When someone tells me I can't. I strongly believe that there's nothing I can't do if I try.* Female, age 16. MBTI type: ENFJ.

TABLE 1. Overexcitability Questionnaire

15. **Does it ever appear to you that the things around you may have a life of their own, and that plants, animals, and all things in nature have their own feelings? Give examples.**   *Yes. For example, in creative writing I've written "Monstrous black clouds casting a mask across the delicate blue sky;" "Compelling the grass to cover within themselves;" "Flowers are closed up, mourning;" "Wind sings out its funeral chant."* Female, age 15. MBTI type: ENFP.

16. **If you come across a difficult idea or concept, how does it become clear to you? Describe what goes on in your head in this case.** *My brain starts to organize different parts of the idea into different drawers, looks at all its parts individually, and then as a whole, spins it around on the tip of my fingers, and eventually understands the idea enough so it becomes clear.* Male, age 17. MBTI type: INFP.

17. **Are you poetically inclined? If so, give an example of what comes to mind when you are in a poetic mood.**   *I am a poet. I think of a form or idea. Then I allow my feelings to write the rest. Example: After reading a poem in which the line "oblong rectangles" appeared, I wrote the poem "4-sided triangles" about apparently unsolvable ideas.* Male, age 16. MBTI type: INTP.

18. **How often do you carry on arguments in your head?   About what sorts of subjects are these arguments?** *Yes. I have arguments and discussions with myself all of the time about anything and everything.* Male, age 15. MBTI type: INFP.

19. **If you ask yourself "Who am I?" what is the answer?** *I am myself. I change for no one and I accept completely what I am.* Male, age 16. MBTI type: INFP.

20. **When you read a book, what attracts your attention the most?** *The intense parts.* Male, age 16. MBTI type: INFP.

21. **Describe what you do when you are just fooling around.**   *I go out and drive in my car in the night and turn out my lights and watch the lightning bugs. Little diamonds among the shrubbery.* Female, age 16. MBTI type: ENFJ.

We also added another question that is not on the Overexcitability Questionnaire: *22. In what ways do your dreams influence you?* Most of the students felt that their dreams were quite important in generating ideas, in having them think about the meaning of life, and in being predictive or explanatory of events in their lives.

We found, in interviewing the students, that they had often had imaginary playmates. Thus I was amused to read in articles by Gary Davis that "Two virtually flawless biographical predictors of adult creativity" seem to be the presence of imaginary playmates and involvement in the theater. Since our students were studying theater, those who also had had imaginary playmates lend credibility to Davis's assertion that such people are headed toward creativity as adults. Here is a typical answer:

Interviewer: Did you ever have an imaginary playmate?

Yeah. I had a guy named John Hutchins. I didn't have any brothers or sisters, and my mother and father worked overtime, and so there was basically just me, me and my animals. I felt really dumb talking to the cat on the porch. But now that I think about it talking to nobody that wasn't there isn't better than talking to a cat. So I was by myself all the time, so I invented this guy named John, and before we moved, we had this really big house. And there's a little corner in the dining room and right by it was a walk-in closet. And right there was where John lived, and he would come out and sit at my little table with me when I got my punishment. And he would protect me from everything and stuff. And I really believed in him. He wasn't imaginary to me. He was real. There was John. John was talking to me. And I thought he was naked, so my dad had to give him some pajamas and everything. And my mom had to wash the pajamas all the time, and he was John. John sat there at dinner with me, and John ate my liver for me. John didn't come up and get the liver, no he didn't. John ate my liver and stuff. There was really a John to me.

He was in my life until I was about nine or ten, when we were getting ready to move because I didn't like my step-dad, and I still don't like him. He still comes around, and I still hate him. I guess I don't hate him, but I don't like him very much. And I couldn't tell my mom because she loved him, and when you love somebody they don't do anything wrong. But he was wrong, because he was drunk all the time. He took my money and stuff. So I sat there and told John, and John was like my psychologist. I would tell him how I felt.

Our experience with this questionnaire was that it enabled us to better understand those who create. Our interviews with the students revealed more about the young creative person than any creativity test or checklist could.

The Need for Qualitative Assessment

A research data base of the Overexcitabilities Questionnaire has been developed in the past few years. Some researchers have explored using the OEQ as a means to identify creative and intellectual students. The rigors of interrater scoring and rating preclude widespread use of such a questionnaire until the number of active researchers grows, but the anecdotal and personal knowledge that we gained seems just as important. This is called *qualitative* assessment, and even the numbers-oriented divergent production researchers are beginning to advocate such. Runco in 1993 noted that several researchers have begun to look at *what* the students say in their ideas, ideas which used to be merely counted for a total fluency score: "The notion that divergent thinking has meaningful qualitative aspects is especially important because of the increased appreciation for the affective components of creativity."

The Myers-Briggs Type Indicator

I included the Myers-Briggs Type Indicator preferences in the response above to illustrate that we found that both the faculty and the students overwhelmingly preferred Intuition (N). (The opposite of Intuition is Sensation (S), trusting the concrete, that which can be touched and seen.) They overwhelmingly turned out to be NFP (Intuitive, Feeling, Perceptive), with Introversion and Extroversion equally divided. Again, not a surprise, but a confirmation that these adolescents were like those studied by Myers and McCaulley for the Myers-Briggs Manual (1985) and were also like adult creative people.

Lysy and Piechowski considered the preference for intuition to be similar to what Dabrowski termed *developmental potential*, an inner propensity toward growth from level to level through conflict. While all Myers-Briggs types individuate, those who prefer intuition predominate among Jungian analysts and even in Jung himself. "Therefore," wrote Lysy and Piechowski, "there seems to be support for the interpretation that growth and transformation are more likely if intuition is well developed."

Since personal growth is a path into the unknown, "Perhaps it is a bit easier for those with strong intuition, who are more comfortable with the unseen, with future possibilities, to follow this course than for those whose intuition is not as well developed," said Lysy and Piechowski. Inner searching produces gut feelings of "I just know it," and the person who trusts intuition trusts the gut. "The inner search, then, for an as-yet-unmanifest self may well be a process more congenial to the individual with strong intuition." My 1995 study of women writers also indicated that the subjects overwhelmingly preferred intuition as compared to a group of women elementary teachers, who decidedly preferred sensing.

These differences in preferences may explain the difficulty creative students have in elementary school. In addition to the conflict between the sensing preferred by most teachers and the intuition so common in creative students is friction between judging and perception: many elementary teachers prefer judging, while the majority of the creative and intuitive students prefer perception. These differences constitute basic incompatibility in preference that may lead to misunderstanding on the part of the teachers and a feeling of rejection for the way one thinks on the part of the students. In *The Developing Child*, Elizabeth Murphy spoke to these differences by suggesting that teachers with one preference offer choice to their students in terms of assignments, and that they be flexible in terms of requirements. An open-ended assignment in an area of interest may satisfy the requirement that the student demonstrate she knows the matters at hand just as thoroughly as twenty work sheets drilling the student in skills she already has demonstrated that she knows by completing the first few items correctly.

The Adjective Check List

Another commonly used checklist is the Adjective Check List (Gough, 1952), 300 words that the person checks as being self-descriptive. The Adjective Check List is not specifically designed to measure creative traits, but a 30-item scale within it was found to relate to personality characteristics of the people studied at the Institute for Personality Assessment and Research. Gough described that research in a 1979 article. I administered the Adjective Check List to our adolescents, and sure enough, they came out as creative personality (CPs). The adjectives that describe a creative personality are *adventurous, ambitious, artistic, assertive, clever, complicated, curious, energetic, enterprising, imaginative, independent, intelligent, inventive, original, possessing wide interests and initiative, progressive, resourceful, self-confident, temperamental, and versatile.* The adjectives that do not describe the creative personality are *affected, cautious, commonplace, conservative, conventional, dissatisfied, honest, mannerly, possessing narrow interests, sincere, submissive, suspicious.* Gough and Heilbrun used these terms in 1983 in The Adjective Check List Manual. Creative personality high scorers are *venturesome, aesthetically reactive, clever, and quick to respond.* Intellectually, they have such characteristics as *wide interests, mental ability, and fluency of ideas.*

Our students also came out on the high end of the Free Child scale in Transactional Analysis. One who scores high on this scale is "ebullient and enterprising, not at all inclined to exercise self-restraint or to postpone gratifications." Those who come in contact with such a person "are swept along whether they like it or not, in a rush toward enjoyment."

Another scale within the Adjective Check List is the Welsh Origence-Intellectence Scales, based on Welsh's 1975 monograph on creativity and intelligence as they relate to personality. Our students turned out high on the High Origence-High Intellectence Scale, A-2. High scorers on this scale are *self-sufficient, strong-willed, original in thought and perceptions, aesthetically sensitive, indifferent to convention,* and *much annoyed by those who are uninsightful, intellectually maladroit, or lacking in perspicacity.* In spite of many talents, the high-scorer on A-2 is scarcely more comfortable with his or her own needs and reactions than with those of other people. Intimacy based on candid sharing of emotionally significant feelings is sensed as dangerous and hence avoided.

Our creative adolescents scored low on the Counseling Readiness Scale (CRS), another topical scale. The male who scores low on this scale is *"less inhibited, more enterprising, and more confident of his ability to attain goals and seek satisfaction; therefore, he is less likely to seek counseling or to feel he needs it."* The female who scores low: *"Not at odds with herself or with others, she feels little need for counseling, nor would counseling serve much purpose."* However, the description of low-scoring females also said that such females are other-directed, gentle and not ambitious. That was certainly not true of our girls, as we observed them work, compose, write, and do art for two weeks.

While this checklist is among the best available, a careful person can see that there are some difficulties in using it to identify and select students for special programs. Checklists serve another purpose, however, and that is for the purpose of description. We administered our creative adolescents the Adjective Check List, and they turned out to be creative in personality. What a surprise, the reader might say. Yet at the very least this description confirmed our identification process throughout our state, for we came up with students who were recommended by their districts on the basis of their creative interests.

Again, the qualitative use of information may be valuable to persons seeking to understand those who are creative. To use a checklist to select for a program is one thing; to use a checklist to describe a person is another. Whether or not one subscribes to the theory behind the checklist is also important. The Myers-Briggs Type Indicator is one example. If one has doubts about the Jungian theory of personality types, the information gleaned from the checklist about the personality of the person may not be seen as valuable information. The Adjective Check List (ACL) is another example, as is the California Psychological Inventory (CPI) and the Minnesota Multiphasic Psychological Inventory (MMPI), the 16 Personality Factors Inventory (16PF), and many others. In the next few chapters, the reader will see that many of the major studies of creative people used these checklists, with varying results.

Cattell High School Personality Questionnaire (HSPQ)

In another study of creative and intellectually gifted youth, Karnes, Chauvin, and Trant administered another personality checklist/inventory which also has an acceptable research base, the Cattell High School Personality Questionnaire, to a group of intellectually gifted students and to a group of students attending special schools for the fine and performing arts. They found that the young fine and performing artists were "tender-minded, reflective, internally restrained, self-assured, but somewhat tense and driven," and that the intellectually gifted students were shown to be "excitable, assertive, enthusiastic, and relaxed or composed."

We administered the HSPQ to our creative adolescents and to a comparison group of students in high school geometry classes. We found some gender differences in the creative youth. The girls were higher than the boys in dominance. The talented boys, however, were higher in tender-mindedness. The talented girls and the comparison girls had no differences, but the creative and comparison boys were different. We published these results in a study called "Androgyny in the Personalities of Talented Teenagers."

The results showed two major differences between the girls and boys, described thus: the talented girls (as well as comparison girls, who were also college-bound) tended toward androgynous characteristics such as tough-mindedness, tough poise, dominance, and aggressiveness. The talented boys tended toward such androgynous characteristics as tender-mindedness and sensitivity. While the girls were aggressive, they were less aggressive than the comparison boys, and the talented boys were more tender-minded than both the talented girls and the comparison girls.

Both the talented girls and the talented boys showed similarities in the dimensions of leadership, school achievement, and creativity, with no significant differences apparent. However, the talented boys showed more creativity than either the talented girls or the comparison girls. This could be an indication of the fields in which the talent was displayed—musical theater, creative writing, and visual arts. When a young man decides to attend a summer institute in these nontraditional fields, he has already indicated self-sufficiency and nonconformity, more so than the girls who decide to do so.

Conjecture as to why the comparison girls and the talented girls are so similar could include reference to an article I published in 1991, where I postulated that women creative in the areas of mathematics, visual arts, and music do not surface as readily as their male counterparts because of the double bind women face in developing their talents as adults. They must provide mentally and physically for caretaking time for children and husband. This need to fulfill family expectations and obligations is often directly counterproductive to the one-mindedness needed for developing one's talents.

This HSPQ androgyny study indicates that even initially, the girls in both groups might be very similar, and the drive and commitment necessary for developing one's talents might be absent as early as the second and third years of high school. The striking similarity between the two groups of girls could be because these girls, whether or not they possess talents in the various domains, are already socialized into the "average" category of behaviors and display no extremes in personality. Other studies to be discussed later also indicate that talented teenage girls do not show marked differences from other girls, especially in terms of the percentage of eating disorders and self-destructive behaviors.

The boys, on the other hand, are already nonconforming by the very act of attending a summer institute in musical theater, writing, and visual arts. Males in the arts have already gone against gender stereotypes and may affect a "gentleman pirate" demeanor as Barron described in 1972. The boys must make a strong emotional commitment to the art in order to even pursue it. Females tend to choose art education over fine arts, often for practical reasons; that is, they can teach, have a steady income, and still raise families. As a result, their commitment to their talent is often given over to domesticity and teaching.

The girls in each group in this sample would be likely to pursue their paths with tough-mindedness. The deciding factors in development of talent would be having the minimum intelligence necessary for functioning in the domain and the requisite talent in writing, musical theater, or visual arts. In fact, the talented girls and comparison girls were differentiated only by the presence of "specific talent in a domain." (See my pyramid model in Chapter 1.)

The talented boys and talented girls were not differentiated except in personality traits which would seem to indicate the presence of androgyny. The talented boys and comparison boys also differed in their tough poise and creativity. As defined by Cattell and Cattell, to possess tough poise is to view the world objectively and to make decisions based on cool, rational thought. The comparison boys scored higher in tough poise while the boys attending the summer institute scored higher in creativity.

Those possessed of much tough poise may appear not to care about others' feelings nor to want to express their own. By contrast, those like our creative boys who score low on tough poise "are guided by their hearts, feelings, and imagination." Tuned in to the emotional aspects of decision-making, they are frequently unable to make decisions based on reason and facts. Those who score low often have higher ratings of creative ability; in fact, the creative boys scored the lowest of all four groups on tough poise, indicating that the hypothesis of androgyny in talented people in the arts may have some basis, as seen in the results of personality testing. John Fraas and I published the results of this study in 1994.

Personality and Behavioral Checklists

Checklists are very popular, except among those who review them for the *Mental Measurements Yearbooks* (MMY). Two of the most popular checklists used to identify students with creative thinking ability are the Williams CAP program and the Renzulli-Hartman Creativity Scale, included in the Scales for Rating the Behavioral Characteristics of Superior Students (SRBCSS). Again, the question is whether what is being asked actually is related to creativity. Let us sample what the reviewers said.

MMY Reviews of Williams CAP

Damarin, a 1985 MMY reviewer of the Williams Creativity Assessment Packet (CAP), reported that the manual was not well-written, that the validation data were scanty and poorly documented, and that he could find only one use for the checklist, to prove that "creativity tests are really measures of susceptibility to experimenter-demand characteristics." Damarin continued: a creative child who is asked to "draw pictures in squares one at a time (no skipping around)" would probably do poorly, especially as the Williams tests penalize the child for skipping answers. A second reviewer, Rosen, dismissed the CAP as containing "a technically uncertain set of instruments whose usefulness is limited by a lack of appropriate information as to validity and reliability," and said that Williams had made "exaggerated claims."

MMY Reviews of Renzulli-Hartman Scales

According to Argulewicz, one reviewer of the entire Scales, "The SRBCSS represents a significant advancement in the expansion of the methodology for identifying intellectually gifted, creative, or talented youth." Of the Creativity Scale, he noted that the validity was determined by comparison with the Torrance Test of Creative Thinking, and that the Creativity Scale correlated with verbal subscales but not with nonverbal subscales. The other reviewer, Rust, said the references in the manual seemed outdated, that concurrent validity was "untested," but that face validity, stability, and retest reliability for fifth graders seemed all right. "In summary, the scales' strengths include their conceptual formation and their ease of administration."

Nevertheless, the average classroom teacher might experience some difficulty in giving the Renzulli-Hartman Creativity Scale because of the number of questions asked in each item, or in technical jargon "the length of the stem." For instance, sample items on the Creativity Scale of the *Scales For Rating The Behavioral Characteristics Of Superior Students* are these:

5. Displays a good deal of intellectual playfulness: fantasizes; imagines ("I wonder what would happen if . . ."); manipulates ideas (i.e., changes, elaborates upon them); is often concerned with adapting, improving and modifying institutions, objects, and systems.
6. Displays a keen sense of humor and sees humor in situations that may not appear to be humorous to others.
7. Is unusually aware of his impulses and more open to the irrational in himself (freer expression of feminine interest for boys, greater than usual amount of independence for girls); shows emotional sensitivity.

10. Criticizes constructively; is unwilling to accept authoritarian pro-nouncements without critical examination.

Mrs. Larson Fills Out a Checklist on Bobby

Remember Mrs. Larson and her puzzlement over Bobby? Even though Bobby's school ability index was one point too low for the cutoff, Mrs. Larson requested the Creativity Scale of the Renzulli-Hartman and has begun filling it out. She's on Item 5. Well, Bobby displays intellectual play-fulness all right, most of the time, but he doesn't seem to fantasize much, though he may do so at home, and Mrs. Larson doesn't know about it, so she can't mark it "sometimes."

Does he manipulate ideas? What does that mean? Change or elaborate on ideas? Well, yes, sometimes. Is he often concerned with institutions and world change? Well, last week when they were talking about World Regions in third grade social studies, he asked where Michelangelo came from, but she just put that down to the turtles on TV, but it could have been that he was interested in aesthetics and art.

Now Mrs. Larson notices that she has four boxes from which to pick only one answer to this entire item; the responses are Seldom or Never, Occasionally, Considerably, and Almost Always. Yet in this one item, num-ber 5, she has been asked about eight different things about this child. Her dilemma illustrates one of the difficulties with the Creativity Scale from the Renzulli-Hartman. At item 6, she checks Considerably, because Bobby does bring in those Calvin and Hobbes cartoons, but she's never seen him frown-ing when other people are laughing, nor has she seen him giggling mania-cally when the others are not laughing, and that's what she thinks that "sees humor in situations that may not appear to be humorous to others" means. (Sense of humor in creative people will be discussed in more detail in Chapter 6.)

Item number 7, "unusually aware of his impulses," could mean that he always asks to go to the bathroom, couldn't it? Or else it could mean that he is quite a conformist, buttoned-up, shy. But then the item asks whether he's "open to the irrational in himself," which could mean that he's unaware of his impulses and acts out a lot. Then the item insinuates that Bobby could be quite feminine, a sissy boy, and Bobby certainly is not that. He's a roughhouser along with the rest of the third grade boys, and is always chosen first for games in the playground. Does he show "emotional sensitivity"? Well, yes, he does. He helps other students, and he asked about that starving child pictured in *Weekly Reader* the other day.

Mrs. Larson, taking an unusual amount of time on this questionnaire because she really cares about Bobby and thinks there's "something there," as teacher lingo goes, has to check "Occasionally" for this item. Mrs. Larson has anguished over the checklist, wondering whether Bobby's criticism is constructive or not, remembering the time he really got angry at the principal interrupting on the intercom just when he was going to do his demonstration of a duck call for show-and-tell, and she decides it is not, checking "occasionally."

Katherine Miller picks up the checklists from Mrs. Larson and adds the scores. The checklist is weighted so that every item counts the same. Even though item 5 asks eight things, and item 4, "Is a high risk taker; is adventurous and speculative," asks about three, every item is weighted the same. The total number supposedly shows the amount of creativity characteristics a child has.

How can we evaluate whether these items predict the potential for creative behavior on the part of the student? Are the items based on research into the characteristics of creative people as they were in their childhoods? And, in even more far-reaching terms, do the ten items on this checklist select for the potentially creative adult? For example, item 1, "Displays a great deal of curiosity about many things; is constantly asking questions about anything and everything," seems more appropriate for intellectual giftedness. The item is probably here on the creativity characteristics checklist because creative students are supposed to have a certain amount of intellectual giftedness, too. But do creative adults have curiosity, and did they, as students, constantly ask questions about anything and everything?

Davis, in a 1989 article, called the Renzulli-Hartman traits "carefully selected and defended," but Renzulli in 1990 also told an audience that not a week passes that he and his colleagues don't get a letter or a phone call telling them how a test user has shortened the stem. Renzulli and his colleagues have undertaken a substantial revision of the SRBCSS; this revision should be used, not the earlier versions. No checklist that has not been renormed within the last ten years should be used.

GIFT, GIFFI, PRIDE

Other checklists or inventories are Davis and Rimm's GIFT, for elementary students; the 1982 GIFFI, I and II, for middle and high school students; and on Davis's How Do You Think test for college students, validated with students of all socioeconomic levels and races. These lists do measure traits that creative people seem to display. Davis in 1997 and Rimm in 1990 were quite positive about the validation results reported, claiming that these checklists are safe and predictive for a school district. They must be scored by the company, though an examination packet is available.

Promising Practices

Personality checklists filled out by the students are entirely different from behavior checklists filled out by teachers in the school system. The latter supposedly show whether or not the student possesses certain researched characteristics and thus is potentially creative. Both our studies and the Karnes, et al. study took such teacher-identified students, then described them, and didn't select people for programs because of what the checklists added up to. As far as I am aware, no school district uses such well-researched, somewhat validated, and relatively reliable instruments as the Myers-Briggs, the Adjective Check List, the 16 PF, or the High School Personality Questionnaire to select students, nor should they.

Selection by means of personality instruments should not be done, but why selection by relatively invalid and unreliable checklists is permitted is beyond me. The problem of assessing young students is a universal one. That such checklists are tallied into weighted scores used to make major decisions about young students' lives bothers me. That school districts use the false promise of objectivity in using such matrices to combine unlike, unrelated, and unreliable data worries me.

Performance Assessment

Baer said that performance assessments, that is, asking experts to look at student products, seem to have promise in assessing creativity. Hennessey and Amabile, in a series of studies described by Hennessey in 1997, recommended storytelling assessment to identify verbal creativity. The mammoth fallout and interest in the Gardner Multiple Intelligence (MI) theory and the ensuing large research grants have yielded much that is useful in assessing creative products. Books by Lazear, the Campbells, and Armstrong have much advice about how to assess by looking directly at intelligence instead of filtering through linguistic and logical-mathematical indicators.

According to Morrison and Dungan, looking at student performance in district- or state-wide contests is a practical, doable assessment opportunity that has the added advantage of comparing students with others outside the school. The highly trained judges at regional music, science, mathematics, art, writing, and sports contests bring a wide background in assessment of similar products. Baer in 1994 noted that expert evaluation—the way creativity is assessed in real life—can be replicated in schools by having panels of experts in the domain look at what the students make or do. Thus there are many ways to assess creativity other than paper and pencil tests.

The assessment of creative potential has many pitfalls, but careful, thorough, and informed people can sidestep these pitfalls with proper attention. One major criticism of this kind of assessment, called authentic, is that it is not validated across the state or the country or internationally, and what is called highly creative in one setting may not have a relationship to what the rest of the world views as creative. Relying upon experts in one school system may not produce the specialist or authoritative judgment that the student would meet with on a wider playing field. What one parent views as worthy of permanent enshrinement on the refrigerator or within a frame may be, to the eyes of objective observers, really an inferior product colored by the eyes of love and adoration, by the halo of parental felicity.

Let us use the students in our summer institute as an example. They learned, in a minimal way, how to write the libretto of an opera. They participated in the frustrating, lengthy, mind-filling creative process. They sat for hours at the piano in practice rooms composing, they acted, made costumes, wrote the story, rehearsed, collaborated, and sweated. Their journals revealed their changed attitudes. The products they produced were novel, original, never seen before. The students did actual work and participated in actual process—they did not just do abstract exercises twice removed from the process. Their work was *authentic*.

I suspect the fluency all the participants gained might have been due to their feeling comfortable and satisfied and pleased with themselves after working together in such an intensive effort for fifteen days. The point is this: we have a mystical belief in tests. If we will just sit back and look at the tests we have given, and stop investing them with magical powers, we would realize that the tests show little, if anything, and cannot do much in five or ten minutes of testing. Our students increased in creativity all right, but two ten-minute tests were woefully inadequate in measuring that increase. Yet with accountability constraints, this is what educators are often asked to do.

Let us take another example. Say there is a boy who can throw a ball from center field to home plate with great and accurate force. Observation would dictate that he would probably do well as a center fielder. Is there any need to give him a paper and pencil test to see whether he has spatial ability? In a similar vein, a better-than-test indicator of enhanced creativity of the adolescents at our summer institute was the observational or portfolio assessment of their work. We considered what they had made while at the institute: many poems, short stories, prints, four amateur but earnest operas, all shown on a videotape. These products were not judged or graded in any way, for the emphasis was on the process they went through, and not on the *quality* of their products. (An assessment of quality should come after many more poems, stories, operas, and prints are produced. However, our instructors were themselves masters in their fields: composers, actors, writers and artists who could have assessed the quality of the products if such judgement had been called for.)

Another type of authentic assessment is the creativity portfolio that a student assembles throughout the years. This could include products made, sketchbooks used, journals, concerts, plays, games, camps attended, and other such records. Whether or not the student demonstrates specific talent in a domain that is great enough to be developed through the process of training expertise, she would at least have a record of creative thoughts and projects and would think of herself as creative. Memory of creative times could be awakened and recalled with pleasure and nostalgia. Picture it! If we had done this as children and teens, no adult among us would be able to say, "I'm not creative," for the proof would be there, in this authentic portfolio of creative experiences gathered while maturing.

Creativity Training

In many industrial, business, school, and psychological settings, an effort to enhance creativity called *creativity training* is taking place. This section looks at a few of the most used methods.

An Example of Divergent Production Training

Guilford listed *fluency, flexibility, elaboration, originality,* and *transformation* as aspects of divergent production. He also listed *synthesis* and *analysis* as well as evaluation, all of which appeared in Bloom's Taxonomy of Educational Objectives: knowledge, comprehension, application, synthesis, analysis, and evaluation. Many creativity enhancement programs use divergent production training.

For example, the Odyssey of the Mind program has an activity for students called *Spontaneous Problems:* Five students enter a room and sit around a table; two trained student judges are already present. The five get a topic, think for a couple of minutes, brainstorm possible items that fit the topic, and then are judged on the fluency (how many), flexibility (how many different categories), and originality (how rare) of their responses. The team with the most points wins.

In an exercise that I use to help students internalize the types of divergent production, the first three steps are similar to those practiced by teams in the Odyssey of the Mind:

TABLE 2. An Exercise in Divergent Production

A lesson in **divergent production** that I often use to illustrate fluency, flexibility, originality, elaboration, and transformation is to have the students brainstorm on, for instance, the topic of Birds.

■ **Fluency**

After dividing students into groups of four or five and explaining exactly what brainstorming is, ask students to "brainstorm birds." The word *brainstorm* has made its way into the popular lexicon, yet few people know its Guilfordian origins as explicated at the State College of Buffalo Creativity Studies Program. The rules of brainstorming are that the participants must go as fast as they can listing ideas as they come to the mind, with a recorder writing them down, and there is to be no judging of answers, as in "That's a really stupid idea" or "No, that doesn't fit" or even "Will you explain that, please?"

■ **Flexibility**

To illustrate *flexibility,* ask them to look at the list and see how many different categories of answers they've come up with. There are **athletic teams** with the nicknames of birds, for example the St. Louis Cardinals or the Baltimore Orioles. There's the **musical group** the Byrds. There are **species** of birds: robin, bluebird, owl, nightingale. There is **food made from the flesh** of birds, turkey for Thanksgiving, turkey stuffing, chicken cacciatore, pheasant under glass. There are **idiomatic sayings** using birds or their products, such as "Don't put all your eggs in one basket" or "A bird in the hand is worth two in the bush."

TABLE 2. An Exercise In Divergent Production

■ **Originality**

To illustrate *originality* or *rarity,* ask them to see which items on their lists they think are most original or rare. They may have the name of a famous professional basketball player, "Larry Bird," or the name of a flower, "Bird of Paradise." If the unusual item does not appear in the lists of the other members in class, call it original.

■ **Elaboration**

To illustrate *elaboration*, ask the students to take drawing paper and draw one of the most interesting items on their list. Each student individually draws something interesting. Ask them to draw with detail and individuality.

■ **Transformation**

To illustrate *transformation*, as a collaborative assignment in divergent production, ask them to exchange drawings and to change the classmate's drawing into something else.

This simple, exercise teaches the students the terminology and has them experience divergent production firsthand—rather trival, but fun.

Creativity Training in College Courses

A few colleges offer courses in creativity. McDonough and McDonough found that of 1,504 colleges, a total of 76, or five percent, offered courses in creativity taught by diverse faculty in engineering, art, education, psychology, music, and philosophy. A conference for professors of creativity courses is offered every summer in Midland, Michigan, at the Northwoods Institute. There the professors share ideas and try out each others' favorite methods for enhancing creativity. Often students from their creativity classes come and demonstrate what they have learned. One group of engineering students from the General Motors Institute demonstrated their uses for industrial sludge; students from a liberal arts college did multi-media presentations in response to their assignment, "Come to class with no clothes on."

Creativity Studies Project

In 1967 Alex F. Osborn undertook a massive effort to deliberately teach to enhance the creative abilities of college students. Osborn, developer of the brainstorming technique and the Creative Problem Solving Process (CPS), directed an advertising agency in New York City before heading up the creativity studies program at the State College of Buffalo. His successor at the college, Sidney J. Parnes, founded the Center for Studies in Creativity. The focus was the art of problem solving (now there is an emphasis on problem finding as well). Students learned the Creative Problem Solving Process, utilizing the intelligence theory of the Structure of the Intellect, combining convergent production with divergent production, in consultation with J.P. Guilford. Parnes in 1987 reported an evaluation of the program. After two years, posttests showed that the students in the experimental group scored significantly better than the control group. They also did exercises in Noller's *Creative Action Book*. Results indicated there were significant differences in students' scores.

The question is whether scoring well on these tests has predictive validity: did the student scoring high do well in other courses, and did he enter a profession where enhanced creative process skills would be useful? In other words, did the creativity training transfer? Parnes said that these tests "required considerable transfer from the kinds of exercises and materials the students used in the classes." The students also were compared with students in English classes, and they received the same grades, even in writing themes which allowed creativity. There were no results reported on math achievement. In nonacademic achievement at the end of two years, the experimental group seemed to be accomplishing more in areas such as leadership, social participation, art, and social service. Recent studies have shown that the graduates have obtained jobs in business, industry, the arts, and education.

Most interesting, though, is who dropped out of the creativity studies program. Parnes and Noller found that the students most likely to drop out were those with arts interests who had thought that the creativity studies project would feed those interests. Most of the students were women, and those who dropped out were interested in music, entertainment, modeling, art, interior decorating, and journalism. Those who stayed in were interested in recreation leadership, mechanics, social service, sports, religious activities and office practice. Parnes said, "Those lower in self-control and higher on 'manic' tendencies (impulsivity, spontaneity, etc.) seemed to seek the quick answer, the novel experience, and when it no longer appeared to be novel and exciting, they tended to drop out of the picture." The dropouts did not like working in the workbooks or the structure of the program, but they did like brainstorming and the game-like atmosphere.

Those in education who use the Creative Problem Solving Model and similar workbooks and materials must remember that Osborn, whose *Applied Imagination* started it all, was interested in increasing the creativity of *business* people. Parnes said that those who dropped out of the creativity studies program were those who might have "limited value in an organization." People who are creative within an organization contribute to the profitability of that organization, and they expect a reward, usually monetary, for their creativity. The ones who stayed in the creativity studies program got better and better on Guilford's tests measuring evaluation ability. Again, the predictive validity of these tests is a question, though it would seem reasonable, especially to those who work in the area of thinking skills, that training in evaluation would help in real-life situations requiring evaluation.

As an artist and not a business person, I have to admit that I nod off when I read creativity training books and programs. Perhaps I would also have dropped out of the Creative Studies Program. It does seem that those who didn't stick it out had interests similar to those people like me have: music, entertainment, the arts. They may have felt they were creative enough already. I would rather be in a play, go to choir practice, write a poem or work on my novel than fill in a workbook to enhance my creativity. I would rather go to our Sunday afternoon writer's group with a new poem for my friends to discuss. Perhaps the value of creativity training books is that they help people who do not consider themselves creative to step into the stream.

A few years ago, I was glad to see I wasn't alone in feeling weird when asked to do workbook exercises and to follow step-by-step processes to make me more creative. Writer S.M. Els was a graduate student trying to write a creative thesis for a degree in education. She tried all the techniques she had been taught in her graduate programs, but none worked, so she made up her own and wrote her thesis on her creative process as a poet and a writer. It became a book called *Into the Deep: A Writer's Look at Creativity.*

To their credit, Isaksen, Puccio, Treffinger, and the other researchers at the Buffalo Creativity Studies program took the studies about drop-outs seriously, looking more closely at the personality preferences of the people who entered both their undergraduate and graduate creativity studies programs. They began to research how people with various personality preferences function and contribute to corporations and organizations. This research is currently being published in scholarly journals.

Creativity Training in the Schools

Various people have asserted that young people and adults can be trained in creativity. They have manufactured programs and exercises in divergent production, to encourage people to improve their flexibility, fluency, and originality, as well as their ability to elaborate and to make transformations. There are many programs from which teachers can teach and which individuals can use to enhance their own sense of creativity. Torrance listed the six most common types of creativity training: teaching specific creative problem solving skills; direct teaching of problem solving and pattern recognition; using guided fantasy and imagery; using thematic fantasy; using creative writing; using Quality Circles. Such programs are linear in that they consist of published directions and exercises. A partial description of some of these programs or systems follows.

TABLE 3. A Sampling of Creativity Training Programs

■ *Divergent Production Testing:* These tests and the pros and cons of their usage have been described in Chapter 3. The practice of testing for divergent production cognition has continued out of a concern for inclusiveness. The problem of "false negatives," or elimination of those who are really creative because they scored low on such tests, is one of the main difficulties. The inclusion of those who score high but who have no creative products or other indicators is a plus, as the high score indicates they are able to function divergently. In 1993 Runco stated that "divergent production tests are very useful estimates of the potential for creative thought."

■ *Creative Problem Solving (CPS):* This granddaddy of all creativity training is the foundation for such programs as Future Problem Solving and Odyssey of the Mind. People work in groups and resolve a "mess" through divergent and convergent processes such as problem finding and solution finding, criteria setting and finally focusing on the one best answer. Treffinger, Isaksen, Feldhusen, and colleagues have produced many training materials, as has Doris Shallcross. Each summer they hold an international creativity conference in Buffalo which thousands of people attend.

TABLE 3. A Sampling of Creativity Training Programs

■ *Gordon's Synectics:* Synectics, putting unlike objects together to form a new object, can be learned at a training center. It is also a popular teaching technique in textbooks about models of teaching.

■ *Meeker's divergent production exercises:* These exercises are found in the *Sourcebooks*. There are basic and advanced levels that contain exercises in all of Guilford's divergent production factors.

■ *Torrance's programs:* Many programs, workbooks, and the like are available at the Torrance Center for Creativity at the University of Georgia, many of them developed by his graduate students and colleagues over the years. A typical book, developed after Torrance wrote extension exercises for a Ginn textbook series, is *Incubation Teaching: Getting Beyond the Aha!* by Torrance and Safter.

■ *Taylor's Talents Unlimited:* Taylor identified nine talent totem poles: academics, productive thinking, communicating, forecasting, decision-making, planning and designing, implementing, human relations, and discerning opportunities. This program was validated by the National Diffusion Network and is widely used in schools.

■ *Williams's ideas for thinking and feeling:* Williams created exercises following the Guilford divergent production aspects.

■ *Samples's metaphorization:* Samples suggested ways to help people form metaphors, noting that almost all theory-making in science is metaphoric.

■ *Eberle's work:* Eberle designed exercises in creative visualization and invented the term SCAMPER, a code for teaching creative thinking: Substitute, Combine, Adapt, Modify, Put to other uses, Eliminate, Rearrange.

■ *Future Problem Solving:* In this international competition based on the Osborn-Parnes model of Creative Problem Solving, students research and propose solutions for world and community problems.

■ *Odyssey of the Mind (OM) competitions:* An international competitive program where teams of students invent and create according to certain problems all have been given.

TABLE 3. A Sampling of Creativity Training Programs

■ *Edwards's* **Drawing on the Right Side of the Brain:** This technique uses upside-down drawing in order for people to see holistically and not form brain codes.

■ *Rico's* **Writing the Natural Way:** Rico pioneered the now-widespread use of webbing to generate ideas and organizational structure. Computer software exists to help in this process.

■ *Invention Competitions:* These are commercially run by various groups, including Invention Museums.

■ *deBono's coRT Lateral Thinking:* Lateral thinking is a packaged program used in thousands of schools internationally. Six "thinking hats" are taught.

■ *Davis's personal transformation:* The Davis program emphasizes affective as well as cognitive aspects of creativity enhancement.

■ *Bagley's and Hess's* **200 Ways of Using Imagery in the Classroom.** This popular book has many guided imagery scripts, useful in all areas.

■ *Crabbe's and Betts's* **Creating More Creative People:** These books, written for the Future Problem Solving program, emphasize creativity training. The exercises are similar in design to those above.

■ *Cameron's* **The Artist's Way:** A 12-step program by a creative writer which combines "morning pages" with meditative techniques. With twelve weeks of exercises about recovering—Recovering a Sense of Connection, Recovering a Sense of Autonomy, Recovering a Sense of Faith—this program speaks to the mid-1990s obsession with dysfunction.

■ *Goldberg's Creativity Exercises:* A series of exercises to help writers break through blocks to writing, including such techniques as "writing practice" and writing in public. This extremely popular program for writers has applications for other fields, just as Edwards's drawing program does.

TABLE 3. A Sampling of Creativity Training Programs

■ *UCONN Confratute:* This annual summer conference at the University of Connecticut has a creativity strand where hundreds of teachers learn how to infuse creativity into their daily work. The work of Renzulli, Reis, and colleagues at the Confratute, published by Creative Learning Press, is the most widely-adopted plan used by schools.

■ *Project Vanguard:* A 30-hour project providing creativity training for teachers to help them identify students with creative potential. The training covers morphological analysis, Synectics, metaphors, analogies, visualization, attribute listing, what if's, inferring, random input, forced input, criteria finding, and the creative problem solving process.

■ *Reynolds's Creativity, Inc.:* This high school extracurricular creativity program utilizes affective techniques and art enhancement exercises to help students probe their inner selves in order to reach their truly creative cores. It has the advantage of cutting to the emotional as a way of reaching the creative. Students respond very positively to this program at our summer institutes for talented teens.

There are many other programs which someone wanting either to infuse creativity training into the curriculum or teach it separately would do well to look into. As one of my graduate students said, it seems as if there's a new catalog of creative thInking materials in the mail each week.

Many reading and math series include such exercises in the teachers' manuals. Publishing companies such as Good Apple, Zephyr, Synectics, Creative Learning Press, and Royal Fireworks specialize in books that help teachers to train divergent thinking and other aspects of creativity. Training in divergent thinking includes such open-ended activities as brainstorming, making up stories, thinking of new and unusual uses for objects, and forcing relationships between unlike objects. In divergent thinking there are no wrong answers (unless you are scoring a divergent thinking test, where fluency earns the highest points), whereas in convergent thinking, there are right—and wrong—answers. Most school learning is concerned with convergent thinking, though one of the influences of the field of creativity training is that more divergent thinking is being taught.

Torrance in 1987 listed six real-life results of creativity training in elementary and secondary schools: increased satisfaction; evidence that academic achievement is not affected by creative performance; writing more creatively in different genres (one student even wrote a novel); growth in personality and the acquisition of a healthy self concept; improvement in attitudes toward mathematics; and an openness to pursuing creative choices.

A hard-nosed pessimist might wonder whether the creativity training was justified for such tenuous results. But attitudinal and conceptual changes are difficult to measure, though they are vastly important in the formation of the necessary intrinsic motivation one needs to produce creative products. Creativity demands emotional risk-taking. To make and to show what one has made is at base an emotional decision and as such, the affective must be valued in any training of creativity. Trust within the group and between members of the group and its leader must be established before any training can be undertaken. Perhaps *training* is not the right word—creativity *experiencing* or creativity *simulation* may more aptly describe the process as students and instructor undertake a journey together.

Creativity Training as Differentiation for the Talented

Special education programs often use creativity training as a means of differentiating the curriculum. Differentiation is the main way of justifying education for the talented. Years ago I heard the rationale for creativity training from a famous speaker at a conference, who said that students with high IQs are rigid, like structure, and are uncomfortable when they are asked to do something that doesn't have a right answer. They are not risk-takers. Thus, they should be taught to be creative through training in divergent thinking.

I am not at all sure that students with high IQs are rigid and like structure; in my work with high IQ students at a school for the gifted in New York City, I found that students' personalities cannot be generalized. They are individuals, kids, humans, and some are rigid and some are flexible. Their IQs did not presuppose rigidity or flexibility. However, this rationale is still heard as the justification for giving creativity training to students with high IQs, yet saying that high IQ kids are rigid is to me *not* justification for using divergent production training in special programs, because if some students receive creativity training, *all* students should receive creativity training.

The science of creativity training is not yet so perfected as to say that some students would benefit more than others. Likewise, on the undergraduate or graduate level, anyone who wants creativity training should receive it. There are few empirical studies as to the value of such training; that research is yet to be completed. There is nothing in the training of fluency, flexibility, elaboration, and originality that justifies it as the special province of classes for high-IQ students. The fun, laughter, easy atmosphere, charged climate, and productivity that result from creativity training should be available to all students.

Creativity Training Is Fun

Let's admit it. Whether or not creativity training is even the province of the schools, creativity training enrichment is fun. Doing the exercises produces laughter, humor, good feeling, and cohesiveness in a group. Even though I don't like to read the workbooks, I love being in a group and doing the training exercises, and so, it appears, does everyone else. I remember taking a group of teachers through the Creative Problem Solving process. On a dank November afternoon in Michigan, no one wanted to be at this required after-school inservice. It was the week of the annual Ohio State-Michigan football game, and our "mess" was the following: "In what ways can we get tickets to the Ohio State-Michigan game?" By the end of the session we were laughing and feeling good, and we had invented a way to get tickets to the game! I still remember how we changed the size of the football field in order to add more seats to the stadium.

Teachers Get More Empathy with Creativity Training

Students are not the only ones who should have creativity training. Teachers need it too. A study done by McDonnell and LeCapitaine in 1985 showed that teachers who received forty hours of group creativity training at Synectics, Inc., in Massachusetts, had statistically significant increases in empathy in comparison to a control group. The teachers also reported that the training helped them in being more open with their students, in listening intently to student responses and ideas, in reinforcing students, and in allowing students to experiment more. The teachers in my graduate education classes might agree, as we often spend the evening laughing and being outrageous as we try out various creativity activities. Sometimes the glee is not for mixed company!

Summary

1. Personality tests are better-validated than behavior checklists. Behavioral checklists used to make decisions about students' lives are problematic.
2. Use of creativity test results to make decisions about students' lives is problematic.
3. Weighing the scores equally on creativity checklists might not be the best idea.
4. Creativity training has grown substantially in the schools in recent years. Many programs are available.
5. Creativity training, while fun, is not sufficient as a curriculum for talent development education.
6. All students should have an opportunity for creativity training.
7. Teachers can benefit from creativity training.
8. Alternative methods of creativity assessment, such as storytelling and performance assessment using already-existing competitions, look promising.

PART III

**Personality and Intellectual Characteristics
of Creative People in Various Domains**

It's spring break, and Katherine has taken Brad to New York City to visit her beloved, eccentric, rich Aunt Margaret. A known supporter of the arts, Margaret is playing hostess to a wondrous mix of artists and thinkers that she has invited to her elegant Central Park West apartment in honor of Katherine's visit. She's invited writers, actors, artists, classical musicians, jazz musicians, choreographers, and dancers. A mathematician will be bringing some of his colleagues, in town for a conference. Also expected is an evolutionary biologist who has recently written a provocative but rather unreadable book about the origins of humanity in offshore shale; his wife, a biologist and researcher, is coming too.

Margaret loves what happens when such diverse people get together. As the evening progress, people who have stayed in their own groups begin to mix more. Someone proposes Charades. The actors love it. They shine. But when a round of Trivial Pursuit begins, the stars are the writers and scientists, who recall every detail that has ever passed through their brains. Then the men start talking about baseball, the good old Brooklyn Dodgers. The dancers are bored with all this. They want to move. One of them finds a Chubby Checker album among Margaret's old records. They begin to twist, adding variations never seen in the sixties.

The visual artists think that baseball and trivia are all right, but Charades? They wouldn't be caught dead. They quietly head to the TV room for the latest video game. With their hand-eye coordination and spatial ability, they are superb. The musicians discuss the inadequacies of Margaret's sound system and esoteric details of stereo equipment in general. One rock musician wanders off to dance.

At some late hour a group of writers gathers around the piano to sing show tunes as one of them plays by ear. They know all the words to these songs, some from as far back as the forties. The dancers keep dancing, moving. The actors join in the singing and really camp it up, with two of them throwing in absurd asides on every long note, in the form of lines from Shakespearean tragedies they've performed. The loft artists are bored and leave early, making a stop at the Cedar Tavern in the Village.

Gradually, the party thins out. At 3:00 AM Margaret, exhausted, goes to bed. Brad has also gone to bed. But Katherine sits in the kitchen with a poet, drinking the last of the bourbon. He is reciting the poem he's just written on a napkin, the one about the stiltedness of salons and cocktail parties. Kathern wonders whether her kids at school will have the opportunity to become as successful as most of the people at the party. Her students seem so young, and their town is far away from New York City.

"Do you think you're creative?" she asks.

"Creative?" he seems taken aback. "Well, sure. I just created this poem, didn't I?"

She explains to him that she is supposed to teach creativity to talented children, and he laughs.

"You can't teach creativity!" he says. "A person is either creative or not creative."

"But you can teach a creative person to be more creative, don't you think?" she says.

"Depends on what they make. A creative person has to make something, just like I just made this poem."

"Of course. It's so simple. It's so clean. The creative person makes something that didn't exist before."

They go round and round, throwing out names—Agnes de Mille, Robert Oppenheimer, Frank Lloyd Wright, Marlon Brando, Virginia Woolf.

"They all made something. A theory, a character, an atomic bomb, a building, a story. It's so simple," Katherine says, more to herself than to the poet.

"De rien," the poet says. "Glad to be of service." The bourbon is gone, and he makes an exaggerated sweeping bow and somewhat unsteadily goes out to the hallway. She presses the elevator button for him and sees him safely on.

Katherine giggles and goes to bed, wishing she had the energy to write it all down, the entire party. All those creative people, together in one room.

If she had written it all down, she'd have given herself a great deal of information about what dancers and scientists and poets are like. Maybe the creative act, that moment of fusion or illumination or realization, is beyond definition or explanation, but creative people can be observed, questions can be answered: What are the intellectual and personality characteristics of creative people in specific domains? What is the relationship of measured IQ to creativity? How do various types of creators—writers, artists, actors, scientists, dancers, mathematicians—differ?

To put it simply, there are two ways to approach creativity. One is to judge a product as creative and then to look at its creator or producer, to see what that person is like. The other is to assess a child's ability through paper and pencil tests or through observation, pronounce him or her potentially or actually more creative than others, on a presumed normal curve of creativity, as a construct which supposedly exists within everyone to some degree or another (explored in Part II).

    Part III looks at studies of people who have produced creative products—visual artists, creative writers, creative mathematicians, creative scientists performance artists, musicians, inventors. What are their backgrounds, their personalities, their experiences, and their ways of looking at the world?

Predictive Behaviors and Crystallizing Experiences

The next six chapters survey the research that's been done on artists, scientists, mathematicians, entrepreneurs, inventors, architects, musicians, composers, actors, and dancers. I have summarized the research and looked at the paths of development within the domain. When one looks at the development of talent, one notices certain patterns that are common to those who enter the same field. In my book Talented Children and Adults, *I called these* predictive behaviors, *for even early in life, practitioners of creativity in a certain domain have undertaken certain practices that are common.*

    Along with these predictive behaviors are certain crystallizing experiences, as Feldman called them. Crystallizing experiences are unique to the individual, while predictive behaviors are common to the field. The crystallizing experience lets the person know that this domain is the one for him and sets him on the path. Since the first edition of this book was published, several hundred of my students have conducted biographical studies. Their assignment was to compare and contrast the person about whom the biographical study was written with the commonalities I found in the lives of these creators in certain domains. To a surprising degree, the students have found that the paths are similar. "Find a writer who didn't have a predictive behavior of voracious and uncritical reading," I challenge them. "Find a scientist who was not rabidly curious, from an early age, about the meaning of life." Few have. I leave you, the reader, with the same challenge as you read biographies after you have read the next few chapters.

Chapter 5

Visual Artists and Architects

What people can make with their hands is a lot better than they are themselves.
—Joseph Brodsky

That which fills my head and my heart must be expressed in drawings or pictures . . . Drawing becomes more and more a passion with me, and it is a passion just like that of a sailor for the sea.
—Vincent Van Gogh

The stereotypical visual artist, with ragged jeans, dirty fingernails, a beard, and a cape or scuffed leather jacket, prowls the streets of the city. Or in a beret with palette in hand, on the banks of the Seine River, he paints a riverscape of people and boulevards in Paris. How much do such stereotypes reflect the truth?

From ancient times to relatively recent ones, the artist was regarded as a craftsman, a solid worker who made art, carved friezes, worked with tools to create useful decorations under the tutelage of a well-known artisan, in his workshop. The Bohemian stereotype arose later, a result of the individualizing and personalizing that came out of the romantic era, the late eighteenth and the nineteenth century.

The Industrial Revolution changed the perceived role of artists in society. Art became a romantic search for abstract beauty, and artists were viewed as romantic figures. The ultimate romantic, Gauguin, who came to art late in life, was actually disdained by elite artists in France and Belgium as a Sunday painter. Having come under the influence of Pissarro, Manet, Monet, and Renoir in 1876, he finally got into his first show in 1880. There, Cezanne noticed his work but considered him derivative, though talented, and showing no obvious originality. Manet's statement that "No one is a painter unless he loves painting more than anything else" was a warning and a challenge to Gauguin. Gauguin's "Study of a Nude" in 1881 finally impressed this group of men. Even though he had been a banker for eleven years, was married, and had five children, Gauguin resigned his position at Bertin's banking house and in 1882 gave up his secure living to become a painter. His wife never forgave him and the family never recovered financially.

From a time when many artists were anonymous—craftsmen under the patronage of the rich—to today, when the rebellious artist is an accepted stereotype, the fascination with artists' lives has continued.

Spatial Intelligence

Howard Gardner, in *Frames of Mind*, made useful differentiations among kinds of intelligence. For example, he identified spatial intelligence as one of his eight frames of mind, and stated that "the centrality of spatial thinking in the visual arts is self-evident." Spatial intelligence is the ability to see the world accurately, and to make and perceive changes and transformations in the physical world. Vincent Van Gogh, as recounted in Irving Stone's *Dear Theo*, expressed the extent to which spatial visualization is important to an artist: "It is at bottom fairly true that a painter as man is too much absorbed by what his eyes see, and is not sufficiently master of the rest of his life."

Spatial visualization ability is the area where strong gender differences have been found, with males outperforming females. Male artists generally score higher than female artists in spatial visualization tasks. However, while few can be visual artists, everyone can cultivate his or her spatial intelligence by learning to see the visual arts with the eye of a connoisseur. While Gardner called *these intelligences*, others have asserted they are *talents*; Gardner said if he had called them talents, people would not have paid so much attention.

While the eight intelligences are hugely popular as a means to plan curriculum, especially in elementary schools, they are still abstract, focusing on the cognitive, the mind. I prefer to differentiate talents by domain of practice. For example, visual artists need spatial intelligence to do their art, but they also need other intelligences in order to be successful in their domain. For example, each artist needs interpersonal intelligence to sell the work, and logical-mathematical intelligence to plan the work. Sternberg's description of intelligence as executive, creative, and practical seems apt when one speaks of how a talented person makes, manages, and functions to be effective in the domain of choice.

Predictive Behaviors for Visual Arts Talent

Since one cannot produce a work of visual art without that aspect of personality called talent, it is logical that early talent be recognized and nurtured. Al Hurwitz, himself a visual artist, noted that certain behavioral and work characteristics are common for visual-arts-talented children. He said that "no child, however talented, can reflect all of the characteristics," but conversely, "it is unlikely . . . that one who lacks all or most of them possesses special talent in art."

Interest in visual arts begins early and emerges through drawing. The young visual artist often moves through the stages of drawing rapidly, just as young musicians move through the mastery of music rapidly. This is called *precocious* development, and when the child is between nine and eleven, she often begins to become frustrated with her development as she begins comparing her efforts with images from mass media. Another behavioral indication the young visual artist displays is the ability to concentrate for a long period of time on an artistic problem, as well as a preference for being alone while doing art.

Such a child is self-directed and does art on her own, away from the art room. Hurwitz commented that the person talented in the visual arts may not fit the common perception of creative people, especially with regard to the personality attribute of risk-taking, for talented young people have "invested a great deal of themselves in developing mastery" and thus, "they are unwilling or unable to experiment in new areas." The child may use art as a retreat, drawing for comfort.

There is also an indication of fluency in the talented young artist; that is, the child often has more ideas than there is time to enact them. Not only does the work itself have details that other children miss, but also, the child will often do multiple drawings. The child may use a drawing to illustrate a point, for drawing to the talented young visual artist is like talking or writing to the talented verbally gifted student.

Hurwitz also listed the characteristics found in the art work of children talented in the visual arts. Among these are realistic representation or verisimilitude. Talented young artists also are able to control their compositions, blending and mixing colors and consciously linking forms and experimenting. Junior and senior high school students will begin to surpass their teachers in realistic representation; they may draw detailed comic strips with narrative structure. Even in young children, the use of detail in drawings is extraordinary. They use their visual memories to enhance the art works they make.

Their extraordinary visual and kinesthetic memories show up at an early age, and they are able to use such recall in filling three-dimensional space, as when playing with clay. Talented young artists practice for hours and use a wide variety of media, not just pencil and paper. They are curious about the possibilities of other media. They are doodlers, improvising with shapes and lines, seeing patterns that appear from negative space. Hurwitz said, "Art functions as an extended conversation between form and imagination."

Hurwitz also differentiated between visual arts talent and critical sensitivity to the arts, saying that the latter is also a visual perception talent, but that it relies more on verbal ability in its expression. He said that the lack of critical sensitivity in the general public is due to the lack of arts appreciation study in the schools. The training of connoisseurs is essential to the maintenance of a domain, for critics, a knowledgeable buying public, and museums and galleries are all necessary for the viability of the visual arts. For the last ten years, there has been a concerted effort by the National Endowment for the Arts—Arts in Education programs to enhance discipline-based art education, in order to train the necessary art appreciators.

Problem-Finding and Visual Artists

A very interesting study of visual artists is Getzels and Csikszentmihalyi's *The Creative Vision* (1976). Choosing 321 sophomore and junior student artists—152 females and 169 males in their early twenties—studying at the Art Institute of Chicago, the researchers tried to determine what personality characteristics these students had as compared to students who were not studying art. Another purpose was to determine how artists find problems. Problem-solving is not the crucial process in creative thinking, but rather, the artist must find a problem to solve.

The study took place over several years, and they have since conducted follow-up studies. They chose to follow thirty-five male fine arts majors because men are most often successful artists. The students were majors in fine art, industrial art, advertising art, and in art education, so the research also yielded some insights into the differences among personalities of students who chose various specialties.

Characteristics of Arts Students

Most of the students in the Getzels and Csikszentmihalyi study were from intact families with conventional religious backgrounds. Over half chose art as a career between the ages of fourteen and nineteen, and more women than men decided on art as a career before age ten. They chose art for self-discovery, self-knowledge, to gain an understanding of others, and to find out what's real and what's not. One young artist said, "I paint because it's necessary . . . it's something you have to say." Another said, "In other kinds of jobs, you rarely see the outcome of what you have been doing. I guess actually the drawing is me. There was charcoal, paint—but without me nothing would have happened." In other words, they chose art for intrinsic reasons that emphasized inner growth, self-discovery, and expression of feelings, rather than for extrinsic reasons that emphasize fame, recognition, and worldly gain.

In choosing art as a career, the students were realistic about their slim chances for financial reward. Older than other college students, they often chose to go to art school after trying college or after working for awhile. The parents of the men disapproved of this decision. One young man said that his father had supported him when he went to college, but now considered him a college dropout; he had to drive a cab to pay for his study at the Art Institute of Chicago. Frank Barron, in his 1972 study, also found that male artists had difficulty in being taken seriously by their families. Research revealed no clear childhood reasons for choosing the visual arts as a career. As Getzels and Csikszentmihalyi stated, "Instead of finding an inevitable destiny springing from a single source," the researchers found "a highly complex formative process—innumerable events slowly building up to a final commitment."

These artists had begun by copying cartoon characters, as children do; their drawings were often done when they experienced feelings of loneliness. This loneliness may have come from their mothers going to work or from the birth of a sibling. They discovered their talent, and that talent gave them a feeling of competence. The male artists remembered their mothers as being "warm and close," but their fathers were remembered as "harsh." Getzels and Csikszentmihalyi said that ". . . when the young artists were adapting to the balance of forces in the family, they used art as a means of identifying with the mother and at the same time establishing their own competence and independence from the father." Their elementary years were remembered as being bleak, but their high school years were a little better. The artists did not participate in athletics, but their competence was beginning to show in the designing of stage sets, posters, and other art works that talented high school students usually do.

More of the young successful artists were oldest sons. Many of them had not done well academically in high school or college. They chose art because it was not a nine-to-five job. One of the artists had been a stutterer, and his skill in drawing gained him acceptance from peers. (Another stutterer was the writer John Updike, who is discussed in Chapter 7). One began drawing when a younger sibling was born. Another used drawing as a way to compete with older siblings. Getzels and Csikszentmihalyi said that young artists stick with drawing because they can control their environment better through drawing than through other means available to them. As their talent develops, they get praise and recognition, motivating them to continue. However, their values change as they realize that art has power to do much more than simply gain them acceptance and praise, for they discover that through art they can interpret the meaning of life and resolve problems.

In IQ, they were similar to college students, but they did less well when speed was required: the authors said, "quickness of response in standard intellectual tasks is not the forte of those who plan to become artists." In visual-spatial perception, there were huge differences between the artists and regular college students. Not surprisingly, spatial perception was outstanding in both males and females, with female artists performing better than female college students. It is interesting to note, however, that the female artists still performed lower in spatial perception tests than the college males, while male artists performed the highest of all.

In aesthetic judgment, both male and female art students scored twice as high as the college students. This was to be expected, though the authors felt that aesthetic judgment does not have much to do with creativity. Aesthetic judgment is more an aspect of becoming a connoisseur, or critic of art—becoming an art historian or a museum curator rather than an artist. In their values, the art students were quite "extreme," as the authors put it. Both women and men artists differed from college students in economic, aesthetic, social, and political values, and women artists differed from female college students on theoretical and religious values as well.

Getzels and Csikszentmihalyi made the analogy that art students are committed to their profession in the way that the clergy are committed to their religions. Art students also have very low economic and social values. Getzels and Csikszentmihalyi postulated that not caring much about society's opinions or money is necessary for people who have careers "in which the only thing they can count on is economic insecurity," and where working alone in a studio constitutes the social milieu.

Artists' Personalities

In personality, both women and men artists were aloof, reserved, introspective, serious, and nonconforming to contemporary social values—that is, "standards of behavior and morality have little hold on them." They had low scores in "superego strength,"or conscience. They were unconventional, subjective, intense, and imaginative. Independent, they preferred to make their own decisions, and their self-sufficiency was high. They were both radical and experimental. The stereotype of the unconventional artist seems to have some basis if the results of this personality assessment are to be believed.

Like other creators, artists exhibited androgynous personalities, meaning that they were not concerned with their actions being viewed as masculine or feminine. The women artists showed more masculine values than women college students of their age, and the men artists had more feminine personalities than male college students. Thus both genders have characteristics that have been traditionally associated with the opposite sex, and they could be considered to fall near the median on the continuum of masculinity to femininity. Women were more tough-minded and men were more tender-minded. The authors expressed this personality characteristic thus: "The psychology of creative men is a feminine psychology by comparison with less creative men; the psychology of creative women is a masculine psychology by comparison with less creative women."

A very interesting result of the statistical correlations the researchers did was the uncovering of the artists' naiveté. The artists were not shrewd. Naiveté, in the sense of creativeness, is openness. The artists were able to be open to new ways of doing things, to see the old things in new ways. This enabled them to find creative problems to solve. They were not blasé about what they experienced, but rather opened themselves to questioning with childlike wonder and awe. As discussed in Chapter 2, viewing the world with naiveté is necessary for the creative process.

Ghiselin referred to it when he said that the creative person is always on the alert for the "the alien, the dangerous," practicing "an imaginative surrender to every novelty that has even the most tenuous credentials." A look at the childlike yet sinister wonder with which the artist Maurice Sendak illustrated childhood fears is an example, as is the dreamwork of Paul Klée and Joan Miró and the circus of Calder. Red Grooms and Jonathan Borofsky also come to mind, with their ingenuous ways of looking at urban life.

Ideally, any work of art also teaches the perceiver to see old things in new ways. The artist approaches the world with newborn eyes and helps the jaded and blasé audience to see again. This is true in all the arts as well as the sciences. Magritte took naiveté to its essence. Gablik said of him, "For Magritte, paintings worth being painted or looked at have no reducible meaning: they are a meaning." Magritte said, "The mind loves the unknown. It loves images whose meaning is unknown, since the meaning of the mind itself is unknown."

Differences among Artists According to Specialty

Getzels and Csikszentmihalyi found that students differed in their values, depending on the specialties they chose. Not surprisingly, fine arts majors cared less for economics and more for aesthetics than the advertising and industrial arts majors. Again, not surprisingly, the advertising arts majors also had higher political values, and art education majors cared more for social issues. Fine arts majors were lowest of the art students in sociability, while the advertising arts majors scored highest. The fine arts majors were the most extreme, being more naive, more imaginative, less conforming, and less conscientious than the other arts students.

The Successful, High Achieving Artists

The authors chose to follow thirty-five male fine arts students through the beginnings of their careers, because as late as the mid 1970s, women fine arts students were less likely to become well-known artists. Getzels and Csikszentmihalyi, using teacher ratings to distinguish high and low achievers, found that the students judged to be high-achieving by their teachers seemed to become successful more by the strength of their personalities than by perceptual or intellectual abilities. All high achievers matched the personality extremes described above: they had low super ego-strength and were aloof, introspective, sensitive, imaginative, self-sufficient, and nonconforming. They all cared little for the economic aspects of life.

Although women were not included in the follow-up study, their success was evaluated while they were in art school, and the findings were contrasted with those for the men. In fact, most women students judged to be successful in art school were so designated on the basis of their high spatial visualization abilities, whereas teachers judged male students as talented on the basis of personality. The authors evaluated the differences this way: art teachers seem to appraise a male student on the basis of long-range possibilities suggested by his personality rather than on his perceptual aptitudes; however, they seem to appraise a female student on the basis of the perceptual skills she actually displays. This may reflect a tacit belief that a man will develop his aptitudes with time, while a woman who does not initially have aptitudes will abandon her aspirations and settle for more traditional pursuits. This differential treatment many still be prevalent.

Consider the career of artist Lee Krasner. The Brooklyn-born daughter of Jewish immigrants wanted to study art but was rejected from the Washington Irving High School for the Arts in Manhattan. Applying for a second time, she was accepted, but was told by her art teachers that she had no talent. She didn't listen and went on to the women's school of Cooper Union, where she interested one of her male teachers by her good work. She began to model (as did Georgia O'Keeffe) for spending money, and was urged to apply to the National Academy of Design. Hating the conservatism and rigor there, she determined to get out early by painting a portrait in *plein air* that the faculty committee would accept. She shocked them with an extremely skilful self-portrait.

Most of her teachers called her a nuisance, aggressive and difficult. She didn't care. She continued to follow her own course and began to have an affair with a fellow student, Russian immigrant Igor Pantuhoff, who became a popular portrait painter and also an alcoholic. She transferred to Hans Hoffman's art school, where her portfolio won her a scholarship. Again she attracted the patronage and attention of the teacher, while with others she continued to be considered too pushy. As she began to have her work accepted into group shows, her reputation as a nonconformist and tough cookie preceded her wherever she went. She was chosen by her teachers for her talent and not for her looks, and by the time she met Jackson Pollock, she was a more advanced artist than he. As his wife, she spent the rest of her life living in the shadow of his growing fame, and her work was not much valued until recently.

Women's search for connectedness dominates their development during and just after their college years, to the detriment of their drive to succeed in their chosen field of creative endeavor. Few if any gender differences are found in creativity until after college, when women must decide how they will manage being mothers, wives, and creators. The double bind hits hard, and this gender difference cuts across all fields and domains. The men creators never seem to wonder how they will manage raising a family and having a career. The women creators always do. That is why many who reached prominence were childless and even lived alone, without a mate.

The Classic Experiment Regarding Problem-Finding in Artists

This 1976 study of visual artists has had wide repercussions because of the emphasis on problem-finding rather than problem-solving. Getzels and Csikszentmihalyi set up an experiment in which they explored students' abilities to find problems to solve via their art. In a studio room, they put twenty-seven objects, for example, a feather, a mannequin, a bunch of grapes, a velvet hat, a glass prism. They asked each of their study group of male fine arts students to come to the studio to rearrange the objects, and then to make a drawing. There were no time constraints, and the directions were that they could do anything they wanted with the objects, "so long as the drawing will be pleasing to you."

While they worked, the students were observed by expert artists and trained psychologists, who first focused on three things: how many objects the students touched; the uniqueness of the objects chosen for the arrangement; and what exploratory behavior the students exhibited. Then, while the students were drawing, the observers focused on how the problem was structured (process), and on the behaviors of the students while they created the works of art. They then interviewed the students, asking them how concerned they had been in finding the right arrangement before, during, and after making the drawing. The researchers also asked art teachers, artists, people in business, and mathematics students to evaluate the originality and craftsmanship of the students' works.

In their longitudinal study of successful and unsuccessful fine arts students, the researchers found that those who had the highest problem-finding orientation were the more successful. Five years after the students had graduated, Getzels and Csikszentmihalyi contacted them again, to see who was successfully pursuing art as a career and who was not. About half, or fifteen of the young men, were in careers at least peripherally related to art and were still painting; about one-fourth had quit painting; about one-fourth said they wanted to paint but were not presently doing so.

Those who were most successful had the following attributes. The successful students had the best grades and ratings in their studio courses, though they may not have had good grades in their academic courses. In family background, both of their parents were likely to be in the professions. They came from higher socioeconomic backgrounds than those who were not successful artists. The authors speculated that a higher socioeconomic status might encourage problem-finding behavior, because if artists have a family to help them financially if times get tough, they feel freer to pursue a marginal career.

Also, their early environments may have included "more sensory and intellectual stimulation."

The personality characteristic most related to success as an artist was low self-sentiment, defined as lacking self-control, lacking a desire to conform to acceptable social behavior, and being unconcerned with social approval. They also found that oldest sons were more likely than middle sons to experience success as artists. Oldest sons were also more likely to have had highly-rated problems, leading the authors to assert that there may be "a peculiar constellation of experiences that firstborn sons undergo, alien especially to middle sons" that leads to a tendency to find the right problems and to be oriented to discovery, as well as to achieving success in art. The Goertzels and Simonton also found similar predominance of older children achieving success, but Sulloway disagreed, saying that the younger-borns throughout history have been more creative and rebellious.

Getzels, in a 1987 follow-up, reported a small positive relationship (.35) between these artists' problem-finding abilities and later success as an artist. A reason for the correlation not being higher may be the currency of the "artist of the moment" or the "in" artist, whose work is popular but not necessarily the best. The quality of the work of a truly talented artist who is high in problem-finding may not be perceived until after his or her death, and true success or eminence in a creative field may not come at all during the artist's lifetime.

This problem-finding orientation led to many other studies that are still going on. Developmental psychologists have postulated that in the Piagetian way of looking at development, the highest form may not be formal operations, but *post*-formal operations, where the person, as an adult, finds problems. Runco edited a book in 1994 that contained many ongoing studies on problem-finding, problem-solving, and their relationship to creativity. He concluded that problem-finding in artists is inextricable from the inner self. That is, the emotional or affective is involved to a great degree, and to separate the emotional from the problem that is found is perhaps impossible.

The Importance of Luck and Other Social Factors for Success

Tannenbaum pointed out that much of the realization of potential comes from factors other than personality or intellect. Following upon his work, I have added the factor of *chance* to my framework for talent development (See Pyramid in Chapter 1). Luck, for example, plays a large part in the realization of potential. Simonton called it being in or putting oneself into *proximity*. For creative people, this involves the very important step of choosing or being chosen by mentors. Luck may also come with the accident of the family into which one is born.

Feldman and I, in an article on parenting, noted that talent seems to run in families. Actors breed actors (the Fondas, the Redgraves, the Sheens, the Baldwins); professors breed professors (Margaret Mead); race car drivers breed race car drivers (the Unsers, the Pettys); athletes breed athletes (the Ripkens, the Roses); artists breed artists (the Wyeths, the Renoirs); writers breed writers (the Cheevers, the Updikes); musicians breed musicians (the Graffmans, the Bachs). The current spate of movies starring the children of movie stars is certainly not a function of heredity, but of proximity of these children to movie making. The fortune of birth has made many of the film stars of today. The social context, luck, chance, and circumstances in which one finds oneself are extremely important, perhaps equally as important as that mysterious possession called talent.

That is, talent is not enough. One must try to improve on one's chances, on one's luck, even if one has had the fortune of being born into a talented family. In order for artists to be successful in realizing their creativity, Getzels and Csikszentmihalyi said they need to do four things:

1. Rent or buy a loft, so they can socialize, show their work, and establish a reputation for being a serious artist—that is, they have made the commitment to renting a working space.
2. Exhibit work in an art show. A group show is acceptable, but a one-person show sponsored by a private art gallery that represents one's work is preferable.
3. Move to New York City, for no artist is taken seriously as a major fine artist in the United States unless he or she has been validated by the New York City art scene. (Los Angeles artists would disagree, and so would other art centers in the United States, but New York City still seems to be *the* place.)
4. Relocate to a provincial art center. This is viewed as a less desirable move that can be made in terms of career visibility. Such centers as Taos in the southwest and Provincetown in the northeast are popular choices. Some artists also take the path of getting a Master of Fine Arts degree from a university or art school, and then of teaching in the academy while doing their art on the side. Doing this is considered a safety step, and the artist takes the risk of being isolated from the trend setters of the art world and stagnating.

These social necessities may go against the personality grain of the creative visual artist, who is an introvert, a loner, an iconoclast, difficult to get along with, and who values aesthetics far more than economics. Getzels and Csikszentmihalyi said that many of the young men, when they moved, took two years to get back into the swing of producing art. Their art works changed in character, style, and size. They experienced depressions and frustrations, caused by the pressures of establishing themselves in different geographies than where they had begun their art. These conflicts affected them and their families. Several of them had spouses who worked or were independently wealthy. The necessity of having a steady breadwinner cannot be overemphasized when looking at the lives of creative artists whose work does not sell. Many of them turn to teaching or to working for arts groups doing short residencies in elementary and secondary schools.

Georgia O'Keeffe's career path was illustrated in Robinson's biography. O'Keeffe had strong ties to New York City's loft culture. A native of Sun Prairie, Wisconsin, she arrived in New York City after studying for a year at the Art Institute of Chicago, and also with a visiting professor from Teacher's College of Columbia University at the University of Virginia. This teacher, Alon Bement, propounded the theories of Arthur Wesley Dow, with whose ideas O'Keeffe was much taken. And so at the age of twenty-seven she came to New York to study with Dow at Columbia. A year later, in 1915, she began taking classes at the Art Students League, and her group of friends began regularly visiting the Alfred Steiglitz gallery called *291*. Anita Pollitzer, one of their mutual friends, showed Steiglitz a group of works O'Keeffe had sent her. O'Keeffe was granted a one-woman show by Steiglitz, who was very impressed by the work.

Although O'Keeffe didn't live in New York City at the time, her connections there were strong, and after her relationship with Steiglitz began, she spent many years in New York City exhibiting at Steiglitz's various galleries before establishing residency in New Mexico. Whether her work would have had its impact without her New York City loft or her most fortunate association with Steiglitz cannot be known. Certainly Steiglitz's falling in love with her, moving in with her and eventually breaking up his marriage for her, as well as his dedication to the promotion of her work, did not harm O'Keeffe's visibility.

The 1997 exhibit at the Metropolitan Museum of Art called "Steiglitz's O'Keeffe" included nudes, photographs of her strong hands, and images of O'Keefe looking mysterious behind high-collared coats. Steiglitz was attracted to her mannish wardrobe and nonconformity, and he made arguably his loveliest works of art about her. Even when they lived apart, he in New York and she in New Mexico, they wrote to each other many times a day. Although O'Keeffe wanted to have children, Steiglitz, who was much older than she and who already had a daughter, refused, saying that she would diffuse her attention to her work if they had children. He told her her work was her child. Thus she never had to experience the double bind of creative women who become mothers.

Artists continue to make their way to New York City. Andy Warhol came from Pittsburgh. Jackson Pollock came from California and points west. The artist Elizabeth Murray grew up in Illinois in an eccentric family that Murray described as "unorthodox" and "goofball," in an interview with Deborah Solomon. She studied at the Art Institute of Chicago and Mills College, where she "spent the whole time fantasizing about moving to New York." She taught in Buffalo for two years and arrived in New York in 1967, where she rented a loft. She got married, had a son, and did the practical thing that women artists seem to do: like O'Keeffe, she taught art, trying to do her own work at night.

Solomon had her first one-woman show in 1976, when she was thirty-six, and her fame began to grow within the New York art world. In addition to her son by her first marriage, she and her second husband had twin daughters when Murray was in her forties; however, by then her career was well established. This is consonant with Foley's work on the careers of artist mothers, which will be discussed later in this chapter. Murray has been called "one of the few true talents to have risen out of the commercial hoopla of the 1980s." Again, the influence of the loft culture of New York City is evident in the path of her success.

The Getzels and Csikszentmihalyi study is only one of the studies of visual artists, and it is unique because of its exploration of problem-finding behavior. Other studies have looked at personality variables and factors contributing to success.

Other Studies of Visual Artists

In 1975, Anne Roe studied artists who had already achieved. Another well known study of visual artists is Barron's 1972 *The Making Of An Artist*. Barron chose students at the San Francisco Art Institute and the Rhode Island School of Design and administered tests of intelligence, personality, and divergent production. To test divergent production, you will recall, is to give a paper and pencil measurement of how fluent, flexible, elaborative, and original a person is. The Myers-Briggs Type Indicator has also been administered to artists, with interesting results. Another study was of accomplished sculptors, conducted by Sloane and Sosniak in 1985 in connection with Bloom's

Development of Talent Research Project at the University of Chicago. A 1986 study by Foley was of painters who were also mothers. Other biographical studies were done by the Goertzels in 1962 and 1978, by Alice Miller in 1990, and by Howard Gardner in 1993. All these studies will be discussed here.

Roe's Findings

What are the psychological aspects of artistic success? Anne Roe's 1975 study of painters took twenty-three male artists who averaged fifty-one years of age—that is, they were long time achievers. Fourteen were from the lower-middle and middle classes. Their fathers' occupations ranged from farmer to usher to brigadier general to businessman, and 25 percent of them had fathers in the visual arts. Most of them had gone to art school, but only 12 percent were college graduates. Their fathers generally disapproved of their choices of professions because being an artist means being poor. Their mothers approved in the sense of wanting their sons to do what they wanted to do. However, the mothers who had suffered the economic deprivations of being themselves wives of artists also disapproved.

In their relationships with their parents, Roe postulated that the artists had "unresolved oedipal problems." The psychoanalytic approach is evident here. Roe also found that 25 percent of them had suffered rejection or social isolation or had serious childhood illnesses. Twenty-five percent of them also had lost a sibling or a parent through death. All of the artists were married or had been married, one four times. The artists objected to the inferior artistry of the stimulus pictures on the Thematic Apperception Test (TAT) and so administering the test was difficult. Her experiences with administering personality tests to creative people are similar to what other psychologists have found. The creative people often looked askance, were sarcastic, and even rebellious about being subjected to pencil and paper analysis. (For example, when I asked women writers to take the Myers-Briggs Type Indicator for a study I did, several of them tried, in the spirit of cooperation, but were unable to complete it, as it is a forced choice instrument, and they hated making the choices.)

Barron Finds Gentleman Pirates

Barron's 1972 *Artists in the Making* was a study of young artists at the San Francisco Art Institute and at the Rhode Island School of Design. Administering psychological and personality tests, Barron found that the art students were similar to those studied in Chicago. They were not interested in making a good impression on other people and were not as well socialized as other students. They cared little about social conformity, but they had a high need to achieve success independently, on their own. They were more flexible in outlook and less cheerful than others. Both women and men were similar.

On the Minnesota Multiphasic Psychological Inventory (MMPI), the art students, both men and women, scored in the pathological ranges on all the scales. This may merely indicate their low need for conformity, for they differed from truly psychotic people in that they were far less rigid. Barron described the male artists as "gentleman pirate" types, showing "an independence of thought and unconventionality" which made their experiences and their conclusions unusual. The flair with which they lived their lives may account for the pirate description. Perhaps they swaggered when they walked, but they also paid attention to nuance and detail and were open to experience, sensitive to the world around them, sensually tuned in.

The women, also, were unconventional, flexible, open, independent; they approached life vigorously and were sensitive to details. However, they differed from male artists in being less flamboyant, more naive, and more introverted. Remember, that's compared to the male artists. In the world, these women artists, compared with other women, would appear to be adventurous, independent, and very willful.

The art students had interests most closely resembling those of musicians, artists, authors and journalists, advertising men, and architects. They rejected occupations such as school superintendent, business education teacher, army officer, and other occupations which call for managing people physically and in practical ways. They were highly dedicated to their work and to their beliefs, as well as very independent. They preferred working alone and often lost themselves in their work. They could visualize their emotional lives.

In other studies that Barron did, described in his 1968 book, *Creativity and Personal Freedom*, he found that highly creative people tended to be pacifists, eschewing violence as a way of expression: "Pacifistic tendencies are related to personality development and are found most prominently in persons whose inner life and creativity are more highly developed." Perhaps this explains the passionate antiwar sentiments of many people in the arts. He also related these pacifistic tendencies to the androgyny of creative people, saying, "It is still the men and not the women among us who decide to go to war."

Barron also did some comparative work, differentiating among painters who were representational artists, abstract expressionists, those who used geometrical forms, and those who used dynamic color in their art. For example, those who painted representational art were often highly verbal, poor at being able to judge the quality of mosaics, unoriginal in inkblot tests, and concerned about social status. Their work was highly rated by the public and by the faculty. Those who were abstract expressionists preferred asymmetry and complexity and were good at judging the quality of mosaics. They got good grades in drawing, but poor ratings from psychologists in originality.

Highly geometrical painters did poorly in writing and drawing in school but were excellent in aesthetic judgment. They were also high in independence and autonomy. Painters who used dynamic colors in their work were rated as spontaneous and independent. They were good at judging the use of color in mosaic designs but poor in judging the use of form. Barron's most quoted finding with regard to these art tests was that the more creative people in all domains preferred complexity and asymmetry in design. In 1995 he said, "Only a person who can live with complexity and contradiction, and who has some confidence that order lies behind what appears to be confusion, would be able to bear . . . discord." He continued:

> The creative intellect . . . is that which is ready to abandon classifications known from the past and to acknowledge in its strongest form the proposition that life, including one's individual life, is pregnant with unheard-of possibilities and may be the vehicle for transformations without precedent . . the creative artist and scientist appear . . . to have experienced an unusual amount of grief and ordeal in life and to have shouldered burdens of pain that most commonly disable the individual for any constructive participation in the human community . . . I suggest that creative individuals are those who have learned to prefer irregularities and apparent disorder and to trust themselves to make a new order.

In 1995 Barron described a ten-year follow-up study of these artists. He found that most were still working at art but none, even those who would be called successful, were close to being able to support themselves with their art. They would work part-time or full-time in jobs that paid the rent and put food on the table, but they considered themselves artists first and foremost. Some would go on welfare periodically. Among creative activities that they had completed since art school were poetry and children's literature, movies, theater, photography, and even pornography.

I have noticed that going to art school seems to be a common thread for musicians and writers as well as artists. It is interesting to speculate on how many rock stars met in art school. Victor Bockris, Rolling Stone Keith Richards's biographer, wrote: "Between 1959 and 1962 John Lennon, Ray Davies, Pete Townshend, Jimmy Page, Ron Wood, and David Bowie had just left, were in, or were about to enter British art schools. Almost every school contained at least one of the men who would go on to become the first generation of pop musicians." To Richards, most of the teachers in art school were "drunks, freaks, and potheads who didn't care what the kids did." One of his teachers said that if he had worked as hard on his art as he did on his music he'd be a successful artist.

One of the people Barron interviewed in his follow-up said that when he transferred, after six years of college in the University of California system, to the San Francisco Art Institute, he found "no rules, basically—so I excelled there, I graduated with honors." A poor student academically because he would test the teachers, and if he didn't like them he wouldn't work for them, he said, "A person should go there just for the experience—it's so loose. Crazy things happened. I felt fulfilled. I felt like an artist when I came out."

This man had a marginal living as a fisherman and plumber, but he had filled 30 journals with autobiographical writing and art work and had helped other people with their creativity. He said, "I consider myself an artist." Barron commented that in this sense, art is a vocation or sacred calling, not an occupation, and one who heeds the call has a certain character, besides interest and talent. "Honesty, at whatever cost, is one of the traits of the artist in his or her art."

The MBTI Shows N and F

The Myers-Briggs Type Indicator has been used to indicate the Jungian-based types of many occupational groups, including scientists, artists, laborers, writers and counselors. The creativity studies with the Indicator were done in conjunction with the Institute for Personality Assessment and Research (IPAR), by Barron, MacKinnon, Gough, Helson, Crutchfield, and others. The Institute studies' subjects were chosen by peer nomination. Among the types of creative people studied were architects, mathematicians, scientists, and writers. The work of the Institute is discussed later in the book.

In addition, Simon in 1979 conducted Myers-Briggs testing on 114 professional fine artists. Here are the most frequent types in descending order:

INFP (Introversion, Intuition, Feeling, Perception)
INFJ (Introversion, Intuition, Feeling, Judging)
ENFP (Extroversion, Intuition, Feeling, Perception)
ENFJ (Extroversion, Intuition, Feeling, Judging)

The predominant preference for intuition (N) and feeling (F) stands out, with artists overwhelmingly preferring intuition as a way of perception. Jung saw that people perceive the world in two ways, sensing or intuiting. The person who uses the intuitive mode prefers to understand the world by the way of the unconscious. A sensing person may describe an orange as "juicy" and "orange," while an intuitive person may describe an orange as "Clockwork" or "Tequila Sunrise." Intuitive persons look towards possibility and may not notice realities. They prefer to make decisions on what may not be seen and heard, but on what may come as a hunch or sudden insight.

Here is how Myers and McCaulley, in the *Manual*, describe the INFP, INFJ, and ENFP personalities.

INFP: Full of enthusiasms and loyalties, but seldom talk of these until they know you well. Care about learning, ideas, language, and independent projects of their own. Tend to undertake too much, then somehow get it done. Friendly, but often too absorbed in what they are doing to be sociable. Little concerned with possessions and physical surroundings.

INFJ: Succeed by perseverance, originality, and desire to do whatever is needed or wanted. Put their best efforts into their work. Quietly forceful, conscientious, concerned for others. Respected for their firm principles. Likely to be honored and followed for their clear convictions as to how best to serve the common good.

ENFP: Warmly enthusiastic, high-spirited, ingenious, imaginative. Able to do almost anything that interests them. Quick with a solution for any difficulty and ready to help anyone with a problem. Often rely on their ability to improvise instead of preparing in advance. Can usually find compelling reasons for whatever they want.

The Myers-Briggs Type Indicator has already been discussed and will be discussed more, as most researchers seem to have given it to the creative people they studied. For now, it seems obvious that artists had definite personality type *preferences* in common; Myers and McCaulley said that "preferences are like handedness; one uses both hands, but reaches first with the preferred hand which is probably more adept."

Goertzel, Goertzel, Goertzel and 700 Famous People

The Goertzels's studies, in 1962 and 1978, were two interesting biographical analyses of eminent people, among them artists. In the 1962 study, 400 people were chosen; in the 1978 study, 300. The people had least two books written about their lives. The Goertzels found common threads among them. They divided the eminent into four groups: the political, the literary, the artistic, and other. The artistic category included sculptors, painters, actors, composers, film directors, dancers, and performers. Of the 1978 group, 75 of 300 fell into this category.

Goertzel, Goertzel, and Goertzel found that those in the artistic category were less likely to have gone to college than others who had biographies written about them; as a corollary, the artistic people were not known as being good students in school, and were not likely to be omnivorous readers. However, they were more likely to have had special schooling, perhaps because their precocity stood out early. Another interesting fact about the artistic group was that more of them were first- and second-generation immigrants than the others.

Another observation was that artists are likely to come from families who had other members who practiced the same art: "There are families who paint, families who sculpt, families who act, families who are musical." They cited the families of Calder, Renoir, Wyeth, Picasso, Charles Aznavour, Charles Ives, Georgia O'Keeffe, Edith Piaf, and Maurice Utrillo. They said that the family backgrounds and emphasis within the family upon the specific creative form did not uphold "the myth of the lonely, temperamental artist starving alone in a garret."

Another artistic family was that of the Van Goghs. Vincent served an apprenticeship in his uncle's gallery, as did his brother Theo. Their sister also seemed to have an interest in art, although Vincent did not believe she should pursue this interest. He wrote, as quoted in *Dear Theo* (Stone, 1937),

> Our sister writes extremely well, and describes a landscape
> or a view of the town as it might have been in a page of a
> modern novel. I always urge her to occupy herself rather

with household matters than with artistic things, for I know that she is too sensitive, and at her age she would find it difficult to develop herself artistically. I am very much afraid that she suffers from a thwarted artistic desire, but she is so full of vitality that she will get over it.

Germaine Greer, in her book about women visual artists through the ages, *The Obstacle Race*, said that most women who were visual artists came from artistic dynasties, and if they did receive training in visual art, their work was often not signed. She also said that easel painting has not been a preferred medium for women, and she wondered why easel painting has gained such credibility as being the most prestigious way for doing graphic arts. Greer said, "Daughters were ruled by love and loyalty; they were more highly praised for virtue and sweetness than for their talent, and they devalued their talent accordingly."

Judy Chicago has spent years trying to recapture a sense of the value of the art that women have traditionally made. In her biography, *Through the Flower*, Chicago described her odyssey through art history and her thrill at discovering that women have always been artists. She wrote, "Much of the work of women possesses a world view, a set of values, and a perception of reality that differs fundamentally from the dominant perspective of our culture." Her exhibit of women creators exemplified through plates, *The Dinner Party*, and her work with women's needlework and weaving are examples. At this writing, *The Dinner Party* still doesn't have a permanent home; perhaps this is a comment that the art that women make is still devalued.

Having a Supportive Husband Helps

In 1996 Foley published her 1986 study of fifteen painters, all mothers of children ages three months to eight years, in regard to their ability to combine mothering and being painters. She found that they were committed to their work but experienced role conflicts. In order to do both, they used child care help in the home or at day care centers, and they had husbands who were extremely supportive of their careers. The women were artists before they became mothers and hence were well-launched on their careers, having galleries to represent them and showing regularly in juried exhibits.

In their personalities, they exhibited the same core traits as the artists elsewhere here described. Foley wrote, "It cannot be said that women artists' commitment and motivation to becoming artists is any less than men's; rather, it appears to be more a difference in the timing of the commitment." The women artists were passionately committed to their careers *and* to their families, and Foley quoted one of them thus:

> Interviewer: What does it mean to you to be an artist?

> Artist: Almost everything! I mean it is me, it's what actually am. I don't just make art. I am it. I live it out . . . I mean my whole life.

Foley found that in her comparison group of mothers who were in professions such as law and business, the conflicts were a little different. While the artist mothers wished that they had time to paint, the mothers in professions wished they had more time with their families. The artist mothers had more flexible schedules, and when their children went to school, they often used the period from 9 A.M. to 3 P.M. to do art. The professional mothers were involved in careers with inflexible hours, and Foley said, "The problem for the professional mother was meeting, rather than defining, the demands." For the artist mothers the conflict came from having to cope every day with allocating time for each role.

The intrinsic rewards of painting made for a certain emotional well-being in the artist mothers, and one of them said, "The most gratifying internal—which is ultimately more important—is if I feel like I've answered a question. To me, each painting I do is like plunging into the abyss and I never know if I'm going to swim out . . . by *swim out of the abyss*, of course, I mean solve the visual problems that each painting has."

Here we see that the conflicts that arose with being a mother and an artist didn't diminish the rewards of doing the art. It should be noted that these women were in the middle and higher socioeconomic levels, did not have to struggle financially, had help with the children, and had supportive spouses. But Foley said even if they hadn't had the financial wherewithal, they would, somehow, somewhere, be making art, "because making art was an integral and vital aspect of these artists' being."

Sculptors Show Commitment

Sloane and Sosniak, in a study published in 1985, chose twelve men and eight women sculptors who had won either Guggenheim Fellowships or the Rome Award. Some of them had studied in the same schools with the same teachers, but none of them had studied with one another. Interviews with the sculptors found no outstanding demographic patterns. As many were first-borns as were later-borns. As many fathers were professionals as were blue-collar workers. As many mothers worked outside the home as inside the home. As many mothers were professionals as were nonprofessionals. As many of the sculptors came from higher socioeconomic levels as from lower socioeconomic and middle levels.

For their elementary school years, the sculptors remembered, as do most of the artists, intense drawing and the emphasis on products, on making the drawings realistic and recognizable representations of what they were drawing. Their social life was normal, playing in the neighborhood with the other kids. Only one of their fathers was a commercial artist, though some of them came from families that went to museums, talked about art, and valued art.

The sculptors didn't remember elementary school art as challenging or even as art. In their out-of-school activities, they were more likely to take music than art lessons. During high school, the sculptors began to gain identity and recognition as artists. Several of them said that they were the best at drawing, or the best at building or welding. They were referred to in their yearbooks as "Rembrandt" or "the class artist." Several of the artists were honor students, good at everything they did, or had several other areas of expertise, such as athletics, music, or journalism. About half the parents were actively helpful in finding teachers or in supplying equipment. The teenagers' work was also displayed and commented on positively.

Taking art in high school was not universal among the sculptors, and some remembered art classes in high school as the class for "flunkies." In many high schools, if students are musicians and play in the band or orchestra, they can't take art classes, and vice versa. This may have precluded the sculptors from taking art, for group music such as band, orchestra, or chorus is a more social activity, and perhaps more socially accepted.

When they graduated from high school these sculptors typically had no idea of what it takes to make art as a professional; they possessed no portfolios, perhaps no high school art classes on their transcripts, and perhaps no letters of recommendation from art professionals or teachers. But somehow they stumbled into four-year art degree programs, and three-quarters of them went on to earn Master of Fine Arts degrees.

They often transferred to find programs that were for fine artists and not for art educators. The teachers they found were professional artists themselves who worked in the field and had access to a network of other artists and connections to the art world. Even a short studio class with a professional artist had great impact. One said, "I mean he was a very important person in the art world. And the fact that he was teaching at that school, it was the spirit of it or something." Another said, "Your teachers were professionals. We went to New York. We saw the shows. I knew what was going on." Another said, "If you don't have contact with someone who is doing good work, how do you know what's possible?"

As they took courses and studied, the competition and exposure to the other students was intense. They all learned from each other. Almost all the sculptors went through a stage of imitating artists, trying to find the essence of what made a Henry Moore or a Jackson Pollock. But the breakthrough to finding their own styles, their own problems, eventually came. One said, "In art you make up your own problems. And the art problems usually come from the immediate history . . . If on the walls of Fifty-seventh Street they're hanging abstract expressionist paintings, the [art student] will usually pick up from that point and say, "Now where do I take Jackson Pollock from here? What do I do next?" The decision to become sculptors came as their works evolved. Often their works became bigger and bigger, more three-dimensional. Most of them were painters before becoming sculptors, probably because art education is very painting-oriented. Some of them shifted to pottery before choosing sculpture.

The decision to commit their careers to making art—to being artists— came, as one sculptor said, ". . . as a progressive or sequential revelation. It's nothing like a blinding flash. It didn't happen at any one time." When they did decide to commit their lives to making art, they did so "ferociously." For some that commitment didn't come for seven or eight years after art school. As one said, "Partially it had to do with really floundering around for personal identity as well as artistic identity." The artists who attained success often felt lucky, but some of them said that their luck was a matter of preparation. They had prepared themselves to be ready to take the chances that came into their paths. "I've had this uncanny luck at always being at the right place at the right time with the right people."

They were still viewed as young artists, even when they had reached forty, and the authors noted that the sculptors' commitment hadn't flagged and that they still were doing what they wanted to do. One of the sculptors said, "Nobody calls me in the morning and says, 'Hey, it's time to mix that concrete, kid.'" . . . You do it because you want to do it."

Recent Research

The vogue for large-scale psychological studies of artists' personality characteristics has passed. Expensive studies of big groups of creative people are not being done. What we're seeing instead is the case study or qualitative research of one person or a small number of people. These often assume that the case is representative of the population. Quantitative research, by contrast, chooses a larger, and random, sample of the population and generalizes from that. The biographical technique of historiometry as practiced by Simonton abstracts generalizations from historical populations such as musicians, writers, artists. For example, in a 1984 book Simonton looked at the biographies of 2,012 philosophers, 690 classical composers, 38 American presidents, and 301 geniuses. We will refer to his findings in Chapters 8 and 9. For our purposes here, however, we will look at two mainstream books on the psychology of creativity.

Pablo Picasso Was Influenced by an Earthquake

Compelling case studies have been done by Swiss psychoanalyst Alice Miller. Among her other books was *The Drama Of The Gifted Child*, in which she conjectured that parental narcissism is a main difficulty that bright children face, for parents often put their own frustrated expectations upon their children. In *The Untouched Key*, in 1990, Miller postulated that the work of visual artists such as Picasso, Kathe Kollwicz, and Seline is the result of childhood trauma. Picasso's *Guernica*, one of the most critiqued, lauded, and famous works of art of the twentieth century, details the beginning of the Spanish Civil War in 1936; while most view it as a representation of the cruelties of war, Miller saw in Picasso's painting the realization of repressed childhood trauma.

Studying Picasso's life, reading all the biographies extant about him, she noted that they all glossed over his childhood, saying that he came from a happy family, his father an artist also. Instead, she found that at the age of three, he had experienced the consequences of a devastating earthquake. Three days after that earthquake his first sister was born. His second sister was born shortly before he began school, and Miller postulated that these two births are what caused him to paint such angry portraits of women throughout his life. She said, "The three-year-old Picasso was painfully reminded of the trauma of his own birth by the horrors of the earthquake, the proximity of death, and the birth of his sister."

These blows, however, were compensated for by his warm and happy home life. Picasso came from an indulgent family; because he so protested going to school, he was permitted to quit his education early, never properly learning mathematics or reading. Miller wrote that these factors combined to make Picasso as creative as he was. She said if his father had not made him feel safe, Picasso could perhaps have become psychotic, and in repressing these childhood traumas, "would have become an upstanding, compulsive functionary in Franco's Spain."

Miller's point in the book is that people respond to childhood trauma with creativity or with destruction. They become creative if there is some warmth in the traumatic environment, and they become destructive if there is no warmth. For example, Hitler's mother stood by and tacitly approved the beatings he received at the hands of his stepfather; there was no warmth; thus he became a destructive adult. Miller's attributing of Picasso's creativity to his reaction to an early childhood earthquake, and to the birth of sisters, is an example of the psychoanalytic point of view about human behavior, wherein one incident is key to understanding a person's later behavior and personality.

Gardner's Case Study of Picasso

Cognitive and developmental psychologist Howard Gardner also did a case study of Picasso as an illustration of spatial intelligence. In *Creating Minds*, Gardner illustrated his theory of development by using the lives of seven creators —six men and one woman. They were all modernists, changing their domain in response to events in the late nineteenth and early twentieth centuries. Gardner said he himself identifies more with the modernists than the postmodernists, as the postmodernists are too anarchic. Simply stated, Gardner's complex theory of the development of creative individuals takes into account three relationships: between the creative child and the adult he becomes; between the creative person and others; and between the creative person and the work he/she does.

He took a lifespan perspective emphasizing these interactions throughout the course of the eminent people's lives in the areas of cognition, personality, motivation, and interaction with the Zeitgeist. Each of the creators worked with the domain's unique symbol system in a way that changed the domain. Gardner also studied how the creators interacted with others in their field. One necessity in each of these cases was that there was some "fruitful asynchrony," that is, something was not quite plumb, but rather askew, and this gave the creator a way to make something never before seen by the domain. In these studies, Gardner noticed that each creator had to make a Faustian bargain with the devil; that is, all was not rosy between them and the world.

In the case of Picasso, Gardner did not make as much of the earthquake incident as Miller did; that is to be expected, as psychoanalysts look for key incidents in childhood and developmental psychologists look at the picture across the whole life. Calling Picasso a prodigy, Gardner documented his life in rural Spain under the direction of his art teacher father; then his schooling in Madrid and Barcelona; and then his arrival in Paris. A tragic incident, the suicide of his friend Carlos Casagemas, inspired the blue period painting, *La Vie*, in 1903. This was Picasso's first defining work. Other key paintings followed: *Les demoiselles d'Avignon* in 1907 took the art world by storm. Gardner compared the impact of *Les demoiselles* to the impact of Stravinsky's *Le sacre du printemps*, as both defined the domain for years to come.

Picasso's friendship with Georges Braque initiated cubism, and the Zeitgeist was prepared through the presence of "Nigerian masks . . . optical illusions in William James's psychology textbook, the discoveries of Einstein, the writings of the symbolist poets . . . cabaret posters . . . the master Cézanne." Side by side the two artists remade art history. For several years they were seldom apart, and rumors of homosexuality abounded. Fame and celebrity came to Picasso and he began to travel, to live high, to flaunt his adulteries, and to collaborate with artists in other genres. Though his work had always had images of bulls, the bulls of the bullfight ring and the bulls of mythology, in the late 1920s and 1930s, these creatures began to appear more than usually in his work.

The bombing of Guernica in 1937 by Franco's German air force shocked the world, as thousands of innocent people were killed. Picasso was inspired to make a huge painting condemning the slaughter. Gardner said, "Seldom in the history of human painting has a single work been so clearly destined to be 'defining' as Picasso's *Guernica*." The painting has been called the most important of the twentieth century. Picasso was fifty-five years old when he painted it, and he was to work for over thirty more years, constantly re-inventing himself and his work, but this painting stands as his masterpiece.

It was Picasso's posthumous show at the Guggenheim Museum in the mid 1980's. As I turned to look backward, down the architectural coiled spiral designed by another modernist, Frank Lloyd Wright, I was struck at how similar these lined-up paintings of grotesque, unsmiling, and deformed women looked. How the aged artist must have hated women to repeat this theme over and over again. Gardner's case study indicated that Picasso increasingly identified with the Minotaur, that mythical beast, half bull and half man, that waited at the center of the labyrinth for the sacrificial maidens. Gardner said, "Those who remained involved with Picasso were likely to meet a bitter fate," as his first wife became insane, one mistress hung herself and another had a break-down, and his second wife committed suicide. The feisty Madame Gilot resist-ed his destructiveness and he even came to show some admiration for her, though he was also jealous of her friendship with Matisse, the man he admired most of all. His horrible treatment of his women and his men friends showed Picasso's cruelty, and his Faustian side (which all creators seem to have, accord-ing to Gardner) was indicated in his ruthless approach to developing his career.

Cross-Fertilization and Cross-Cultural Influences among Artists

Picasso's repeating theme of the Minotaur had a profound influence on a young American artist in New York City in the 1930s. His name was Jackson Pollock. Pollock went to see *Guernica* in 1939 when it came to a gallery in New York as a fund-raiser for refugees from the Spanish Civil War, going many times and making many sketches. He began to take the sketches to his Jungian analyst and to realize that his own childhood bestiary, of chickens and snakes and coyotes, had a place in his art despite what his teachers said. Picasso's images gave Pollock permission to work with his own dreams and images. Biographers Naifeh and Smith said, "Jackson recognized in Picasso's art the mutating images of his own unconscious."

Picasso, in *Les demoiselles d'Avignon*, changed prostitutes into creatures with African masks for faces, and in *Girl Before a Mirror* imagined breasts like vegetables; Pollock began to make similar transformational creatures. The image that struck him most was the bull, and Pollock was dumbstruck by the coinci-dence, for "Picasso had fixated on the very same animal that had prowled and terrorized Jackson's unconscious since childhood." Pollock then went beyond Picasso and combined the bull image with images drawn from Native American lore. The modernist was being used by the postmodernist, the expressionist by the abstract expressionist. Such cross-fertilization is common in the development of any domain as in this case, where one artist drew from another's images and went on to transform the domain. The visual arts were never the same after Picasso; the visual arts were never the same after Pollock. And so it goes.

Architects

Is the architect an artist or a scientist? A businessman or an aesthete? The answer, of course, is all of the above. Architects are hybrid creators; combining the characteristics of almost all the creative types, they provide a spicy addition to the creativity brew.

The Institute for Personality Assessment and Research (IPAR) studied architects in addition to writers, research scientists, inventors, and the like. Using the system of peer nomination, a group of architects was invited to be interviewed and tested. MacKinnon discussed the results in *In Search of Effectiveness*, and Barron described follow-up studies and a few typical cases in *No Rootless Flower*. Among the architects were Philip Johnson, I.M. Pei, Eliel Saarinen, Louis Kahn, Pietro Belluschi, A. Quincy Jones, and Richard Neutra.

Not surprisingly, the architects had personality characteristics similar to both scientists and artists. Independence, intuition, a theoretical orientation, a preference for complexity, originality, and openness to experience or naiveté were characteristic of them. Through a trait analysis, these top ten traits were observed in architects: (1) originality; (2) aesthetic sensitivity; (3) sense of destiny; (4) responsiveness to ideas; (5) cognitive flexibility; (6) independence; (7) inquisitiveness as a habit of mind; (8) sense of personal identity; (9) intellectual competence; (10) valuing of intellectual pursuits.

All of the architects were highly creative and respected in their fields. They had a sense of destiny common to most creative producers. MacKinnon said, "With a marked degree of resoluteness and almost inevitably a measure of egotism, the creative person typically considers himself to be destined to do what he is doing, or intends to be doing, with his life." The architects felt their work was worthy even though many had experienced great frustration and depression. They had passed through the adolescent period having attained a strong sense of ego identity, even though their adolescences, like those of other creative people, were characterized by confusion and conflict. MacKinnon said that they often had teachers and parents who emphasized a tolerance for ambiguity and kept them open to possibility. Most of them made their decision to become architects after high school, but a few waited until after college.

Among the personality tests they gave was the Myers-Briggs Type Indicator. MacKinnon noted that all the architects preferred P (perception). He said, "A preference for the perceptive attitude results in a life that is more open to experience both from within and from without, and characterized by flexibility and spontaneity." Likewise, they all preferred N (intuition) as a means of viewing possibilities. The adult creators studied by psychologists overwhelmingly prefer intuition. MacKinnon said, "In contrast to an estimated 25 per cent of the general population who are intuitive, 90 per cent of the creative writers, 92 percent of the mathematicians, 93 per cent of the research scientists, and 100 per cent of the architects are intuitive as measured by this test." The architects were evenly divided in their preference for thinking and feeling.

Other tests were administered as well. In values, the architects most valued aesthetics and the theoretical. They were able to make unusual and odd mental associations, and they preferred complexity. On the California Psychological Inventory, they came out as dominant, caring about social status, self-confident, not especially sociable or participating in social activities, outspoken, self-centered, aggressive, unconventional, strongly motivated to achieve, and feminine. Since all the architects were males, this last characteristic points to androgyny. MacKinnon commented:

> The evidence is clear: The more creative a person is the more he reveals an openness to his own feelings and emotions, a sensitive intellect and understanding self-awareness, and wide-ranging interests including many which in the American culture are thought of as feminine. In the realm of sexual identification and interests, our creative subjects appear to give more expression to the feminine side of their nature than do less creative persons.

He noted that Jung would say that creative people are not "so completely identified with their masculine *persona* roles as to blind themselves to or to deny expression to the more feminine traits of the *anima*." However, this tendency to androgyny may have led, in the architects and in other creative people, to "considerable psychic stress and turmoil."

Barron conducted the twenty-year follow-up study of the architects in 1978 and discussed his findings in his 1995 book. He noted that some had continued to be successful while others were still struggling to make a living as architects. He listed their thoughts about the future of architecture as a profession, noting that most of them thought that architecture had become more of a business due to overwhelming government regulation and rampant rising costs. The architects who survived were often heads of or employed by large firms with sophisticated business methods. They felt that the profession of architect required less artistic creativity than it had in the past.

However, a different view emerges from Charlie Rose's June, 1997, interview with the Israeli architect who created the Montreal World's Fair Habitat '67, Moshe Safdie. When asked what he looks for when a young architect comes to him for a job, Safdie replied, "The drawings." He said that the drawings are like a confessional. When one looks at the drawings, he has a sense of what the person is about. The second thing Safdie looks for is in the eyes of the young architect. This is a sense of social commitment, a commitment to create a better human environment.

Barron asked architects in his study to evaluate their own creativity. Typical responses were these:

- I'm a poet in materials.
- I let the building express itself.
- I have a strong feeling for form; I know how to refine, to redo things.
- I have a strong feeling for color.
- I am able to incorporate the other arts in my architecture.
- I can scuttle conventionality and do original work.
- I am able to achieve complete integration of many facets; I can express a single idea in structure, circulation, visual form.
- My structures are free of turmoil and noise.
- My work represents myself completely.

Barron concluded, "These clearly were people who had a high opinion of themselves and their own importance. And why should they not?" The still-successful architects were now in their 60s, and Barron noted that they had begun well; they had come from families with artistic and musical interests, and their parents were often foreign-born. In their childhoods, they had been encouraged to use their imagination in play and had spent much time drawing, reading, hiking, building things, playing music. They liked to play alone, preferring individual over team sports. They felt inferior in childhood, especially physically, and reported doubts about their athletic ability. Their parents were often described as severe, and their mothers were the dominant parent.

The architects matured late sexually and they often did not have their first sexual experience until they were in their twenties. All except one eventually married, and they had an average of three children. However, Barron said, "Even in adulthood, many had not achieved sexual intimacy in an enduring relationship," and they said they were not interested in sex as a motive in their lives. They had selected architecture after considering careers in art or in science. The reason for selecting architecture was to help society, a reason of social commitment. They reported that early on, they had a relationship with an important mentor who inspired them to be architects, often in summer internships or as students of sparkling teachers. The difficulty in finding commissions was their most disappointing early experience. They valued courses in the other arts as well as in visual arts as giving them a broad view of the world. As they progressed in their careers, they continued to value relationships with older architects.

Those who were disappointed after early careers significant enough to have them be nominated to be studied by IPAR were described by Barron thus: "embittered, talented people, some with sheer bad luck in their stories, others with foolish misreckoning, and still others with little talent after all, though with a love for building and design." Barron noted that some of these unsuccessful talented architects had struggled with family tragedies, alcoholism, and depression. Some of their 1958 tests had shown unusually high levels of psychopathology, which led Barron to comment: "The failures usually had manifested the seeds of serious problems of personal adjustment, and they had to expend a lot of their energy in just keeping themselves together."

Dudek and Hall in 1991 conducted the third follow up study of these architects. Seventy, or 78 per cent, of the surviving architects responded. Some were from comparison groups studied at IPAR. They showed five characteristics that helped them be so productive for so long: commitment or drive, high skillfulness and mastery, a continued pleasure in and sensitivity to aesthetics, good business ability, and an ability to delegate responsibility. They continued to work after their age mates had long retired, and Dudek and Hall commented that their drive to create kept them going. Their work was their life. "The desire to succeed, the image of oneself as a winner, and the joy of doing, the pleasure of being engaged in an activity to which one is totally committed" were the main factors in their continued creativity.

Frank Lloyd Wright

A case example of how these characteristics worked in the childhood of one of the United States's most creative people of the century, Frank Lloyd Wright, will illustrate. In his stunningly poetic *Autobiography* (1932/1943/1977), which he revised many times, Wright detailed the experiences that made him a creative, productive adult. In describing his early years, he referred to himself in the third person, as "the boy" or "he," and only began to refer to himself as "I" in recounting when at the age of eighteen he broke away from his home ties and left Madison, Wisconsin, for Chicago.

Wright's mother, Anna, was a schoolteacher from an immigrant Welsh Unitarian family that valued Education with a capital "E." She found her ideal educated mate in Frank's father, whom she met near their family valley in

Wisconsin, where he worked for awhile as a circuit rider and music teacher. When they married, Anna was in her late twenties, her husband in his mid-forties. Frank's father was a dilettante, "tirelessly educating himself, first at Amherst, then to practice medicine, soon found by him to be no genuine science. Then the law, but again—disillusion." The specter of the ineffectual father seems apparent here. Finally taking up the call to be a Baptist preacher, he moved the family back to the Weymouth, Massachusetts, when Frank was three years old and his sister was one.

But the mother's loyalties swerved from the father to the son after Frank was born, and they were to continue that way. Anna's "extraordinary devotion to the child disconcerted the father," and the father began to recede into the background in her affections, for she "now loved something more, something created out of her own fervor of love and desire. A means to realize her vision." They lived in genteel poverty in Massachusetts when Frank was seven years old. His father took his consolation from music, playing into the night alone in the empty church on the organ. Frank would have to pump "with all his strength at the lever" and would be "crying bitterly as he did so." But Wright came to love music through these nocturnal experiences.

Meanwhile, Anna became very interested in the Froebel methods of education, similar to our present emphasis on manipulatives and concrete experiences for young children. She brought home gifts of blocks and paper in geometric shapes to the young boy and encouraged him to play with them for hours. She had in mind that he was to build buildings, and besides helping him with these manipulative maple blocks, she hung his room with drawings of English cathedrals. The family moved back to Madison, Wisconsin, and one April, when Frank was eleven, his Uncle Frank came to take him to the family Valley to work on the farm. Frank worked there every year from April to September, when he would go back to Madison to school.

At the farm he protested about the heavy labor, the milking of cows, the chopping of wood. He often ran away but was always brought back. One of his uncles pinched his flabby upper arm and told him that he must work so hard he would "add tired to tired—and add it again," and Frank saw his physical and mental strength grow. He learned that "work is an adventure that makes strong men and finishes weak ones." He was a dreamy boy, a reader, a lover of music, imagining the time away, and his summers at the family farm, while strengthening him physically, also provided him solitary time as he worked to the rhythm of machinery or ranged in the woods listening for the tinkle of the bells of the cows he had been sent to find. He said that his uncle, seeing him go into a trance of dreamy thought, would shout, "Frank, come back! Come back, Frank!" The freedom to range the woods was described thus: "One eleven-year-old was turning to inner experience for what he heard, touched, or saw."

Back to school each September in Madison, Wright and a friend who was crippled and mercilessly teased by the other boys formed a comradeship of outsiders. The two boys were odd and didn't fit into the group of other boys. They read and read together in secret hideouts, basements, and attics, and even read the forbidden Nickel Library books. They developed crushes on the girlfriends of Frank's sister and spent a lot of time tinkering and inventing things. Wright said, "Both Frank and Robie had real passion for invention, and were banged, pinched, stained or marred or were 'had' somewhere by perpetual invention going on." Designing and drawing always, they invented a water-velocipede, a catamaran, a cross-gun, bows and arrows, a bob-sled, kites, a water-wheel, a scroll-saw, a turning lathe. Their real life was lived outside of school. Wright said, "But—of the schooling itself? Not a thing he can remember! A blank! Except colorful experiences that had nothing academic about them."

The boys were enterprising as well, going into partnership with another boy and forming a printing firm. They began publishing a newspaper in their mid-teens, and Wright again commented that the formal education going on simultaneously with all these wonderful enterprises meant nothing: "But the schooling! Trying to find traces of it in that growing experience ends in finding none. What became of it? Why did it contribute so little to this consciousness-of-existence?" Wright said that even though his memories of school were so negative, school perhaps was not purely harmful, for one of the purposes of school is to civilize wild young people, and if the school can't do it, perhaps the art school can

> You can't let boys run wild while they are growing. They have to be roped and tied to something so their parents can go about their business. Why not a snubbing post or— school, then? A youth must be slowed-up, held in hand. Caged—yes—mortified too. Broken to harness as colts are broken, or there would be nothing left but to make an "artist" of him. Send him to an Art Institute.

Wright's imaginational intensity was so strong that once he imagined that his mother was going to have a party for him and his friends. He began talking of it to his friends, describing the food and the presents there would be at the party. They believed him, and when they came in their Sunday best, his mother was quite surprised to see them. But when they said they had come to a party, she looked at Frank, understood, and made a party, even getting Frank's father to play for them on his violin. She went along with her beloved son, even though they were poor. Frank's intensity of imagination was so great, he didn't think he was lying to his friends; he believed his own fantasy. His real life was the life of his imagination.

During the summers he helped fix and improve the farm machinery; he recalled that the rhythms of the farm became an opportunity to internally compose music: "All machinery makes some recurrent noise, some clack or beat above the hum that can be made into the rhythm of song movement—a rhythm that is the obvious poetry in the mathematics of this universe." His apprenticeship pumping the organ for his distracted father paid off in his being able to relate the structure of music to the pounding of machinery.

He said, "After one thousand two hundred and sixty todays and tomorrows like those yesterdays" he turned sixteen and prepared to enter the University of Wisconsin. The farm experiences left him with "a self-confidence in his own strength called courage" and with no fear but that of people. He was very shy with girls: "The sight of a girl would send him scampering like a scared young stag." Meanwhile, his father and mother were not getting along. His scholarly father was now teaching himself Sanskrit and escaping into his music, and their poverty was so overwhelming that his mother would wait at dinnertime to eat what the family had left on their plates. Wright had become so muscular and strong that at age sixteen, when his father tried to beat him, he held his father down on the floor until his father promised he would beat him no more.

Anna asked the father to leave as things began to be unbearable, and "Father disappeared. Never seen again by his wife and children." He took only his violin and his clothes. The marriage was quietly dissolved, and the family felt great disgrace and shame. Wright felt his mother had been dealt a great injustice, as divorced women were not usually found in society, especially divorced wives of ministers. She kept working in an engineer's office and kept pushing him, getting him a job with a civil engineer at the University of Wisconsin. Wright entered college then, to study civil engineering. He said that he was glad he was spared what was called architectural schooling at the time and that he instead got a practical education in civil engineering. He continued his voracious reading and dreaming and kissed a girl for the first time. At college, he was still an outsider, and he never graduated. He left Madison for Chicago, feeling a "sense of shame in accepting the mother's sacrifices for so little in return."

During college he experienced an event that was to haunt his vivid dreams for years afterwards. A new wing on the state capitol building collapsed because of the criminal negligence of the architect. Wright said the horrible carnage "never entirely left" his consciousness. In Chicago he began as an apprentice but then broke off to found his own firm in Oak Park. The achievements of his adulthood are legend.

Thus went the childhood of one of the world's foremost architects. He was encouraged to be creative, to dream, to range freely. He had artistic parents interested in education. He was provided with music lessons, tools, and books, even though his parents were very poor. His mother suggested architecture to him at an early age, and then moved heaven and earth to influence him in that direction. He was engaged in many projects and had a few friends who were interested in the same things. His father was viewed by the son as ineffectual, and the mother was viewed as a major influence in his creativity. In his family mythology, the attainment of an education was emphasized, as well as an ethic of hard work. The family experienced hardship and took it in stride. Wright was not chided for being odd; rather, his family encouraged him. All of these seeds of his later accomplishment were planted in his early years.

These studies of architects demonstrate a remarkable consistency in characteristics over their life span. From early to late they continued to be creative producers. The drive and the will to create continued in the architects such as Philip Johnson and I.M. Pei, just as it did in the visual artists such as Manet and Picasso.

Summary

1. The visual artists showed independence, intellect, passion, persistence, and a rejection of conventional economic values.
2. Their talent for art was often not formally developed until after high school.
3. Gender differences were apparent in spatial ability and treatment by teachers.
4. Chance or luck and proximity to a loft culture was necessary in the realization of their promise.
5. Visual artists and architects preferred intuition and perception. Visual artists preferred feeling, while architects were evenly divided between feeling and thinking.
6. They sometimes experienced childhood trauma.
7. The careers of visual artists and architects follow a somewhat predictable developmental path.
8. Younger artists and architects mine the work of older artists and transform the domain.

Chapter 6

Creative Writers

A writer is someone born with a gift. An athlete can run. A painter can paint. A writer has a facility with words. A good writer can also think. Isn't that enough to define a writer by?
—Cynthia Ozick

If people only knew what lies at the heart of my novels! What a tumult of desires these carefully written pages conceal! I sometimes have a loathing for the furious cravings that give me no peace except when I am working.
—Julian Green

I know my troubled nature and have tried to contain it along creative lines.
—John Cheever

A writer's self-consciousness, for which he is much scorned, is really a mode of interestedness, that inevitably turns outward.
—John Updike

According to a recent survey of single people which asked what were the most desirable occupations for a mate, poet was near the top, as was novelist. In stating this preference for "writer as spouse," were these men and women choosing a fantasy? A stereotype that has little to do with reality? For the truth is that writers write. They write obsessively and at odd hours, and they require a solitude that excludes the spouse, along with everyone else. A poet, novelist, and playwright once told me that his wife left him because he spent so many hours all alone, writing, and she wanted him to be more sociable.

Perhaps those survey respondents thought marriage to a writer would be exciting. Imagine the thrill of sitting beside Coleridge as he wrote "Kubla Khan" sprung full-blown from his unconscious, in a rush of opium-induced inspiration! But the truth, according to biographers, is that Coleridge had written several drafts of "Kubla Khan" before this reputed inspired visit of the Muse. And to watch a writer write is, well, as boring as watching a bear hibernate. Most movies and plays about writers have focused on their personal lives, for seeing them do their work is not very exciting. The process of production of their art is solitary. Not romantic at all.

What leads to someone choosing such a lonely life? Creative writers—poets, playwrights, novelists, story writers, essayists—have definite personality characteristics. Not the least among them is an urge to communicate to the world what they think, as well as to discover, through writing, what they think. The reason someone becomes a writer, as Joyce Carol Oates said in *(Woman) Writer*, is that the person needs to "verify experience by way of language." It is that simple. The writer needs to write, and "experience itself is not authentic," Oates said, "until it has been transcribed by way of language." In other words, the writer knows what she thinks only after she has written it down. Katherine Anne Porter in her *Paris Review* interview said, "This thing between me and my writing is the strongest bond I have ever had—stronger than any bond or any engagement with any human being or with any other work I've ever done."

Writers are different from one another, of course. Poets differ from novelists, essayists differ from playwrights. Simonton in 1986 showed that writers and poets were apt to be from the city and have nonreligious, small families, with nonsupportive fathers and unhappy home environments; not surprisingly, the writers were voracious readers. Simonton calculated that poets reach their peaks of productivity at about age thirty-nine, and prose fiction and nonfiction writers peaked at around age forty-three. He wrote, in 1984, "Twice as much of a poet's lifetime output comes from the twenties as is the case for novelists," but this may vary according to the type of work being written. Lyric poets (like creative mathematicians) tended to peak early, and many died young. Simonton said, "This youthfulness of poetic and mathematical creativity makes it feasible for poets and mathematicians to die at tragically early ages and still find a place in the annals of history."

Poet and critic Donald Hall may have an explanation for the youthful curve of poetic production. In *Their Ancient Glittering Eyes* he spoke of going with his wife, poet Jane Kenyon, to visit the aged poet Archibald Macleish, whose sixty-year-old son had recently died. When Hall asked Macleish if he had written about his son's death, Macleish replied that he had been unable to write poems for several years now. Hall reflected:

> One problem for the old poet, I thought that day, arises from loss of short-term memory. Some poets write well in their fifties, even in their sixties, but few later . . . When you're writing a poem, you carry it with you day and night, for months or even years, often underneath the surface of waking thought; when you walk the dog or drive the car, a word for that poem may enter your consciousness when you do not know that you are thinking of it. When short-term memory fails, you lose that part of your brain that works when you don't know it's working.

Writers often write across genres. Is Tess Gallagher a poet or a short story writer? Was Raymond Carver a short story writer or a poet? John Updike is a prolific reviewer, essayist, and poet as well as novelist and short story writer. So is Joyce Carol Oates, whose yearly production of novels, poetry, short stories, nonfiction, and essays is nothing short of frightening to other, less productive writers. (Yet some writers don't cross genres. The poet David Citino told me that everything he tries to write comes out as a poem.) The ability to cross genres is an example of what Gruber called a "network of enterprises," all feeding each other. Gruber used this term with references to the many related projects of scientist Charles Darwin, but it applies equally well to writers and other creators.

In *Frames of Mind*, Gardner listed linguistic intelligence as one of the types of intelligence. In his discussion of linguistic intelligence, he spoke of the different kinds of writers, asserting that the poet composes in the most difficult of the verbal arts, one that requires the greater verbal or linguistic intelligence. The poet must have these three language talents: an ability to sense the several meanings of words, an ability to position the words so that their meanings resonate with words on other lines, or a spatial ability with words, and an ability to catch, in an imagistic way, the feelings that made the poet want to make the poem.

Gardner further differentiated among the various types of creative writers. The novelist wants to "wrest the essence, the real truth" from life. The writer of narratives wants to show the reader what he has experienced or envisioned. Translation is possible for plays, novels, and essays, but not for poems. Poetry is what is untranslatable, as Frost said.

Who are the poets and writers of today? A *Directory of American Poets and Fiction Writers* lists names and addresses of contemporary poets and fiction writers who have published at least one novel, or three short stories, or twelve poems in at least three different literary publications, or they must have won literary awards, or any combination of these. About 6,600 American writers have met these qualifications. There is a lively literary world in America, even with the consolidation and commercialization of major publishing houses. While the sensational aspects of the lives of poets and writers will always draw attention, these and the others who are writing, alone in their rooms, collecting rejection letters, are the real story of the creative writer.

In 1995 I presented a study of themes in the lives of women writers, all of whom are listed in the above-mentioned *Directory*. Later I revised the study to include male writers as well. These are the themes in their lives arranged according to the environmental suns in the Pyramid of Talent Development in Chapter 1, mentioned here as I describe them in detail in the book, *Psychology of Writers,* the manuscript of which I am completing at the time of this writing.

Themes under the Sun of *Home*

- (1) unconventional families and family traumas;

- (2) predictive behavior of extensive early reading;

- (3) predictive behavior of early publication, keeping journals, writing to make sense of things;

- (4) incidence of depression and/or acts such as use of alcohol, drugs, or the like;

- (5) being in an occupation different from their parents.

Themes under the Sun of *Community and Culture*

- (1) feeling of marginalization or being an outsider, and a resulting need to have their group's story told (e.g., minorities, lesbians, regional writers, writers from lower socioeconomic class, writers of different immigration groups);

Themes under the Sun of *School*

- (1) nurturing of talents by both male and female teachers and mentors;

- (2) attendance at prestigious colleges, majoring in English literature;

- (3) learning how to get along in the profession (tacit knowledge);

Themes under the Sun of *Chance*

- (1) residence in New York City at some point, especially among the most prominent;

Themes under the Sun of *Gender*

- (1) history of divorce, especially among the women;

- (2) conflict with combining motherhood and careers in writing;

- (3) societal expectations of femininity incongruent with their essential personalities.

Writers also have individual and specific creative processes and habits unique to each.

The creative writer also seems to have certain core personality attributes. The following seem to be present to different degrees in many writers: (1) independence/nonconformity; (2) drive and resiliency; (3) courage/ risk-taking; (4) ambition/envy; (5) concern with philosophical matters; (6) frankness often expressed in political or social activism; (7) androgyny; (8) introversion; (9) psychopathology; (10) depression; (11) empathy; (12) intensity; (13) sense of humor; (14) trust in intuition and perceptiveness that comes out in an attitude of naiveté; and (15) energy transmitted into productivity. Some of these will be discussed here, as they have surfaced in many of the major studies of writers.

Barron's and Other Studies of Creative Writers

Donald MacKinnon, in 1978, described the work of the Institute for Personality Assessment and Research (IPAR) at the University of California at Berkeley. IPAR was formed after World War II. MacKinnon directed this Institute, after serving with the Office of Special Services on its assessment staff. The OSS used personality assessment to determine the qualifications of those who would be spies, counterspies, resistance leaders, and those who would perform "irregular warfare." In 1949 the Rockefeller Foundation granted funds to start IPAR, with the purpose of determining which people were most highly effective and what made them that way. Among the people studied were writers, architects, engineering students, women mathematicians, inventors, and research scientists, all chosen by peer nomination. Researchers at IPAR included Barron, MacKinnon, Gough, Helson, and Crutchfield, among others. In 1968 and 1995, Barron described their study of writers.

At IPAR, Frank Barron and his colleagues asked literature and drama professors at the University of California for the names of the most creative of outstanding contemporary writers. They invited those sixty-six writers to participate on campus in extensive testing and interviewing, and these studies pioneered some of the tests and interview techniques still used in studying human behavior, for example, the Q-sort method of interviewing and the Barron-Welsh Art Scale for evaluating works of art. Writers studied included Truman Capote, Frank O'Connor, Norman Mailer, Muriel Rukeyser, William Carlos Williams, MacKinlay Kantor, Jessamyn West, A.B. Guthrie, Jr., Andrew Lytle, Robert Duncan, Bill Mauldin, and Kenneth Rexroth.

Tests and interviews were conducted off campus with such writers as W.H. Auden, Marianne Moore, Michael McClure, Arthur Koestler, and Sean O'Faolain. Also among these writers was Saul Bellow, who told George Garrett about being paid ten thousand dollars to go to Berkeley and take psychological tests: "They had Capote there, too—and what they ended up with was the feeling that writers had more willpower . . . And if *that's* all, it doesn't tell you anything, except maybe that discipline helps." Bellow's comment illustrates the way most artists view being studied by psychologists.

Barron discussed this study in *No Rootless Flower*, in which he wrote of trying to probe the relationship between reason and imagination: "It was a painful and taxing responsibility to ask these writers, many of whom had suffered much in their own creative lives, to probe deeply into themselves and to answer the questions . . . seemingly irrelevant and unworthy questions." Of poet William Carlos Williams' M.D. seeming to enjoy being studied, Barron wrote, "This made me very happy. The only solace for the psychological researcher who presumes to look—with the subject's consent and help . . . into the depths of another's being is that it may be beneficial to the person as well as contribute to experience and knowledge."

After extensive testing and interviewing, some qualities of writers emerged. Not surprisingly, the writers scored high in verbal intelligence, with creative writers scoring 156 on the Terman Concept Mastery Test. Compare this to the average of 137 scored by the gifted population Terman observed in his famous longitudinal study, begun in 1922 and still being carried on at Stanford University. Captains in the Air Force scored 60, and the general population scored lower than that. In addition to possessing striking verbal intelligence, the writers were found to be independent and unconventional, possessing traits which seem to be core characteristics of most creative people, not only writers. (Getzels and Csikszentmihalyi found that the visual artists they studied were also independent and not conventional.) Writers were interested in all the arts and felt strong reactions to various media, such as paintings. For example, whenever Ginsberg visited a new city, he went to the museums and took detailed notes about the works of art there.

Many creative people are good at several fields; for example, musicians often are painters, writers often musicians. In particular, writers also seem to have a fondness for late night singing of old songs, and of course, they also seem to be able to remember all the words. When I was chair of the literature panel of the Ohio Arts Council, other panel members, all writers, brought their guitars, banjos, and harmonicas to our annual meetings in Columbus, and we regularly sang late into the night. Several played professionally. Root-Bernstein called this "correlative talents."

Another term for one who crosses over into other talent areas is "polymath." Many, if not most, talented people have unusual abilities in several areas. They can also think in different domains without having one interfere with another; rather, they work in such a way that each area informs the other. The writers William Carlos Williams and Anton Chekhov were doctors; Einstein, Max Planck, Paul Klée, and Aldous Huxley were also musicians; Michelangelo, Galileo, Margaret Mead, and George Washington Carver were poets; Saint-Saens, Stephen Sondheim, M.C. Escher, and Edna St. Vincent Millay were fascinated with mathematics.

What constitutes writing talent is most often a matter of peer judgment, although there is a large popular following for many writers who would not be judged talented by other writers. The writers Barron studied were not just wishful thinkers about writing: they were productive human beings. It cannot be overemphasized that one does not become a writer by wishing. One must write. Anyone can put pen to paper or fingers to word processor and call himself a writer; in this way, writing seems more accessible for the aspiring creator than playing concert piano or painting in oil. The writers also aspired to fame, to recognition by the public and by their peers. However, peer recognition is more important than public recognition. This also characterizes other creative producers. The "loft culture" that Getzels and Csikszentmihalyi talked about also exists in the writing world. Writers keep in touch with each other and often seek to establish themselves through public readings, which, unfortunately, are frequently attended only by other writers.

Ironically, while writers obviously need other writers, they are also threatened by them. The ambition needed to survive is often relentlessly ignored by the general and publishing public and seems to be accompanied by envy and insecurity in the face of others' success. For example, the writer T. Corraghesan Boyle said he wants to be "the most famous writer alive and the greatest writer ever." But the other side of this extraordinarily confident man is glimpsed in his novel *East is East*, for he modeled the character Ruth after himself, giving her the same anxieties and "petty jealousies" that he felt as a young writer studying at the famous Iowa Writer's Workshop.

Poet Molly Peacock made no apology for her ambition:

From when I was a little girl I wanted to be an artist, and I said to myself, "Somehow I'm getting out of Buffalo, New York." I had a drive to get out of that house and that town. That takes ambition, and my ambition is located in that very early desire to succeed. Of course, you can't be published in *The New Yorker* without a drive to succeed. But also you can't be published in issue one, volume one, of a brand new, teeny-tiny literary enterprise without a similar hunger for success. I think people who don't discuss their ambition contribute to a veil of deception and a mythology that does not serve writers, and certainly not women. Ambition is a fact of anyone's life who aspires to anything.

Writers need ambition, as do other creative producers, but that ambition often produces horrible feelings of inadequacy and anxiety as one writer compares himself with other writers. Writer's conferences are breeding grounds for the mosquitoes of the swamp of self-regard. They often engender jealousy and anxiety among the participants, who may see each other as rivals. In addition to this inherent competition, writers also face a caste system in many workshops. For instance, at the Bread Loaf Writer's Conference, a two-week conference held in Vermont every August, writers are divided into ranked divisions, with Auditors (those who won't have manuscript conferences) and Contributors (those who will have manuscript conferences with a writer who is featured as a teacher) at the bottom. These struggling writers are not permitted to socialize with the Fellows, Associates, and Senior writers who have their parties in a certain cabin. Sometimes a Contributor or Auditor may have an affair with someone on a higher rung and be invited to this cabin.

Rumor has it one struggling young poet had such a violent reaction to the snootiness at this conference that he chained himself to a tree and tried to commit suicide. Social stratification exists in all professions, not only writing, and people know on which levels they rest. However, even with all the tension and self-hatred the conference engendered, the year I attended, 1977, I had a chance to study with Toni Morrison and to hear her read from *Song of Solomon*; I heard Irving's *The World According to Garp*, O'Brien's *Cacciato*, and Gardner's *On Moral Fiction* in manuscript. My roommate had a chance to study with Maxine Kumin.

In addition to the need/fear relationships among writers, writers value productivity. As in any creative profession, writers must be productive in order to achieve the senior ranks. Here are examples from several powerhouses. For example, the prolific John Updike doesn't know how many books he has written:

> But do I count just the forty hardcover volumes that the obliging firm of Alfred A. Knopf has published? What about the five slim books for children, and the out-of-print paperback "Olinger Stories," or the peculiar but precious quasi novel entitled "Too Far to Go" in this country and "Your Lover Just Called" in Great Britain, containing linked short stories, not all of which have appeared in other collections? And what of the many limited editions, binding together material often, that is not between hard covers anywhere?

To try to count the numbers of books that the author Joyce Carol Oates has written is similarly difficult. Her web site listed 80 books and 47 special publications. Another example is Stephen King, whom *Time Magazine* referred to as King, Inc.: since 1973 he has published over 40 books, including novels, short story collections, and chapbooks. This doesn't count the works of Richard Bachman, one of the pseudonyms King uses. He has written multitudes of introductions, commentaries, and blurbs as well as screenplays, television scripts, and mini-series. He has also worked as a director, screenwriter, executive producer and actor. He owns a radio station in Bangor, Maine, and plays in a rock band. In an interview with King, Joseph B. Mauceri said, " There was a troubled time in his life when King seemed to retreat to a tower of melancholy and solitude. In fact, he claimed that he would not write or publish anything for years. However, he could not escape his nature. Stephen King is a writer."

John Sayles is another amazing example of a productive writer. Sending a short story blind to *The Atlantic,* he caught the attention of the editor and later turned the story into his first novel, *Pride of the Bimbos*. He followed with a second novel, *Union Dues*, which was nominated for a National Book Award and the National Book Critics Circle Award. He received two O'Henry Awards for his short stories, collected in *The Anarchists' Convention*, and set to work writing a play and over two dozen screenplays and making films. He has written rock videos for Bruce Springsteen and a third novel, *Los Gusanos*.

His film *Return of the Secaucus Seven* is a cult favorite that may have been noticed by Lawrence Kasdan, whose *The Big Chill* is remarkably similar. Other small films, *Lianna* and *Baby, It's You,* followed. *Brother From A Small Planet*, *Matewan*, and *Eight Men Out* were bigger successes. Among his recent films is *Lone Star* (1996), *The Secret of Roan Inish* (1995), *Passion Fish* (1992), and *City of Hope* (1991). One of the quintessential Sayles actors, David Stathairn, who is in what could be called Sayles's repertory company and has played, among other characters, the sheriff in *Matewan*, described Sayles as a kind, workaholic genius. Sayles has raised money for his many films through writing and revising other people's screenplays for more commercial projects.

There are other writers, though, who have written little; at least not as much as the writers above; at least hardly anything like the output of writers like Isaac Asimov, Ray Bradbury, May Sarton, or James Michener. One of these is William Styron, who has had a relatively modest output, J.D. Salinger, who has not produced for many years, and Frank Conroy, who has had hardly any output at all. All of these writers are revered, some would say, in disproportion to their amount of publication. Styron said that when he finished *The Confessions of Nat Turner*, he experienced an "almost blind rush of creativity, with no rewriting at all." He then wryly stated, in an interview with Mandelbaum, "You only wonder why it doesn't happen more often. I wish it did. I would have more books."

The writers studied at the University of California were concerned with the meaning of life and the search for truth and beauty, and they furthermore were particularly concerned about behaving in an ethically consistent fashion. Supposedly this is the lofty purpose of literature, and that the writers searched for truth and beauty is not surprising. From Shelley's "beauty is truth, truth beauty" to John Gardner's *On Moral Fiction*, the purpose has been put forth that literature is a way to morally explicate and uphold human values. This is not to say, however, that literature is written expressly to set forth doctrines, for any such literature would, and does, seem dogmatic. (And teachers who insist that students come up with the "one true meaning" of a literary composition are just as dogmatic.) Rather, the writer uses experience as a search for meaning and not meaning itself. The writers' act of writing is, itself, a search for meaning. As John Gardner said,

> Out of the artist's imagination, as out of nature's inexhaustible well, pours one thing after another. The artist composes, writes, or paints just as he dreams, seizing whatever swims close to his net. This, not the world seen directly, is his raw material. This shimmering mess of loves and hates— fishing trips taken long ago with Uncle Ralph, a 1940 green Chevrolet, a war, a vague sense of what makes a novel, a symphony, a photograph—this is the clay the artist must shape into an object worthy of our attention; that is, our tears, our laughter, our thought.

Since writers often take aesthetic pleasure in the texture of the paper, the placement of the type, the sewing of the binding, and the spacing of the headings, it is not surprising that several of the fine small presses are owned and run by writers. An interview with the novelist Don DeLillo by Passaro noted DeLillo's love of how sentences are constructed and how words are juxtaposed: "Not just how they sound and how they mean, but even what they look like." Working on a manual typewriter gives DeLillo's writing "an almost sculptural feeling of pressing new words into blank paper."

Poetry is often made into high quality, hand-set, hand-sewn books that provide the eye and the finger with as much aesthetic pleasure as they do the mind with poetic delight. These *chapbooks* are small, exquisitely-printed books with fewer than 30 pages. Many writers are also collectors of rare and fine books. Larry McMurtry, another Pulitzer Prize winning writer, is well known for his large rare book collection, and many writers collect first editions, chapbooks, and *broadsides*, poems set in the manner of old handbills. One of my greatest pleasures is discovering a first edition at the local library sale or at Goodwill of a first novel by a writer who has since become famous. Last month I found one of John Irving's first novels, *Setting Free the Bears*, bought it for seventy cents; I came home, looked it up and found it was worth several hundred dollars!

Barron, in observing that the writer is independent in thought and judgment, frank and candid in dealings with others, implied that the writer may value freedom of expression more than the feelings of others. Indeed, writers throughout the world have often been the first to be thrown into jail or sent into exile for what they have written and said. Solzhenitsyn and Brodsky were sent to Siberia for what they wrote. The British writer Salman Rushdie, sentenced to death by the Ayatollah of Iran for his novel *Satanic Verses*, had to go into hiding in 1989.

The writers' organization PEN has a Freedom To Write Committee, a watchdog group concerned about writers throughout the world being persecuted for expressing themselves. In 1990, nine of the eleven panelists on the National Endowment of the Arts literature panel resigned in protest over the antiobscenity pledge the U.S. government was threatening to require the grant awardees to sign. (Congress eventually voted that awardees won't be required to sign such pledges.) At a less lofty level, young creative writers often publish frank underground newspapers that are the bane of their teachers and school administrators.

Writers attract the interest of others, probably because of their ability to say what they think. I ran into a best-selling author from my home town, Robert Traver (*Anatomy of a Murder*, 1955), outside of the university library a year before his death. The best-known citizen of Ishpeming, Michigan, by then in his eighties, was as opinionated as ever. As we chatted, he talked about the evils of the city and the beauties of the wilderness of the Upper Peninsula. He held forth on the timeless tranquilities of nature and the filth and noisiness of the city, sounding for all that summer's day like Wordsworth proclaiming "the world is too much with us." The grizzled old man was almost blind, but he still read avidly, and still wrote.

With his straightforwardness and adamance, Traver was much like the writers in the Barron study, who were found to be frank people who needed to communicate and were likely to take risks in doing so. Through psychological testing the study also found that the writers showed a desire to achieve through their work, and not through conformity to a social group. They had presence, they wanted to achieve social status, and they liked themselves.

Barron's team of researchers divided the writers into three groups: distinguished writers, student writers, and representative writers (those who had achieved financial success and popular recognition but were not considered distinguished). In independence of judgment, the distinguished writers scored well above the general population. In this, popular writers are like popular elected officials, for studies have shown that leaders chosen by the people generally are a little more intelligent than the general population, but not so intelligent that the populace cannot identify with them.

In flexibility, the student writers scored higher than the distinguished writers, who in turn scored higher than the representative or commercially successful writers. That student writers were more like the distinguished writers in this quality may be attributed to identification and life-style imitation, Barron postulated, since distinguished writers retain their independence and flexibility.

Creative Writers and Deviance

According to Barron, creative writers were "markedly deviant" from the general population. In particular, distinguished writers tended to be schizoid, depressive, hysterical, or psychopathic, and not to have rigid sex role expectations. Barron said, "In brief, if one is to take these test results seriously, the writers appear to be both sicker and healthier psychologically than people in general." That is, the writers may have had psychological problems, but they also had inner strength to help them. Barron said, "This jibes rather well with their social behavior . . . They are clearly effective people who handle themselves with pride and distinctiveness, but the face they turn to the world is sometimes one of pain, often of protest, sometimes of distance and withdrawal, and certainly they are emotional."

Psychoanalysts and psychologists have often stated that writers write because of deep-seated pathologies. Freud, in "Creative Writers and Day-Dreaming," theorized that writers use their personal childhood fantasies. Ernst Kris wrote, in *Psychoanalytic Explorations in Art*, that writers write because of "regression in service of the ego."

More recently, Rothenberg has dealt with the mind of the writer in *The*

Emerging Goddess and *Creativity and Madness*. In over 2,000 hours of interviews, including some with award-winning writers, he formulated a theory of the creative process in writers which he called the janusian process, after the Roman god Janus, the two-faced god. He also studied the creative process in people who were not writers but who had been given an assignment to write a novel or poem.

The writers (and scientists and visual artists) were able to hold opposites in their minds while creating and to see the possibilities of working with these opposites. Thesis becomes antithesis and both are integrated into the theme of the work. Irony, metaphor, ambiguity, and creative tension are hallmarks of the janusian process. These are organic and are seen by the writer as crucial to the meaning of the work. The shadow becomes the ego and vice-versa. Both are within the one, and the writer's purpose embraces both. For example, when considering the theme of a novel, one writer said he got the idea while reading Erik Erikson's work on Martin Luther, and it occurred to him to write about a revolutionary hero who "was responsible for the deaths of hundreds of people, but he himself would kill only one person with his own hand—and this was the one person who had been very kind to him and the one person he loved."

Rothenberg also studied a comparison group. They were matched for success, age, and sex, but their managers had secretly notated that they were not very creative. The group was given an assignment to write a creative prose work for a certain amount of money. They proceeded to make outlines, think of suitable endings, take detailed notes in journals. Rothenberg conducted ongoing discussions about their works in progress, just as he did with the creative writers. Some of the people actually completed these works of the imagination, but they produced no janusian twists, what Rothenberg called "simultaneous antitheses." Most gave up before completing the works. The ability to see the other side and its creative possibilities is what differentiated the two.

Rothenberg said that the *janusian* process is used in the beginning and during the generation of ideas, but that later, a *homospatial* process is used by writers. This is a process of *synaesthesia,* where metaphors are created by superimposing unlike elements upon the same space. Thus the writer combines what is seen in the mind's eye, the mind's ear, the mind's touch. Sounds have color and sights have sound. Tastes have texture and movement. Artists, writers, and scientists consciously develop this metaphorization process, but it also rises spontaneously. He said, "The homospatial process leads to effective literary double meanings and directly produces poetic rhymes, assonances, and alliterations."

Kay Jamison, in a study of 39 British writers and 8 artists, found that 38 percent of them had been treated for affective illness whereas in the normal population less than 5 percent are. They also reported mental problems, including hospitalization in their first-degree relatives to a greater extent than in the normal population. Jamison said that psychiatrists should be cautious in their diagnoses and prescriptions of drugs, since the states of creativity are similar to those reported by people with mood disorders. The side-effects of commonly prescribed drugs may damage the creative process. Several of the writers stopped taking lithium because of its deadening effects on their creative thinking.

According to Alice Miller in *The Untouched Key* (already discussed with reference to her theories on Picasso's creativity), writer-philosopher Friedrich Nietzsche, after the death of his father and his brother, grew up as the only male in a house full of women who taught him self-denial and silenced his curiosity. Miller wrote, "Friedrich Nietzsche needed his entire philosophy to shield himself from knowing and telling what really happened to him." Miller said that for years she has been trying to tell the world that poets, writers, and painters told the "encoded" stories of childhood trauma in their works, but that no one would listen to her. She believes that the denial of evidence is due in part to the revelation of "forbidden knowledge" of the idealization that children put upon their parents—in other words, the lies children tell themselves about their parents, to compensate for the parents' failings.

In 1988, in *The Literary Mind*, psychologist Leo Schneiderman proposed that Faulkner wrote because of ego defects, including low self-esteem caused by an overprotective mother and a rejecting father. Schneiderman said also that Lillian Hellman wrote out of narcissistic "chronic rage" that resulted from "material deprivation;" Tennessee Williams, to compensate for his incestual feelings towards his mother and sister; Flannery O'Connor, out of guilt for getting ill with lupus in her late twenties and being dependent on her mother during adulthood; John Cheever, because of "early withdrawal of parental empathy;" Vladimir Nabokov, longing for his presexual days; Jorge Luis Borges, because of oncoming blindness and his shame after a series of crises in his family's fortunes in Buenos Aires; Samuel Beckett wrote out of a "character disorder marked by extreme rigidity and self-centeredness;" and the playwright Harold Pinter writes out of "regression to a past that was as emotionally deprived as is the present." Schneiderman said, "Great literary art is a synthesis of technical skill with tremendous fear, rage, or other powerful emotions, and . . . the fundamental character of great writers reveals significant failure along developmental lines, that is, a basic lack of maturity."

The Myers-Briggs and Writers

In conjunction with other studies of writers at the Institute for Personality Assessment and Research were those using the Myers-Briggs Type Indicator (MBTI), a personality type indicator that has been used to examine the characteristics of scientists, artists, laborers, writers, counselors, and many more. Writers tested with the Myers-Briggs were found overwhelmingly to be introverted, intuitive, feeling, and perceptive—INFP. These findings, consonant with other studies done by the Myers group, showed writers to be similar to artists. Most striking was that writers much preferred to use their intuitive and perceptive powers over their sensing and judging capabilities. Such persons who prefer introversion, intuition, feeling and perception, according to Myers and McCaulley, show inner strength, especially with regard to their personal values, and are reserved. They look for a type of job that provides satisfaction rather than money, and can be perfectionistic about their work. They are interested in ideas, often reflecting on the disparities between ideals and realities. Extroverts in this category are more outgoing and can be persuasive about their passions, while their preference for intuition and feeling allows them to trust their inner selves.

Barron's study also noted that creative writers are not good cooperators or committee members; they do not have a great need for harmony, nor do they seek easy praise. Indeed, anyone who submits manuscripts time after time after time—and most writers have this experience—must be patient, resilient, and stubborn.

The Biographical Approaches

While the Barron study combined testing and interviews, there are other approaches that have been used to study writers, such as the case study approach. Another is Simonton's historiometric approach. The first would be to take a few random biographies of writers, which could be called case studies (though not in the strict psychological sense). The other would be to take many biographies and extrapolate from them, as the Goertzels did, or to apply statistical techniques to their analysis—the technique called historiometry, as Simonton did—and see what researchers have found.

The Goertzels's studies documented seven hundred eminent persons who had at least two books written about them. The 1978 study included eighty-two literary people: forty-seven fiction and drama writers, twelve nonfiction writers, thirteen poets, and ten editors and publishers.

The Goertzels found more only children among writers than among artists, politicians, or others in the study. The writers, not surprisingly, were voracious early readers. About half the writers hated school, teachers, and school curricula. Literary people were twice as likely to attempt or commit suicide than subjects of biographies. Also, literary people were less likely to come from literary families than were artistic, business, or political people to come from families established in their respective areas. Two-thirds of the writers described their childhood home life as unhappy, while less than half of the other eminent people so described their early years. Literary people were also more likely to have alcoholic parents.

An aspect of the family life of writers not mentioned by the Goertzels but noted by playwright Arthur Miller, in his 1987 autobiography, *Timebends*, was that many writers have had ineffectual fathers. He said, "It would strike me years later how many male writers had fathers who had actually failed or whom the sons had perceived as failures." He went on to list Faulkner, Fitzgerald, Hemingway, Thomas Wolfe, Poe, Steinbeck, Melville, Whitman, Chekhov, Hawthorne, Strindberg, and Dostoyevsky, and said, "The list is too long to consign the phenomenon to idiosyncratic accident."

This aspect of the writer's life, Miller thought, led the American writer to seek to create a new order, springing "as though from the ground itself," of self-made men "quite like the businessmen they despise," and he called the American male writers, "fatherless men abandoned by a past that they in turn reject, the better to write not the Great American Novel or Play, but verily the First." The writer T. Corraghesan Boyle said about his father, "I tried to understand him, but he was usually extremely morose and insensibly drunk, like his father before him," and said that his grandfather had put his father into an orphanage.

In an article about Boyle, Friend said that Boyle's recent novels ". . . have featured a foredoomed search for a missing father." The poet Robert Bly said at the 1991 James Wright Poetry Festival that it took him years to put the word "stagger" in a poem about his father, whose alcoholism filled him with shame. The novelist John Irving's father disappeared from his life, and the absent father has been a theme in his work. Both talented sons of Duke Wolff have felt so betrayed by their father that Tobias, in *This Boy's Life*, and Geoffrey, in *The Duke of Deception*, have forever memorialized this heedless father.

Dick Allen said his becoming a poet is a direct result of his family dynamics—"The shaping forces of a domineering mother and an acquiescent father who were locked in a relationship fulfilling her need to control and his to be controlled." He said that almost every poet he knows comes from such a relationship, and that his life as a professor is a continuation, as he is ". . . protected by the mother-university just as my father was protected by his mother-wife."

The father of novelist, short-story writer and poet Sheila Robert was an alcoholic; her story "Next Time" deals with that alcoholism and its effect on her family. Poet Frank O'Hara's mother was alcoholic, as was Anne Rice's. Writer Scott Sanders said his alcoholic father "drank with a fearful thirst." Sanders was afraid that everyone would know the family secret. "The house trembled . . . I was not able to write openly about my father's drinking until well after his death." It is not known whether writers had more alcoholism in their families than other people. Perhaps their responses to the alcoholic environment were different; perhaps they responded with greater overexcitability or intensity.

The search for the missing father is not just the search of sons. Mary Gordon's memoir, *The Shadow Man*, is ample proof that women writers undergo such a search also. Gordon grew up with a belief that her father was a pious Catholic, a misunderstood poet, a Harvard man who had fallen upon hard times. He had indeed fallen upon hard times, but he was an immigrant Jew to Lorain/Cleveland, Ohio, who had never graduated from high school, the head writer for a hack pre-*Playboy* magazine called *Hot Dog*, a man with false-everything, not counting his false teeth. Gordon researched in available archives, census demographics, local histories and oral memories to find the truth.

The Goertzels observed yet another aspect of an unhappy home life among writers: more literary people had marriages that ended in divorce than others in the study, and yet more of the writers never married in the first place. Perhaps the twin phenomena of fewer marriages and more divorces have something to do with sexual divergence; of the twenty-one people identified as sexually divergent in the Goertzels' study, twenty were literary people. In addition, the writers were often ill as children, or handicapped, or "homely." The Goertzels noted, "Their photographs as children and adults are less attractive than those of politicians, athletes, and performers."

Their childhoods and adult lives were judged to be more "lonely, unhappy, and difficult" than others'. On the positive side, they were as children very sensuous, reacting profoundly to visual, olfactory, and tactile sensations. But even this sensitivity worked against them; writers as small children "were intensely responsive to the emotional climate in their homes" and were "acute observers of the family dramas being played out before their eyes."

(Overexcitability and the Dabrowski theory are discussed in Chapter 4.)

Tobias Wolff's memoir, *This Boy's Life*, also made into a movie, detailed his early life with his mother, the two of them "on the road" so to speak, until his mother married a very uncongenial stepfather. Their life in a northwest town was described in vivid detail by Wolff, who almost became an Eagle scout, yet ran with a gang who stole, drank, and did drugs. Wolff, realizing he had to get out, faked his credentials on an application to a prep school in the East. Once there, he flunked out. Meanwhile, his real father, a con man who pretended to come from a blue-blooded Eastern family, and his brother Geoffrey, who also became a writer, were living in comparative ease in the East, ignoring the traumas Tobias was enduring. Tobias forgave his father's neglect, rationalizing that he must have been very busy, until he himself held his own newborn son in his arms; he then felt overwhelming anger toward the man.

Writers often retreat from the world by reading and fantasizing, and when they were young, they didn't need as much companionship as other children. One of the young writers who studied at the aforementioned summer institute described his reading behavior as compulsive and constant. "If my friends knew how I behave when I read, they would be surprised." Often reading in the woods under a tree, he would imagine himself a character in the book, even talking out loud, "No, don't do that! You'll get killed!" Also, he rewarded himself for doing some homework by reading a chapter of a novel, then doing more homework, then reading a chapter, then doing more homework. This behavior, uncovered by the Dabrowski Overexcitabilities Questionnaire (OEQ), revealed an intense imaginational and intellectual reaction to the written word.

Writers weren't popular with their peers. In fact, they often provoked dislike and rejection from peers, adults, and teachers, often because of their outspokenness. Although peaceful children, they often had to be pushed into doing physical activities or studying subjects they didn't like, such as math and science. The writers also are not joiners of social causes, except to contribute (but not to hold office) and are content to be alone much of the time, though they do like to socialize with other writers occasionally.

Midcentury Writers: The Academicians

Other biographies bear interesting witness to the lives of creative writers. The psychotherapist Eileen Simpson's memoir, *Poets In Their Youth*, which included stories about several of the United States' foremost modern poets

(Simpson was married to John Berryman), gave interesting insight into the social lives of poets and novelists. Berryman, Caroline Gordon, Robert Lowell, Jean Stafford, Delmore Schwartz, R. P. Blackmur, Mark Van Doren, Randall Jarrell, Allen Tate, Theodore Roethke, Saul Bellow, Robert Fitzgerald, Edmund Wilson, and others crossed paths in the 1940s and 1950s. Simpson's documentation showed that even for these prestigious college-educated poets, the way was tough.

Applying for grants, living on one-year appointments at various universities, hoping to win contests or to get manuscripts published by major houses, the poets described by Simpson were in the 1950s like other poets are now. How many people today have read books by these famous poets or novelists? Or by the poets writing today? Being published does not ensure being read. Poets have an especially rough time in the United States, where poetry is not popular. Recently on a plane I sat next to a well-educated radio commentator. When we got to talking about modern poetry, he looked at me strangely and said, "I bet I can't name one contemporary poet alive today. I remember Shelley and Keats from high school, but that's all."

Several of the poets described by Simpson had major bouts with mental illness. Lowell was institutionalized often for manic-depression (before the use of lithium). Schwartz was diagnosed as a paranoid schizophrenic. Tate was rumored to be a philanderer. Stafford was institutionalized for alcoholism; Roethke, for mental illness and alcoholism. Berryman himself was an alcoholic depressive who, after several suicide attempts, died in 1972 after jumping off a high bridge into the Mississippi River. Jarrell also was alleged to have committed suicide by jumping in front of a car on a lonely road one dark night.

Alcohol was a major part of the social lives of these writers; indeed, addiction to alcohol figures in the lives of many creative writers, artists, and performers. In 1995, Simonton observed, "Among creative writers, the rates of alcoholism clearly exceed those found in the general population." A struggling young musician, talking about excessive drinking among his artistic friends, claimed, "Alcohol is at least as important as love." But the writers studied by Simpson were established as the elite of the nation. Praised by the academy, they were the heirs of Eliot and Yeats, the founders and editors and writers for the most prestigious literary and political journals: *The Nation, The Partisan Review, The Sewanee Review, The Kenyon Review.*

They were the inventors and purveyors of the New Criticism. If there were any accolades to be given to poets and novelists, they received them.

They sat on the Library of Congress advisory committees and dedicated themselves to lives of thought and writing. Yet their personal lives were anything but pleasant, anything but happy.

Simpson documented that Schwartz, Lowell, and Berryman all had strong mothers who were hard to please and absent, dead, or ineffectual fathers. Berryman's father committed suicide at the age of thirty-nine. In order to get his mother's attention, John would often feign fainting spells or leap onto a parapet and threaten suicide.

Delmore Schwartz's mother was a strong Jewish traditionalist. When her younger son married a non-Jewish woman, she said he would be "better off dead." Delmore also married a woman who was not Jewish; Simpson wrote, "Anticipating an hysterical attack, Delmore might well not have told her." Robert Lowell's mother was the only one he would let rescue him when he was thrown into jail during a manic bout he suffered while visiting his old Kenyon College roommate from Indiana. She came and collected him to an institution back home in Massachusetts.

Midcentury Writers: The Beats

While these writers produced that which was accepted by academics in the 1940s, '50s and '60s, the Beats were writing rebellious poetry and prose with a jazz beat and a downtown air. Kerouac, Cassady, Ginsberg, Ferlinghetti, and Burroughs shocked and thrilled the youth of the age. They wrote about jazz and heroin and addiction and being free, on the road in automobiles and motorcycles, and about the decline of America. Ginsberg's landmark poem, "Howl," published by City Lights in 1956, began the San Francisco renaissance. Barry Miles's biography of the poet, *Ginsberg*, tells of the profound influence Ginsberg had on a whole generation of youth and writers in America and throughout the world. Ginsberg's revolutionary "saxophone line" style, his call for the legalization of marijuana and for stopping discrimination against homosexuals, echoed throughout the 1970s and blended with the anti-Vietnam War movement.

Ginsberg crossed paths with many of the great writers of the world, beginning at Columbia University, where he studied under Mark Van Doren and Lionel Trilling. Later, exiled to Paterson, New Jersey, after his hospitalization for mental illness, he came under the tutelage of William Carlos Williams. Then came his residence in various apartments in Manhattan, where the Beat generation began to formulate its theories of art. He hung around with theater people such as Judith Malina and Julian Beck at the San Remo Bar in Greenwich Village, where the term "beat" was first applied. Miles wrote about the group.

> They explored the sinister, the criminal, and the forbidden. They rejected the conformist consumer society of America in the late forties but were not thinking in terms of rebelling against it. The Beat Generation began with personal exploration. "It wasn't a political or social rebellion," Ginsberg said. "Everybody had some form of break in their consciousness or an experience or a taste of a large consciousness or 'sator.' They had all read Spengler's *Decline of the West*, and took it for granted that civilization was collapsing around them. The atomic bomb had just been dropped on Japan and that, to them, was proof enough. The early Beats had no hope of trying to change society."

By the time he died in 1997, Ginsberg had hobnobbed with Bob Dylan, the Rolling Stones, and the Beatles. He had founded a literary movement and been kicked out of Cuba and Czechoslovakia for his advocacy of homosexuality and for his frank diaries. He had lived in Mexico, Tangier and India. He was decried for writing obscenity. He was in Stan Grof's and Timothy Leary's LSD experiments and had experimented with many other drugs as well, especially the hallucinogens. He had meditated naked, changing "Om" in public places, had met Ezra Pound, and had marched in many antiwar protests. He had tried to levitate the Pentagon. He had become a Buddhist and had helped to found a Buddhist poetry center in Boulder, Colorado, the Jack Kerouac School of Disembodied Poetics. He had given readings all over the world.

Ginsberg also had spent a few years working in advertising promotion, an educational experience which enabled him to effectively, tirelessly, and ceaselessly promote his own works and those of his friends. Self-promotion or promotion by friends is necessary to the realization of the creative writer's hope to have an audience for what is written, and promotion is often undervalued in the realization of creative writing talent.

As Getzels and Csikszentmihalyi noted, the loft is important in the socialization and professionalizing of the visual artist; to creative writers, the literary agent and a group of connected friends is equally as important. Many literary works are first published by small presses, and many books of poetry are published by one friend for another. Where self-publication is looked down on in academic fields, it often occurs in literary fields. Ferlinghetti founded City Lights expressly to publish his own, Ginsberg's, and other Beats' works. Ginsberg loyally continued with City Lights, even when he could have made much more money publishing with mainstream publishers.

I myself was publisher and editor of a small literary press in the late 1970s and early 1980s. I published poems, with illustrations, by many poets, among them Nick Muska, Larry Smith, Robert Fox, Howard McCord, Peg Lauber, Linda Hasselstrom, Judith Lindenau, Joel Lipman, Bruce Severy, Carol Pierman and David Shevin. Dorothy Linden illustrated many of the poems. I solicited poems from poets who were my friends and also accepted poems sent to me by submission. And why not publish good poets who were my friends? To do so is an old and respected literary tradition.

For example, in a 1990 essay on the Scribner's publishing house, called "I, Who Knew Nothing, Was In Charge," Charles Scribner, Jr., said that throughout its early years, Scribner's was "a staunch Princeton house." It is quite a sport among literary people to watch how connections and friendships bloom into publications and contracts, and in fact, *Esquire* published a tongue-in-cheek family tree on just that subject a few years ago, and *Spy* magazine had a column called "Logrolling," featuring blurbs by one friend for another, and then the corresponding jacket blurb by the other friend for the first friend.

The Beats continue to engage the imaginations of would-be rebels. The black clothes of today's rock and roll punk youth who identify with the restless spirit of the Beats, the smoky coffeehouses on any college campus, continue to engage the spirit of young people, even though the Beat movement, like World War II, has celebrated its golden anniversary.

Midcentury Writers: The Women

The 1960s also found the U.S. poetic world with two suicidal women poets, called "confessional" by their male detractors (though confession was the mode of discourse in poetry long before them). Anne Sexton and Sylvia Plath wrote their longing lyrics and the literary world waited, with bated breath, as they played out their sad destinies. Sylvia Plath died by putting her head in an oven in 1963, and Anne Sexton gassed herself in her garage.

Their works often spoke of the typical conflict experienced by women. As Foley found in her 1996 study of artist mothers, and as Belenky, Clinchy, Goldberger, Tarule, and Gilligan found, women with children experience great conflict in finding time, inclination, support, and social approval for doing the strenuous work needed to have a successful career and to have a family. Both Margaret Drabble and Tillie Olsen told of writing in the middle of the night before the children got up.

Such writers as Adrienne Rich, Margaret Atwood, Joyce Carol Oates and Anne Tyler demonstrate that productivity, persistence, and prolificacy are of crucial importance in maintaining the writer's vision. Oates, in "(Woman) Writer," noted that most women writers write because they have to, and do not view themselves as "woman writers." Virginia Woolf, in *A Writer's Diary*, described the hard work of getting it right:

> I write two pages of arrant nonsense, after straining; I write variations of every sentence; compromises; bad shots; possibilities; till my writing book is like a lunatic's dream. Then I trust to some inspiration on re-reading; and pencil them into some sense. Still, I am not satisfied.

Women as well as men put down one sentence after another, writing toward completion. Woolf wrote, "I have just finished, with this very nib-ful of ink, the last sentence of *The Waves* . . . Yes, it was the greatest stretch of mind I ever knew."

Women writers are no different from other women creators in that they experience the same guilt, doubt, and conflict with raising children and having a writing career as other women in their chosen careers. They also fight to be taken seriously as creators. "Don't call me a poetess," said one woman poet. "I am a poet. A poetess is a maiden spinster publishing verses in the church bulletin."

Writers and Depression

In early 1990 Pulitzer Prize-winning author William Styron wrote an op-ed piece for *The New York Times* about the cavalier treatment of the suicide of Primo Levi, the Italian writer. In this letter, Styron confessed to having been suicidal himself, and from this grew one of the major bestsellers of 1990, Styron's account of depression, *Darkness Visible: A Memoir of Madness*. Styron wrote that in his early sixties he had fallen into deep depression after stopping drinking. He was hospitalized for his mental condition, but it was not until later that he realized his psychiatrist had over-prescribed medication, thereby exacerbating the very condition being treated.

Styron named other writers and artists who had suffered from debilitating depression: Albert Camus, Romain Gary, Jean Seberg and Randall Jarrell, among others. Styron wrote that although it was denied by biographers and family, Jarrell "almost certainly killed himself. He did so not because he was a coward, nor out of any moral feebleness, but because he was afflicted with a depression that was so devastating that he could no longer endure the pain of it." Others who suffered depression were poet Hart Crane, Vincent Van Gogh, Virginia Woolf, abstract expressionist Mark Rothko, photographer Diane Arbus, playwright William Inge, and humorist Art Buchwald. Of the origins of such depression, Styron wrote:

> When one thinks of these doomed and splendidly creative men and women, one is drawn to contemplate their child-hoods, where, to the best of anyone's knowledge, the seeds of the illness take strong root; could any of them have had a hint, then, of the psyche's perishability, its exquisite fragili-ty? And why were they destroyed, while others—similarly stricken—struggled through?

Styron pointed to the childhood roots of his own depression. Even as an adult he had never fully mourned the death of his mother when he was thirteen. On the night on which he had earlier decided he would commit suicide, he was in his living room listening to classical music when he heard a Bach tune his mother had hummed. In an extremely distraught state of excitement and emo-tion, Styron woke his wife and begged her to take him to the hospital; he began his recovery upon hearing a song which unleashed his feelings of loss.

Woolf, in her *Diary*, wrote often of "black moods" that were lifted through writing. Composing *To The Lighthouse* was especially therapeutic because of the hold her parents had on her:

> November 28, 1928. Father's birthday. He would have been 96, 96, yes, today; and could have been 96, like other people one has known: but mercifully was not. His life would have entirely ended mine. What would have happened? No writ-ing; no books;—inconceivable. I used to think of him and mother daily; but writing the Lighthouse laid them in my mind. And now he comes back sometimes, but differently. (I believe this to be true—that I was obsessed by them both, unhealthily; and writing of him was a necessary act.)

Jamison, author of *Touched With Fire: Manic-Depressive Illness and the Artistic Temperament*, found that artists, poets, and writers were 35 times more likely to seek treatment for serious mood disorders than the average person, and of these three groups, poets suffered the severest forms of disturbance. Jamison gave diagrams of the genealogies and documented manic-depressive illness in the first-degree relatives of writers Herman Melville, Samuel Taylor Coleridge, Virginia Woolf, Ernest Hemingway, Mary Wollstonecraft and her daughter Mary Shelley, Samuel Johnson, James Boswell, Lord Byron, Alfred, Lord Tennyson, and Henry, Alice, and William James. Poets were especially struck with such illness. To the following diagram based on Jamison's research I have added novelist Michael Dorris, who committed suicide at the age of 52 while this revision was being prepared.

TABLE 4. Poets & Writers with Depression or Manic-Depression

✳= Asylum or psychiatric institution; ❖ = Suicide attempt; ☞ = Suicide

POETS	WRITERS
✳ Antonin Artaud	Hans Christian Andersen
❖ Charles Baudelaire	Honoré de Balzac
✳ ☞ John Berryman	James Barrie
William Blake	James Boswell
✳ Louise Bogan	John Bunyan
Rupert Brooke	Samuel Clemens
Robert Burns	❖ Joseph Conrad
George Gordon	Charles Dickens
Lord Byron	❖ Isak Dinesen
☞ Paul Celan	Ralph Waldo Emerson
☞ Thomas Chatterton	✳ William Faulkner
Samuel Taylor Coleridge	✳ F. Scott Fitzgerald
✳ William Collins	Nikolai Gogol
❖✳ William Cowper	❖ Maxim Gorky
☞ Hart Crane	Kenneth Grahame
Emily Dickinson	✳ ☞ Ernest Hemingway
✳ T.S. Eliot	❖✳ Hermann Hesse
Anne Finch	Henrik Ibsen
Oliver Goldsmith	❖✳ William Inge
Thomas Gray	Henry James
Gerard Manley Hopkins	William James

TABLE 4. Poets & Writers with Depression or Manic-Depression

✳= Asylum or psychiatric institution; ❖ = Suicide attempt; ☛ = Suicide

POETS	WRITERS
✳ ☛ Randall Jarrell	✳ Charles Lamb
Samuel Johnson	❖✳ Malcolm Lowry
John Keats	Herman Melville
☛ Vachel Lindsay	❖✳ Eugene O'Neill
James Russell Lowell	Francis Parkman
✳ Robert Lowell	Mary Shelley
Louis MacNiece	✳ Jean Stafford
❖✳ Osip Mandelstam	Robert Louis Stevenson
✳ Edna St. Vincent Millay	August Strindberg
✳ Boris Pasternak	Leo Tolstoy
☛ Cesare Pavese	Ivan Turgenev
✳ ☛ Sylvia Plath	✳ Tennessee Williams
❖ Edgar Allan Poe	❖ Mary Wollstonecraft
✳ Ezra Pound	✳ ☛ Virginia Woolf
Alexander Pushkin	Emile Zola
✳ Theodore Roethke	
✳ Delmore Schwartz	☛ Michael Dorris
✳ ☛Anne Sexton	
❖ Percy Bysshe Shelley	
❖✳ Sara Teasdale	
Alfred, Lord Tennyson	
Dylan Thomas	
Walt Whitman	

Andreason studied twenty-seven male and three female faculty at the University of Iowa Writers' Workshop over a period of fifteen years, comparing them to a group of hospital administrators, lawyers, social workers, and the like. The average age of both groups was 38 years. Bipolar manic depressive affective disorder was found in 80% of the writers and in 30% of the comparison group, which itself had a higher than usual incidence of affective disorder. Two-thirds of the writers had sought psychiatric help. Two of the thirty writers committed suicide during the 15 years of the study. Andreason studied the first-degree relatives of the writers and found that almost half of the members of the families of the writers also had occupations that emphasized creativity, such as teaching music or dance, though they may not have been in the writing field. This indicates that there may be a general creativity factor that is genetically transmitted. The verbal intelligence of the family members was no higher than that of the comparison group, about 125. Andreason had predicted schizophrenia but instead found manic depression; she noted that writers said they wrote during the long periods between episodes, rather than during the highs and lows characteristic of bipolar disorder. According to Andreason, "Affective disorder may be both a `hereditary taint' and a hereditary gift."

Ginsberg, suffering extreme self-doubt and almost arrested for burglary, checked himself into the New York Psychiatric Institute. (Incidentally, tests given at this time showed Ginsberg's IQ to be "near genius level," according to Miles.) Ginsberg's childhood in New Jersey had been odd to say the least. His mother, a paranoid schizophrenic, was often institutionalized; Allen himself had to take her to the institution once. At home, she liked to be "natural," often striding around the house in the nude. Ginsberg's father was the well-known poet Louis Ginsberg, a teacher who tried to keep life somewhat normal for Allen and his brother. Ginsberg's moving 1961 poem "Kaddish" is an artistic revelation of his family's trials, an anguished expression of regret that when his insane mother died in a mental hospital, they were not able to summon ten Jewish men to say the Jewish prayer for the dead, Kaddish.

John Cheever struggled also, and wrote in the diaries published posthumously in *The New Yorker* in 1991:

> I must convince myself that writing is not, for a man of my disposition, a self-destructive vocation. I hope and think it is not, but I am not genuinely sure. It has given me money and renown, but I suspect that it may have something to do with my drinking habits. The excitement of alcohol and the excitement of fantasy are very similar.

The 1991 suicide of the Pulitzer Prize-winning novelist Jerzy Kosinski brought this letter from the playwright Kenneth Brown:

> Jerzy Kosinski was a friend of mine, hence the enclosed poem. He committed suicide recently by pulling a plastic bag over his head and sitting in a hot tub and suffocating. It was a great shock to me. We used to sit in the saloons late at

night and talk about his childhood. The Nazis killed his family when he was about eight years old, and he became a street urchin for awhile. Have you read *The Painted Bird*? He adored the SS troops because they were tall and clean and handsome with shiny boots and black uniforms. It haunted him all his life; he had enormous guilt about his success and his survival, worried about having become a Nazi equivalent through his fame and fortune. I tried to reassure him that his work was a weapon against fascism. Alas, what I said was not enough. I guess nothing would have been enough.

Highly verbal, highly conceptual, highly opinionated, often nonconforming, frank, highly driven, writers are prone to self-abusive and self-destructive behavior even as they are enriching the lives of their readers. But this is not always the case, and there are many writers whose lives are not lived so tragically, or who have, as Styron said, "struggled through."

The picture that emerges can perhaps be summarized in the words of E.L. Doctorow, who said in the 1988 interview with George Plimpton for *Paris Review*, "A writer's life is so hazardous that anything he does is bad for him. Anything that happens to him is bad: failure's bad, success is bad; impoverishment is bad, money is very, very bad. Nothing good can happen." Plimpton responded to Doctorow's statement with: "Except the act of writing itself." Doctorow replied:

> Except the act of writing. So if he shoots birds and animals and anything else he can find, you've got to give him that. And if he/she drinks, you give him/her that too, unless the work is affected. For all of us, there's an intimate connection between the struggle to write and the ability to survive on a daily basis as a human being. So we have a high rate of self-destruction. Do you mean to punish ourselves for writing? For the transgression? I don't know.

"Except the act of writing itself." This statement perhaps illustrates the intrinsic nature of writing talent. The writer does not know what he or she thinks until it's written down. There is something in the very act itself that heals, relieves frustration, and satisfies the need for communication and self-expression.

Like visual artists, writers write because they must, and not because they think it would be fun to be a writer. The high incidence of depression would seem to be an indication of the intense sensitivity with which creative people apprehend the world. It is as if the senses were tuned louder, stronger, higher, and so the task becomes to communicate the experience of both pain and joy. The creative person's products become consumable commodities for the public, but these very products are the stuff of life for the creative person. What John Gardner called a "fishing trip with Uncle Ralph" becomes the epitome of fishing trips, and "Big Two-Hearted River" is born, at the expense of excruciating pain for the writer, the pain of self-revelation, and of immense power and joy, the power and joy of saying something that makes people say, "Yes, that's true. That's true."

A Sense of Humor

I am including a discussion of what it means to have a sense of humor within this chapter on creative writers, because humor is essentially verbal talent. While there are physical humorists such as Jerry Lewis or the Three Stooges, they are actors, using their bodies; actors and dancers, the physically talented, are covered in Chapter 10.

Most checklists for academic talent and for creativity include an item, "Shows a sense of humor." Teachers are asked to check whether a potentially creatively or intellectually talented child has a sense of humor. This is a ridiculously-phrased screening question, since every child has a sense of humor, a sort of compass that points out what's funny. (And every adult has a sense of humor, too.) What the checklists seem to be getting at is whether or not the child has a highly developed sense of humor, or a sense of humor that is more mature than that of others of the same age.

Humor is developmental and cultural. What we laugh at in our society is not what is laughed at in another society, and if we went to a comedy club in Japan or India we would probably not laugh; we would miss the point, even if we could understand the language, for humor—especially stand-up comedy, written humor and political cartoons—often relies on idioms of the language. When we learn a foreign language, the idioms are the most difficult to master. Any society's humorists are often not understood in another country or society, even if they speak the same language. When we say that a mark of academic talent or creativity is having a sense of humor, we probably mean that the child has advanced verbal development and can appreciate and understand humor that older children understand.

Many of the admired humorists in our society have been writers even if they also performed as comedians: Mark Twain, James Thurber, E.B. White, Tom Wolfe, Damon Runyon, Groucho Marx, Kurt Vonnegut, Jr., Dave Barry, Joseph Heller, Roy Blount, Jr., Calvin Trillin, Garrison Keillor, Erma Bombeck, Steve Allen, and Woody Allen are examples. Comedians who have not been writers have hired writers to make their humor come alive in language.

Humor, distinguishable from jokes and comedy, is what helps people cope with incongruities and maintain balance in situations that are threatening and dangerous. Chafe labeled humor a "disabling mechanism" that works in two ways. "First, the very act of laughter disables us, and we are unable to do anything else while laughing—we can't do push-ups and we can't run and we can't read and we can't talk." Secondarily, the act of laughing is so pleasurable that we seek it out by attending shows where people we consider humorous are performing, or we attend movies starring our favorite funny people, or we watch television sitcoms. We enjoy being around people who make us laugh.

We prefer different types of humor. Some people like joke-cracking physical humor and practical jokes; others like witty satire. We also have preferences about jokes. The best-selling book by talk-show hostess Rosie O'Donnell of jokes children sent her contains many knock knock jokes and others that show the developmental level of humor. I sometimes stand helplessly trapped while the office "joker" tells me a joke that "rolled 'em on the floor" at the Elks Club. I giggle politely and leave. Later, curled up with a Thurber anthology, I choke with laughter over the story about the banquet speaker.

Chafe pointed out that humor helps us deal with taboo topics in a socially acceptable way, thereby disabling us in a second way: mentally. Jokes make explicit the contexts and definitions of words and symbols and help us to see the ambiguities. To "get" a joke in any culture demands a dense schema, a high ability to play with meanings of words. That is perhaps why "sense of humor" appears on checklists. We have noticed the verbal ability of young high IQ children, and "sense of humor" is another way to emphasize the verbal content. Therefore, I propose we take "sense of humor" off our creativity checklists and substitute something more specific. For example, "has dense verbal schema and so can make puns, jokes, analogies, that are humorous." Or, "Has a sense of humor that is verbally advanced for his age."

Summary

This is what we know about creative writers:
1. They are often early readers.
2. They have often experienced childhood trauma and may suffer from depression.
3. They used early reading and writing to escape.
4. They have high conceptual and verbal intelligence.
5. They are independent, nonconforming, and not interested in joining groups.
6. They value self-expression and are productive.
7. They are often driven, able to take rejection, and like to work alone for long periods of time.
8. They often have difficulty with alcohol.
9. They prefer writing as their mode of expression of emotions and feelings.
10. They often have advanced verbal senses of humor.

Chapter 7

Creative Writers: Children with Extraordinary Writing Talent

Sweet aromas fill the stallion's heart
Eyes of blue, hide of white
Glimmering with its sweat
On the run, under burning sun.
As quick as a shimmering, sunny stream.
Panting wildly, wildly panting
Suede rabbit hops in its way.

—nine-year-old girl

Music . . . the most amazing thing about music is that you can't describe the tonal quality of a sound. Before you say anything, make sure you're not giving me any of that scientific stuff about waveforms, attacks, decays, sustains, and releases. A sound is relative to the ear, and those words are relative to an idea a computer showed a bunch of scientists who don't even know how to carry a tune . . .
—eleven-year-old boy

This chapter continues the study of writers, but with an emphasis on children. Little work has been done on the juvenilia of eminent writers, and in fact little work has been done on the quality of youthful creative production in most of the arts. In particular, there is sparse analysis of what makes children's writing good, with the consequence that much excellent work goes unmarked as such. Parents or teachers may say to a youngster, "Oh, that's a very nice poem!" without knowing or appreciating the aspects of the writing that make it truly remarkable. Hence I believe that writing prodigy occurs more frequently than is commonly thought.

The material presented in this chapter comes from two areas of study. The first is my examination of the writings, partially presented here, of seven children: four were selected from 400 students in a Manhattan school for high IQ children, where the mean IQ was 140+; and three were brought to my attention by professional writers, parents, or administrators. From these writers, as well as from many years' observations, I have generated sixteen characteristics of quality juvenile writing. Secondly, I have also studied childhood biographies of well-known authors, to determine, if possible, the early situational factors that lead to success as an adult writer. Parts of this study have been published in 1989 and 1991.

What exactly is a child prodigy? In *Nature's Gambit*, David Feldman asserted that the youthful talents of child prodigies emerge with the "fortuitous convergence of highly specific individual proclivities with specific environmental receptivity." In other words, a child prodigy gets that way through the extremely lucky combination of a very strong inner impulse toward an activity, and an environment that is supportive. For his six case studies, Feldman defined "prodigy" as a child of ten or younger who produced work on the level of an adult professional. A conflicting definition is proposed by Radford in *Child Prodigies and Exceptional Early Achievers*: prodigies may be older than ten and their achievements need not have "lasting merit." He said, "Indeed, if the work of children is always to be measured against the highest adult standards, there would probably be none who could be called prodigies at all." However, *The Random House Dictionary of English Language* defines a prodigy simply as "a child or young person having extraordinary talent or ability."

For Feldman, with his emphasis on environment and the fortuitous, the prodigy phenomenon is obviously more than just an effect of high IQ or of special neurological makeup, as in the case of idiots savants; rather, prodigies are those who manifest high ability in one specialized field of intellectual development. The three disciplines in which prodigies most frequently occur are mathematics, chess, and music. Most prodigies are found in music and in chess, fewer in mathematics, fewer still in art, and very few in writing. Feldman, who studied only one writing prodigy, asserted the following:

> For the most part, writing is not a domain where prodigious achievement occurs. Serious child writers are uncommon for at least two reasons. The field itself has few organized supports or strategies for instruction in the craft . . . [and] child

writers may be rare because children normally lack the kind of experience, insight, and understanding that writers are expected to convey in their works.

However, my data conflict with Feldman's; there are more children than Feldman thought who write at an adult level of competence. I have come into contact with such children in the course of my work in the schools, as have many of my colleagues, both writers and teachers. The following poem was written by a nine-year-old girl enrolled in a school for high-IQ children, but her ability far surpassed those of her peers. A letter from her mother in 1995 said she had graduated from high school, where she had been editor of the paper, and was now writing novels and continuing with her voracious reading.

> Sweet aromas fill the stallion's heart
> Eyes of blue, hide of white
> Glimmering with its sweat
> On the run, under burning sun.
> As quick as a shimmering, sunny stream.
> Panting wildly, wildly panting
> Suede rabbit hops in its way.

This poem illustrates unusual linguistic precociousness in the repetition of consonant and vowel sounds (assonance and consonance), the sophisticated rhythms ("Eyes of blue, hide of white" / "on the run, under burning sun;" "Panting wildly, wildly panting;" the improbable images ("suede"). "Sweet aromas" in the horse's heart creates an initial paradox. It is not logical that there would be aromas in a horse's heart, but this girl pays no attention to the logic. The second line uses the repetitive device of parallel structure to create a rhythm. The third line sets up a visual image that is answered in line five—"glimmering" and "shimmering." In the fourth line, the letters r, u, and n are repeated in various melodic combinations: "run," "under," "burning;" then "run" resolves into "sun," which is repeated in the next line, in an alliterative phrase, "shimmering sunny stream." The urgency of the reversed phrases in the fifth line, "panting wildly, wildly panting," keeps the excitement of the poem. Then, when a suede rabbit hops, we can feel the danger inherent in that ordinary situation. The word "suede" is unusual, in no way the typical cliché in rabbit description.

After looking at such children's writing, I have listed sixteen qualities their work often shows:

Qualities Found in the Writing of Children Who Display Extraordinary Talent

1. The use of paradox
2. The use of parallel structure
3. The use of rhythm
4. The use of visual imagery
5. Unusual melodic combinations
6. Unusual use of figures of speech–alliteration, personification, assonance
7. Confidence with reverse structure
8. Unusual adjectives and adverbs
9. A feeling of movement
10. Uncanny wisdom
11. Sophisticated syntax—hyphens, parentheses, appositive
12. Prose lyricism
13. Displaying a natural ear for language
14. Sense of humor
15. Philosophical or moral bent
16. A willingness to play with words

Here are six haikus. Three are by an adult professional, and three are by a child. Can you tell whose is whose? The young poet was featured on an episode of *Nova* called "Child's Play," in 1984, when she was eight years old and in second grade. The adult professional is Bernard Einbond, a professor of literature who in 1988 won the Japan Airlines Haiku contest over thousands of entries. His haikus below are taken from *The Coming Indoors and Other Poems*.

Treading glory lane
To see it end in flood
Or go up in flame

Delectable crumb—
the quickness of a sparrow—
indignant pigeon.

At day's end, straying
the ocean's edge, tang
salt on my lips.

Tides of the ocean long
serving the moon's every whim of
leaving skeletons.

In the crowded train,
two women seated apart
who must be sisters.

Words without meaning
Rebel without a cause
Constant paradox.

The child wrote these: Tread glory lane, At days end, straying, and Words without meaning.

Let's take a few more examples from children in New York City, Ohio, Michigan, and New Jersey. Some of the writings were sent to me, some I discovered, and some were shown to me by teachers, parents, and professional writers. The children were Caucasian, Asian, Hispanic, and African American, girls and boys, though mostly girls. (In contrast to my gender study, Feldman's finds boys are more often identified as prodigies, most likely for reasons of cultural selection and support.)

The next poem, by a six-year-old, was given to me by her mother when I did a workshop in New Jersey. The girl wrote it while riding in a car during a rainstorm.

Ripples of Liquid Caterpillars
Ripples of liquid caterpillars
Roll down my window
They travel slowly
Shedding old transparent skins
How sad
They will not stop long enough
To want to see
Their winged reflections
In the sunshine.

This poignant reflection, with its automatic repetitions of the letters I, l, r, s, t, and o, uses a logic that is also paradoxical. It is not that they won't see their winged reflections, but that they will not want to see them. And how did caterpillars turn into butterflies in just the length of a rainstorm? The meditative, almost-Buddhist quality of the poem should not go unnoticed, either.

Here is another example by the girl who wrote the haikus, written when she was nine:

Star Poem
I am picked up by a star
And flung on to Saturn's turning ring
The star begins to throb
And turns bright red.
All the heavenly bodies turn to fire.
They are rejoicing in the birth of a sunset.
The stars toss me into the sunset.
It is a joy,

It contains all the dreams
People will dream tonight.
A sunset is a dream keeper.

The movement in this poem—the flinging, tossing, turning, throbbing, picking up—is immediately evident. The attributing to the star of an ability to pick someone up is an unusual personification. Usually children's personification takes the form of animals becoming people. The rings and stars and heavenly bodies and sunsets are all in the skies, evocative of the dream being portrayed here. The progression from beginning to end of this work, from being picked up by a star, being flung onto a ring of Saturn, being witness to a sunset being born, and then being tossed into that sunset, which paradoxically keeps the dreams of people, is reminiscent of the wisdom of the psalmists.

The next two examples, given to me by a writer from Teachers and Writers Collaborative in New York City, were written by a junior high school boy from a poverty-stricken area in the South Bronx:

Expression
A comedy of errors,
throughout changing time
you live. Die all in one maze
you run, hide still it all ends
the same. Life is an everchanging
play that blossoms and closes
then dies.
Just a comedy of errors,
Forever a comedy.

Sin-Eater
A clear pure soul of simple logic.
You milk the moment,
Taking a deliberate pace of time.
You don't seem to quit as
You pull the trigger.
He's dead. You're glad. It's
over. You touch him.
Blood smears your fingers.
Running crazy, you feel a sharp pain.
It skips through your mind,

You forget. You're in a war.
You're dead. Simple, isn't it

Again, these poems show a sense of music and rhythm, of heard phrases turned upon themselves in different contexts, of macabre details (common among junior high boys), perhaps a reflection of the circumstances in which the boy finds himself in his neighborhood. But the talent is evident: "clear pure soul of simple logic" stands out as a measured musical phrase. The use of "a deliberate pace" in reference to time and not to walking shows that the writer has absorbed and heard the common language and is able to put it into an artistic context. The echo of "a poor player that struts and frets his hour upon the stage" is heard in the writer's "Life is an everchanging / play that blossoms and closes / then dies."Above all, these poems show a natural ear for language that makes this boy's poetry stand out as exceptional in the context of his classmates whose poems in the anthology are typical of children's poems.

Here is another example by an eight-year-old girl:

Colorful Wildlife
Colorful wildlife is a beautiful violet sun
covering the earth with warm rays.
Wild sweet music all at once.
It is really Phasiphe.
Love, love all around.
Phasiphe Phasiphe Phasiphe
All Phasiphe

This poem was written spontaneously, in response to a jar in the Metropolitan Museum of Art. What stands out about it is the repetition of the word "Phasiphe." The child demonstrates a sense of playfulness with an intriguing word. The willingness to play with words and a joy in pure sound is a mark of all writers, especially poets. This girl early shows such a joy—and a fearlessness. She doesn't know what Phasiphe means, but she is willing to ascribe adjectival powers to the word.

Prose Talent

What about prose? Does extraordinary talent exist among child writers of prose? If so, what are the characteristics of such writing? On my first day on the job as a coordinator for gifted programs, a principal came to me with the following composition and asked that most common question: "Do you think this child is gifted?" I did indeed. This reminiscence was written by an eight-year-old from a small rural town in northwest Ohio.

The Dog Who Stayed with Me

Jimmy, me, and Carol were excited today. It was time to meet under my apple tree. We often, after we met, played in the empty house next door (which was for sale), and brought Teddy to play too. It was one Sunday morning, a chilly one, too. We hardly met that day. But we met inside my house instead of under the frozen, cold apple-tree, pale blue frozen sky, cold icicles of sun falling on us. We were very chilly as we instead went into the empty house with Teddy, who was kept overnight by Carol. "Rudy!" Ma yelled at me, "Get away. Here comes the moving truck." I didn't have time to ask questions. I just ran in to get Teddy if dad meant moving in the empty house. Carol said, "Rudy! Look!" A little setter, just a baby, leaped out of the car (behind the moving truck) and ran to my arms. "Why, hello, there!" Carol said, scratching the setter puppy's red-shining back, "Rudy, ball time!" I chattered my teeth, as another sun-icicle fell on my head. The wind furiously blew, and almost knocked the puppy out of my arms. "Come on," puppy!" and I tried to run without jolting the puppy. But I was so cold I couldn't help it. "Rudalas, come!" Dad yelled, and he saw the puppy. "Bring it in, but hurry!" I flung open the door and put the setter down upstairs in my warm bedroom. I ran downstairs, and the puppy followed. I got some meat scraps and a small, low bowl of milk. I teased him and held out the meat. He didn't need teasing, though. He followed me anyway. "Come on, Caboose." I began to call him Caboose. "Little Red Caboose," I often said. He followed me like a caboose and was fed. I went to bed, and below my bed I heard Caboose lapping up the milk and snapping the meat. I fell asleep at last, for Caboose's lullaby of panting was wonderful. His panting was like a lullaby. Next morning was school. I flung up my coat, and caught it. Last of all, I patted Caboose. But every time I turned my back, he whined. He leaped up and followed me. I didn't even know until I entered the school, for the marble-tile on the halls made Caboose's

> claws go click, click. When I got to school, Mrs. Dainty, my fourth grade teacher, just about died. "Don't you ever bring pets to school without my permission," she said.

This prose piece by an eight-year-old displays remarkable use of syntax. The sentence, "We often, after we met," shows an understanding of grammatical apposition. The use of parentheses, as in (which was for sale) and (behind the moving truck), is unusual. The use of the hyphen in the words "apple-tree, "red-shining back," and "marble-tile" also is unusual. These words may or may not be hyphenated in common usage, and in fact their hyphenation suggests that the writer has read prose works where the hyphen, the parenthesis, and the use of apposition is common. Perhaps nineteenth century or early twentieth-century novels? The lyricism of the child—"under the frozen, cold apple-tree, pale blue frozen sky, cold icicles of sun falling on us," and "lullaby of panting,"—is adult in quality. Many adult professional writers strive for such lyricism, whereas this child, composing this piece after church and before dinner, effortlessly wrote this way. "I chattered my teeth" again suggests that she knows that teeth chatter, but not that they do so by themselves. The "lapping" and "snapping" of the dog show a sense of parallel structure and prose rhyme.

The next prose piece is mature in subject matter and shows a remarkable sophistication. An entire third grade class of verbally talented students wrote novels, but this nine-year-old girls' stood out. When I asked her for permission to use her story in this book, she assented, with reservations: she thought this piece was too childish. I disagreed.

> Petrova Polinski was a thirty-seven year old Russian immigrant to America. She was poor and depressed. She had black hair and eyes and wasn't really short or tall. There were always rings of weariness from hard work under her eyes. Her situation was like that of a tiny weather beaten rowboat in the middle of a raging storm, far from any help. Her pathetic sighs of self pity made you feel very sorry for her and her family. Now that she, Petrova Polinski, had actually COME to America, she wished she was back in Russia. Everybody back home had said that in America the streets were paved with gold. Instead they were paved with sweat, hard work, and poverty. She hardly spoke her language and didn't read or write it either. She could only pin her hopes of a better life on

her children, of whom there were five. She sighed and then
her baby cried. Then she sank into a shabby chair with stuffing protruding from beneath the cover and closed her eyes.

The baby wailed again. Suddenly she jumped up and went
over to the cupboard, took out the last crust of bread, threw it
at the baby and screamed, "THERE! Now eat it!" She walked
back to her chair, sank down and began to reflect on her situation again. Why was it that some people, no matter how hard
they worked, never had any money? Why was it that people
who never worked were so rich? If He (God) was really there,
then why didn't He give them a good life? She was beginning
not to believe in Him. It wasn't fair. She never had a moment
to rest. And why didn't her husband at least DO something?

Then came the voice of her six-year-old daughter Olga.
"Mama, Papa's coming home. Let me help you get dinner.
Papa'll be hungry."

This story goes on about Petrova and her family, but already, in its first few
lines, one can see the maturity of the writer, in both style and substance. "Her
situation was like that of a tiny weather-beaten rowboat in the middle of a rag-
ing storm, far from any help. Her pathetic sighs of self pity . . ." And again,
in the narrator's wondering about why some people are poor and some are
rich, and why hard work doesn't pay, the nine-year-old author is asking questions great novelists have struggled with, from Tolstoy to Roth. This child's
work showed the frankness and concern with moral questions that writers are
known for, so it was no surprise when she was chosen to be a child reporter
during the 1988 presidential campaign. I turned on my television one
Saturday, and saw her on national television addressing Dan Quayle: "You
mean that if my father raped me and I got pregnant, you wouldn't let me get
an abortion?" Quayle sputtered in amazement.

Another characteristic of good literature that is most difficult for children
is uncanny wisdom. This is the quality that we look for in the literature that
we read, and its lack is the reason that we usually don't give credence to literature by children. What wisdom can children have? Wisdom is acquired by
experience. The subject matter of the poems and stories by children is usually childlike. The plots of the stories are predictable, with space ships for the
boys and mysteries for the girls. There are monsters and fantasies. The poems
are also about the concerns of the children writing them. Maturity is essential
in literary quality. No Nobel Prize for literature will, nor should, go to a child,

or even a young adult of prodigious talent. But talent does exist, and sometimes children display wisdom not won by age. Observe the following excerpts from essays by an eleven-year-old boy in my writing group. This sixth grader's extraordinary writing talent had been recognized by his teachers since second grade. He is a polymath, also a talented composer and musician. When I said I wanted to use these excerpts in a talk I was giving, he said he had changed his opinions in the meantime, but I was welcome to use them.

Philosophy

If I could put a Bronx cheer on paper, I would. Philosophy is a fake. It's just a bunch of ordinary people capitalizing words and writing theories about things they know nothing about. Sometimes I make up theories. I spend a lot of time with them and play around with them, but I keep forgetting them and they will never get on paper.

Actually, I do remember one faintly, about the universe as a constantly changing picture God wants to frame in his living room. When everybody in the whole universe is doing the right thing, the picture will stop moving, and God will go and buy a frame, and put it upon his wall. If you find this theory interesting, you are probably the kind of person who sits in his or her room and reads German epic poetry.

Music

. . . the most amazing thing about music is that you can't describe the tonal quality of a sound. Before you say anything, make sure you're not giving me any of that scientific stuff about waveforms, attacks, decays, sustains, and releases. A sound is relative to the ear, and those words are relative to an idea a computer showed a bunch of scientists who don't even know how to carry a tune . . .

Lyrics

Before I tell you anything, I have to tell you something. From where I see it, there are two kinds of writing. The first is the kind I like, which is in fact writing as if you were speaking. The second kind would be prose or verse following a rigid structure, using fancy words and stuff.

Lyrics are the other kind of writing in its extreme form and in verse. I admire good lyricists because I cannot write verse at all, let alone using fancy words . . . Good lyrics depend on the type of music they are sung to. For example, if I was commissioned to write lyrics for a country or folk tune, I'd write simple-minded lyrics.

Sometimes wonderful lyrics are ruined by the type of music they are sung to: Here's a song everybody knows: "Row, row, row your boat / Gently down the stream, / Merrily, merrily, merrily, merrily / Life is but a dream." Now take a closer look at these lyrics and absorb what they mean. See what I mean? They are beautiful lyrics. It's the music that makes them corny.

Bugs

Bugs are the most annoying things on the face of this earth. Sometimes I think bugs just spend the winter thinking of gross things they can do to me. Once when I was about 5.33333333 1/3, I was walking near my country house or someplace that had a lot of bugs. Without warning, those disgusting tiny green aphids or gnats or something made a beeline for my eyes and I was rubbing them out for the rest of the week. I used to have brown eyes. I'm not kidding . . . Since God made more insects than humans in this world, we can conclude that He meant for them to be the dominant species. Therefore, I believe that we should honor the bugs by giving them the entire turnip and spinach crop every year.

These extraordinary diary entries show not only wisdom but humor. A sense of humor is one of the marks of the verbally advanced child. (see Chapter 6)

Predictive Behaviors in Children with Writing Talent

What predictive behaviors do children with such talent have in common? I have surveyed published adult poets and unpublished young poets about their youth and have found that they all read—a lot; that their parents read to them—a lot; that they admired words and expression by words. One nine-year-old girl said that writing "is a sometimes better way to express feelings, than words and actions. It also helps me to think logically." I also found that they read early. Research on early readers has shown that they have parents who answered their questions, who spent much time with them, reading to them, and who were readers themselves (Roedell, Jackson, and Robinson, 1980). One of the girls, age nine, said that her mother was now reading Shakespeare with her—"the real stuff and not the watered-down stuff."

I have a hunch that further study of the Dabrowski theory's overexcitabilities by Piechowski and his colleagues will show that writers engage the written word with an intensity that is often interactive, almost physical. One example is a young writer in our study of creative adolescents, who spoke out loud to the characters when reading an exciting book. Another example is from Green's *Diary*, where he described Andre Gide reading from *Solugub*: "His voice reminds one of a bird of prey; it suddenly pounces on a word, swoops off with it, and feasts on it. Then he lowers his book and smiles as though he had really eaten something delicious."

Whether or not these young writers will become well-known novelists, poets, essayists, is impossible to say. Few well-known child prodigies become adult geniuses. Mozart is an exception. The sun of chance plays a large part in the flowering of creativity, as well as in the honoring and rewarding of it. It is precisely because we cannot predict which child will be of great benefit to society as an adult artist that we must nurture the talents of all talented children.

Bloom, in *Developing Talent in Young People*, noted that talented children who become successful adult professionals study their field to the point of "automaticity." Musicians practice, athletes practice, mathematicians practice, chess players practice, all to acquire higher and higher levels of performance that become automatic. The notion that prodigy springs full-blown without specific practice in the field is false. Idiot savantism may do so, but not prodigy. However, the practice must soon come from interest, engagement, and motivation on the part of the young talented person. Being forced to practice only works until the practice takes hold. This is true in other fields as well: the tennis champion Andre Agassiz's father, a tennis coach, insisted that Agassiz serve thousands of balls per day, seven days per week. Tiger Woods began to notice and focus on golf while still in his high chair; his parents then put a golf ball in his crib so he could swat at it, developing hand-eye coordination. Perhaps writers practice the use of words and thus develop automaticity when they are read to and when they read, as well as when they write. Parents often nurture and direct their children in the fields in which the parents themselves have interest and talent. The talented child is then taught by a teacher, who passes on what knowledge he or she can, and then the teacher passes the child to another, more masterful, teacher. That is the path of talent development and of prodigy.

On the other hand, some thinkers such as Chomsky, Jung, Roszak, Hillman, and Bloom have postulated that this early mastery in prodigies is a knowledge of form that has come about through intuition, or through archetypal or innate knowledge, or even through reincarnation. In their adolescent years, spontaneity in young writers often gives way to conformity. But, as studies from Galton's *Hereditary Genius* to the present have shown, some writers come from "eminent" families who themselves are erudite, extremely literate, and encouraging, or at least tolerant of the voluminous reading these writers did in childhood. It is also true that some writers came from unerudite families, and in fact, the Goertzels found that only one adult poet who had had a biography written about him had a parent who was a poet. Allen Ginsberg would have been another; Ginsberg's father was the poet Louis Ginsberg, who was also a high school teacher.

In adolescence, potential writers should acquire the knowledge that they need—being "divergent producers," they now become the necessary "convergent producers." Adolescence is a stage of life that all people, creative or not, talented or not, must go through. In youngsters with writing talent, the compulsive reading usually continues, and the study of literary works becomes more formalized as they approach adulthood. Young adult writers become older adult writers, and their wisdom and experience become part of the literature they create. That is the good thing about literary talent. Precocity or prodigy is not necessary for adult achievement, since most literary achievers continue writing throughout their lives, though precocity or prodigy is often predictive, as the biographies of writers tell us.

Bamberger in a 1986 essay discussed the development of young musicians. She observed a self-conscious stage, a "midlife crisis" through which young musicians must pass if they are to progress from "early prodigiousness to adult artistry." Many factors may enter in, including a dislike of practice, caring too much what others think, and having too many other activities. Csikszentmihalyi, Rathunde, and Whalen, in *Talented Teens,* noted that students who continued with their talent areas were often not sexually active, did not have part-time jobs, had a small group of friends with the same interests, and did not mind spending time alone. To pass through the midlife crisis of adolescence also requires a regular return to the pleasurable state of trancelike concentration, or "flow," while doing the work. Since reading is the activity that most people mention as producing flow, young writers may not be at such great risk as students in other domains.

Famous Writers As Children

I do not remember when I could not read.
—Benjamin Franklin

There were books in the study, books in the drawing room, books in the cloak-room, books (two deep) in the great bookcase on the landing, books in a bed-room, books piled as high as my shoulder in the cistern attic, books of all kinds reflecting every transient stage of my parents' interest, books readable and unreadable, books suitable for a child and books most emphatically not. Nothing was forbidden me.
—C.S. Lewis

Will these writing talents become manifest as the children reach adulthood? Working backwards, I asked the question, what were famous writers like as children? What was their interaction with the written word? A look at the juvenilia and early life of a sample of prominent writers, using a biographical approach, is illustrative that many prominent writers wrote and read young.

George Eliot

In *George Eliot's Life as Related in Her Letters and Journals*, Cross in 1903 described her father, a strong, powerful, middle-aged man, sitting in his leather chair with his six-year-old daughter. "The child turns over the book with pictures that she wishes her father to explain to her—or that perhaps she prefers explaining to him." There was little children's literature in their home, but Mary Ann Evans (George Eliot) recalled "her passionate delight and total absorption in *Aesop's Fables* . . . the possession of which had opened new worlds to her imagination." When she went to school at eight, "she read everything she could lay hands on, greatly troubling the soul of her mother by the consumption of candles as well as of eyesight in her bedroom." One book had to be returned before she could read it to the end, and she wrote the rest of the story out for herself. This is one example of the delight that young writers take in the act of reading.

Stephen Crane

Stephen Crane began work as a journalist at the age of fifteen, writing legibly and fast because the salary of a compositor depended on speed and legibility. Berryman's 1950 biography, *Stephen Crane*, noted that Crane's mother "encouraged the boy's reading with worthy narratives like the Rev. James Dixon's tour of America," while his sister, a schoolteacher, gave him a more "rakish" book called *Sir Wilfred's Seven Flights*. His sister had a great desire to write, and she encouraged him: "From his dissertation at eight on Little Goodie Brighteyes she followed his stories and verses with pride for four years." Crane devoured Westerns, war books, the Frank series, and other paperbacks. He led his gang in play based on the stories in the books. He attended college for only one year; Berryman said that the extent and breadth of his reading has been understated.

Jane Austen

Jane Austen, unlike most children in Georgian England, grew up in a home that had no restrictions on reading or on the subject matters of conversations. Her earliest writings were parodies and satires, and her satirical slant pervaded all of her work later on. Halperin, in his 1986 biography, *The Life of Jane Austen,* counted that her juvenilia total about 90,000 words, all mostly written to amuse her younger brother, Charles, and her older brother Frank, away in the Navy. The juvenilia illustrate that Austen was, even as a young girl, well-read. "Richardson was her favourite novelist, and she knew his works intimately, but she read all the fiction she could get her hands on."

Sinclair Lewis

Sinclair Lewis was the son of a doctor in Minnesota. Shorer's 1961 biography, *Sinclair Lewis*, noted that there were about 300 books in the house, including Scott, Dickens, Goethe, Milton, Beattie, Collins, Gray, and Young. These books "formed the boy's earliest literary preferences and the subjects for his reverie." Lewis graduated from grammar school seventeenth in a class of eighteen; he was poor at spelling and handwriting. By his junior year in high school, he had started his diaries and was an "omnivorous, unsystematic reader." He opened the diary with a list of books, about fifty of them, that he had read during the summer, including Kipling, Thackeray, George Eliot, Victor Hugo, and "trash," as Schorer called it. He read "continually and often guiltily ('Wasted a lot of time reading tonight' is a kind of refrain in the diary during the high-school years)."

Dylan Thomas

Fitzgibbon, in his 1965 biography, *The Life of Dylan Thomas*, said that Thomas taught himself to read from comic books. When he was four, his father, a schoolteacher, used to read him Shakespeare. Thomas's mother used to tell him not to read Shakespeare to a little child, and the elder Thomas would say, "He'll understand it. It'll be just the same as if I were reading ordinary things."

His sister said, "He wrote a poem, a most interesting little poem, about the kitchen sink. And then another about an onion. That kind of thing."

Thomas Wolfe

Nowell, in his 1960 biography, *Thomas Wolfe,* noted that Wolfe attributed his becoming a writer to a great urge within him, nurtured by his father, a stonecutter with "great respect and veneration for literature." (Once again, observe the prodigy-producing phenomenon of "highly specific individual proclivities with specific environmental receptivity" described by Feldman.) His father had a very good memory, reciting such works as Hamlet's Soliloquy, Macbeth, Mark Antony's Funeral Oration, and Gray's "Elegy." Wolfe was also a great reader as a child. Between five and eleven he read every book in the public library of their small town.

Virginia Woolf

Virginia Woolf's literary family is well known. When she was a child of nine she produced a newspaper called *The Hyde Park Gate News*, illustrated by her sister, Vanessa. The two Stephens sisters read books aloud to each other, then reviewed the books in the newspaper; with childlike fascination they included in their reviews the number of deaths in each story. Their reading material included Thackeray, Richardson, Eliot, and most of the Victorian writers. Virginia was avid for praise from her parents; their "Rather clever, I think," overjoyed her. The children produced this newspaper well into their teenage years. But by then, "the charm and fun of the earlier numbers has evaporated. Occasionally a phrase, a joke, a turn of speech anticipates her adult style; but the general impression is rather flat," according to Bell, in his 1972 *Virginia Woolf.* Bell noted that Woolf changed as she entered adolescence: "She is still writing for an adult audience; but now she has reached a self-conscious age and plays for safety."

Tennessee Williams

Spoto, in his 1985 biography, *The Kindness of Strangers*, noted that Tennessee Williams' mother read stories, plays, acted out tall tales, recited Scottish and English ballads, told stories about folk heroes such as Annie Oakley and Davy Crockett, and sang hymns to her children. Bible tales were told by neighbors. The black maid sang spirituals, hymns, and lullabies. He soon began making up his own stories. He was small and sickly and teased by the children at school, and solitary reading became his refuge. By the time he was nine, he had read at least two of Dickens's books, some of Scott's Waverly novels, and some Shakespeare. A few years later his mother bought him a typewriter, and he began to write poems, stories, and articles. His junior high school newspaper published many of these. He also contributed to his high school newspaper and yearbook. His grades were average, but he was already entering literary contests.

The Brontë Family

The Brontë family—Emily, Charlotte, and their less famous brother and sister, Quentin and Vanessa—created little books that were written beneath magnifying glasses, in an invented language known only to them. These long sagas told tales of fantasy, a genre then, as now, of great interest to children. The Brontës all became adult writers of various degrees of success. Their early interest in books and writing seems typical in the lives of writers, as does their early, intense interest in reading. Radford discussed the early lives of Alexander Pope, Samuel Johnson, Thomas Chatterton, and Daisy Ashford (who wrote a critically acclaimed novel, in 1890, at nine, and stopped producing at thirteen), and their early interaction with books was also apparent.

Harry Crews

The writer Harry Crews, who grew up in a sharecropper family in abject poverty, also interacted with books, but his book was the Sears Roebuck catalog. He would look at the "Wish Book" and make up stories about the "perfect" people there, telling the stories to his cousin. In his book *A Childhood*, excerpted in the 1987 anthology *American Childhoods*, Crews wrote that "fabrication became a way of life," and he described how these stories helped him "understand the way we lived" and helped him form a defense against it. His imaginative life as a child "was no doubt the first step in a life devoted primarily to men and women and children who never lived anywhere but in my imagination. I have found in them infinitely more order and beauty and satisfaction than I ever have in the people who move about me in the real world."

John Updike and C.S. Lewis

Besides a childhood environment filled with books and words, health factors can affect whether a person becomes a writer. The winner of the Pulitzer Prize in 1982 for *Rabbit Is Rich* and in 1991 for *Rabbit At Rest*, Updike is a prolific novelist, essayist, reviewer, and poet. An only child, the son of a high school teacher (many creative adults have teacher-parents) and of a writer mother whose typewriter clacking in the living room was one of the sounds of his childhood, Updike as a child suffered from stuttering and psoriasis. Of the influence of the psoriasis on his writing, Updike said, in his 1989 memoir, *Self-Consciousness*:

> Only psoriasis could have taken a very average little boy, and furthermore, a boy who loved the average, the daily, the safely hidden, and made him into a prolific, adaptable, ruthless-enough writer. What was my creativity, my relentless need to produce, but a parody of my skin's embarrassing overproduction? Was not my thick literary skin, which shrugged off rejection slips and patronizing reviews by the sheaf, a superior version of my poor vulnerable own, and my shamelessness on the page a distraction from my real shame?

The stuttering made him careful of his spoken words, and so he poured his thoughts out on paper. He called his stuttering "this anxious guilty blockage of the throat," and said that despite the impediment, he has "managed to maneuver several millions of words around it." His amazing productivity was detailed in Chapter 6.

C.S. Lewis also suffered from a physical disability that he called "extreme manual clumsiness" in his 1955 memoir, *Surprised by Joy*:

> What drove me to write was the extreme manual clumsiness from which I have always suffered. I attribute it to a physical defect which my brother and I both inherit from our father; we have only one joint in the thumb. The upper joint (that furthest from the nail) is visible, but it is a mere sham; we cannot bend

> it. But whatever the cause, nature laid on me from birth an
> utter incapacity to make anything. With pencil and pen I was
> handy enough . . . but with a tool or a bat or a gun, a sleeve
> link or corkscrew, I have always been unteachable. It was this
> that forced me to write. I longed to make things, ships, hous-
> es, engines. Many sheets of cardboard and pairs of scissors I
> spoiled, only to turn from my hopeless failures in tears. As a
> last resource . . . I was driven to write stories instead; little
> dreaming to what a world of happiness I was being admitted.
> You can do more with a castle in a story than with the best
> cardboard castle that ever stood on a nursery table.

Another reason that young writers write was pointed out by Updike. He said that
it was the thought of his words in print that motivated him: "To be in print was
to be saved." Updike, like most young writers, spent "dreamless endless solitary
afternoons" reading nineteenth century novels, books of humor, and mysteries.
He did not recall that his reading interfered with his social or academic life, and
he graduated president of his small-town Pennsylvania high school class with a
scholarship to Harvard, even with the stuttering and the psoriasis. Lewis, also,
spent "endless rainy afternoons" reading, taking "volume after volume from the
shelves. I had always the same certainty of finding a book that was new to me
as a man who walks into a field has of finding a new blade of grass."

Graham Greene

Graham Greene's childhood is a good illustration of the high emotionality and
strong imagination that incipient writers show. He liked to be sick, and his
biographer Norman Sherry, in the 1989 Volume I of *The Life of Graham
Greene*, revealed: "Minor ailments pleased him for they confined him to bed
and brought him a sense of peace, endless time, and a night-light burning in
his bedroom, a feeling of security." He had fears of darkness, of bats, of the
footsteps of strangers, of drowning, and of touching the feathers of birds. All
of these appear in his novels. This "sensitivity toward animate and inanimate
nature was apparent when Greene was only four years old."

Even though he grew up in a large family with older brothers, younger
sisters and relatives and servants about, Greene as a child stayed a loner, a
secretive child who kept his terrors to himself. When he was seven, he discovered he could read: the book was *Dixon Breet, Detective*. He didn't want anyone to know, so he read the book in the attic. His parents thought he couldn't

read and were concerned, all the more so since the child was unwilling to read basal textbooks, such books as *Reading Without Tears*, with their childish approach to reading. But from *Dixon Breet* on, Greene read "with absorption and intelligence." He read widely and said that one of the advantages of being the headmaster's son was that during holidays he could read from the many books in the school library.

Greene said that only in childhood does reading have a "powerful influence on people." He recalled "the missed heartbeat, the appalled glee" he experienced when he first read Dracula: "the memory is salt with the taste of blood, for I had picked my lip while reading and it wouldn't stop bleeding." But he said that reading had other importance apart from providing excitement, fear and escape: "In childhood all books are books of divination, telling us about the future, and like the fortune-teller who sees a long journey in the cards or death by water they influence the future." Greene expressed his belief that early reading has more influence on conduct than any religious teaching, and said that the books for children in the early twentieth century (he was born in 1904) not only provided adventure and excitement and the strangeness of foreign lands, they instilled standards of heroism, idealism, courage and self-sacrifice.

At age ten, when he moved from prep school to junior school, he realized that the world was not as he had gathered from his reading. While the loss of innocence and childhood illusions is part of the normal process of maturing, in Greene's case the abruptness of his awakening to reality was traumatic. Even at an early age, there was a strangeness about him: as a child Greene invented a language of his own called the "lollabobble dialect." Schoolmates thought he was "very different and perhaps a bit bonkers."

He early demonstrated a great sympathy for people that would make him weep. He was quoted as saying, "I remember the fear I felt that my mother would read us a story about some children who were sent into a forest by a wicked uncle to be murdered, but the murderer repented and left them to die of exposure and afterwards the birds covered their bodies with leaves. I dreaded the story because I was afraid of weeping." His biographer said that this "imaginative sympathy with the predicaments of others helped to make him a novelist." Even until his death in 1991 he would weep at a sad movie.

Greene shed some light on the life of a young boy who is about to become a world-class writer in an essay in the *Spectator* in 1923:

> Against the background of visits to grandparents, of examinations and lessons and children's parties, the tragic drama of childhood is played, the attempt to understand what is

happening, to cut through adult lies, which are not regarded as lies simply because they are spoken to a child, to piece together the scraps of conversation, the hints through open doors, the clues on dressing-tables, to understand. Your whole future is threatened by these lowered voices, these consultations . . . the quarrels in the neighboring room, but you are told nothing, you are patted on the head and scolded, kissed and lied to and sent to bed.

Thus it can be seen from these examples that adult writers can have been poor spellers, poor handwriters, and just plain poor. It can also be seen that the childhoods of writers helped form their later passions for words.

To recognize which children have talent and to nurture that talent is essential. Though family interest and encouragement is essential also, perhaps the identification of potential will encourage the families and schools to supply the environments within which the potential can grow. The necessary library cards, the quiet places in which to write, the supportive and not overly evaluative atmosphere, the reading aloud and discussing of literature together (perhaps the turning off of the TV), can all be encouraged by those who discover young children with the potential shown here.

Summary

1. Young talented writers may appear more often than some researchers have shown.
2. This talent seems to occur in all socioeconomic and ethnic groups.
3. There are at least sixteen qualities found in the writing of talented young writers.
4. A look at the childhoods of writers who became well-known as adults shows that they often were early readers and that they read a lot.
5. Talented children often go through a developmental crisis in adolescence as they move into formal operations.

Chapter 8

Creative Scientists, Mathematicians, Inventors and Entrepreneurs

I still can't get over it that you can sit at your desk and noodle around with equations and try out ideas and put together physical principles that may or may not be right, and every once in a while, you can say something about the real world. You can predict the result of an experiment, or a new particle, or say something about the forces of nature or about the way the universe evolves—and all out of pure thought.

—Steven Weinberg

Most of the scientific insights that are considered beautiful bring together seemingly unconnected phenomena in a surprisingly compact way or express the fundamental features of a large number of natural occurrences with one single system of thought. A significant scientific insight is an objective experience and must be reproducible, checked by repeated tests.

—Victor Weisskopf

There he is, immortalized in many teenage movies—the nerd. His shirt pocket lined with a plastic pen holder, his glasses held with an elastic band around the back of his head, his high-water pants and clumsy shoes, his plaid shirt, his floppy leather belt clasped just below his breast, the shock of red hair, and with an earnest gaze through thick glasses, he is a whiz at math or science or computers. But the last thing a teen who is academically talented wants to be called is a nerd. Often such students avoid the special program for academically talented students because of that stereotype.

According to Anne Roe, the personal problems of young scientists include the following: the lack of in-groups, or groups where they will be accepted; the conflict between students' values and family values, if parents and siblings devalue science; the development of verbal abilities in the early grades; and the attitudes of the schools, where teachers often dismiss off-the-wall, non-conforming ideas. These problems are similar to those that any creative youth suffers.

And what about the girl who is a whiz, a creative young scientist or mathematician? She is thought to be so rare, unless she is Asian, that she is not even stereotyped. Brody, reporting on Johns Hopkins University's Study of Mathematically Precocious Youth (see also Stanley and Benbow) showed that those few girls who qualified for radical acceleration (the ratio is 20 boys to one girl) had mothers with Ph.D.s who didn't work outside the home. She also found that these girls were predominantly Asian.

People who are good in mathematics and science have what Gardner called "logical-mathematical intelligence," one of his eight frames of mind. The development of logical-mathematical intelligence seems to be what Piaget had in mind when he traced childhood development from sensorimotor to pre-operational to concrete to formal operational stages. People academically talented in mathematics have certain abilities that seem to make up what Krutetskii, in *The Psychology of Mathematical Abilities in Schoolchildren* (1976), called a "mathematical cast of mind." Gardner said they have a good memory for mathematics and science and the ability to solve problems in their heads, often intuitively skipping steps to come up with the right answers; the ability to perceive a process of mathematical reasoning and to recreate it; and the ability to make new problems and solve them. The ability to be creative in mathematics is, Gardner said, the ability to be "absolutely rigorous and perennially skeptical: no fact can be accepted unless it has been proved rigorously by steps that are derived from universally accepted first principles."

Scientists, on the other hand, don't deal with such abstractions as mathematicians do; they use mathematics as a tool. Mathematicians find joy and fulfillment in the beauty of mathematics for its own sake, or the elegance of the proof, while scientists find joy and fulfillment in considering the true nature of physical reality. Scientists want to unlock the secrets of nature, and they are motivated by their beliefs in underlying universal themes or patterns in nature. The theoretical physicist Viktor Weisskopf, in his memoir, *The Joy of Insight*, said that collaboration among scientists is necessary because "there is a danger of being led astray by complicated mathematics if one does not have close collaborators who can check each step."

Gardner went so far as to say, "Science itself is virtually a religion, a set of beliefs that scientists embrace with a zealot's conviction." Scientists, equipped with mathematics, observational powers, and technical knowledge, are often motivated by the hope or even mystical conviction that their beliefs will be proven to be right, as they perform their experiments on the physical world. These interests emerge when children are quite young, so talent for mathematics and science can be discovered early.

Predictive Behaviors for Science and Mathematics

What have psychologists and biographers discovered about creative scientists and mathematicians? What is the creative scientist or mathematician really like? Fortunately, many of the psychologists who have studied the personalities of creative people have focused on scientists, and many studies have used both tests and a biographical approach. We now know much about the personalities of scientists. Cattell and Drevdahl in their research using The 16 Personality Factor Questionnaire (16 PF) found that creative artists and writers had personalities similar to those of creative scientists, except that scientists had more emotional stability than artists and writers.

In 1968, almost a thousand young scientists who were competing in a national science talent search were compared with some two hundred writers, architects, mathematicians, and scientists who had been studied at the Berkeley Institute for Personality Assessment and Research (IPAR). The study, by Parloff, Datta, Kleman, and Handlon, compared scores on the California Psychological Inventory (CPI), and found that the young scientists scored highest on "Disciplined Effectiveness," a measure of self-control; in making a good impression; in having a sense of well being; in achieving by way of conforming; in being tolerant; and in being sociable, responsible, and intellectually efficient.

The creative adult scientists, however, were not so apt to be so conforming or dependable, and the authors posited that this difference between adolescent scientists and creative adults was a practical adaptation used by the adolescents to get on in the world. A creative adult who is eccentric and demanding is treated with more tolerance than is the "brash, unrecognized adolescent." They also asserted that the job of the adolescent creative scientist is to have the discipline to "learn principles, heuristics, and basic information, which he may then proceed to reintegrate and reorganize in a constructively creative fashion."

MacKinnon pointed out that this picture of the disciplined, self-controlled, conforming adolescent science student was not that of the stereotypical bohemian creative adolescent. However, while young scientists may be conforming and self-disciplined, they also have been found early on to incorporate their science interest into their play. As children, they had collections of rocks, insects, spiders and the like; they had a parent, a relative, a family friend, or a teacher who encouraged them and who talked to them about their interests; and they had a sense of wonder about nature and its manifestations. A case in point is the description of early family fun by Jonathan Weiner, a science writer, who told a story about making a computer from Dixie cups with his father and brother. He said, "I still recall our delight as we sat around the kitchen table and watched the Dixie cup computer making better and better moves until by the end of the evening it trounced us every time. (Evenings like this are not for everyone)."

Vera John-Steiner, in *Notebooks of the Mind*, which contains a discussion of scientific thinking as revealed by interviews, biographies, autobiographies, and the notebooks of scientists, said that young scientists have "informal apprenticeships of the mind." For example, Einstein hated the discipline of the secondary school, and instead turned to reading and thinking and talking with people such as his Uncle Jakob, a sound engineer who played algebraic games with his young nephew and who made mathematics fun. Uncle Jakob called x "a little animal whose name we don't know," according to Clark, Einstein's biographer.

The childhoods of Einstein and of scientist Edward Teller were remarkably similar. Einstein was born in 1879 in Germany and grew up there, and Teller, born in 1908, grew up in Hungary. Teller, like Einstein, was thought at first to be mentally slow. Einstein did not speak well until about age six, and Teller did not speak until about age three. However, by the age of four, "The words gushed forth in polysyllables, understandable phrases, complete sentences," according to his biographers, Blumberg and Panos. Before age 6, Teller showed his precocity in mathematics by putting himself to sleep with multiplication problems, asking himself the number of seconds in a minute, hour, day, week, and year. However, a few years later, he was bored in math class: "His keen interest in mathematics had propelled him into the realm of basic algebra, and he was so far ahead of the class that he seemed apathetic." His grade school teacher ignored him when he tried to answer questions, for Teller was so advanced that the teacher assumed he was repeating the class and hence knew all the answers. Similarly, Einstein was demonstrating precocity in mathematics by the age of nine.

Both boys were interested in other subjects as well. Both were readers,

Teller especially liking Jules Verne's science fiction. Both began musical instruction at age six, Einstein the violin and Teller the piano. Before long, Teller was playing so well that his mother, a talented musician, had hopes that he would become a concert pianist. As a young teen he would often become "engrossed for hours at time in the sonatas and fugues of Bach, Beethoven, and Mozart." Interestingly, Einstein was roughly the same age, fourteen, when he discovered the mathematical structure of music through the works of Mozart. And at fourteen Teller was plunging into Einstein's book on relativity.

It is an odd fact that there were several other Hungarians who grew up along the same river valley in Hungary at the same time, an era of political unrest. These boys didn't know each other then, and later, when they met, they joked they must have come from Mars. Others were Eugene Wigner, a 1963 Nobel Laureate; Leo Szilard, who in 1942 with Fermi produced the world's first controlled nuclear reaction; Theodor Von Karmann, an aeronautical engineer; and John Von Neumann, considered one of the finest mathematicians in the world. All these boys came from families that were close, who valued education and who provided a stimulating intellectual atmosphere in the home.

Both Teller and Einstein had the influence of a university mentor. Teller's father feared that his love of mathematics would lead him to be a poorly paid and low-status mathematics teacher. However, he contacted a mathematics instructor at the University, Leopold Klug, who appraised Teller's aptitude for mathematics. Klug brought Edward a copy of Euler's *Geometry* and discussed the book with him. After several visits, Klug told Teller's father, "Your son is exceptional." For Edward the meetings were inspirational and he began to want to emulate Klug. Einstein's parents took in a boarder, Max Talmey, a medical student. Talmey called the Einstein home "happy, comfortable, and cheerful" and wrote a book on his impressions of the twelve-year-old Einstein. Max gave the child Bernstein's books on physical science, Buchner's *Force and Matter,* and Spieker's *Geometry*, a textbook. Talmey said,

> After a short time, a few months, he had worked through the whole book of Spieker. He thereupon devoted himself to higher mathematics, studying all by himself Lubsen's excellent works on the subject . . . Soon the flight of his mathematical genius was so high that I could no longer follow. Thereafter philosophy was often a subject of our conversations. I recommended to him the reading of Kant. At that time he was still a child, only thirteen years old, yet Kant's works, incomprehensible to ordinary mortals, seemed to be clear to him.

Teller often helped his older sister with her mathematics homework; Einstein did likewise with his younger sister. Both men stayed extremely close to their sisters throughout their lives. Einstein called his sister Maja his "constant companion and unfailing confidant." Both boys wanted to be physicists but their fathers were afraid they wouldn't be able to make a living, and so they persuaded them to enroll in engineering school. Both were from Jewish backgrounds that were not particularly religious. Both fled the Nazis to come to the United States during World War II. Both boys, strong in mathematics, chose to become theoretical physicists.

Niels Bohr and Viktor Weisskopf had similar childhoods. As a child, Weisskopf's mother insisted he take lessons and participate in musical groups. As a teenager, he was strongly attracted to music, but "in the end, science won." He said, "My father had wanted me to be something practical, like an engineer, but I knew that I wanted to work in physics." Bohr's father was a professor of physiology and his mother came from a wealthy Jewish family. This highly cultured childhood led him to follow his father's footsteps and become a professor himself.

Three theoretical physicists born in the U.S., Richard Feynman and the Oppenheimer brothers, had similar backgrounds as well: the early interest and precocity in mathematics, the influence of the practical father who spends time with the son discussing science and mathematics, the obsession with the meaning of life in the cosmos, the strong suns of family and school, the connections to important mentors, the early publication of their research and a continued trajectory toward eminence as the Zeitgeist needed their contributions and talents because of the world war.

Intelligence of Scientists and Mathematicians

Why did Einstein and Teller choose science as opposed to mathematics? Is there some disposition of personality toward one or the other? Research reported by Tannenbaum and Bloom has found that young mathematicians and young scientists do differ; however, both need a certain threshold of general intelligence. According to Tannenbaum, "After the scientist's first job, IQ influences positional recognition directly, regardless of first job prestige, educational background, and scholarly performance." Simonton said that people in the physical sciences have the highest IQs, with physics Ph.D.s having IQs of about 140. People in the biological sciences have "somewhat less Olympian minds," and those in the social sciences are even lower in IQ.

Simonton said that merely learning what is essential in the physical sciences requires high intelligence. For instance, Einstein's field, theoretical physics, requires more basic intelligence than Freud's field of psychoanalysis. Simonton said, in *Genius, Creativity, and Leadership,*

> Thus it is not utterly preposterous to suggest that Einstein and Oppenheimer may have been equally bright and that both were the intellectual superiors of Freud. Both Einstein and Freud were revolutionaries, but Freud revolutionized a field that requires less intrinsic intelligence. Oppenheimer may have surpassed Freud in raw brain power, but the field of physics demands more, so Freud is a revolutionary, Oppenheimer is only an advancer.

You are probably feeling a little intimidated right about now, whether you know your IQ or not. You may believe you have been predestined to achieve according to your IQ. But remember that Simonton didn't say which IQ test was used, nor what it measured, and also, stay tuned for the test scores of innovative inventors. IQ tests were made by scientists, for scientists. Do not ascribe mystical properties to pencil and paper tests.

Young scientists also showed early differences, according to specialty, with biologists preferring hobbies and books related to nature. For example, a plant geneticist I know had gardens in his family's backyard from an early age. Young physical scientists often like to work with mechanical toys and gadgets, and young social scientists are often spellbound readers. Terman's follow-up studies confirmed that scientists had what Tannenbaum called "an early and persistent interest in science." Science students were interested in the causes of things, were daydreamers, liked to solve mental puzzles, and liked art that was symbolic and music that had classical structures. They liked to read science books, to build models, and to take walks in nature.

The high school interests of these often-solitary students tended toward science clubs, science experiments, and the solving of scientific problems. Science teachers frequently had great influence on them. Brandwein studied about a thousand New York City high school science students and found that they had high IQs, were predisposed to like science, and had teachers who inspired them. These teachers themselves were science achievers, active professionals in their learned societies, active also in curriculum writing; they had hobbies associated with science, such as memberships in hiking clubs or birdwatching societies.

Young mathematicians also display their talent early, and they also have high IQs, high spatial visualization ability, and high verbal ability. Krutetskii studied 200 children and found that the able and very able students had six characteristics which surfaced early, the abilities to do the following: (1) to grasp the structure of a problem, separating extraneous information from essential information; (2) to easily find abstract principles within problems; (3) to skip steps in the process of solving problems and still come out with the right answer; (4) to appreciate elegant mathematical solutions; (5) to be flexible and to solve the same problem in many ways; and (6) to remember essential features of problems, even many months later. For the latter, a young mathematician might exclaim in the middle of a solution, "Oh, we had this problem last summer!"

Krutetskii also found that mathematical talent comes in four varieties: the analytic, the geometric, and two types of harmonic abilities. Young mathematicians with analytic talent have strong verbal-logical abilities and weak spatial abilities. Those with geometric talent have strong spatial visualization abilities and weak verbal-logical abilities. Both types of harmonic ability math students have strong verbal, logical, and spatial visualization ability. Krutetskii emphasized that the ability to calculate is not a prerequisite for strong mathematical talent. However, analytic ability is a prerequisite for strong mathematical talent, for mathematics requires the ability to think abstractly.

School behaviors predictive of mathematical talent are that the student may volunteer to collect money, run for treasurer of a club or class, do the statistics for the sports teams, or appear at the door of the math teacher just to talk about a certain problem. The mathematically talented student may join the math club. Richard Feynman won state-wide awards in mathematics in high school. Challenger Astronaut Judith Resnik appeared in her yearbook from Firestone High School in Akron, Ohio, as the only female member of the math club. Her teacher for Advanced Placement Calculus saved her papers as models of excellence for other students. She was the valedictorian of her class.

Gruber on Darwin

The seminal psychological study in the field of creativity in science is Howard Gruber's study of Charles Darwin. In *Darwin on Man*, Gruber asserted that the detailed study of one life was necessary to uncover the essence of scientific creativity. Gruber studied the development of Darwin's theory of evolution, utilizing Darwin's notebooks of 1837 to 1838, written after his famous voyage to the Galapagos on the *Beagle* in 1831-1836. Gruber wrote that scientific creativity takes courage, "brave and patient struggle under conditions of adversity," and that it does not come about through a few moments of insight, but from a long and laborious process of thinking, revising, and reformulating.

Darwin waited until 1859, when he published his *Origin of Species,* to make public his belief that natural selection through the survival of the fittest operated to transmute species. Alfred Wallace had written Darwin a letter in 1858 about his field observations in the South Sea islands. This precipitated Darwin's writing, finally, of the book, for Darwin was well aware of the social consequences of coming out with such a theory. Wallace's work caused Darwin to try to act first. Wallace was also influenced by Malthus's work, and the Linnaean Society gave both men credit at the same time for publishing the theory of natural selection. (However, Wallace stopped short of saying that human intelligence had evolved through natural selection.) Gruber called Darwin's delay in publishing his theory a "grand detour" of twenty-three years, a delay that was illustrative of the psychological process of creativity in people.

For example, a scientist is taught to use the scientific method, to gather data and to form a hypothesis and to construct an experiment to prove or disprove that hypothesis. Gruber called this view of the scientific process "the rationalist myth" and said that a person who takes hold of one theory or one point of view discovers hypotheses "with difficulty." Darwin's notebooks showed that he worked differently. Gruber said that Darwin's life showed that while the hypothesis was in the air, so to speak, certain events in his life were necessary before the hypothesis could be formed.

Darwin had written in his notebooks about natural selection, but through a long growth process encompassing both the forming of a dense schema (or much data gathering), and the process of coming to equilibration, Darwin didn't fully realize what he had found until much later. Gruber said that "novel ideas can be forgotten until the structure of which they are to become a part is sufficiently complete to stabilize them." Another way of stating this could be found in the popular saying that when the student is ready the teacher will come, implying that people take in much but don't fully remember it or utilize it until they are ready.

Gruber also spoke about a "network of enterprises" contributing to the formulation of a scientific theory, or of any theory. (I mentioned the "network of enterprises" in Chapter 6, when I talked about writers writing across genres.) While Darwin was delayed in publishing his *Origin of Species*, he spent eight years studying barnacles; he wrote many articles and papers; he continued to accumulate geological and biological information. He delayed also in publishing *The Descent of Man* in 1871, for he was fully aware that the suggestion that man also had evolved would be explosive, invoking the ire of the church. And so between 1859 and 1871, he published many works, accumulated more evidence, and wrote, thought and spoke on related topics. He lived his life and continued to consider. His theories did not spring instantaneously, but came to fruition after many related projects brought them to being—a "network of enterprises."

Gruber concluded that creativity, or creative thought, is the "work of purposeful beings." Those who say that creative thought arises from chance or the Zeitgeist are only partially correct, as are those who say that creative thought arises from unconscious processes, and internal, not rational, mechanisms such as night dreams and daydreams. He said that while both of these are necessary and important, the scientific creator is "governed by a ruling passion" that informs all of his activities. When Darwin went to the zoo, he found behavior that informed his theory; when he went to the opera, he did the same. Darwin was seeing everything in the context of the theory he was hatching. However, since he was working on this theory over a long period of time, he was able to take such events not as proof of his theory, but as part of the fabric.

According to Gruber, Darwin was able to scrap useless information without scrapping everything:

> Darwin's work was divided into a number of separate enterprises, each with a life of its own. This type of organization has several constructive functions. It permits the thinker to change his ideas in one domain without scrapping everything he believes. In this way he can go on working purposefully on a broad range of subjects without the disruptive effects that would ensue if every new idea and even every doubt immediately required a reorganization of the whole system of thought.

A scientist combines personal imagery (for example, Darwin's images of the wedge and the irregularly branching tree) that has been developed through intense exposure to the natural world, with empirical data-gathering. Gruber said that this intense gathering of knowledge must be "private and personal, even when the desired end product is the public knowledge of science." A density of personal experience is necessary, and each simple idea has much density. The scientist develops his theory as a means to put coherence to the enormous amount of information that is coming in.

Darwin claimed that his schooling was not important, but in looking at his school life, Gruber found that Darwin had been informally exposed to all that he would later propose as theories. Darwin's grandfather, Erasmus, was also part of his development. The family itself was interested and involved in science. At Cambridge, "informal contact with some of his professors and some fellow students was the most important part of his education. Has it ever been otherwise?" The foundations were laid, and Darwin himself had as a mentor or idealized role model Alexander von Humboldt, who had sailed to the Tenebrides.

When Darwin took on the post of naturalist on the *Beagle*, he was already well-prepared by his family milieu and his school interests. Then he undertook the five-year task of taking notes, collecting specimens, making sketches. Sailing on the *Beagle* was not chance or luck, but what Gruber called "the exploitation of an opportunity that fitted in perfectly with his own well-developed purposes." Darwin began as a geologist and ended as an evolutionist. During this process he went through many phases, and he ended up challenging the very beliefs of the society about the origins of biological systems. He did not do this through a moment of insight or a rigorous application of the five steps of the scientific process, but through the process of a life-long creative production.

Simonton's Historiometric Studies

Other interesting and comprehensive work in the area of scientific creativity has been that of Simonton. He has been working in the field of historiometry, or the mathematical translation of biographical information, with the Goertzels' 1962 and 1978 data, and other data from people like Roe and Cox, helping to define what constitutes genius in creativity, as in his 1995 book, *Greatness: Who Makes History and Why*. His other books, *Genius, Creativity, and Leadership* and *Scientific Genius*, were also explications of his work with historiometric methods to study creative lives. Simonton has developed what he called the chance-configuration theory of the development of creativity in science. Briefly translated, there are two steps in the creative process in science. First is the making of a theory or configuration. This step is inner, intuitive, associative, meditative, and more likely generated in solitude than through group brainstorming. The second step is more public, changing this subconscious idea into something that can be communicated or published.

Simonton held that on one personality dimension, all creative scientists are alike: they are devoted to work. That is, their motivation differentiates them from others. And if someone is devoted to his life's work, huge productivity is more likely. He said Darwin could claim 119 publications at the close of his career; Einstein 248; and, in psychology, Galton 227; Binet 277; James 307; Freud, 330; and Maslow, 165. Edison may be best known for his incandescent light bulb and phonograph, but all told he held 1,093 patents—still the record of the United States Patent Office. However, it would seem that all creative people are devoted to work, not only scientists, as we have seen already with visual artists and writers and as we shall see with musicians, actors, and dancers. Piechowski once told me that this view of scientific productivity as being a mark of genius may be particularly American: "Productivity may be a byproduct of genius but is not its fundamental characteristic."

Simonton's data led him to conclude that scientific productivity has an age curve, beginning in the scientist's twenties and reaching its highest point in the late thirties or early forties, then tapering off. Botanists and disease specialists are most productive in their early thirties. Bacteriologists, physiologists, pathologists, and general medical scientists are most productive in their late thirties. Chemists peak in their late twenties. Mathematicians and physicists peak in their early thirties. Geologists and astronomers reach their peak productivity in their late thirties. Theoretical mathematicians and physicists, if they have not made their contributions by the time they are in their late twenties, will probably never do so. Putting these age constraints on scientists' peaks of productivity is frightening to some people, but Simonton derived these numbers from statistical analyses of the lives of scientists. Individual cases differ. Simonton further wrote that this characteristic of early productivity holds true for other creative people as well, including artists, writers, and musicians. He said, "Early productivity is one of the single best predictors of later productivity in all domains of creativity."

However, Darwin's delay in publicly announcing his theory points out that this age curve may be misleading. Darwin once advised a colleague that he should hold his theory in mind, but should not publish it until the data he gathered supported the theory. The age curves shown by extant biographies may be misleading for women, also. Women may be prevented from producing at such young ages by the double bind, that of bearing children and taking most of the responsibility for the houschold, as well as being creatively productive in their career. This timeline holds true for males, but women may have a different career pattern, peaking in productivity later than men tend to.

A 1996 study by Sandra Hanson called *Lost Talent: Women in the Sciences* utilized sophisticated statistical techniques to analyze large databases, as Simonton did. The High School and Beyond (HSB) data collected by the National Center for Educational Statistics; the National Educational Longitudinal Study (NELS) and the Longitudinal Study of American Youth (LSAY) were analyzed. Results showed that although young women and men have similar experiences in the sciences up until tenth grade, the males were more likely to stay in science and continue taking the courses. Course-taking is a necessary behavior in the development of science talent. Home support for science course-taking was higher for the men, and young women who were taking science courses were twice as likely to have a baby or to marry within two years after high school.

The women who continued in the science pipeline leading to the Ph.D. were less likely to date than the women who stepped out of the pipeline. Those who continued also had lower self-concepts than the other women. This corresponds with the findings of Csikszentmihalyi, Rathunde, and Whalen, who found that the teenage students who continued to develop their talent were less precocious in sexual behavior, tended to date in groups, and liked to work alone on projects. Other evidence that girls may be influenced by the urge for popularity with peers and for acceptance by attractive males— urges which may cause them to downplay their intelligence and eventually drop out from developing their science, mathematical, and other academic talents—was shown by Tomlinson-Keasy and Little when they found that a pursuit of social goals and popularity had a negative effect on the development of intellectual skills.

In two current longitudinal studies of very bright women, Westinghouse science award winners, and valedictorians from Illinois, Subotnik and Arnold noted that after ten years, most of the women who had intended to pursue science careers had left the field, for reasons having primarily to do with love relationships. Subotnik and Arnold said, "Like most male-dominated occupations, research science adheres to an unforgiving career schedule." They quoted Nobel laureate Rosalyn Yalow: "It's difficult in a field that changes as rapidly as science to drop out for a number of years and then hope to return without major retraining." Until the culture of science itself changes, the presence of women who must balance childbearing and career pursuits will probably continue to be problematic.

There may be great consequences for dropping out to care for one's children and then again picking up a career in science or mathematics (or any creative field). The necessary track record for eminence may not be produced. When I have said this to my female students, they have often replied, "Who cares about eminence? I want to be happy and raise my family." This constant conflict between raising children and working on a career is common to all women in all domains. There is no research evidence that men go through this struggle.

Those who begin their productivity early often continue in it. They refuse to acknowledge retirement, and they retain their enthusiasm for scientific research, as well as the publication of their research, much later than less creative scientists. They are more likely to have their careers ended by illness or death than by a lack of ideas. Simonton said that those who publish more, also publish the most high-quality papers, just as those who submit the most grant proposals get the most grants. In other words, quantity is needed for success and recognition. Simonton called this the "constant-probability-of-success model," and it also applies to the careers of those in literature and music. Often, the creator cannot choose which idea, which composition, is the best one among all the others being created. But if one continues to produce, something is bound to "hit." Simonton said, "The most prolific and successful creators get their first hit earlier and their last hit later."

Family and Educational Factors

What about the suns of school and home in scientists' and mathematicians' life paths? Simonton's search through the biographies yielded an odd fact: many creative people have lost a parent, a phenomenon called by Simonton "the orphanhood effect." Of course, one must take into account that the persons about whom the biographies were written often lived in a time where life span was not as long as it is now. But orphanhood also comes about from parental absence caused by disease, alcoholism, divorce, or abandonment.

Why do some people become creative in the absence of a parent, and others destructive? Factors to consider are the child's intellectual capacity, the cultural enrichment in the home environment, the birth order, role models, formal education, and the Zeitgeist of the times. As we have already noted, Alice Miller has asserted that whether an adult will be creative or destructive is determined by how childhood trauma was received and dealt with. Creative scientists and mathematicians, though, seem to have had more stable homes than artists, especially writers.

Choice of college is important to potential scientists and mathematicians. If the student attends a college that is not elite, not demanding, located in a backwater away from the action, the chances that the young scientist will make major achievements in science are slight. This is important, and illustrates that counseling for scientifically talented students is necessary. How much education is enough for scientific creativity? The attainment of the Ph.D. at a young age is almost *de rigueur*, although many of the scientifically creative made their contributions before they attained their Ph.D.s, including Einstein. If the student qualifies to get into a highly competitive college and does not go because of finances, counselors should be aware that admission is the important thing, and that the finances will follow once admission is achieved.

Birth order is also important. Firstborns make up more than half of active scientists. (This figure includes only children, who are somewhat different from firstborns.) The reasons for the achievement of only children and firstborns are obvious: the child is exposed to exclusive adult care, whereas subsequent children have to deal with a more complex family environment from the moment of birth. Of second-borns and other younger siblings, there is more of a chance to achieve scientifically if the birth order is spaced at about five years between children.

Later-born children who have lost an older sibling are also more likely to achieve creatively than those who have intact families. The research on the achievement of first-borns often makes middle children angry, for they achieve also; note that the first sentence of this paragraph implies that almost half of active scientists are born second or later. Sulloway in 1996 published extensive research on birth order, asserting that last-borns are rebels, the ones who often do groundbreaking scientific work. He used Darwin and many other scientists and revolutionaries as his examples.

Researchers have found that scientists and mathematicians more often come from stable homes, with stronger father influences, than do other creative types. Another positive benefit is that the parents of the scientific achievers allowed the child to be present when adults were around and to interact with these adults. In fact, the young people met professionals in the fields in which they would achieve in their childhood homes. This was as true of musicians and writers as of scientists. Middle class and professional homes were most likely to have these cultural environments. The existence of such casual role models is important for young creatives.

More formal ones are also needed. Subotnik and her colleagues, in studying Westinghouse Science Talent Search winners, found that the mentor is extremely crucial to the full development of scientific talent. To be recognized and selected by a mentor is essential to the young scientist who seeks to compete in the top echelon of scientists. The young scientist must be both deferential and unafraid to challenge the mentor in dialogue and analysis. Simonton described the structuring of such role model relationships. In science, an apprenticeship, a form of role-modeling, is necessary. For example, Nobel prize winners have studied under other Nobel prize winners (and sometimes married their daughters); such associations enhance the opportunities of winning the prize. Simonton said that the scientist mentor should be about twenty years older, but never less than ten years older. The mentor should still be in the intuitive stage of creativity, not the analytic stage of later years. Instructive as the role model is, however, there is a danger if the student becomes too imitative of the mentor and does not strike out on his own.

A note to school counselors, teachers, and parents of scientifically and mathematically talented students: the influence of the right school, the right mentor, and the right environment for the nurturing of scientific creativity is crucial, and such placement should be a priority of school counselors, who are often content to advise bright creative scientists to attend the local community college or state university, rather than seek scholarships at more competitive institutions. Many worthy students from rural areas are deterred by the myth that they can't afford a competitive college, but frequently, where there's a will, there's a way. For instance, when one scientifically talented young man from a small town was accepted to M.I.T., the coordinator for programs for the talented at his high school contacted the M.I.T. alumni group in the state, and money was found.

Another social institution, the church, has less of an influence than school and family. The role of formal religion in the lives of scientists is often minimal. The least they could say was that they didn't object to it, though very few scientists have come from dogmatic, fundamentalist, rules-filled denominations. Requiring the scientifically creative to attend church, wear a tie, and join activities may hamper the creative instincts of the young man or woman. While most scientists are seeking the meaning of nature in their own disciplines and fields, they often reject or pay minimal lip service to institutionalized religions in order to carry on their scientific inquiries.

Schools, of course, can also suppress. Again, as Brandwein showed, teachers should emphasize inquiry learning rather than rote learning, should encourage independent reading and study, and should recognize the importance of self-instruction. Perhaps the reason that both Einstein and Darwin disclaimed the influence of formal education in their lives was that lecture was the primary method of discourse in German gymnasiums and British public schools. Most creative people speak of their schooling negatively, but they speak of their learning, most of it self-taught, positively. (See Chapter 11 for what creative writers thought of their schooling.)

Another factor that contributes to scientific creativity is what Simonton called *marginality*, one of the meanings of which is to live in two cultures. Significant numbers of creative people have been first or second generation immigrants, able to straddle two cultures and to see things in new ways, not in old, timeworn ways. In 1995, Simonton said a good example is that of the Jews, who are eminent to an extent that exceeds their percentage in the population. "This prominence holds especially for mathematicians, physicists, chemists, biomedical researchers, economists, lawyers, violin virtuosos, chess champions, and faculty members at prestigious universities."

Another theory for why so many scientists are Jewish came from Abba Eban in 1955. Clark quoted Eban thus: "The Hebrew mind has been obsessed for centuries by a concept of order and harmony in universal design." Eban continued, "The search for laws hitherto unknown which govern cosmic forces; the doctrine of a relative harmony in nature; the idea of a calculable relationship between matter and energy" have all contributed to Jewish interest in science.

Another type of marginality Simonton talked about is professional marginality, or being skilled in two professions. In fact, many contributions to science have been made by people who have switched from one field to another. This would seem to be evidence against the "earlier the better," for when one switches fields, one is older, past one's early bloom, yet switching fields permits people to combine and to see in new ways, perhaps becoming younger mentally. However, a third type of marginality, geographical marginality, or coming from the provinces, operates against creativity rather than for it. Being away from the action, so to speak, does not contribute to either aesthetic or scientific creativity, because such creators have little access to those who can help them along. Simonton urged such creators to hurry to a cultural center, for it is difficult to influence a field from the countryside.

The outsider mentality caused by marginality in religion, in sexual orientation, in race or ethnicity, in social acceptability because of disabilities or quirks, often enables creative people to create at the same time that it causes them social discomfort. This seems odd, but it is true. One sees differently from the outside, from the threshold, and seeing differently, naively, is often inspiration for making things new, and changing the commonplace from a new point of view.

The Influence of the Zeitgeist

The researchers and thinkers about creativity also postulate that certain times and places are better, historically, for scientific or other creativity. Simonton noted, for example, that great advances in biological knowledge take place the generation after advances in medicine, chemistry, and geology. Politically, a sense of nationalism enhances creative production, while large empires do not. One generation after the overthrow of an empire, though, scientific creativity is on the upswing. This is because diversity increases the number of ingredients or ideas that go into a scientific discovery. However, great upheaval, such as that found in the Middle East or in Africa, with revolts, shootings, rebellions, and terrorist activities, do not produce the climate for scientific innovation.

The best proof of the power of the Zeitgeist is when multiple inventions happen—when two or more scientists come up with the same invention or creation. Simonton cited the near-simultaneous invention of calculus by Newton and Leibniz, and the manufacture of oxygen by Priestley and Scheele; Gruber discussed the proposing of the theory of evolution by both Wallace and Darwin. Gardner, Feldman, Gruber, Csikszentmihalyi, and Tannenbaum also discussed the importance of the social and political climate, the very time in history, the progression of inventions, making it necessary for these discoveries to be made. It is as if they are inevitable, and thus proof that scientific creativity is not chance, but destiny.

Csikszentmihalyi in 1988 argued the same point, saying, "We cannot study creativity by isolating individuals and their works from the social and historical milieu in which their actions are carried out." Gardner, in a 1993 case study of Freud's career as a creative person, argued that Freud's work could not have been done without the milieu of Vienna at that time in history, the early twentieth century. Likewise, the period of the Renaissance in Florence is often cited as being especially fertile for creativity. Simonton argued, though, that in all cases, one of the discoveries is always more completely designed and described than the others that come during the same time period. For instance, many people tried to invent photography, but only one came upon the daguerreotype.

The production of multiples by scientists working separately is often used to suggest that the arts demand a higher level of creativity. The artist supposedly creates from nothing, and the artistic product cannot be duplicated. There is only one Michelangelo, and only he could have created the particular ceiling of the Sistine Chapel loved by millions. There was only one Faulkner, and only Faulkner could have created his particular Yaknapatawpha County in Mississippi. There was only one Beethoven, and the Fifth Symphony could not have been created by anyone else.

These works of art would not exist if their creators had not existed. Did the world need a ceiling, a county, four notes that resonated throughout ensuing history? We have these creations because of the inner visions and even inner needs of their creators. Artists also participate in the synchronicity of the Zeitgeist. Van Gogh said, "Do you know what I think of pretty often? That if I do not succeed, all the same what I have worked on will be carried on; not directly, but one isn't alone in believing in things that are true. And what does it matter personally then?"

Weisskopf ruminated on the difference in creativity between the arts and the sciences. "In art it is impossible to separate form from content, whereas it is often pedagogically useful in science." In science, the work of many people contributes to "a single edifice" which is called "the scientific world view." While art also grows out of cultural and historical trends, art stands alone. That is, in science we definitely know more than we did a hundred years ago. In art, a work produced a hundred years ago is as valuable as, if not more valuable than, a work produced today. A tendency toward more refinement exists in both art and science. If he were asked today, Newton would admit that Einstein advanced his theories. In science, more complexity "is connected to a genuine increase of insight into nature. The increased sophistication of art may lead to a wider scope of subject matter and a greater variety of creative forms, but hardly to more powerful forces of artistic expression."

The world needed a polio vaccine, a phonograph, a steam engine, a theory of evolution. The world needed geometry, calculus, and quantum theory. The world needed space travel and will need time travel. Scientific creativity has invented these when they were needed. Buckminster Fuller's timeline of inventions in *Critical Path* is a case in point. Fuller showed the "Chronology of Scientific Discoveries and Artifacts" and the "Chronological Inventory of Prominent Scientific, Technological, Economic, and Political World Events, 1895 to Date," placing his own inventions and discoveries in chronological order with the Zeitgeist of the times and of the places. He showed the rapid acceleration of inventions and their impingement on world history, using his own life span as an example.

Fuller said that there is a lag of twenty-two years between an invention and public use of that invention, and that is why we are on a critical path. In his last book, *Grunch of Giants*, Fuller advanced the hope that there would be "bloodless socioeconomic reorientation" made between nations by young business people in pin-striped suits, straddling continents in propounding international technological sharing and commerce. But he asks, "Can it be successfully accomplished before the only-instinctively-operating fear and ignorance preclude success, by one individual, authorized or unauthorized, pushing the first button of chain-reacting, all-buttons-pushing, atomic, race-irradiated suicide?"

We still ask the same question today. The existence of nuclear capabilities in so many countries with histories of instability and revolution is frightening. So also is the cavalier setting on fire of oil fields in Kuwait. And the careless burning of Amazonian forests. The hole in the ozone and smog in cities where diesel is the primary fuel come to mind. Will the benevolent use of the inventions and discoveries of creative mathematicians and scientists get to all the peoples of the world in time?

Studies of Mathematicians

Helson's Study of Creative Female Mathematicians

With the preponderance of male subjects in studies of creative people, it is refreshing to discuss Ravenna Helson's study of creative women mathematicians. Helson found her subjects to be essentially like other creative people, especially women and men creative writers.

Forty-four female mathematicians were studied at the IPAR Project at the University of California at Berkeley. They had been nominated by peers and listed in directories of Ph.D.s who had completed their degrees between 1950 and 1960. The criterion for labeling these women *creative* was the quality of their work. Calling them marginal in the profession of mathematics, Helson noted that several of them did not hold academic posts or positions in research institutions, but did their work at home. Their average age was forty-one, one-third were Jewish, and foreign cultural influence (European and Canadian) was strong, as it is with male mathematicians. They were administered tests such as the California Psychological Inventory (CPI) and the Minnesota Multiphasic Psychological Inventory (MMPI).

These creative female mathematicians had superior intellect and great perseverance. They were adaptive and sensitive to the new and to the unforeseen. Their temperaments were subdued but still individualistic. A clinical Q-sort revealed still more characteristics descriptive of the creative mathematicians. They were independent and autonomous, taking pride in their objectivity and rationality while still being able to form associations and think in new ways. They were seen as being dramatic personalities, even histrionic, and as moody and nonconforming rebels.

In addition, a comparison study was done between creative women mathematicians and other women mathematicians. The creatives were found to perform in a manner superior to the others, in that they received their Ph.D.s earlier, submitted papers for publication before their Ph.D.s, and they received more fellowships and grants after graduate school. The creative women were higher in flexibility and lower in achievement orientation and in cooperation, showing that they preferred to make their own ways of doing things. They did not enjoy the routine details of working in a highly structured environment. The creative women mathematicians seemed to be preoccupied with themselves, showed more autonomy, and could be described as temperamental.

Self-descriptions showed that they were more involved in research than the comparison women mathematicians, and their thought processes seemed to be less overtly conscious. Describing themselves as "inventive and ingenious," they were less interested in salary, promotion, and teaching. In their leisure time, the creative women had intellectual pursuits such as listening to classical music, taking nature walks, going to the theater, and reading. They seem to have simplified their lives, doing the few things they cared about greatly. Homemaking and research occupied most of their time, while the comparison women spent much time in administrative duties, teaching, political activity, and community work.

Creative subjects scored higher on the Terman Concept Mastery Test than the comparison women. Their score was 144. (The Stanford Gifted subjects scored 137, industrial research scientists scored 118, and military officers scored 60.) Creative male mathematicians scored 148. In mechanical reasoning, the creative and comparison women did not differ, and they both scored lower than men. The average IQs on the Wechsler Adult Intelligence Scale (WAIS) of the women mathematicians were similar to those of the men, in the low 130s. [Note: research scientists also had average IQs in the low 130s.]

Helson observed that these women seemed to be more identified with their professional fathers than the comparison group of women. Both groups often came from families of girls, and the creative women, especially, seemed to have few brothers. She noted, "A number of the women mathematicians seem to have been adopted as the 'son' of an intellectual father."

The creative female mathematicians differed from the creative male mathematicians studied. The creative males were higher on social ascendancy, or a desire to rise on the social ladder, as well as intellectual efficiency, or how fast and clearly they could express themselves. Interestingly enough, the comparison males and females were quite similar. Helson wrote, "The creative women described themselves as nonadventurous and inner-focused."

The fact that this late-1960s study was of people who had received their Ph.D.s in the 1940s and '50s may have something to do with the large gender differences found between creative male and creative female mathematicians. However, more recent studies, unfortunately, have shown the same differences. Eccles and her colleagues have shown that mathematical attitudes in the family contribute to females achieving less in mathematics. Mothers' attitudes towards the probability of mathematical success seem to be crucial. Mothers say to their daughters, "Well, I was never good in math either," and to their sons, "Boys have math ability."

In fact, the Terman studies of high IQ students showed that parents rated their boys as having higher ability in mathematics and mechanics and their girls as having higher ability in drama and music. Studies at Johns Hopkins University of mathematically talented students showed that parents expected their boys to enter math-related occupations but expected their daughters to enter traditional female occupations and then stop for awhile to have children.

Helson theorized that there may be biological or societal causes for the gender differences. A comparison study with creative women writers showed that the two groups of creative women were remarkably similar. Interestingly enough, she also found that the creative male writers were more like the creative women mathematicians and women writers than they were like the creative male mathematicians. This led to Helson describing the creative male mathematicians as people who stood alone. "They [creative male mathematicians] have a personality in which there is relatively more social assurance and assertiveness and less conflict with conventional channels of expression and achievement."

The male writers, like the females, paid more attention to unconscious processes than to mastery and initiative. However, male mathematicians and writers emphasized their ambition to a greater extent than the creative women, who emphasized that they would be willing to put aside other things in order to write or do mathematics. Helson did further studies and came up with the hypothesis that there are two creative styles: high in ego-assertiveness, or the need to push oneself in the world; and low in ego-assertiveness. Women creators seem to be the latter, while men may be either.

The creative women mathematicians worked at home, did not have prestigious academic posts, did not teach graduate students. In fact, their lifestyles were more similar to those of the writers than of their male mathematical counterparts. The low ego-assertiveness style does not publish many papers, nor is it productive in the way that Simonton said creative scientists must be. Helson said that the creative women mathematicians may have been more productive, but the institutions had trouble with their ambivalent and aloof personalities. These glaring differences between creative women mathematicians and creative male mathematicians speak to the continuing difficulty of women in achieving in creative fields because of their double bind, the continuing social expectation that they work the second shift at home as well as the first shift at their creative work. Unfortunately, as of this writing, as indicated by the recent studies with women in science, little seems to have changed.

The SMPY Studies and the Iowa studies

The Study of Mathematically Precocious Youth (SMPY) by Stanley, Benbow, and their colleagues, and the studies at the University of Iowa by Colangelo, Assouline, Kerr, and others, have yielded information about young highly talented math students. Even at age 13, these students resemble adult mathematicians in their values and career interests. They were highly theoretical and had a great interest and much background knowledge about careers in math and science. In high school, they had enough strength of personality to fend off the social challenges caused by their high ability.

Verbally talented students have more trouble and are less popular. The mathematically talented youth were more outgoing, mature, and independent. They came from small families with well-educated parents who were often professionals. The parents were often older and very child-oriented. Few of the families had experienced divorce. The family as a whole came together to support the mathematical or science talent of the precocious child. Their toys were often educational toys, puzzles, and many books. As they went into high school, they often skipped grades, and they took the most challenging courses. Their favorite courses were in mathematics and science.

By college, about a third of the girls had dropped out of the mathematics and science tracks and no longer aspired to get a Ph.D. This is despite the fact that the girls had better academic records and grades than the boys. The students most likely to be underachievers were boys from families where both parents had not finished college. The most important variable in this brew was the level of challenge in their high school and college courses. Those who took and succeeded in the most challenging courses were often those who continued in college to take the courses necessary to obtain the Ph.D. and to enter the world of mathematics or science. Benbow and Lubinski said that acceleration of these talented students (that is, permitting them to take higher level courses or even skip high school) has been shown to be a strategy that is quite beneficial. Not permitting highly talented students to accelerate could be called "educational malpractice."

Insight in Mathematicians and Scientists

Besides having optimal family, school, community, gender, and chance factors, as well as having the personality attributes and the intellectual abilities (as in my Pyramid model), it is necessary for thinkers in these fields to produce insights as part of their creative processes. Studies by psychologists of insight have been collected by Sternberg and Davidson in *The Nature of Insight*. An essay by Seifert and her colleagues described several types of insight. Insight was defined as being able to perceive intuitively the inner nature of things. Intuition is, as studies have shown, the preferred mode of perception by creative mathematicians and scientists as defined by such instruments as the Myers-Briggs Type Indicator (MBTI).

One perspective was called the "Wizard Merlin" perspective, which described the leaps that such thinkers as theoretical physicist Richard Feynman made. Gleick's biography of Feynman documented his extreme precocity in mathematics. Feynman's process of problem solving was described by his friend Murry Gell-Mann: "You write down the problem. You think very hard." [Gell-Mann shuts his eyes and presses his knuckles periodically to his forehead.] "Then you write down the answer."

The Prepared-Mind perspective on scientific and mathematical insight follows the four steps that Wallas wrote about in 1926. Insight is information-processing: First there is the mental preparation. Second is incubation. Third is illumination. Fourth is verification. Insight, which comes during the first and second phases, can be helped by study and knowledge. When a person reaches an impasse or comes to a dead end, he is forced to consider all possible information stored in memory. During this down-time of incubation, an accidental stimulus might occur which leads the person to re-consider the path taken, called by Seibert and her colleagues "opportunistic assimilation."

The mystical descriptions of the incubation phase use such words as "subconscious," "unconscious," "spontaneous" and "unexpected" to describe the appearance of the insight. Psychological research has begun to show that these may not be so unexpected. Even Feynman, the genius-wizard-magician, received his insights as a result of an accidental encounter with a previously forgotten aspect of the problem. Gleick described how Feynman gained insight into a complex physics problem after someone mentioned that one type of particle rather than another might be crucial to the interaction he was trying to decipher. Seifert and her colleagues have broken down Wallas's traditional four steps into these categories:

    I. Substages of the Preparation Phase
      a. Confrontation with a problem
      b. Construal of failure
      c. Storage of failure indices in memory
      d. Suspension of initial processing

    II. Substages of the Incubation Phase
      a. Intermediate incubation
      b. External exposure to new information
      c. Retrieval of failure indices

    III. Substages of the Illumination Phase
      a. Interpretation and assimilation
      b. Insight

The de-mystifying of the scientific creative process is proceeding apace as more cognitive psychologists conduct more experiments to show what happens in the mind while scientists and mathematicians solve problems. The finding of problems to solve also involves insight.

Inventors

The work of MacKinnon and Colangelo and his colleagues, researchers who have studied inventors, will be presented here.

Donald MacKinnon was head of the famous Institute for Personality Assessment at the University of California at Berkeley, which sponsored many of the studies described in this book. MacKinnon's specialties were the study of inventors and of architects. Colangelo has also done a study of inventors.

Inventors have spatial intelligence, in Gardner's terms, or figural intelligence in Guilford's terms. This type of intelligence is the ability to manipulate objects in space, from parallel-parking a bus to figuring out gears and levers or the drawings that accompany children's toys on Christmas eve. Mary Meeker said that most jobs in the U.S. government's directory require figural intelligence as opposed to semantic (linguistic) or symbolic intelligence, but that figural intelligence is not as valued as linguistic, or semantic, intelligence (logical-mathematical) in our society. We send the students who have figural or spatial intelligence to vocational school.

MacKinnon, in *In Search of Human Effectiveness*, said there are three major types of inventors. First are those who are employed by business and industry, working as researchers and known as captive inventors. Second are those who work on their own, known as independent inventors. This latter type may be self-employed as inventors or may invent in their spare time, after working at another job. In this, independent inventors are similar to creative people in the arts, who are often unable to find employment or to support themselves with their art—e.g., poets, novelists, actors, visual artists, musicians. A third type is the basic inventor, who creates truly radical new things in such fields as telecommunications, printing, or explosives.

Of the forty-five research scientists who were studied at IPAR, twenty-seven were inventors. To be designated an inventor, the research scientist had to have obtained a patent, applied for a patent, or made a disclosure. About half were independent inventors. No basic inventors were found. A major difference in the two groups was that all the captive inventors were highly educated, most with Ph.D.s, with fathers who were professionals or semi-professionals, while the independent inventors had fewer professional fathers and more fathers in the skilled trades. Only three of the independent inventors had completed a bachelor's degree, and only half had completed high school.

They were administered the Terman Concept Mastery Test, which does not test spatial or figural intelligence. The captive inventors had a mean score of 119, the independent inventors a mean score of 51, the lowest among the groups tested. However, there was little difference in the number of patents held. This was surprising, since people employed by corporations to be inventors should presumably know the ropes better, and should go through the formal channels of obtaining patents more often than people who invent in their spare time. In fact, who held the most patents? It was not a research scientist with a Ph.D.; rather, it was an independent inventor. This great discrepancy between people who achieve as inventors and people who score well on a verbal test illustrates the great harm done to figurally intelligent people by evaluating their intelligence via IQ tests.

MacKinnon's group, in analyzing the two types of inventors according to personality and preference, devised eight categories of industrial research scientists. They were Type I, The Zealot; Type II, The Initiator; Type III, The Diagnostician; Type IV, The Scholar; Type V, The Artificer; Type VI, The Esthetician; Type VII, The Methodologist; Type VIII, The Independent. They concluded that the research inventors were mainly Initiators and Diagnosticians, as were the independent inventors. The Initiators were described as having the ability to focus quickly and generate ideas when a research problem is presented. Other people find them exciting, and they are willing to give time. They consider themselves "relatively free of doctrinaire bias—methodological or substantive." They are good team players, described by the observers as "ambitious, well-organized, industrious, a good leader, and efficient."

The Diagnosticians were good evaluators, able to diagnose problems and to improvise quick answers when research runs into trouble. Patient with others when they make mistakes, they are described as "forceful and self-assured in manner, and unselfish and free from self-seeking and narcissistic striving."

Independent inventors, not surprisingly, had high self-confidence and self-esteem, and a willingness to troubleshoot and to plunge in. MacKinnon theorized that this personality aggressiveness may have contributed to their low test scores, since they guessed wrong answers as often as right ones. The captive inventors, while less cautious than their colleagues who are employed by industry but who don't invent, were much more cautious in taking the tests, and didn't guess as often.

Another analysis of inventors was done by Colangelo and others, who studied mechanical inventiveness and inventors. The group was made up of thirty-four inventors who held patents and who ranged in age from forty-four to eighty-two years. These inventors had certain patterns in their lives: (1) They had extremely happy childhoods and came from intact homes, probably because they grew up at a time when divorce was less likely; ninety-five per-cent of them viewed their families as very close. (2) They had very strong reli-gious ties. (3) During their childhoods, they all had some area to tinker in, and about two-thirds of them came from farming backgrounds. (4) Many of their inventions came about as ways to cut down on time done in chores. (5) They were married, and their wives were very supportive of their work. (6) They had few outside hobbies, and viewed their work as their fun. Their inventions were always on their minds. (7) They were politically conservative, risk-tak-ers in their inventions, but "normal" in all other areas—family, religion, pol-itics, dress. They were strongly independent.

Colangelo and his colleagues undertook a study comparing these inventors to students who had attended a summer inventions workshop as well as stu-dents who had scored high on the American College Test. They found that the students who had attended the summer inventions workshop and the inventors were equally as innovative, and both were more inventive than the high-scor-ing, academically-achieving students. The inventors believed that too much schooling would ruin a person's good ideas. Also, they cautioned young inven-tors to keep their ideas to themselves, for two reasons: to avoid theft, and to avoid society's sometimes dampening effect, for most inventors had difficul-ties in realizing or selling their ideas. These inventors would seem to be simi-lar to the maverick or the independent inventors that MacKinnon studied.

MacKinnon noted that most of the major inventions in the twentieth cen-tury have been made by independent or individual inventors, operating with neither support from industry nor financial backing. These inventions were such things as air conditioning, automatic transmissions, bakelite, the ball-point pen, the catalytic cracking of petroleum, cellophane, chromium plating, cinerama, the cotton picker, the cyclotron, domestic gas refrigeration, electric precipitation, the electron microscope, the gyro-compass, the hardening of liquid fats, the helicopter, insulin, the jet engine, Kodachrome, magnetic recording, penicillin, the Polaroid camera, power steering, quick freezing, radio, the safety razor, the self-winding wrist watch, streptomycin, the Sulzer loom, titanium, xerography, and the zip fastener.

Entrepreneurs

Of my mental cycles, I devote maybe ten percent to business. Business isn't that complicated. I wouldn't want to put it on my business card. When I read about great scientists like, say, Crick and Watson and how they discovered

DNA, I get a lot of pleasure. Stories of business success don't interest me in the same way. Part of my skill is understanding technology and business. So let's just say I'm a technologist.

—Bill Gates

The entrepreneur is stereotyped as ruthless, loving money, loving risk, and taking risk. Studies of entrepreneurs have shown that they do have some characteristics in common. Roberson-Saunders found that entrepreneurs are focused and controlled from within, they have a high need for achievement, and they are risk-takers. Individual entrepreneurs differ, of course, and there are gender differences also. Many male entrepreneurs come from families who are well-off; that is, they are used to living well. Their role model for being an entrepreneur is often their own father or another relative they knew well in childhood. They have at least some college, usually a bachelor's degree. They are married and have children.

Female entrepreneurs were usually first-borns and from the middle class, often divorced. Minority entrepreneurs often came from lower to middle income backgrounds and likewise were first borns who had attended college. Entrepreneurs often choose to go off on their own because they lack opportunities for advancement at their present jobs and they want to make more money. When they start their first company they are about 30 years old. Minority entrepreneurs had more difficulty obtaining initial funding from banks and financial institutions.

Successful African-American entrepreneurs said that racism was their main obstacle, with access to capital related to racism. They also lacked the role model of a successful father or relative, as most had come from blue collar backgrounds; this, they felt, was why they began their entrepreneurial careers later than other entrepreneurs.

In a study of personality preference of entrepreneurs, Reynierse in 1997 compared the Myers Briggs Type Indicator preferences to 159 entrepreneurs and compared with those of 404 small business owners, owners, 387 business managers, 1,024 lower-level managers, and 479 business executives. Results showed that business entrepreneurs and managers are quite different and represent opposing perspectives of their worlds. They summarized what has been found so far about entrepreneurs and managers:

TABLE 5. Myers-Briggs Type Indicator Preferences of Entrepreneurs and Managers: (Summarized in Reynierse, 1997)	
Extroversion-Introversion (E-I)	1. Entrepreneurs more extroverted than managers. 2. Entrepreneurs more frequently E than managers and small business owners.
Sensing-Intuition (S-N)	1. Entrepreneurs highly innovative (N), executives more functional (S). 2. Entrepreneurs more frequently N than managers and small business owners.
Thinking-Feeling (T-F)	1. Entrepreneurs & managers more frequently T than small business managers. 2. Management at all levels have higher frequencies of T.
Judging-Perceiving (J-P)	1. Management at all levels have higher frequencies of J. 2. Entrepreneurs have higher levels of P.

Reynierse theorized that the P preference would be found in entrepreneurs, as P's have generally been thought to be innovative and creative: "Although entrepreneurial P managers may be a source of discomfort within bureaucratic J organizations, in a business environment where change is perpetual and stability and control an illusion, they are probably essential for any organization to remain competitive."

He said that the mindsets of entrepreneurs and managers are often radically different. The entrepreneur ". . . has an external orientation that promotes opportunity recognition (E), tends to be innovative and can detect patterns and shifts (N), and is highly flexible, promoting an action orientation and responsiveness to change (P)." Business managers ". . . have an inward orientation toward their own practices (I), are particularly attentive to immediate events within their span of control and influence (S), and generally adhere to internal policies, structure, and plans, a commitment that is antagonistic to flexibility, action, and change (J)."

Intuition (N), as with other creative people, seems crucial in the personalities of entrepreneurs as well. Reynierse noted that the frequency of N increases with level of management, with proportionately more Ns in higher levels: "Both business entrepreneurs and business executives tend to be visionary Ns." That small business owners have more preference for F may reflect their preference for working closely with individuals and caring about them. The Sensing Perceiving (SP) combination is very rare and not much is known about such a person. He thought perhaps this is because these people often hate to take personality tests and do so only when required by their bosses.

Another study of 100 entrepreneurs by Miner in 1997 showed four personality types holding promise for succeeding as an entrepreneur: personal achiever, empathic super salesperson, real manager, and expert idea generator. In 1996 Kets de Vries presented a case study of a 44-year-old entrepreneur undergoing psychotherapy. The study gave insight into how an entrepreneur is made. Characteristics included a need for control, a sense of distrust, a desire for applause, and a need to resort to primitive defense mechanisms. The entrepreneur exhibited narcissistic tendencies, was reactive, and had difficulties with self-esteem. The author concluded that "running a business appears to not necessarily be a rational process, but more a retrospective rationalizing of decisions."

Studies have also been done of women entrepreneurs. In 1996 Langan-Fox and Roth published a study of 60 Australian women entrepreneurs. The women were motivated by a need for power and influence, by their ability to obtain influence and to have power, by resistance to being subordinate, by an internal locus of control, and by a need to achieve. They thought there are three psychological types of female entrepreneurs: the need achiever, the pragmatic, and the managerial. A lust for power was highest in the need achiever and the managerial women entrepreneurs. In 1993 Brodsky also reported a study on 41 female entrepreneurs as compared to 47 corporate managers. Managers were more trusting and required lower levels of control than the entrepreneurs, who wanted to define their own work situations. Although managers viewed the corporate environment as safe and supportive, entrepreneurs considered it confining.

Entrepreneurs across cultures are remarkably the same. In 1993, a cross-cultural study of entrepreneurs in India and the U.S. was reported by Stimpson, Narayanan, and Shanthakumar. In the US both male and female entrepreneurs had higher scores on innovation, achievement, and personal control than non-entrepreneurs. Also, female entrepreneurs and non-entrepreneurs both had higher self-confidence scores than their male counterparts. In India, both male and female entrepreneurs scored higher than non-entrepreneurs on personal control.

J. Paul Getty, Warren Buffett, and Bill Gates

Let's look at some individual entrepreneurs who became known as the richest men in the world. The lives of J. Paul Getty, Warren Buffett, and Bill Gates have striking similarities. Getty was an oil baron and takeover specialist; Buffett is a financier; Gates owns a software company. All three came from families that already had a comfortable way of life. Getty's father was a wealthy attorney in Minneapolis; Buffett's father was a Congressman and a stockbroker; Gates's mother is a banker and his father, a prominent Seattle lawyer.

All three were discipline problems in school. Getty's parents pulled him out of the local high school and put him into a military academy in Los Angeles. Buffett experienced trauma when the family moved from Omaha to Washington, D.C., and he had a difficult adjustment. When he finally came to permanently live with his parents in Washington, D.C., he paid more attention to his five paper routes and the profit they brought him than to his studies, and his parents had to intervene. Gates was a cut-up, bored in his local public school; worried about his educational future, his parents, when he was in seventh grade, placed him in a private boys' school with high academic standards and a comfortability in working with bright, eccentric boys.

All three demonstrated early their ability in mathematics and their affinity for the fields in which they would make their money. In his 1976 autobiography, Getty described a trip to Indian territory (Oklahoma) in 1903 where his father, George Getty, had to take care of a client's legal problems. The trip introduced the Gettys to the oil frenzy. Getty wrote: "There are men—albeit they are few and far between—who seem to have an uncanny affinity with oil in its natural state. By some mysterious instinct, they appear to sense its presence even when the pool is thousands of feet below ground." Getty's father had this instinct.

In 1904, at the age of eleven, the young Getty witnessed his first oil well come in. At the age of 16 he began to work for his father's oil company from the bottom, as a roustabout. "I could expect no preferential treatment because I was the Boss's son. I would have to hold my own with the other men, take my share of the orders, and do my share of the work." He went to college during the year and worked summers in the oil fields. He spent a year at Oxford University in Great Britain reading political science and economics, thinking he would try for the diplomatic corps.

His father wanted his only child to come into the business and persuaded him to try wildcat oil operating for one year. On a stipend of $100 per month, he scouted for promising leases. Nothing came his way until the end of the year. Getty persuaded a banker friend to stand in for him at the bidding in order to intimidate the other bidders into believing that a major oil company had interest in the property. The well was built and produced 700 barrels a day. By the age of 24 Getty was his own millionaire. He said, "Anyone who starts from scratch—even someone like me, who started from scratch but with family wealth behind him—is likely to regard the figure and the label as ultimates and ends in themselves."

Bill Gates met his future partner at Microsoft, Paul Allen, at Lakeside School, which had connections with an infant computer company. Students in the honors mathematics class were invited to play with the computers and to experiment with programming them. The two boys fell in love with computers. Gates straightened up his academic act. He was so quick he barely needed to study, and he would become so obsessed with computer programming he would sneak out at night and go back to the computer company, where he worked out programming problems and created, among other things, a scheduling program for the school.

Gates displayed the classic characteristics of the underachieving gifted boy who does homework only for the classes he likes. The private school was good for him. He became a straight-A student and received a perfect 800 on his SAT mathematics test, becoming a National Merit Finalist. Admitted to Harvard, Princeton, and Yale, he chose Harvard. He continued working with Allen, who was in college back in Washington, on BASIC programming, learning the other languages as well (COBOL, PASCAL, etc.).

His biographers, Manes and Andrews, commented that at Harvard he rarely attended class except for the first day, but he would study for the final and receive an A or B. After he illegally used the graduate school computers and amassed great amounts of user time, Harvard considered kicking him out.

His non-academics at Harvard also included a heavy dose of poker playing. He took a leave from Harvard after six semesters to move to Albuquerque to develop the software business with Allen. He never returned.

Warren Buffett's mathematical ability was so keen that he began to buy low and sell high at age six, when he bought a six pack of Coke for a quarter and sold it for five cents a can. He always had what his biographer Kilpatrick called "an auditor's instinct—the ability to get at the real numbers, not the supposed numbers passed along by others." He skipped a grade in elementary school. His mathematical ability took its form in an interest in finance and the stock market, and he bought his first stocks at age eleven. He had been following the stock market and at the age of eight he began reading books on investment which his father had around the house. He also began following the horses while in middle school and published a betting sheet, selling it for a quarter.

His fascination for mathematics and his interest in money bordered on obsessive. In church he would calculate the longevity of the hymn writers to see whether they lived longer than other people. In high school he and a friend set up a pinball machine business, and he had several paper routes. His grades in junior high were poor, improving only when his congressman father threatened to take away his paper routes. He also worked at a golf course retrieving lost golf balls. While still in high school he saved enough money to buy a 40-acre farm in Nebraska. He briefly attended the Wharton School of Business but transferred back to the University of Nebraska, graduating at age 19. Rejected by the Harvard Business School, he enrolled in the Columbia Business School, where his academic record was excellent: he graduated with a master's degree in economics at age 20. He is a world class bridge player.

All three were readers from a young age and continued to enjoy reading throughout their lives. Getty experienced a real quandary when his father asked him to take over the business, as he loved his reading of political science and economics. He disdained the rah-rah social life and lack of academic rigor at UCLA, but "Oxford was, for me, an ideal place to study. Students were considered and treated as mature, responsible individuals, not as untrustworthy adolescents. The underlying philosophy was that if a student desired an education, he would obtain it without constant, niggling supervision."

Reading was emphasized in the family. Gates said in a *Playboy* interview, "When I was young, we used to read books over the summer and get little colored bookmarks for each one. There were girls who had read maybe 15 books. I'd read 30. Numbers two through 99 were all girls, and there I was at number one. I thought, Well, this is weird, this is very strange. I also liked taking tests. I happened to be good at it. Certain subjects came easily, like math. All the science stuff. I would just read the textbooks the first few days of class." When Buffett would play basketball with his high school friends, he was known for abstractedly taking a break to go off to the sidelines for awhile to read the *Wall Street Journal*. He would then come back into the game. Even now he rarely watches television, saving his time for reading and studying.

However, they were somewhat different in their mating behavior and love lives. Getty had five wives and five divorces as well as many mistresses. He was always attractive to, and attracted to, women. "I was anything but the ideal husband . . . I'm afraid I gave more time and attention to oil wells and proxy-fights than to home and fireside. My autocratic tendencies were no less apparent in my personal life than in business." On the other hand, neither Gates nor Buffett were popular with the ladies. Marrying late, Buffett separated from his wife in the late 1970s. He lives with a woman in Omaha. Gates had a reputation among women as being somewhat strange, and he did not marry until his mid-thirties. He said he was surprised when he met his wife-to-be. "Amazingly, she made me feel like getting married. Now that is unusual! It's against my past rational thinking on the topic."

All were workaholics, driven to compete and to win. Their shrewdness in contract matters, in protecting their interests, and in slyly, ruthlessly beating all competitors is legendary. These adult behaviors were also predicted in childhood—in Getty, in his striving to prove himself to Oklahoma wildcatters even though he was a rich kid, son of the boss; in Buffett's willingness to leave a stockbroker position and start his own business in his bedroom, not even telling his investors where their money was being spent, but just to trust him; in Gates's reputation, even among his childhood friends, for screaming arguments that lasted for hours, often ending in disdainful putdowns of "stupid" or "dumb" ideas. Gates says, though, that he wants people to stand up to him and argue it out, as that is where the problems are solved.

The need for independence, control, and being the boss shows strongly in all of them. All were hands-on managers, setting examples by working long hours and modeling obsessiveness for their employees. While Getty liked the fast life of cars, yachts, and blondes in his limited free time, both Gates and Buffett seem to have trouble enjoying their billions, living rather modestly, with few opulent indulgences. Buffett still lives in his modest neighborhood in Omaha; Gates lives near his parents where his large house has many electronic devices, and though he loves fast cars and buys the software rights to great art, he does not own a private airplane and often flies coach.

Getty's interest in art led to his endowing of the Los Angeles Getty Art Museum and to the Getty Foundation funding of discipline-based art education. Gates plans to give most of his money away when he reaches his fifties. Buffett also plans to give most of his money away, leaving little to his children. Gates has similar plans: "I don't believe in burdening any children I might have." He'll give them a million dollars, but not a billion. Getty gave up his fast cars and yacht-buying habits and said of himself, "Those who wish to call (or consider) me frugal, parsimonious—or even miserly—are welcome to do so . . . I long ago outgrew the neon-lighted suit worn by those who believe they should make a great show of wasting money for no other reason than to demonstrate that they can afford to be wastrels."

I interviewed California business consultant Jerome Stein about entrepreneurs who are not as famous as these three. He said that even in moderately successful entrepreneurs, the maverick quality stands out, as well as the intuitive insight and independence. In what consists the creativity of entrepreneurs? Their personality characteristics of risk-taking, their high mathematical intelligence, their obsessiveness and passion for their work, and their ability to see their fields in new ways are part of this.

The insight and ability to foresee what will be needed is a great part of their personalities. While the computer mavens were building hardware, Gates and Allen saw the need for software for those machines, and positioned themselves by legally protecting their compositions, their creations of computer programs that would run on the machines being built. While the world was gearing up to exploit fossil fuels for the running of the machines necessary for an industrial society, Getty was scouting for that fuel and protecting his interests through complicated and ruthless maneuvers for control. While the stock market was falling and everyone was selling, Buffett was buying low, keeping his acquisitions until they recovered and creating a portfolio of solid, performing stocks that continue to climb. While other stocks were splitting, Buffett's never did, and today one share of his company costs almost $40,000. The creativity of the entrepreneurs consists of insight, intuition, and sheer guts, combined with canniness, cunning, and a deep knowledge of their domain.

Summary

1. As a general rule, scientists and mathematicians have more formal education than people in the arts.

2. They demonstrate an early aptitude and love for the field.

3. They are motivated less by external concerns than by internal concerns, or the desire to know.

4. As children, they are encouraged by parents or teachers.

5. They begin producing early and produce in quantity.

6. Their personalities vary from reserved to aggressive.

7. The family environment was happier than that of those pursuing the arts and literature.

8. Women were underemployed and experienced conflict between raising children and pursuing a science career.

9. Young scientists and mathematicians were more conforming than older scientists and mathematicians.

10. There was a need for supportive and connected mentors.

11. The societally-recognized creativeness of their work depends on the historical milieu, or Zeitgeist. Were they in the right place at the right time?

12. Inventors were often from rural areas and had conservative backgrounds. They demonstrated their risk-taking through their inventions and not in their lives.

13. Entrepreneurs across races, cultures, and gender seem to have similar personality characteristics.

14. J. Paul Getty, Warren Buffett, and Bill Gates have many similarities and a few differences in their biographical paths.

Chapter 9

Musicians, Conductors, and Composers

Of music so delicate, soft, and intense
It was felt like an odor within the sense
—Shelley

I have always been opposed to "background music." How can one converse
about trivialities at a party or even engage in serious work if, at the same time,
the deepest expressions of life and death, sorrow and elation, fill the room?
—Viktor Weisskopf

What comes to mind when you picture a musician? Do you see a young boy
forced to practice his piano lesson, who plays a tape recording of himself so
he can escape to play baseball? Or a young girl lugging her cello to school for
orchestra rehearsal or down the street for her private lesson? Or a garage band
practicing at all hours of the night, waking you up and inspiring you to call
the police? Or do you see young Van Cliburn wowing them in Moscow, making the evening news?

Whatever you see, it is probably an image that includes practice.
Musicians practice. They take private lessons. They play alone. They play in
groups. Even if they are in school groups—choirs, bands, orchestras—they
must take private lessons in order to further themselves in their music.
Schools have the responsibility to identify students who are musically gifted
and to serve them through music programs, but no child who has musical talent will proceed very far unless she has private teachers. While this could be
said to be true for visual arts talent as well, few young talented visual artists
take private lessons. Few young talented creative writers take private lessons.
Few young talented scientists and mathematicians take private lessons, but all

young people who are talented in music must if they are to succeed.

Much has been written on musical talent, especially in the genres of auto-biography and biography. Musical intelligence, another of Gardner's eight "frames of mind," is characterized by acute hearing ability, or audition, as well as the ability to understand the organization of rhythms. Many have likened musical intelligence to mathematical intelligence, but Gardner point-ed out that this ignores the emotional impact of music, and the musically tal-ented person's ability to evoke emotion. Most of us listen to music because of the wordless emotion caused to well up within us.

Gardner also noted that musical illiteracy is acceptable in our society, and that little training in music, beyond basic singing and reading of notes in ele-mentary school, happens: "Music occupies a relatively low niche in our cul-ture, and so musical illiteracy is acceptable." I once asked a group of about a hundred educators how many could read music, and five raised their hands. Four were music teachers. The rest could not read music, even though many of them were elementary teachers who had taken a mandatory course in music literacy. Our knowledge of classical music is also poor.

However, the power of music to move us cannot be disputed. Few people have not had moist eyes when hearing some tune or another. I once wrote a newspaper column on what makes us spontaneously weep, and most people whom I asked said they got tears in their eyes when hearing children sing, hearing an old love song, singing the national anthem, or singing a favorite hymn.

Predictive Behaviors for Musical Talent

Musical talent often shows up early, and if a family has a keyboard instru-ment, the musically talented child will probably be picking out tunes at a young age. Michael Howe and his colleagues, in a study of how early musi-cal talent is manifested, found childhood spontaneous singing was observed at an earlier age in those who later became the most accomplished young musicians. The age at which parent and child first listened to music together tended to be lower for the most successful, and they were more likely than the others to have had a keyboard instrument in their home from an early age.

Musical prodigy, or the ability to perform at an adult professional level, shows itself as more complex and more advanced at a young age than simple musical talent. In Great Britain, the Gulbenkian Foundation's 1978 report about training young musicians adopted several definitions of musical talent.

Children who are gifted are those who have the potential to become performers; among them are those who can become stars, and the British termed these children "outstandingly gifted." Britain distinguishes between degrees of musical talent, and as we do in the United States, the school takes a role in identification when musical talent isn't identified by parents and friends.

There are crosscultural differences in attitudes toward talent. In Japan, for example, talent is not thought of as arising in a child; talent is trained. Suzuki, in *Nurtured By Love,* advocated the nurturing of musical talent from early infancy in a system of talent education called The Suzuki Method. He wasn't interested in definitions of talent, claiming that any child who learns to speak can learn music. Repetition of the correct, as in learning a foreign language, is necessary. "Ability is one thing we have to produce (or work for) ourselves. That means to repeat and repeat an action until it becomes a part of ourselves." Tone-deaf children are not hopeless, either, as is commonly thought in the United States. Suzuki said that children who are tone-deaf, in singing the scale, usually sing *fa,* the fourth note, a little high. "I found out that one has to teach them a new *fa.* If they have learned the wrong *fa* by hearing it five thousand times, one must make them listen to the right *fa* six thousand or seven thousand times." The children listen to the correct interval between *mi* and *fa* many thousands of times, and "the right *fa* becomes easier and more natural for that child, so in the end he always produces it. The result is that he is no longer tone deaf. It takes six or seven months to achieve this with a child of six."

With the Suzuki method, a parent, usually the mother, works closely with the child in the acquisition of the rudimentary musical skills necessary to playing the violin. (Suzuki instruction on piano and cello is also available.) In one application of the technique, mothers of infants are first taught to play one piece on a tiny violin that is sized to the child. The child listens to recordings of the piece but does not play at first; training begins when the child asks for the violin. The first song is a set of variations on "Twinkle, Twinkle Little Star." This, it is to be emphasized, is a training method based on the philosophy that musical intelligence can be taught. Since Asian education utilizes drill and practice to the point of mastery, Westerners often wonder whether such education creates automatons or maestros.

Gardner, in an article called "Learning Chinese Style," shared his observations about repetition and practice. He noted that young Chinese students were taught calligraphy, repeating over and over certain patterns and figures. The differences between U.S. education and its emphasis on early exploratory activities in art and early Chinese art education were so great, he wondered whether the Chinese children would be able to transfer their training to free-hand drawings, so he asked them to draw a portrait of him with their calligraphy brushes. They were able to do so, with several of the ten-year-olds making recognizable portraits. Gardner said, "Chinese children were not simply tied to schemata. They can depart from a formula when so requested."

Standardized Tests

Schools should never use IQ tests as a screen in identifying music talent, but should use the musical aptitude measures that have been validated over the years. These can be used to identify talent in youth from musically deprived families, where the school is the only agency that identifies the child. In the United States and Great Britain, standardized tests have been developed to identify music talent in young people. These are such tests as the Seashore Measures, which were developed for the Eastman School of Music in 1919, the Gordon Primary Measures of Music Audiation (PMMA) developed in 1979, and the Gordon Intermediate Measures of Music Audition (IMMA) developed in 1982.

Recently a coordinator of programs for the talented wanted to change his district's identification procedures to reflect the Multiple Intelligences (MI) approach. He asked me what tests he should use to identify musical talent. I sang a note and asked him to sing the same note. He could not match my pitch. "You can't get into my choir," I said. Musical talent is most truly found by looking *directly* at the intelligence, not by filtering the assessment through linguistic or logical-mathematical, paper and pencil tests.

Developmental Research

Bamberger said that musically talented children go through a "midlife crisis" in their adolescent years. Young musically talented children approach music holistically, using many strategies quite naturally as they approach music. The crisis comes when the child comes to consciousness, becomes more self-critical and reflective about music. This time is a "period of serious cognitive reorganization . . . there can be neither return to imitation and the unreflective, spontaneous 'intuitions' of childhood, nor a simple 'fix-up.'"

A similar scenario of cognitive reorganization was described by pianist Lorin Hollander in 1987. A child prodigy whose father was a violinist, Hollander at three years was handed a violin by his father. The rebellious child smashed it "coldly and empirically" and then began to play only the notes on the piano that his father couldn't reach on his violin, F below middle C. He gave his first concert in kindergarten, for a pageant called "Circus," and when he was eleven, he first played a concert in Carnegie Hall. He noted that he himself had gone through the Erikson stages (see Chapter One). "Following [Erik] Erikson's nicely laid out cycles, while continuing to perform I have three or four times undergone profound changes in my personality and, I believe, in the actual dynamics of my nervous system."

This transition from the promise of prodigy to the artistry of the adult musical artist is developmental, and Bamberger likened it to Piaget's concept of disequilibrium falling to equilibration and then to a reorganizing of schemata. She said that the mid-life crisis is a process of reorganizing, during which the child learns to analyze and synthesize musical knowledge.

Choosing a Career in Music

While there are many who have high accomplishment in music, it takes a special breed of person to face the stiff competition that a career in music necessitates throughout one's professional life. A career in music means that one must practice, take lessons from ever more advanced teachers, audition, and win over all entrants, only to receive what is often a low salary. And like creative writers who take jobs in university writing departments and visual artists who teach in art, musicians often become music teachers in order to support themselves. Hence many performers "moonlight" during the day, as typists or underwriters or waiters, while school music teachers often gig in orchestras or bands at night.

Many of us know musicians of many trades by day (including teaching) whose weekend nights end at 3:00 a.m., after the bars close. Their families barely see them, but the supplementary salary helps them stay in a profession that feeds the soul more efficiently than it does the body. In addition, the classically trained musician must take any job that comes along, must audition for faraway symphonies and obscure chamber groups. A friend of mine plays the flute in a symphony orchestra in underdeveloped Latin America. Young and fresh out of music school, she could find work in music only with this faraway symphony.

Perhaps all of this indicates that we have trained too many musicians, as discussed in Chapter 1, where reasons of quantity for valuing creativity were cited. Perhaps our conservatories and music departments are turning out students who are unemployable. But perhaps the real problem is a lack of appreciation and employment for highly-trained musicians because as a society we are musically illiterate. A flip through the radio stations in any urban or rural area will illustrate the types of music and musicians our society supports. Depending on geography, rock 'n' roll—golden oldies, soft rock, hard rock, Top 40—or country music of several varieties will be prevalent. The lower end of the dial will have perhaps one jazz station and one public radio station that plays the chestnuts of classical music. Little new classical music hits the airways. Nor does much innovative music of any genre. My point is that as listeners we are untrained, even lazy, and unable to appreciate what our countless fine musicians would like to play for us.

When a young person chooses any of the arts as a career, it is often with the knowledge that our society does not really support its young artists. For the past few years, politicians have been asking why the government should support funding for the National Endowment for the Arts, and the funding has been drastically cut. Yet these same critics would probably not dispute the necessity for the government to support young scientists with scholarships and grants and research jobs. In some ways, young creative artists are less valued in our society than young scientists and mathematicians. This is not necessarily true in other countries. While traveling in Finland, for example, I met the director of the regional theater in Lahti. His theater, subsidized by the government, employed forty full-time actors.

The arts, all of them, are necessary for human well-being. Pleasure as well as the knowledge of ourselves that we get from the arts cannot be duplicated in any other human enterprise. A person who does not get satisfaction from the arts has an impoverished soul. The arts feed our spirituality, speak to our humanness and our universal similarity, bridge continents and languages. Yet often the arts are the first to be cut from school programs, because they are viewed as extraneous to educational experience, even though when children remember what they learned in school, it is often what they learned in arts: projects, concerts, plays, physical performances they gave in sports, editorials they wrote for the school newspaper.

Personality Attributes of Musicians

Several studies of personality attributes of musicians have been conducted. (Personality attributes form the base of the Pyramid of Talent Development, you will recall.)

Kemp, in several studies using the Cattell High School Personality Questionnaire (HSPQ) and the 16 Personality Factors Questionnaire (16 PF), studied several hundred performers and composers in Great Britain, as well as student teachers of music. Suitable control groups of nonmusicians were also tested.

Secondary school musicians were found to be significantly different from nonmusicians in these personality factors: they were more intelligent, more dominant, more conscientious, more individualistic, more self-sufficient, and more controlled. They were less emotionally stable, less happy-go-lucky, and less outgoing. The more talented musicians who were attending conservatories were less outgoing and less adventurous than secondary school musicians. The more talented musicians were also more excitable (perhaps an emotional overexcitability) and both more individualistic and more apprehensive.

Adult professional musicians were more outgoing, more intelligent, more individualistic, more imaginative, more forthright, and more self-sufficient. Male musicians were shown to be less emotionally stable than male nonmusicians. They also were more suspicious and radical. Why this was so is not spelled out, but perhaps it is because professional musicians have had to weather great competition from peers, always checking to see who might be gaining on them, and they also need great personal drive and passion for their music. Women professional music performers were found to be more dominant and more tense than the comparison females. Again, drive and passion are needed for success in musical performance, and the women would need to be more like men performers than like other females.

Kemp also did a most interesting study of music teachers and performers, using the 16 PF. Musicians who were studying to be teachers were more extroverted and outgoing and less sensitive to criticism than those who wanted to be performers. The music teachers also found conforming to be easier. According to Kemp, "This movement away from the high levels of introversion and sensitivity known to characterize the music student allows the student teacher to withstand the rough and tumble of classroom existence." People who become music teachers showed their conservatism in their tendency to "cling to the well-worn methods of music teaching embedded within their own music education."

The necessity for teachers to be outgoing, more outgoing than performers, may be a problem for those who have spent many hours alone in practice rooms training for performance. Kemp wrote, "Music teachers who, over several years, will have spent long periods in the solitary confinement of the practice room focusing on their own personal musical development, may find it difficult to readjust to the interests and learning difficulties of others." He thought that the "rich, colorful and imaginative inner mental life" of musicians "renders them self-sufficient and detached from others." They may not be able to manage the behavior of students. But choosing teaching may be the right choice for musicians for whom performance is too demanding.

Wubbenhorst did a comparison study of personality types and psychological androgyny of about a hundred graduate students studying to be music educators and performers. He used the Myers-Briggs Type Indicator (MBTI) and the Bem Sex Roles Inventory (BSRI). Both groups preferred ENF (Extroversion, Intuition, and Feeling). However, on Judging and Perceiving the students came out in the middle, at 50-50, and so, on the recommendations of Myers and McCaulley, who had a sense of the direction of the tip of the scales, they were scored as preferring Judging. Both groups also turned out to be psychologically androgynous on the BSRI.

Again we see that these musicians were similar to other creative people studied in that they prefer Intuition (N). The androgyny in the personalities of creative people "suggests a strong connection between Intuition-Feeling and androgyny," according to Wubbenhorst: "The reported high levels of androgyny among the musician subjects in this study suggest support for Bem's gender schema theory, in which an androgynous individual is able to move freely across sex-role behaviors when organizing and processing information." This ability allows them to have flexibility, which may be viewed as an enhancement or an advantage in the classroom and on the performance stage.

Buttsworth and Smith looked at personalities of several hundred Australian musicians in 1995. The 16 Personality Factors (16 PF) Questionnaire was administered. The musicians sang and played keyboards, strings, woodwinds and brass. The performing musicians were less intelligent and more emotionally stable, sensitive, and conservative when compared with the nonmusician group. Male musicians were more sensitive and shrewd than female counterparts. Brass players were more suspicious, imaginative, apprehensive, and radical than singers and more extroverted and less anxious and creative than string players. Keyboard players were more warmhearted, emotionally stable, and shrewd than were the others, perhaps because they had to be so adaptable to changing roles of soloist, accompanist, or ensemble player. Singers were more distrustful, imaginative, anxious, and extreme than the instrumental musicians.

The study uncovered some resentments among section players. The string players viewed the brass section as alcoholic, loud, and rowdy, while the brass viewed the strings as effete, oversensitive, and conceited. The authors theorized that brass players more often play solo parts than members of a string section, and the aggressiveness shown may be necessary for solo performers. How players and instruments are matched remains a matter of conjecture; do the personalities of the players determine the instrument they play, or do their personalities change as they get more experience playing in the instrumental section?

Dyce and O'Connor published a study of the personality characteristics of 150 popular rock and country bass players, guitarists, and drummers. The performers completed the Interpersonal Circumplex questionnaire. Popular performers tended to be significantly more extroverted, arrogant, and dominant when compared to university students, and more neurotic than the rest of the population. The authors hypothesized that the neuroticism might be caused by the nomadic lifestyle and employment instability. Neuroticism might also be necessary for conveying passion when performing music. The popular musicians also showed more openness to experience in the realm of fantasy, and seemed to be more imaginative than the general population.

Personalities of Composers

Composers also differed from performers and teachers. Kemp published a study of student composers and compared them with music students who did not compose music and who were not interested in doing so. He also administered the 16 PF questionnaire to members of the Composers Guild of Great Britain, comparing them with professional musicians who did not do any composing. Male professional and student composers were found to be more aloof, dominant, sensitive, and controlled. They were imaginative and self-sufficient. The only difference between the students and the professionals was that the professionals had higher IQs. Female professional composers were also dominant and self-sufficient. Composers were the most extreme in all the personality factors.

Shyness

Shyness is a heritable quality of temperament and personality that is present in many creative people. While one study described above, using the personality preference instrument, the Myers-Briggs Type Indicator, indicated that performers and music teachers prefer extroversion, it is commonly known that many creators, including composers, prefer introversion. Shyness is related to introversion, and it is also an aspect of neuroticism. Sulloway commented, "Extroverts are characterized by a lively sociability that contrasts with the introvert's reserved and quiet manner. Shy people are *anxiously* introverted, which is why they are uneasy in the presence of strangers." Sulloway related shyness to birth order, saying that it is more common to laterborns, who were often taunted and criticized by older siblings.

However, shyness occurs no matter what one's birth position in the family. For musicians, shyness might be overcome by the playing of music, speaking in another language, the language of music, using another code for communication. Jenny Boyd described how Mick Fleetwood courted her when they were teenagers. "I remember when I first met Mick Fleetwood, he was extremely shy and found it difficult to carry on a conversation. He used to telephone me, say hello, then put down the phone receiver next to his drum kit, which he would then begin to play, while I listened for the next forty-five minutes." The anxiety and tension shy people feel can be assuaged through metaphor, whether musical, artistic, poetic, or physical.

Attributes Necessary for Conductors

The profession of conductor requires certain skills and attributes. Among these are a deep knowledge of music and the social skills of being able to be perceived as a leader. The conductor D. Polkow quoted Solti as saying, "A first-class conductor is a combination of intelligence, psychology, and intuition, or knowing how to ride the possibilities of the moment—being able to feel the hearts and minds of your players." Solti wanted to be a conductor ever since as a child prodigy musician in Hungary, he heard Beethoven's Fifth Symphony. "That concert made my life," he said. This crystallizing experience sealed his fate. Solti said that determination and drive are key personality characteristics:

> You must have talent and determination, or endurance. The really first-class conductors have these qualities. You must be able to suffer through all of the obstacles, and work very hard. You have to pursue conducting as your single ambition and know that somebody, somewhere, someday, will give you a chance. And when you get that damn chance, you must be ready. Go and do it. Go and pester people. I did the same.

And get whatever experience you can get, however you can get it. I am quite certain that true talent does not go unnoticed.

Lebrecht, author of *The Maestro Myth: Great Conductors in Pursuit of Power,* found that exceptional conductors must have

- a keen ear;

- the charisma to motivate musicians from the very first time they meet;

- the determination to get their own way;

- high organizational ability;

- physical and mental fitness;

- unswerving ambition;

- a forceful intelligence;

- an instinctive sense of order which helps them to organize scattered notes to the artistic core;

- the ability to interpret a score and convey that meaning to musicians and audience.

Rudolf said that conductors need older mentors who will initiate them into the requirements of the conductor's world: "Young conductors usually need the approval of older colleagues." He noted that the initial success of a conductor is "rarely the result of publicity but rather word-of-mouth communication within the profession." For example, Wagar noted that Dennis Russell Davies, when he was a piano major at the Juilliard School, met Luciano Berio, and "through Luciano I got to meet some very important musicians and composers."

Conductors often discover that their talents on their musical instruments are not enough to propel them to the top levels of instrumental performance, and that their conducting talents are greater than their performance talents. Davies said, "I began to see that though I was a good pianist I wasn't ever going to be winning the Moscow Tchaikovsky Competition. Some of the gifts I had were much more suited to conducting." In fact, the conductor often has to bear the resentment of both the musicians who play the music and the composers who write it. Rudolf commented that the musicians often resent "the dictator on the podium." The composer Igor Stravinsky said, "Conducting, like politics, does not attract original minds . . . it is more a field for the making of careers and the exploitation of personalities . . . than a profession for the application of exact and standardized disciplines." Stravinsky likened conductors to politicians and diplomats:

> A conductor may actually be less well equipped for his work than the best of his players, but no one except the players need know it, and his career is not dependent on them in any case, but on the society women to whom he must toady and to whom his musical qualities are of secondary importance . . . his first skill has to be in the game of power politics.

Because so much of the work of conductors is repetitive, Stravinsky thought that they often "develop an occupational indifference to music." He called them "intermediaries" and "social parasites living on the creations of others," and said conductors are delinquents, "too quickly rusticated and lost to the new musical ideas" of their time. In fact, Solti said that he was unable to understand contemporary composers and said that he was too old to learn. The social and organizational talents of the conductor often take precedence, for the conductor must get to know prominent, wealthy, and influential people and persuade them to support and further the interests of the orchestra.

On the importance of chance and seizing it when it comes, several conductors emphasized that often, as in the case of Esa-Pekka Salonen, conductor of the Los Angeles Philharmonic Orchestra, and Leonard Bernstein, late conductor of the New York Philharmonic Orchestra, the opportunity, if not taken, may not come again. Wagar quoted Catherine Comet, one of the few women conductors, who said:

> I don't know how a conductor makes it . . . that has always been something of a mystery to me. You have to study a lot and be ready because somehow everybody gets chances. But you have to be ready for it when it comes . . . these chances never happen at the perfect moment with six months notice. They just sort of happen suddenly and you really have to be ready for them . . . chances come like a big bang . . . so study as much as you can even though it can be frustrating . . . conducting is a crazy profession. Don't do it unless you are really crazy also . . . to be a conductor you have to be obsessed with music.

The conductor must be able to inspire the often recalcitrant musicians by "taking charge," as Victoria Bond noted in a discussion of why there are so few women conductors. Adult men may not want a woman to take charge over them. Musicians appreciate a conductor who can give them inspiration and a feeling after the concert that the whole orchestra has shared the accomplishment. Solti said that the conductor must always remember that "music is a totally abstract art" and the conductor must have such force of personality that he "can take his abstract image and put it above other people's." The conductor Herbert Blomstedt, who studied at the Royal College of Music in Sweden, said that the conductor must have "psychic energy" in order to convey the composer's intent.

A conductor needs a phenomenal memory for music. Salonen's chance came in London when he was very young. He essentially experienced the understudy phenomenon, stepping in and conducting when a conductor got sick. The word passed, and people flew to London to see how he did. He did well. Within a year he had memorized thirty symphonies. Some conductors have photographic memories, and study the scores with grave intent. Others even conduct without the scores in front of them, having memorized entire compositions. The conductor Charles Dutoit said, "Conducting should always be controlled by the brain in a way which enables you to put the shape of a movement into context."

Few conductors, unlike Salonen, are composers themselves. When Salonen heard one of his compositions performed on the radio, he reacted like a composer, berating the conductor for not understanding the piece. His wife reminded him that composers were doing the same to him, and he realized that the profession of conductor carried a great responsibility to the intent of the composer. Salonen said that when he was studying composing, "I looked at conductors as the main enemies of music," but he turned to conducting after "feeling the pull of Bruckner and Beethoven, not to mention the 20th century classics, and they just took over."

In other words, the conductor must have what Lebrecht described as "an aspiration to compose, conduct and instruct, an irresistible charisma" and a formidable intellect that can range "across the warp and woof of Western thought." Ewen said that the conductor's ability to interpret must awaken the audience from "musical sleep" so that "spiritual enrichment" takes place. The conductor is a cross between a high priest and a chief executive. And most importantly, the conductor must love music deeply. As Herbert Blomstedt put it, "After a concert I feel exhilarated and want to do it again. I never get tired of making music." And as Esa-Pekka Salonen said, "Sometimes I have these funny moments of joy. I'm studying the score and I suddenly realize how great the music is, and I'm overcome by very powerful feelings of euphoria."

Again and again we see, in the anecdotal comments of musicians, the great pleasure and passion they have for their music. Composers, performers, and conductors have at least one thread in common. They love music. Music arouses great emotions within their souls.

Intelligence of Musicians

How intelligent are musicians? Kemp commented on the higher IQs of music students, saying that although earlier researchers had reported no consistent relationship between intelligence and musical aptitude, later studies have shown that "even when the music students were compared with the under-graduate norms their level [of measured intelligence] was marginally higher." These data suggested to him that music students "choose to pursue music in preference to other academic studies because of a strong motivation towards music rather than any lack of intellectual capacity." In other words, their intelligence indicated that the musicians were capable of entering other professions, but they chose music because they wanted it. (Incidentally, Kemp also said that many adult musicians use their intelligence to leave music for more lucrative professions.) In fact, there is a basic assumption in schools that music students tend to be smart. When the band director addressed parents of fifth graders at my son's school, he said that an advantage of playing in the band is that a child's peers are the kids who are often on the honor roll.

When people ask me how to get their children through middle and high school intact, I often tell them to get their children into the band or orchestra; the entire school often revolves around instrumental music periods, and students' schedules will be such that they will be in classes with good students. A high school band director told me that the grade point average of students in all his bands is 3.2 on a 4-point scale. Whether bright students join music groups because they are good at it or because their parents make them is not known. Since it is well documented that a high IQ is positively related to high grades, these observations would seem to support Kemp's study.

Development of Talent in the Domain of Music

Talent development in music takes certain developmental paths. Whether the musician is to play classical music or popular music, the paths have certain commonalities.

Sosniak's Study of Concert Pianists

Results of The Development of Talent Research Project, centered at the University of Chicago, were edited by Benjamin Bloom and published in *Developing Talent in Young People*. The project defined talent as high-level demonstrated ability, rather than as a natural aptitude. They asked the most outstanding young (under age forty) creative producers in several fields to participate. The Project sought to answer these questions:

> How were the outstanding persons in art and music, in athletics, in various fields of scholarship, and in industry, government, and other areas of human endeavor discovered, developed, and encouraged? Do these very talented individuals achieve because of innate and rare qualities and/or as the result of special training and encouragement?

Sosniak's contribution to the project was her study of twenty-one concert pianists who had received international recognition in piano competitions. The study focused on the three obvious phases in the development of talent in piano: the early, middle, and adult years. The group had no outstanding physical characteristics or interests; they were as likely to go hiking in their free time as to read romantic novels. Sixteen of them were male, five were female, and all were Caucasian. They were mostly only or older children from middle-class families; 80 percent of them had parents who were professional or white-collar. (This means that 20 percent of them came from homes that were not professional or white-collar.) Half were from urban areas, half from small and middle-sized towns around the country. Their families appreciated music, and music was in the home, though their parents may or may not have played an instrument. Their families thought music lessons were a good thing for children to have.

However, most families think that. Sosniak pointed out that 69 percent of all families thought that learning a musical instrument was good for children to do, 79 percent of all families have a habit of listening to music, and 44 percent of families had at least one amateur musician. This made the families of these future concert pianists almost indistinguishable from the normal families. What explained the achievements of these young pianists?

Stage One: The Early Years of Talent Development in Music

What did the early years show about the development of the talent of these pianists?

1. They came from homes where music was respected, even valued, and often there were amateur players in the household.
2. Music lessons were considered a necessary part of growing up, and the children were expected to take lessons. Their parents scheduled lessons for the children, and the children went.
3. The teachers were such that the children liked going to music lessons. The families chose teachers that were good teachers, who conveyed a love of music to their students.
4. The families expected the young musicians to practice, to spend time in preparing their piano lessons. It was part of the family script, the family ethos. Once the commitment was made and the students were found to be talented, the family expected they would practice. Other children of their ages spent a lot less time at lessons. The students also liked the piano, and liked practicing. Often siblings were also given music lessons, but the ones with the most drive were the ones who achieved the most.
5. The lessons began early enough that the routine of practice had been made part of the family schedule before the other activities normal to young children came up, before the scout troops and the sports teams and the other lessons. Their practice was already a set part of their days.
6. The young pianists were called such, and got the label of "pianist" by their friends, by adults in the community, and by audiences, even before they were teenagers.

Sosniak pointed out the importance of these early years in developing habits of motivation, discipline, and self-concept in the young pianists. Their aspirations to become pianists had a foundation in the family commitment to the playing of the piano as worthwhile and valuable, and in the family's physical and financial and psychological support of that commitment.

Stage Two: The Middle Years of Talent Development in Music

As the young pianists reached adolescence, the playing of the piano became the playing of music with the piano as the instrument for the music. Aesthetic appreciation was beginning.

1. The young pianists' practices and music lessons were now part of daily and weekly habit.
2. About twenty hours or more a week were spent in their practices, music, and other activities in learning to be musicians. Sosniak said that this was "at least equivalent to a half-time job."
3. The young pianists were engaged and involved in their playing.
4. Music lessons took place at least once a week, and their teachers were also dedicated and knew a lot about music. The teachers pushed the students to have precision in their playing, and they also encouraged the students to learn more than the mechanics.
5. During this time, other options were narrowed, and decisions were made that focused on music rather than on other choices. Families making long-distance moves to be near the best learning environment and choosing for the young musician a limited general education, in order to focus more on music, were two dramatic examples of such narrowing of options.
6. The whole family was affected by the budding career of the young pianist. Perhaps other children in the family were negatively affected by this intense commitment of the family's time, of the family's monetary resources, and of the family's change in lifestyle.
7. The student moved into the world of music from the world of the family; the teacher became more important, as did the competition of peers for motivating the music and for providing the student with feedback as to his or her worth as a pianist.

Stage Three: The Musician as Adult

Finding a master teacher and being accepted as a student by this master teacher were crucial steps in the development of adult piano talent. Such teachers don't advertise for students, operating instead within informal networks of lesser teachers. I often use the movie *Madame Sousatzka* in my classes as a classic illustration of this pattern of talent development in musicians—and in other top youthful performers. Madame Sousatzka, a middle-level piano teacher, struggled to keep her prize pupils, who moved on to other teachers when they felt ready. The movie explored the teacher's emotional difficulties and those of her students as they made their transitions.

Sosniak's study found that being a student of a master teacher meant more than just taking lessons; it meant adopting a style and a sense of musical repertoire, and a raising in standards of musicianship and performance. The master teachers expected discipline and commitment. The students were expected to practice at least four and as many as seven hours per day between lessons. Because the master teachers were often on tour, lessons lasted longer than an hour, and could be as far apart as three weeks or a month. The master teachers did not tolerate excuses or sloppy preparation. The students had moved from their parents' sacrifices and the expectations of their homes to the world of music professionals. Having closed their other options of study, they were in select music conservatories or schools where their teachers were located.

As a final step in talent development, the teachers then themselves became lesser gods to the mature young pianists, and were seen as coaches as the students began to pursue their own careers, aggressively seeking the correct venues and contests and awards in order to enhance their visibility as musicians. Many continued to take as well as give lessons.

However, the path to musical creativity may not be as cut-and-dried or age-related as stated here. Crosscultural anomalies exist. Take the case of master sitar player Ravi Shankar. As described in Boyd's book, *Musicians in Tune*, Shankar was from a theatrical family from Benares, India. They began to tour the world and ended up being headquartered in Paris. He early demonstrated talent in acting and in dancing, and as his family toured, he got used to the partying, the accolades, and the four-star hotels. He began to fool with the sitar, but he had no teacher, and so he copied, watched, and played by ear. In 1935, one of the greatest musicians of India came to be a soloist with the group. "I was bowled over. He looked very ordinary, but there was some inner fire in him that felt like a volcano." The musician was with them for only ten and a half months, "but within that period he changed the course of my life."

Shankar was viewed as being talented in poetry, dance, music, and painting, and everyone told him everything he did was wonderful. "He was the first one who said to me, 'You are nothing; you can never do anything like this; you are like a butterfly; you are like a jack-of-all-trades; you have to do one thing properly, and I will teach you if you leave everything and come with me.'" Shankar thought about it for over a year and finally went back to India at the age of eighteen. He stayed with his teacher for more than seven years.

"I lived in the house next to him, a very creaky old house with flies, scorpions, snakes, and even wolves at night. It was very uncomfortable and I suffered very much." Shankar went on to become one of the great masters of the sitar.

Shankar's method of composing influenced the contemporary composer Philip Glass, who met Shankar while studying with Nadia Boulanger in Paris. Glass described their collaboration in his book, *Music by Philip Glass*. The two worked on the score of a movie together. Shankar would come to the composing sessions, drink tea, tune his sitar, ask Glass to play the string drone, the tamboura, and then Shankar would sing the music to Glass and Glass would notate it. "If the piece was, say, three minutes long, he would first sing the entire three-minute flute part, then the entire three-minute violin part, and so on." Shankar's knowledge of the raga was so ingrained that he could spontaneously compose after a period of meditation, calming, and praying.

The Indian tradition of music education which Shankar underwent teaches the musician to improvise: "As an Indian performing artist, I create spontaneously. Because we improvise all the time, we create on the spot, it's like an unfolding raga." The training emphasizes learning the raga from the guru. The musician follows a format, but it is really an ingrained structure. "We don't say this is A and this is B. It just comes out, sometimes in long durations, sometimes in short durations, which we are also controlling." Before a performance Shankar washes, puts on clean clothes, meditates, and prays. "Then sitting there after tuning, it's already in my head, and now it's physical, so with the first note I merge into that raga." He does not think about what note he's playing: "A raga at that time is like a person, like making love, in the sense that the whole raga merges with me and we become one."

Glass said that Shankar's way of music making profoundly affected him. When Glass would try to transcribe the music Shankar was singing to him, he would put in bar lines. Shankar would say, "All the notes are equal." Finally Glass took out the bar lines altogether. "And there, before my eyes, I could see what Alla Rakha had been trying to tell me. Instead of distinct groupings of eighth notes, a steady stream of rhythmic pulses stood revealed. Delighted, I exclaimed to Alla Rakha: 'All the notes are equal!'" Later, when Shankar came to be a visiting professor in New York City, Glass studied with him again, and his contact with Indian music opened up for him his new musical language.

As in visual artists (Picasso's use of the bull influencing Jackson Pollock's use of the bull) and in writers (Pound's translation of Japanese Zen poets influencing contemporary poets like Bly and Wright), and in scientists (advances in quantum mechanics in Switzerland influencing theoretical physicists in the United States), musicians also learn from peers from other cultures. One culture can influence another, as talented composers and musicians communicate in the code of music, which is universal to those who want to learn.

Biographical Studies

The memoir, the case study, and the historiometric study of biography all provide qualitative and quantitative illustrations that illuminate musical talent development and musical genius. Following are several examples.

The pattern of the family giving up many things for the sake of the musical talent of the child is quite common, according to Jean Bamberger, who studies musical prodigies. Bamberger also validated that the young musicians must practice before school, after school, on weekends. Understandably, the conflicts of the necessity for practice and the demand to live a normal life are difficult for young musicians and may contribute to their giving up music during adolescence. Burt Bacharach gave up music from ages twelve to sixteen, but his mother's encouragement and his early, rigorous training made him come back to composing and playing. Another conflict occurs when the young musician tries to balance a broad general education and professional music education.

Mentors, teachers, and other supporters are crucial to musical development. The cellist Pablo Casals throughout his life was grateful to his mother for her devotion to his musical talent; she was instrumental in his attending music school in Barcelona, far away from the tiny Spanish village where the family lived. Composer and conductor Leonard Bernstein studied with Serge Koussevitzky, Fritz Reiner, Heinrich Gebhard, Isabella Vengerova, and Aaron Copland. The successful conductor and composer, like the successful scientist, depends largely on mentors.

The role of imitation and duplication of others' works in composing is also an important means of developing musical talent. Beethoven's composing career has been divided, by musicologists, into three periods: the imitative, the heroic, and the introspective. The first works by even the greatest composers came from practice, imitation, and learning what had gone before in order to free the composers for the great works they would make in their more mature compositions. Thus, musical ideas are transmitted from one generation to the next.

Simonton's Studies of Composers

Simonton, using historiometry, studied 696 classical composers. In *Genius, Creativity, and Leadership,* he said that the composers tended to compose their best-known melodies between their thirty-third and forty-third years, peaking in production of famous tunes at about age thirty-nine. However, their most melodically original works appeared later, when the influence of the Zeitgeist, or historical milieu, upon their works tended to diminish. At this later stage they felt freer to go against the temper of the times, and they created their most melodically original works after age fifty-six. Bach's "Art of the Fugue" and the music Beethoven composed in his Third Period (the last five piano sonatas, the *Missa Solemnis,* and the Ninth Symphony among others) are examples of this more innovative music.

Simonton also pointed out that longevity pays off in long-lasting fame. Those who become most famous had the longest careers, were the most prolific, and were born a long time ago. Like scientists, composers who attained the most eminence tended to begin their productivity earlier, tended to produce more, and tended to have long careers. Within those long careers, however, quality of life had a direct influence on quality of composition. When Simonton studied ten of the most famous composers, examining the aesthetic merit of their compositions, he found that the most artistically original music was composed when they were in most pain, facing hard life challenges such as family deaths, job insecurities, moving, troubles in their marriages, legal problems, and political upheavals in their countries. The composers' life circumstances and emotional stress influenced their melodies.

Life at Juilliard

Judith Kogan, in a memoir called *Nothing But The Best: The Struggle For Perfection At The Juilliard School,* described the education of the world's finest young musicians who study at New York City's Juilliard School at Lincoln Center. Juilliard students believe they are the elite young players of the world, and both students and administration "seem to think that students at any other conservatory (except, maybe, the Curtis Institute of Music in Philadelphia) couldn't get into Juilliard and therefore can't play." Kogan said:

> Juilliard is the universe where the world starts and stops. Its windows sealed, Juilliard is cut off from the world even physically. The tie that binds is music, and the force that cre-

ates order is ability. Some invisible hand ranks people. Ability loosely corresponds to technical proficiency. In some ways, the focus on ability blinds people to music itself. In some ways, music is appreciated not as something beautiful but as a tool of commerce. Professional motivation is more important than artistic, the glamour of personality more important than the art of music.

The 750 talented musicians fought for the eighty-four practice rooms, where they practiced eight, ten hours a day, confining their social lives "to those who do the same thing at the same level of proficiency." Students at Juilliard knew each other by the instruments they played, by how well they played the instruments, and by who their teachers were. They practiced, practiced, practiced. Kogan said, "Practicing is an integral part of living for them, different from eating and breathing only in that they ate and breathed before they walked."

The practice makes the students feel secure. If one practices something forty times, one feels more secure than if one practices something thirty times. The practice becomes a way of avoiding the real world: ". . . the hassles of life in New York City, the agony of adolescence and young adulthood, the pain of a shaky or battered ego, the unpredictability of a course in an unstable profession, where one can pick up the instrument and sound heavenly one day and hellish the next." If the students leave the practice room for a bathroom break, they may come back and find that another obsessive practicer has taken the practice room.

In the research on the development of expertise, in whatever field, practice is deemed to be essential. Again, as mentioned in Chapter 2, the person learns the task to the point of automaticity. There is some evidence that such attention to practice by musicians is a key to success. In a study of 257 young musicians ages 8 to 18, Sloboda and colleagues found a strong relationship between musical achievement and the amount of formal practice. High achievers had more consistent patterns of practice and did their practicing of technique in the morning. The researchers concluded that formal practice seems to be a major determinant of musical achievement.

After the competitions, the rivalries, the hours in the cafeteria, the required ear training and chorus classes, and the egos of the temperamental teachers, the students from Juilliard graduated and found that those who were their rivals were now their friends, for they had all come through, and now they had only to put Juilliard on their resumes in order to attract notice. But it is still not easy for graduates of one of the best schools in the world. The students joined the thousands of musicians living in the neighborhood of Lincoln Center.

Kogan said, "Hardly anyone ends up with a solo career. Some earn spots in orchestras, some in principal seats. Some teach, some free-lance and some do both. Some leave music entirely. Some reach the top and are disenchanted. Some drift into new careers and find contentment." The real world demands a new kind of commitment, and the excessive discipline that has been imbued into the recent graduate will carry over into all aspects of life. However, according to Kogan, "The commitment must be seen as something one has chosen. The musician who sees the commitment as a sacrifice will always be bitter."

Despite her frank description of the demands of a profession in music, Kogan, who ended up in another profession, found that the ultimate discovery in a talented musician's life is a personal, even spiritual one. The musician ultimately discovers the basic and simple truth: he loves the music. She discovers that it was all worth it, for the music.

Folk and Popular Musicians

Folk music, jazz, ethnic music—all contribute to the music of classical composers. The Finnish composer Sibelius wrote at the time of a great language shift, with a movement to overthrow the official Swedish language and replace it with vernacular Finnish. The tone poem "Finlandia," within the larger work of the same name, is based on a folk tune. Bela Bartok's work is another example of the incorporation of folk music into formal musical structures, as is the work of Copland. The derivative nature of much creative work is evident in the work of musicians, as it is in the work of other artists. Much creative work is elaboration or extending, and much is "piggybacking," in the words of creativity training. The musical composer masters the structures and the forms necessary in order to either put them aside or to use them with variation.

Folk music has not only influenced classical musicians; it has influenced popular musicians as well. Social movements also influence musicians. Rock musician Bonnie Raitt described going to a Quaker summer camp where her counselors played the Kingston Trio, the Weavers, Joan Baez, Bob Dylan, and Peter, Paul, and Mary. Then blues music began to influence her: "I had to choose whether to spend my allowance on the new Bob Dylan, Beatles, or Muddy Waters record." Paul Kanter of the Jefferson Airplane described entering the 1960s after the white-bread 1950s. "We were middle-class kids with no problems compared to other people in the world." They went to college, "drifting without any idea of what we wanted to do." Then, in 1961, 1962, and

1963, "you saw all these people making music and social movements circling around them from the peace movement to the civil rights movement." Folk singers such as Pete Seeger began to influence the youth with a feeling of social consciousness. The music of the Civil Rights movement—images of black people and white people holding hands and swaying to the gospel sounds of "We Shall Overcome"—filled the media.

The Influence of African Americans on Contemporary Music

The research on talent development does not often include, however, the major contribution of the United States to world music. That is the influence of African Americans. That contribution was developed in a completely different way from the way of formal training described above. In fact, Haskins noted that the influence of African Americans on world music has been an influence of the poor, the disenfranchised, the untaught and untutored. When Africans were brought forcefully, as slaves, to the United States, they communicated with each other by way of drums and chants, until the plantation owners banned the use of drums. They developed ways to subvert this order, one of which was to tap their heels on the floor in certain rhythms. Once the Africans were Christianized, churches became a source of singing and music, using call and response similar to that used on ships by the Irish and British sailors, and in the fields by the laborers and the foremen. They also brought with them, besides the drums, the banjo and the bones.

Haskins said in his book, *Black Music in America,* that it is traditional in many societies that the "most expressive and emotional music forms in society" come from the lower classes, and that it was the lot of the Africans who were brought here "to be the peasant class, and thus to furnish the sub-soil of our national music." The same is true in Argentina, where the tango is the national music. The tango arose from the urban working classes, from the hordes of immigrants, mostly men from Italy and Spain, who came, and worked to send money back to the Old Country. Lonely and mournful, they spent much time in bodegas and in rooming houses, where they played their bandoleons and guitars and danced with each other while waiting for their turns with the prostitutes.

Thus, the creativity of uneducated musicians takes the form of popular music. Black musicians were thought not to be able to achieve competence in classical forms, and much prejudice prevented them even studying. Those who did achieve competence were not permitted to sing or play in orchestras or solo concerts. This continued even into 1935, when the Daughters of the American Revolution did not permit Marian Anderson, a contralto, to sing at Constitution Hall. Eleanor Roosevelt made arrangements for her to sing on the steps of the Lincoln Memorial, "but it was a comparatively small blow against racism," Haskins commented. Female black opera singers such as Leontyne Price and Jessye Norman were the exception rather than the rule. Sarah Vaughn was found weeping in her dressing room after singing for a state dinner at the White House. When asked why, she said she had come to Washington, D.C., twenty years earlier and couldn't find a hotel room, yet now she was singing in the White House. She was weeping from joy after great frustration.

The music that African-American popular musicians brought to the world was within the world's collective unconscious, according to Boyd. She quoted B.B. King as saying that the blues and the feelings it brings are at the core of most popular music. King said, "When I sing blues today I still get some of the spiritual feeling; it's a thin line between blues and gospel . . . and the roots of all music that I hear, especially in the Western world, seem to fit into the music that I play. So if I border the line of rock, or soul, country, or any other kind of music, I can incorporate it into the blues because there's a place there."

To illustrate the mammoth influence and role that African American musicians have played on the world of music, here is a partial list of black musicians who made American music unique:

- Scott Joplin (1868-1917) Ragtime Composer

- W.C. Handy (1873 1958) Blues

- James Reese Europe (1881-1919) 369th Infantry Band

- Buddy Bolden (1868-1931) New Orleans Jazz

- Jelly Roll Morton (1885-1941) New Orleans, Chicago Jazz

- Ma Rainey (1886-1939) Classic blues singer

- Louis Armstrong (1900-1971) Jazz trumpeter

- Duke Ellington (1899- 1974) Swing, jazz composer

- Billie Holiday (1915-1959) Jazz singer

- William Grant Still (1895-1970) Composer

- Charlie "Yardbird" Parker (1920-1955) Be Bop

- Nat "King" Cole (1919-1965) Ballads, jazz

- Mahalia Jackson (1911-1972) Spirituals

- Bo Diddley (1928-) Rhythm & Blues

- Miles Davis (1926-) Trumpet player, Cool jazz

- Ray Charles (1929-) Soul

- James Brown (1934-) Soul

- Smokey Robinson (1940-) Motown

- Aretha Franklin (1942-) Church Soul

- Stevie Wonder (1950-) Composer, Singer

- Quincy Jones (1933-) Composer

- The Marsalis brothers. Wynton, Brandon. Composers, Conductors

This list could go on and on: what about Bessie Smith, Thelonious Monk, Chuck Berry, Art Tatum, Dizzy Gillespie, Erroll Garner, Billie Eckstine, Jimi Hendrix, The Supremes, Wilson Pickett, Bob Marley, Harry Belafonte, Bobby McFerrin, Muddy Waters, for example? Would Elvis Presley, the Rolling Stones and the Beatles have made such an impact without the influence of Bo Diddley and Chuck Berry?

Rap musicians have a great contemporary influence as well. Teddy Pendergrass commented that rap speaks to the contemporary African American youth: "Rap music is one of those serious art forms." Rap star Ice-T said he began to create rap music in order to help his friends, to tell them what he saw. He thought it would be too depressing, but when he recorded "Six in the Morning," people "freaked. What I do is very easy for me to do." He just looks around and records what he sees. Irish singer Sinead O'Connor commented that hip-hop music is the most powerful and honest form of music because it brings people together. "Any form of music that has come out of Africa—soul music, people like James Brown, hip-hop—are the biggest communicators. It's got so many messages within its rhythms, within the drumbeats, as well as its words." (These quotes were from Boyd's book, written in the early 1990s, before the violence that hit the world of rap music in the late 1990s.)

Only two of the seminal figures on the list above had a rigorous formal education in music: Wynton Marsalis attended Juilliard, and William Grant Still attended Oberlin. Still directed the NBC Symphony Orchestra, on radio, and it was not widely known that the conductor was black, for there would have been repercussions. The Marsalis family is an example of a prototypical musical family, with all the children playing instruments under the influence of their jazz musician father. However, the process of becoming a musician must always entail practice and the influence of other musicians. The evidence of discrimination and prejudice in the lives of African American musicians is everywhere. For example, after the Civil War, it was thought that blacks, especially black men, were not capable of reading music.

Smokey Robinson, in his autobiography, *Smokey*, discussed the influence of black music: "When Motown first started hitting . . . writers were calling us 'white bread soul,' saying that we were pandering to middle-class America by homogenizing gut-bucket black music." Robinson mentioned the Contours, Levi Stubbs, David Ruffin, and Martha Reeves, who "sounded like the real deal to me." Then, in the seventies, people said that Soul's golden age was gone, but that only meant that it was changing, and such composers and musicians as Al Green, Teddy Pendergrass, and Stevie Wonder, who composed the influential *Songs In The Key of Life*, came to the forefront. Disco was the rage, and the contemporary musicians Van McCoy, Hal Davis, and Harvey Fuqua again changed soul music. Robinson cited such musicians of the eighties as Michael Jackson, Prince, Terrence Trent D'Arby as doing the same to popular music. He said,

> That's the point: funk doesn't die, it develops. It was here before us and it'll be here after us. It's changed—by technology, by instrumentation—yet it hasn't changed. Dinah Washington tried to get over with the same sort of big ballads Whitney Houston is singing now. Black music in America has always reached out to everyone. That's its very nature—to include, not exclude. Like the religious roots from which it springs, it's a music of gratitude and generosity. Black musicians—singers and writers and producers— have always dreamed the Tin Pan Alley dream of mainstream hits. Why not?

Robinson commented that the music industry was racist, saying that it was not fair that his songs had to hit the top of the black charts before being permitted to cross over to the white charts. "That's like having to work your way from the back of the bus." In speaking about black artists' influence, he said, "Black artists have adapted, altered, deepened, and, in many instances, discovered the future for American culture at large. That's been especially true in music." This illustrates the influence of socioeconomic and cultural values on the development of creativity.

Improvisation and Creativity

But, you may be asking, all of this describes the development of talent, and not of creativity. Isn't creativity more loose, more free? All that Sosniak's study and Kogan's memoir described was practice, competition, striving in an effort to learn how to use the musical instrument. How is this creativity? Many musicians and devoted listeners would insist that the instrumentalist who has mastered the technique so that the soul of the music can come through is as creative as the person who puts the notes down on the page, just as the actor would insist he is as creative as the playwright. However, without entering the debate of who is more creative, we will now take a look at composers and improvisators, who do sit with the blank page at the piano, and who do put notes on the page, and who do go through what we have conventionally called the creative process.

The difference between improvisation and composing can be illustrated through scenes from the life of composer and conductor, Andre Previn. Previn's done it all. He's been a successful composer of scores for movies; he was a successful jazz pianist with his own trio; he has been a songwriter; he has risen in the ranks of orchestral conductors to conduct world class orchestras. Born in Berlin in 1929, Previn was the son of an enthusiastic amateur musician who took his son to concerts. Previn felt pure joy in hearing a symphony at the age of five, and from then on he pursued music as a career. In Bookspan and Yodkey's biography, *Andre Previn*, he said of his childhood: "I think we musicians have always had rather selfish childhoods. The luxury of having a unilateral talent, which makes one's future life inevitable, is wonderful, but it also makes you selfish." He said he was insular and had a narrow perspective. "I myself was always so concerned with being a musician, with becoming a good musician, with becoming a better musician, with learning this and with learning that, that even my areas of amusement and leisure time, even my play time seemed to be connected inevitably with music." He said he never even looked at what was happening in the world at large.

Pianist Gary Graffman, in his memoir, *I Really Should Be Practicing,* said that his best friends were always musicians. As high school students they would go down to the jazz clubs in Greenwich Village or meet at their homes and play for each other. The insular world of the talented individual is often restricted to others who have similar talents and thus similar interests.

Previn was so classically trained he couldn't improvise. Fleeing Hitler, his family moved when he was a young child to Los Angeles, where Previn came under the influence of American pop culture, especially jazz. At fourteen he heard a scratchy recording of "Sweet Lorraine" by blind black piano player, Art Tatum. He "just fell apart. It was unbelievable." Previn scoured the stores for "Sweet Lorraine" and found that it was just a "pleasant, folksy little tune." Wondering where all the notes came from, it dawned on him that Tatum himself had added them to the arrangement. "He'd taken that puerile thirty-two-bar melody and made ingenious music out of it." Previn became fascinated. He found a recording of the Tatum version of the song; playing it over and over, he began to write out, note by note, every song on the album. In so doing he used up several packs of needles.

> The process was a long and a painstaking one, for Tatum's playing was crammed with fists full of notes and harmonic changes that might look like mistakes on paper if you hadn't heard them first. Here was a musical magician whose illusions remain to this day something of a mystery to his fellows. No less a jazz pianist than Oscar Peterson . . . tells of being stunned by his first hearing of a Tatum record; Peterson at first refused to believe anything but that he'd heard two pianists and a bass player, not just one man on one piano.

Previn finally finished notating the music, and he had page after page; sometimes just a few bars would take over a page of notation as he listened to Tatum. Then he began to practice the music as though it were Mozart, with meticulous attention to each note and rhythm, for he didn't understand how jazz worked. He thought that reading notated music was how to do it. He finally learned Tatum's songs and would practice them for hours. Then he realized that jazz was about improvisation, making things up: "A jazz player had to be his own composer and play not premeditatively but make up his music on the spot. Improvisation. That's what jazz was all about."

Rock 'n' roll musicians also improvise. Phil Collins described how the band Genesis composed their songs. When the band would enter the studio they would often have written nothing for the group, because they were all solo artists as well, and they saved their compositions for their own albums. "We go in and just turn everything on and start playing, and we improvise and improvise for days until something works." Collins would tape everything and the group would listen back. Someone would say, "That sounds interesting. What happened there?" To write songs by such a process the group needed to be uninhibited, to trust the others, and to take risks. The others can't mind if someone starts to sing out of tune, trying to reach a note in a melody that hasn't been written yet. "We all know we've got to let our trousers down without worrying about it." Such a process of trust, improvisation, and chemistry can only happen in certain bands. "And that's what makes the band great, at least the experience of doing that. It's very enjoyable because you're creating something out of nothing," Collins said. (Quoted in Boyd's book, *Musicians in Tune*.)

Session drummer Peter Erskine commented that nowadays young jazz musicians are taught to repeat common notes or phrases, "get them under their fingers so when they're improvising, they're really just recycling a lot of scales they've played before many, many times." When jazz guitarist John Abercrombie taught these young people, he would take a tune and play it in half-notes so that the young musicians would not be able to play what their muscle memory in their fingers knew. "You have to be very creative then because every note has to be a good choice." Keith Strickland of the B-52s described improvisation as being similar to children's play. "Being in touch with the child in you is part of the whole creative process. I don't feel that I write songs as much as I make them up; it's playing the way you do in your childhood." He said that a musician has to be very open and nonjudgmental when doing this. "We do that as a band; we go through the improvisational process; we jam, allowing anything to happen." (Quoted in Boyd's book, *Musicians in Tune*.)

New age jazz saxophone player Paul Horn spoke about improvising as a peak experience. "When I started to improvise, I found I could get up and play music, with thoughts coming, and these thoughts could be translated into musical terms." He would hear with his inner ear and this sound would connect down his arms into his fingers. "Intellectually, by the time you've even thought about it, you're eight beats later." Horn said that playing jazz is very fulfilling because the musician never gets bored. "It comes out different every time." He said that the energy in improvising is "a spiritual thing" because the musician can transcend the intellect and get into the here and now. "Jazz comes as close as you can to the spiritual" (Quoted in Boyd).

Composer Charles Ives grew up as the son of a music teacher and band leader. His memory was filled with church songs, community songs, patriotic songs. He and his father would compose together for church choirs and community bands. Often the amateur players and singers would be out of tune. Ives composed tunes where the singers would sing in one key and the accompanist would play in another. Biographer Jan Swafford noted that even as a teenager, Ives would go against conventional composition techniques into improvisation. Swafford said, "From the beginning of his creative life his searching imagination prodded at conventions in ways sometimes clumsy, sometimes fresh and effective." As a teenaged organist in Danbury, Connecticut, Ives performed many pieces, for example, *Variations on "America,"* as improvisations before writing them down.

Is formal study of the medium, or achieving a basic level of expertise in the medium, necessary for truly creative products to be produced? The British aesthetician Robert Abbs would say yes, even though the ears of the world's jazz lovers would disagree. Abbs believed that only people who are trained in their fields can be receptive to the ideas that come to them, and can transform these ideas into useable symbols. In *A is for Aesthetic* Abbs wrote:

> Stravinsky, Tippett and Wagner . . . we can see that these gifts from the unconscious came to individuals who were highly accomplished in musical composition and who were already consciously engaged with a particular problem. Only someone who formally understood musical chords could actually hear "the pure triad of E flat major" and only someone who had mastered the art of composition in his own culture could musically record it.

Abbs's comments imply that there is some music that is of a higher form than other music, and implies that "true" originality comes in creating classical music. Others would assert that "true" creativity comes in having no notes in front of you, only a melody in your head, and in being able to transform that melody into jazz, folk, pop, rap, or rock. The improvisational musician Stephen Nachmanivitch began his book, *Free Play,* with these words:

I am a musician. One of the things I love best is to give totally improvised solo concerts on violin and viola. There is
something energizing and challenging about being one-to-one
with the audience and creating a piece of work that has both
the freshness of the fleeting moment and—when everything is
working—the structural tautness and symmetry of a living
organism. It can be a remarkable and often moving experience
in direct communication.

Why Are there so Few Women Composers?

In an interview for a book called *The Creative Experience* edited by Rosner
and Abt, Aaron Copland discussed creativity in composing. Copland spoke of
music being a language that expresses emotions at all times, but the composer
becomes aware that he is feeling such an emotion only when he begins singing
or playing a sad song, for example, and he wonders then why he is feeling sad.
The lack of awareness in the mind of the composer about his feelings seems to
create an abstractness. A person cannot compose when he is too depressed,
because creating art is a positive statement, and the composer has to feel that
he is accomplishing something. If a composer composes when he is depressed,
he then becomes elated so that he can express his depression. A composer
might also compose to get rid of repressed anger. To create a chord that is for-
tissimo and dissonant is an expression of anger. Then Copland went on:

> One of the reasons why cultivated music is one of the glories
> of mankind, one of the real achievements of mankind, is that
> we are dealing in amorphous, highly abstract material without
> any specific thought content. Incidentally it's one of the mys-
> teries of music that there have been no great women com-
> posers. There have been great women singers, pianists, vio-
> linists, who interpret marvelously well, but for some reason or
> other, no outstanding composers. People have made an analo-
> gy between the fact that there have been no great women
> mathematicians and no great women composers. Perhaps it's
> the inability to handle abstract material that defeats them

Women in music, except for the necessary sopranos, mezzo-sopranos, and
contraltos, seem to have been relegated to the same place as were blacks.
Even those who were rigorously trained became helpmates and muses. Alma

Mahler, the wife of Gustav Mahler, is an example. She was classically trained in turn-of-the-century Vienna, a prime time for creativity. She was a serious composer who studied with other composers there. But Monson, her biographer, called her a "muse," an inspiration to male creatives. Monson said, "She might have become an important composer; had she been born a century later, she could have been a conductor. As it was, she devoted her life to men whom she considered to be geniuses." After Gustav Mahler died, Alma married Walter Gropius, who founded the Bauhaus, and later she married Franz Werfel, a writer. She also had long affairs with the composer Alexander von Zemlinsky, Arnold Schoenberg's teacher, with Ossip Gabrilowitsch, a pianist, and with Oscar Kokoschka, the artist.

The last male bastion in music seems to be conducting—there are few Sarah Caldwells—but today women composers can be found. Copland probably would have been surprised that the Pulitzer Prize in 1991 was won by a woman composer, Shulamit Ran, who won for her *Symphony*. Ran, a professor at the University of Chicago, said of her art, "I think music must reflect life, or at least life as the composer sees it," and "I want my music to challenge both the mind and the heart, and to do so in equal fashion."

Marilyn Shrude

Marilyn Shrude, a Professor of Music and Director of the MidAmerican Center for Contemporary Music at Bowling Green State University in Ohio, is another successful composer. Born in 1946, she has a doctorate in music from Northwestern University and is mid-career. Her music, composed for large and small ensembles, has been performed in almost every state in the U.S. as well as in Korea, Switzerland, Germany, the Soviet Union, Canada, Belgium, the Netherlands, France, Japan, Taiwan, Poland, Spain, Austria, and Australia. She has received two Individual Artist Fellowships from the Ohio Arts Council, and she is a board member with the International Alliance for Women in Music. She has received a Kennedy Center Freidheim Award, been named a Woman of Achievement by Women In The Communications Industry (WICI), received the ASCAP/Chamber Music America Award for Adventursesome Programming, and an Ohioana Award for contributions to the cultural life of Ohio. In 1997 she received an Academy Award in Music from the American Academy of Arts and Letters. The citation from the Academy said,

Marilyn Shrude's music is imaginative, poetic, at times gentle, at other times powerful. With few notes, she can write a universe of beautiful sounds that soon cascade into harmonies of grandiose gesture, such as in the Saxophone Concerto. Her colorful instrumentation enhances all her ideas, and the elegant scores immediately give images of her wonderful conceptions, melodic lines, counterpoint, and fresh sonorities. All these devices come from a refined, sophisticated ear. Her works are perfectly constructed, genuine, and at all times musical.

In an interview, Marilyn described that she grew up in an ethnic Catholic Polish and Lebanese family Chicago and entered the convent as a high school student at age fifteen. She always composed music, though it wasn't particularly valued or noticed. Her middle and late adolescence were times of concentrated effort in music. She took lessons on three instruments, and since she was in a convent and had decided to become a music teacher, she had intensive study—more intensive than if she had been in a regular high school with all its distractions. Shrude's career as a composer began formally during her graduate work at Northwestern University, when she took a course in composition. She was the only woman in the composition class at the time, the early seventies.

She practiced all three instruments and also spent a lot of time singing. She had been playing the organ for Masses since the age of eleven. The simultaneous and intensive training in religion and music led her to doubt her talent: because humility was required of a religious girl, she could never think her work was good. When she emerged from the convent, she had to work through many feelings so that she could accept her talent. Though many of her teachers and mentors were supportive, the years in the convent had given her a weak self-concept. Composing was not encouraged because it was vain, and women were not to be proud.

"I always had the urge to write music, and did so since the age of ten; I did it on my own, mostly for school programs. People knew I did it, but it was never encouraged. They rarely looked at it. I had very little professional feedback on it whatsoever." Shrude taught music in a high school for a few years after she left the convent. Then she decided to quit teaching and go to graduate school at Northwestern, where she met her husband, saxophonist John Sampen.

She was in residency at Northwestern for one year while she got her master's degree, and then she went back to teaching school. They married and moved to Kansas, and Marilyn found herself without a composition teacher. The three years in Kansas were spent teaching herself composition by listening to contemporary works. She views this as an exploratory period where she was gaining literacy, trying out ideas, imitating. She sometimes studied with a good friend on the faculty of the university where her husband was teaching, but she was essentially teaching herself. The couple returned to Northwestern to pursue doctorates. When she got back to Northwestern, she found that her relationship to her mentor on the composition faculty had changed. She had grown. She was not as needful as she had been. She began to strike out on her own.

Shrude talked about the necessity for a composer to know people who perform music. Many of the strides she made as a composer were the result of having good performers to write for. However, her main struggle is that of time, for she and John have two children.

Like Copland, Marilyn Shrude expresses her emotions through her compositions. Even when she has started a composition ostensibly to solve a technical problem, she finds later that the music essentially turns out to have expressed what she has been struggling with emotionally. I think that most creative artists would agree with that assessment.

Most of her pieces are narratives, even though the story is not apparent. The form of "A Window Always Open On The Sea," composed early in 1990, is shaped by lines from a poem by Michael Mott. Michael and his wife were neighbors and good friends of Shrude and Sampen when Michael's wife was dying of cancer. Shrude's father had recently died, and Shrude's sister-in-law was dying of cancer. This piece turned out to be "a working out of all these deaths." She dated the piece the day her sister-in-law died. For Shrude, composing is the expression of emotions, no matter how the piece starts out.

She doesn't compose on a computer or on a piano, but at her table. She tries things on the piano, but says, "You get to a point where you know how things work. I can hear the sounds in my head." She works in the lengthiest blocks of time she can get. Like most artists in any genre, she composes because she must. She often uses poetic texts in her compositions. Howard McCord's "Arctic Desert" (1979) was one, "Lines From Tennyson" (1984) and "I Wandered Lonely As A Cloud" (1989) were others.

Other works include "Psalms for David" (1983); "Genesis: Notes To The Unborn" (1975); "Four Meditations; To A Mother And Her Firstborn" (1975); "Solidarnosc" (1982); "Drifting Over A Red Place" (1982); "Interior Spaces" (1987); and "Renewing The Myth" (1988) and "Amish" (1989), the theme music for the nationally-syndicated PBS series *Cooking from Quilt Country, Cooking from the Heartland, Marcia Adams' Kitchen*. "A Gift of Memories" (1992) was based on Wordsworth's poetry and was written on commission from the Cleveland Chamber Symphony at the death of her mother. "Concerto for Alto Saxophone and Wind Ensemble" (1994), "Into Light" (1994), for the Interlochen World Youth Symphony Orchestra, "Notturno: In Memoriam Toru Takemitsu" (1996), for violin, alto saxophone and piano, and "Eight Bagatelles" (1997), for two pianos, are other important recent works.

In the past few years she has been composing mainly on commission. She rarely submits her pieces to competitions or blindly to publishing houses. She has a network of fellow musicians all over the country. "I know a lot of people all over and they're helpful. They sometimes give you favors that you don't even expect." As codirector of the New Music & Art Festival, she annually listens to each of the five hundred submissions that the Festival attracts, from all over the world. Twenty compositions are chosen for performance. She agrees that it can be difficult and costly for composers, especially for younger people, to have their work performed well. Often a composer must find some performers, hire them and organize a studio performance. A good tape can be worthwhile for opening doors to festivals, contests, and the like.

Marilyn Shrude is a mother, which has put her on a timeline different from that of other composers. Like the artist mothers in Foley's study, Shrude has had to make modifications in order to combine parenting with composing. The value of having a supportive husband cannot be underestimated, for their children always come first. "We've done pretty well at trying to accommodate each others' schedules, even with young children, though it's been difficult."

Whether having children has stymied her career doesn't matter to Shrude. "Having children who are young adults has been a new and enjoyable phase of the parenting process." She can't imagine not having children. "I love having children. It's so enriching. If I didn't have children I'd be more reclusive. I wouldn't have to schedule myself to cook, to take them to places. When I'm alone, I let my duties go and don't seek out social contacts." Letting go of one's children when they become young adults is one of the most difficult aspects of parenting. "Growing into a relationship which is no longer parent/child has its own set of difficulties, but the rewards are great." She has never thought that she would have been better off childless, nor has she been resentful that the demands of motherhood interfere with her creative work.

To return to the question of whether improvisation is more or less creative than composing, Shrude said that many improvisational artists can "speak but not read and write. To be able to read the music and to write it down is to know the full language of music. Music is a language. Some people read and some people write and some people do all of it."

Shrude considers herself competitive but not obsessed. There are things she should go for, but she doesn't. Like most creators, she enjoys having her work recognized by her peers. And to be performed by a major orchestra such as the Chicago Symphony or the New York Philharmonic is always a goal.

Mid-career, Shrude does not exhibit the anxiety or drive usually observed in composers. Perhaps the balance she has achieved is the result of her being a mother. The serenity with which she views her life and her accomplishments seems to reflect an aspect of the creative female personality that hasn't been explored in research.

Foley's study showed that the artist mothers, while they were often in a frenzy trying to get everything done, felt enormous serenity in doing their work. Foley, contrasting artists with professional women in law, medicine, and business, found that the artists, perhaps because they were able to express their emotions through their art work, seemed to have less emotional stress. In fact, their emotional stress came from having their responsibilities as mothers interfere with their emotional need to work in their art. When one of the artist-mothers was not able to work for ten months because of a complicated pregnancy, she said, "Honestly, I'm sort of tearing my hair out about not having painted for that length of time." One of the professional mothers spoke of "going nuts" when she was at home with her children for too long, and of escaping into her workplace where the demands were predictable and appointed. The professionals had been high academic achievers who felt accomplishment in achieving a product, a sale, or a contract. By contrast, the artists valued the "process" of painting, which provided "escape and relief of tension and the return of mental tranquility."

The artist, no matter what genre he works in, uses his art as an expression of emotion, and when he is deprived of that expression, he feels conflict and tension. Boyd quoted jazz drummer Robin Horn, who said that when he hasn't practiced for a week, "I start to become a real uptight son of a bitch." He said that the music has to come out. "It has to be satisfied and nurtured. I have a really strong inner drive. It's like an inner voice that nags at me. When I've finished playing, after about an hour, I feel a thousand times better." Ultimately, what making music is about, for these players, composers, conductors, and performers, is passion, a love of the medium, and a natural proclivity to express emotion through music.

Summary

1. The development of musical talent takes much practice, work, and hard training.
2. There are crosscultural differences in talent development. Asians, for example, emphasize repetition, drill, and training, and Americans emphasize inspiration and improvisation.
3. Musicians exhibit certain personality attributes, and these may differ by whether a musician is a composer, a performer, or a conductor.
4. The whole family is affected in the development of great musical talent. The family may move to cities with better teachers, and siblings may be affected by the emphasis on developing one child's talent.
5. Young, talented musicians often undergo a midlife crisis in adolescence as they move from natural expression to learning the structure and mechanics of music.
6. Musicians are similar in personality to other creative people, with slight variations among types of musicians. Composers and conductors have the most extreme personalities.
7. African Americans have produced a music heritage that has affected popular music and jazz worldwide.
8. Improvisation and formal composition require different skills.
9. Women composers exist.
10. Musicians find the expression of their emotion through music healing and fulfilling. The practice is not considered drudgery, as with nonmusicians. This practice often leads to the immense joy and freedom and wholeness of being able to express the emotions through musical skill. Music performers, music composers, and musical conductors alike feel this joy as they do their craft and art.

Chapter 10

Physical Performers:
Actors, Dancers, and Athletes

The qualities above all necessary to a great actor: in my view he must have a great deal of judgment. He must have in himself an unmoved and disinterested onlooker.
—Diderot

I know a woman, lovely in her bones,
When small birds sighed, she would sigh back at them;
Ah, when she moved, she moved more ways than one.
—Theodore Roethke

I don't remember a time when I wasn't moving.
—Judith Jamison

She is so dramatic about everything. Even the least bit of criticism sends her into a tirade of histrionics. She talks to her dolls a lot and makes up elaborate scenarios taking place in distant lands, where she plays all the roles. And him! He can't stop moving. He can't sit still. Teachers get angry and may even call him hyperactive. They say he has a lot of energy. When the chorus sings, he moves to the music, and even does so in church.

Children like this are incipient actors, dancers, or athletes. As such, they are interpreters, like music performers. Some questions asked in the previous chapter arise in regard to these performers, too: are choreographers and playwrights the creative ones, and actors and dancers are merely tools of the words and patterns? Let's investigate.

Performers

Think back for a week. Can you count how many actors you have watched perform? If you watched one hour of commercial television, you saw approximately fourteen minutes of commercials. On each commercial actors appeared. In each dramatic show you watched actors. Did you go to a store where salesmen took care of your wishes? They were probably performing for you. Perhaps they didn't *really* like you that much. Did you watch a professional sports game where someone spiked a ball in the end zone or lay moaning on the court after fouling someone? They were probably acting, giving a performance for the crowd.

Did you see your favorite political figure give a speech? Acting. No doubt that sincerity belied other concerns, perhaps a vote on a bill or a domestic situation. Did you teach this week? Were you truly so intensely involved with the students as you pretended to be? Did you tell someone a story, or did someone tell you a story? Chances are good that role-playing was part of your week as you heard or told stories: "And then he said . . . And then she did . . . Can you believe it?" Even though you might not have gone to the theater this week, you saw or did a performance. Acting is everywhere, for in its basic definition, acting is pretending. One self pretends it is another self. This pretense is socially desired and approved of by all concerned. If we were our raw selves and acted out instead of acting, the world would be ruled by emotion, and social convention would take a back seat.

For the purposes of defining talents, school people have narrowly circumscribed performing to acting and music. Yet athletes are as much performers as are the actors and musicians. In most schools each team of athletes receives special equipment, special coaches, and, in some places, elaborate stadiums and arenas in which they can show their stuff. Formally trained actors have trouble finding jobs, everyone knows, so why develop those talents? Yet few athletes play beyond high school, except in community leagues. While athletes are often admired and treated as special, actors have reputations as being unconventional, not conforming to classroom expectations. It is not easy to love a classroom actor. The biographies of many actors reveal they were class clowns, cut-ups, rebels, or outsiders in the social whirls of their schools.

Of Gardner's frames of intelligence, bodily-kinesthetic intelligence is what actors, dancers, and athletes exhibit. However, the personal intelligences enable actors and dancers to interpret the world through their bodily actions. Athletes are performers also. The dramatic spike of the ball in the end zone, or hanging on to the rim of the basket just for a millisecond? Performing for the crowd. Bodily-kinesthetic intelligence is "skilled use of the body" that has evolved in humans over millions of years. Westerners have divorced the mental from the physical and speak of the body as separate from the soul or the heart. Recent thought has attempted to reconcile the two, as people have been urged to exercise and research has shown that physical activity is positively related to longevity.

Richard Schechner said there are four spheres of performance: (1) entertainment, which includes the arts and the display of satisfying or beautiful actions; (2) healing, which includes the bedside manner, the actions of the shaman, and interactive psychotherapy; (3) education, which includes the political purpose of exhorting, persuading, and convincing people to change their minds; and (4) ritualizing, which includes the liturgical services of churches and the ceremonial pomp of graduations, weddings, and holidays.

Schechner noted that most live performance happens not in a theater but "as religious practice, political demonstration, popular entertainment, sports match, or intimate face-to-face encounter." He said that performers in all areas must undergo rigorous physical training and must buy into the physical ideal that the field of performance values. "Rigorous exercises reshape their bodies—this is as true of kathakali [a Hindu performance form] as of football, of ballet as of shamanism."

All forms of performance are called *play*, a term which in theater indicates the script the actors perform; in athletics, a special move that is rehearsed over and over again by the person or team; in music, the physical interaction of the body with the instrument. All play is serious, though in our society we use the term to indicate a lack of seriousness: "Stop playing and come in and do your homework." "Want to play stick ball?" "Do you play bridge?" "I just want to play on my vacation; I'm burned out."

Play involves movement. "The chess player made a brilliant move and beat his opponent." 'Move! Move!' the coach shouted to his players during practice." "He made a move on her at the disco." In order to perform the required movement, the player's body must often be changed permanently or temporarily. The ballet dancer must turn her feet. The football player must bulk up. The actor must diet and exercise to maintain the physical ideal for the ingenue or leading man. The center of balance within the body must be broken down and then rebuilt. Schechner said there are four genres of play: games, sports, art, and religion. In each of these the player must be put into a state of disequilibrium: "Each genre deforms and reforms the body by introducing disequilibrium, a problem to be solved by a new balancing specific to the genre." The body is deconstructed and then reconstructed according to the rules of the form that is being played.

James Sloan Allen, in a 1992 essay about the education of performers at the Juilliard School, noted that performers are often impatient with a liberal arts education: because they are so concerned with the practice necessary for performance, they do not see the relevance of studying literature, mathematics, or science. He noted the similarities between the performers in the arts and athletes. Both need original endowments of great physical talent, and they depend on health professionals to keep them in physical shape for their performances. Both athletes and artists play, train, exercise, drill, practice, compete, and study with coaches. Both are called players. Both have mentors who exert phenomenal influence on them. Both must be able to work with groups and must understand teamwork: "However intensely performers study individually, they usually consummate their artistry collectively, in ensembles— the true solo is a rarity." Both athletes and performers show their mettle in competitive situations. Performing in competitions is their reason for being— the performance. "A performance is a test of capacities between what the creator has created and what the performer can perform," Allen said.

Performers must also have good memories. This is not required of creators to the degree that it is required of performers. Creators might have good long-term memory for digits or words, but performers have what is called *active memory*. While memorizing has lost its emphasis in most of education, performers must know how to memorize, for "who but a performer has to memorize anything like the score of a symphony or a concerto, the choreography of a ballet, or the role of Hamlet?" The performer begins with the work, and the license to embellish or to improvise is a limited license, because the original work is always there, and straying too far from it negates it: "Although a performer can stamp a work with an individual performance style and surprise a creator with performing insights, the work is almost always there, waiting to be learned and performed."

To put the work into active memory, the performer must practice, in order to acquire automaticity. Arduous practice and rehearsal are required. Intense concentration is required. Musicians respond intuitively to sounds, actors to emotional innuendo, dancers and athletes to spatial patterns. They may thus become preoccupied with the "how to," with the practicality of technique, and may become quite narrow in their orientation to the world. That is the challenge of the educator of performers.

Mainstream educators of the talented are often required to identify performers, but they leave their training up to experts in the domains of creative performance. One main difference between performing artists and creative artists is that "whatever their innate talent, most performers . . . depend equally on teachable skills." Schools for the performing arts owe their existence to this need for expert training. There is a distance between the composer and the choreographer, the playwright or screenwriter and the actor, and that distance is marked by the necessity for performers such as actors and dancers to combine bodily and emotional intelligence. Allen commented on the necessity in all performers to have physical dexterity and extreme discipline:

> Performing artists must make the fingers move with flawless precision, the voice perfectly hit the note, the body move fluidly, the limbs fly, breathing come at will, tear ducts submit to command. And their polished performances can be astonishing; the pianist whose hands race across the keyboard capturing every harmonic nuance and never missing a note; the dancer who spins blindly *en pointe*, then soars as if suspended in air to land on a dime; the actor who dissolves the stage and enfolds the audience in a drama of verisimilitude; the singer who holds F above high C until the house comes down. So demanding are the physical expectations of performance as to remove performers from the guild of artists and send them into the ranks of athletes.

Thus, the use of the body in performance has been recognized, and how the body should be used is defined according to the field in which the performer works.

Predictive Behaviors for Acting

The field of the education of the talented lists visual and performing arts as one of its concerns on most definitions, but the visual arts seem to be discussed more. The checklists in the field do list characteristics that may mark acting talent, but to my knowledge such checklists are seldom used as educators seek for more global cognitive characteristics such as high IQ, or they seek to identify global creativity by using checklists that emphasize cognitive fluency, flexibility, and the like. My view is that more specific predictive behaviors should be described and sought. Kough listed these characteristics that may mark acting talent in elementary school:

> ## TABLE 6. Kough's List of Characteristics of Dramatic Talent in Young Children
>
> 1. Readily shifts into the role of another character.
> 2. Shows interest in dramatic activities.
> 3. Uses voice to reflect changes of idea and mood.
> 4. Understands and portrays the conflict in a situation when given the opportunity to act out a dramatic event.
> 5. Communicates feelings by means of facial expressions, gestures, and bodily movements.
> 6. Enjoys evoking emotional responses from listeners.
> 7. Shows unusual ability to dramatize feelings and experiences.
> 8. Moves a dramatic situation to a climax and brings it to a well-timed conclusion when telling a story.
> 9. Gets a good deal of satisfaction and happiness from play-acting or dramatizing.
> 10. Writes original plays or makes up plays from stories.
> 11. Can imitate others. Mimics people and animals.

Renzulli and his colleagues also made a "Dramatics Characteristics Scale" in their 1976 *Scales for Rating the Behavioral Characteristics of Superior Students* (The "Creativity Characteristics Scale" was discussed in Chapter 4). This contains ten characteristics such as "Volunteers to participate in classroom plays or skits," and "Handles body with ease and poise for his particular age," or "Is able to evoke an emotional response from listeners—can get people to laugh, to frown, to feel tense, etc." These items are tallied on a Likert scale, with a weighted total. (Note: weighting totals may not be desirable, because they indicate the number of characteristics a student has, and no one knows how many characteristics predict for adult acting talent.)

Such checklists as these target talents in a specific domain. Schools should routinely try to notice such talents in order to specifically develop them through opportunities in theater, speech, performance, and acting.

I was an administrator at the Hunter College Elementary School in New York City. Because our students had high IQs and were precociously verbal, casting agents would often request to see our children in order to invite them to audition for theater, film, and television roles. I'd show the agents around, and they would peek into classrooms and point, "That one." I would give them the names of the children's parents. The "look" came first; the assessment of acting talent followed. Similarly, acting talent in musical theater is often of secondary importance. The best singers, not the best actors, often get the best role, although at the top levels, both singing and acting talent must be present. Such prior emphases—on looks and on musical talents—may lead the actor to despair. The actor leads a precarious existence in the realm of ego, with rejection almost surely inevitable. One constructs one's portraits of characters from observation of others cycled through one's self, and so Bates noted that actors are probably both the most extroverted and most introverted of all artists.

Although theatrical children often come from theatrical families, such as the Redgraves, the Fondas, the Bernhardts, the Sheens, and the phenomenally successful Culkin children, it is also interesting to note that many of the parents at the Hunter College Elementary School who refused to let their children audition for the casting agents were people from the theater and film industries. "I saw what can happen to child actors," one said. They also had experienced the "stage mother" phenomenon: many parents impose upon their children their own desire for fame and fortune by submitting them to try-outs and auditions. Judy Garland's mother is an example; she permitted Judy to take amphetamines and depressants in order that movie schedules be met, according to Edwards' biography. Patty Duke's stepparents are another example. After committing her birth mother to an institution, they adopted her and changed her name from Anna to Patty in order to conform to studio wishes. Both Garland and Duke suffered from mental difficulties later in life. Most often, though, the child actor does not become the adult actor. Early promise or even achievement is not enough in the acting profession. Other factors, most often chance, intervene.

What do biographies show about the childhoods of people who became known as actors during their adulthood? Biographies often show the actors had childhood turmoil such as moving often (John Wayne, Marlon Brando, Wally Cox), death of a parent (James Dean), parental alcoholism (Greta Garbo), and the like. We do not know whether actors experienced more turmoil than other artists such as writers. Chances are if you pick up a biography of an actor you will find an unconventional childhood. Jack Nicholson, for example, grew up thinking his grandmother was his mother, while his real mother, a dancer who had had Jack without being married to his father, lived far across the country with her husband and other children. Such deception laid the foundation for the duplicity practiced by the actor.

In *The Way of the Actor*, Brian Bates said that actors, when they are young, often adopt the role of humorist to get by taunts and teasing. Bates said actors' stories of their youths often have in common "the experience of being an 'outsider.' Different. Struggling to belong. And while it would be facile to accept them as representative accounts of the actors' childhoods, it is striking that they have such a similar theme." The outsider role could be imposed from without or within; the actors could have been conscious rebels, such as Marlon Brando or Jack Nicholson, or they could have been painfully shy and rejected by peers, as were Meryl Streep and Dustin Hoffman. The young actor may turn to acting as a way of healing hurts. The opportunity to play a role may give a chance to create metaphors for situations which are too raw to explore outright. Often these metaphors are healing or insightful for the viewers as well. The arts as self-therapy often function in metaphorical, healing ways.

More than 80 master's degree programs, 300-plus bachelor's degree programs, and several hundred non-degree conservatory programs train actors. Few make a living from acting, yet the humanistic training they receive in the world's greatest literature and drama is in itself intrinsically valuable to them as humans. While acting is an art, highly developed in people who have studied it and who perform for our pleasure and enlightenment, the humanistic quality of acting is necessary for our very survival as human beings who must perform or act in various settings. Acting is not mere faking; one must act in order to survive. Hornby differentiated among manipulative acting, which is acting to get someone else to do something (e.g., buy a product, vote for a candidate) and acting as an art, which, when done well, touches our deepest being with glimpses of what the actor shows about human nature. Yet our attitude towards actors and acting is highly ambivalent, for we don't want our salesmen, our athletes, our political candidates, our teachers to admit they are also actors.

The actor who performs acting as either manipulation or as an art must probe human nature in order to pretend. Such pretense is based on close observation of humankind and its physicality and people's outward expression of inward conditions. The most admired and highest paid creative people are certain movie stars, some of whom command millions of dollars for a few scenes in a motion picture. Yet one of these, Marlon Brando, has been quoted by Schickel as saying he thinks acting is not even a profession worthy of a man. Even while he devalued his profession, Brando collected the money given him for acting.

However, others have been more eloquent about the mental and physical artistry that comprises acting creativity. Like singers, they are dependent upon their instruments, their voices and their bodies, but unlike singers, their material is other people, not notes on a page. Marlon Brando in his autobiography described sitting in a phone booth on the Lower East Side of Manhattan, studying the people approaching as if to memorize their gaits and expressions.

The MacArthur Award winner Bill Irwin is an actor who was trained as a clown. In describing one of the classes Irwin taught, Shekerjian said,

> The first students arrive and from a distance try to copy his motions. They fail miserably. Irwin's too good to be casually imitated. Every inch of him understands movement and exactly how much can fit in the space of a split second. His gestures are lean, tight, targeted, spare. He wastes nothing. His concepts are neat, not epic. And when you're not laughing at his antic behavior, you are dazzled by its elegance.

Irwin begins by observing people's behavior. The shuffle of a bag lady, or the quick moves of the hustler with shells, or the waiter who gives the specials of the day, are all material for the actor. He stores all these motions "in some remote but active corner of his mind," and practices at home in front of a mirror.

The comedian Buster Keaton earned his living, and got his laughs, by keeping completely silent, no matter what was done to him; he would be beaten up on stage and never show expression. Keaton's early life was spent on stage with his vaudeville parents. His father would beat the young Keaton on stage, and Keaton's act was to show no reaction. Keaton lost his ability to smile for the camera: "If something tickled me and I started to grin, the old man would hiss, 'Face! Face!' That meant freeze the puss. The longer I held it, why, if we got a laugh the blank pan or the puzzled pose would double it. He kept after me, never let up, and in a few years it was automatic. Then when I'd step on stage or in front of a camera, I couldn't smile. Still can't" (quoted in Alice Miller, 1990).

Stanislavski, one of the founders of the Moscow Art Theater, described his training as an actor in turn-of-the-century Moscow in his 1936 *An Actor Prepares*. His tenets of acting came to be known as the Stanislavski Method, later shortened to The Method when Lee Strasberg began his Actors Theater in New York City. Now Stanislavski's technique is simply called Method acting. Stanislavsky detailed the processes by which acting is made an art; in these processes, one can see the great influence of psychoanalysis on the acting profession.

1. Acting is made an art through the use of the subconscious.
2. Acting is made an art through the actions that the actor takes in even something as simple as taking a seat on a chair.
3. Acting is made an art through the actor's use of imagination to turn the words of the playwright into believable reality, for the playwright cannot put into directions all that the actor must do.
4. Acting is made an art through the actor's concentration of attention so that the actor is unaware of the audience, and through observation and paying attention to how people act in real life.
5. Acting is made an art through rigorous physical training, such as muscle relaxation and conditioning.
6. Acting is made an art through breaking a piece to be acted into its units and its objectives, marked by buoys in a "channel" that "points the true course of creativeness."
7. Acting is made an art through a process of inner probing into the psyche with a sense of faith that the performance will be as true as it can be at this stage of the actor's life. Stanislavski spoke of truth as being related to the actor's inner vision:

> What we mean by truth in the theater is the scenic truth which an actor must make use of in his moments of creativeness. Try always to begin by working from the inside, both on the factual and imaginary parts of a play and its setting. Put life into all the imagined circumstances and actions until you have completely satisfied your sense of truth, and until you have awakened a sense of faith in the reality of your sensations. This process is what we call justification of a part.

8. The actor must use emotion memory, recapturing within himself feelings he has had, in order to interpret the character at hand, but always acting as an artist, in his own person. The actor plays himself, but "in an infinite variety of combinations . . . which have been smelted in the furnace" of the emotion memory.
9. Acting is made an art through communion with the inner self and with the other actors on stage. This is not communication, but a deeper connection, almost spiritual. (Perhaps this aspect of the actor's creativity is evidenced by the reputedly large numbers of love affairs between actors during rehearsals or filming or the run of the

play, and the quick breaking up thereafter.)

10. Acting is made an art through adaptation to each circumstance, so that manipulation of the situation can take place. For example, an actor who wants to get the part of a bully will not appear recessive, or the actor in a situation where she must attract the attention of her mother across the street will project her voice, even though her mother is not really across the street but across the stage.

    After all these aspects of the actor's art, Stanislavski said there is still one more, and that is the most important one:

11. Acting is made an art through the inner motive to play the instrument that the actor has developed of herself. Furthermore, three aspects of the character being portrayed must be balanced: the emotions, the will, and the intellect. To strive for balance among these three is the inner goal of the actor, who must then create an "unbroken line" between the audience and the stage, from morning until night in all aspects of his life, and thus never waver from the inner concentration that playing requires.

Stanislavski called this the "inner creative state," and warned that even when playing an old part, the actor must prepare himself to do it with renewed fervor.

> The inner preparation for a part is as follows: instead of rushing into his dressing-room at the last moment, an actor should (especially if he has a big part) arrive there two hours ahead of his entrance and begin to get himself in form. You know that a sculptor kneads his clay before he begins to use it, and a singer warms up his voice before his concert. We need to do something similar to tune our inner strings, to test the keys, the pedals and the stops.

In all works that she performs, the actor must always look for the super-objective that the work projects. Great authors such as Dostoyevsky, Tolstoy, and Chekhov write about human themes, and these themes are the main artery of their work, "providing nourishment both to it and the actors." In bad plays, or in lesser works, the actor must still try to find the super-objective, and to make it deeper and sharper.

The actor cannot always have inspiration or instinct to play a part, and that is where discipline and training come in. How to get inspiration was described this way:

> Therefore put your thought on what arouses your inner
> motive forces, what makes for your inner creative mood.
> Think of your super-objective and the through line of action
> that leads up to it. In short, have in your mind everything that
> can be consciously controlled and that will lead you to the
> subconscious. That is the best possible preparation for inspi-
> ration. But never try for a direct approach to inspiration for
> its own sake. It will result in physical contortion and the
> opposite of everything you desire.

That, to the Moscow Art Theater, was the summary of creativity in acting. As
it was later interpreted by the New York Method acting studios, Stanislavski's
Method became the ultimate expression of the true, inner self. Psychoanalysis
and the ensuing belief that the actor was a true artist, not merely a skilled imi-
tator or a charming mimic, began to influence theater just as such a romantic
shift took place in other arts. By the 1950s, Method acting, with its dictate that
to be a true artist one had to suffer and to bare one's soul, had become a great
influence on many actors. Marlon Brando's portrayal of Stanley Kowalski in
Tennessee Williams' *A Streetcar Named Desire* became, to many, the epitome
of the achievement of the Method actor. Richard Schickel, in his 1986 critique
of the cult of celebrity, *Intimate Strangers*, said that Brando "brought the spirit of modernism over from literature and painting (where, increasingly, the
subject of the work was the work itself) and brought it to performance."

Here's a telling but apocryphal story about Sir Laurence Olivier and
Dustin Hoffman filming *Marathon Man*. Hoffman stayed up all night, running
himself into exhaustion in preparation for the shoot the next day, immersing
himself in the actual physical experience of the character. The day after the
shoot, Hoffman collapsed exhausted in a chair, bleary-eyed and rubber-mus-
cled. Olivier came over to him and said, "You know, there's an easier way. It's
called acting." This illustrates the basic controversy within the acting profession of emotional reality versus technique. Brando and Hoffman, DeNiro and
Streep are reputed to search for the emotional reality of the character in their
preparation for their roles. Actors such as Cary Grant and Laurence Olivier
relied on technique and training. British actors are known for the latter;
American actors for the former. Following are some comments made by
actors on acting in the anthology of the same title, a series of essays collected by Cole and Chinoy.

Actors on Acting

Laurence Olivier

In his essay, Sir Laurence Olivier called acting "the art of persuasion." When asked about communicating a sense of danger to the audience, Olivier said that he was not very conscious of how this "caged animal" feeling that he gave to audiences and other actors worked, but that the particular play he was in had a lot to do with it. He said, "Othello, of course, screams for it." He also said he watched other actors for ideas. He imitated Sid Field for his comedic sense, borrowing "freely and unashamedly," and admired all his colleagues for their differences. He learned "stern professionalism" from Noel Coward, timing from Rex Harrison, and naturalistic acting from Alfred Lunt. Olivier said, "I think the most interesting thing to see is that an actor is most successful when not only all his virtues but all his disadvantages come into useful play in a part." Olivier thought his hands flung about too much while he acted, and he tried to control them, but he said that sometimes he just had to let go.

Michael Redgrave

The British actor Michael Redgrave—whose daughters Vanessa and Lynn and son Colin are also actors—wrote about what he called "The Stanislavski Myth:" the religious fervor that had grown up throughout the world whenever Stanislavski was mentioned. Speaking of the immense impact that "that thunder-clap of a name" had on the theatrical world, Redgrave said that any actor reading Stanislavski's book would be filled with great self-doubt; however, the book would also bring the actor into reconciliation with his own necessary exhibitionism.

Stanislavski urged actors to seek their characters in themselves and to do away with cliché. The temptation of the actor to act with cliché is great, and audiences often want cliché. Of the two types of acting then in England, the one where the effect springs from the cause, and the one where the effect seeks out the cause, Redgrave said that the latter was more popular. He said, "It is very seldom that we see a production in which more than a few actors are faithful to the actor, the director, and their artistic conscience." Without this commitment, actors become casual laborers and not artists.

Stella Adler

Before the Actors Theater, there was the Group Theater in the 1930s in New York City. The Group Theater modified the Stanislavski system. Besides emphasis on the actor's self-awareness and preparation in his craft, the Group Theater brought together the whole company. One of its founders, Stella Adler, said, "This theater demanded a basic understanding of a complex artistic principle; that all people connected with this theater, the actor, designer, playwright, director, etc., had of necessity to arrive at a single point of view which the theme of the play also expressed."

Again, the influence of the new fad of psychoanalysis can be seen, in that the actor was viewed as having personal problems that the whole group could help solve. As the actor got immersed in the whole process of the theater, he was sometimes reeducated and clarified. By 1934 the Group Theater had modified Stanislavski's system to emphasize the actor's clarity of actions rather than the actor's inner life. Adler said, "Now emphasis was put on the circumstances of the play and a much stronger use of the actor's need to find greater justification in the use of these circumstances and a more conscious use of them." Even if an actor was insufficiently aware of his unconscious feelings, for acting was considered a process of bringing up the unconscious and making it conscious so it can be used, and the actor can be freed emotionally, the Group Theater process of rehearsing scenes would help him: "Each scene was given an architectural solidity which was difficult for anyone to break down, and no matter what their individual acting problems were, they nevertheless helped enormously to achieve the ensemble excellence."

The Group Theater was built on the idea of ensemble; that is, no one actor was more important than another actor, but all were essential cogs in the machine, parts of the whole, members of the collective. This idea coincided with the worldwide rise of socialism as a political system. The presence at this time of the left wing attraction to communism is evident in the theories of the Group Theater; they felt that the whole company must live together in a commune-like existence. In fact, many of them were later accused of being Communists and blacklisted during the infamous McCarthy hearings of the House UnAmerican Activities Committee in the 1950s.

Judith Malina

By the 1960s, Judith Malina and Julian Beck had founded The Living Theater. Malina and Beck modified the purpose of the theater to include dramatic social consciousness, for they believed that theater transformed the participants as well as the audience. Many of the plays were staged with students, factory workers, school children, and other nonactors, since acting technique was less important than the social message of the play. The public outcry after they produced Kenneth Brown's *The Brig* in 1963, a raw and disturbing portrait of life in Marine Corps prisons, may have contributed to social changes in brigs in the Marines (Brown, 1990). Malina's diaries, written at the age of twenty-one, in 1947, indicated that even early on she was not a Stanislavskian. Malpede quoted Malina as saying,

> For years I have refuted Stanislavski's sense memory theory
> . . . I played the last scene of *Iphigenia in Aulis* in a conscious
> attempt to demonstrate that I could play the famous tearful
> plea with my mind empty of all but the most prosaic thoughts.
> I said: A painter does not weep when he paints a weeping figure. Yet I exploited my own emotional turmoil when I played
> Cassandra. And in the role of Mildred Luce, driven mad by
> the loss of two sons in the war. What alternatives can I find to
> the sense memories of grief? Does the actor exhibit his peculiar emotion the way the freak exhibits his distorted physique?

In a later note, Malina wrote that she was not protesting against "realism" but the "fake mimicry" that is acting falsely. Actors in the Living Theater spoke of being changed utterly by their work there. The emotional impact of the plays was often so strong that the audience joined the actors in protest, marching out of the theater with them. The lines between stage and audience became blurred. In one play performed in Italy and Brazil, where Malina and Beck were in prison for three months, an actor was hung from a parrot perch and electric shock applied. Malpede, in *Women in Theatre*, said of the Living Theater productions, "The scene is a brutally naturalistic moment in an otherwise imagistic play; Judith says it is meant to wake us from our trance and make us face the reality of daily torture in prisons throughout the world." Malina saw the actor's art as showing the audience that he really believes what he's saying, in order that they listen very carefully, "to see whether they are in accord with it."

Peter Brook

Peter Brook was called a *Wunderkind* when he was young. Born in Great Britain, he went at the age of seventeen to Oxford and became a film and stage director of international repute. He and Paul Scofield founded the Theater of Cruelty. In 1987 I was privileged to sit through all twelve hours of his *Mahabarata* at the Brooklyn Academy of Music, and in my journal the next day, I wrote: "I woke up this morning to dreams of Ganesh and the mythological characters of Hinduism, they became so real to me yesterday at the production. I was talking with the Elephant King and rooting for Vishnu. I have not been so moved by a production since I saw Sam Shepard's *Buried Child* at the Pittsburgh Public Theater years ago." (In 1991, Brook released a shortened movie of the *Mahabarata*, only six hours long.)

That spring I went again to the Brooklyn Academy of Music to see Brook's production of Chekhov's *The Cherry Orchard*, and I wrote, "I sat three feet from where Academy Award-winner Linda Hunt entered, and saw her gather herself for her entrance. She focused her attention, took a deep breath, closed her eyes into a squint, opened them wide, and burst onto the stage. Shivered as the doors closed in the final scene. We, the audience, were locked in. We sat sadly and breathlessly. We could hear the axes chop, chop, chop their way to progress. The genius of the playwright, the genius of the director, the genius of the actor all came together last night."

The Theater of Cruelty emphasizes improvisation and the collective lives of the actors in company. Brook's company for *The Mahabarata* included actors of every ethnicity possible. In writing about the art of acting, Brook, in *Actors on Acting,* said: "Acting begins with a tiny inner movement so slight that it is almost completely invisible." He went on to say that stage actors have an awareness of this tiny inner movement because of what is required with a live audience, but film actors often have to act with a camera as an audience. This is why stage actors can be film actors, but film actors often have difficulty becoming stage actors. The camera lens is able to pick up the tiny inner movement much more acutely than a live audience is.

Brook said that this flicker, this tiny movement, is often present instinctually in young actors. Child actors "can give subtle and complex incarnations that are the despair of those who have evolved their skill over the years." Then something happens, and later on, the child actors "build up their barriers to themselves" and find that touching the essential is difficult if not impossible. This would seem to relate to Bamberger's developmental theory of music talent fulfillment and the presence of the mid-life crisis in adolescent performers, as discussed in Chapters 7 and 9.

Brook also criticized the Method actor, saying that he can be spontaneous only, and base his actions on observation. For Brook this means that the

Method actor cannot draw on "any deep creativity." The creativity of acting comes from improvisation, when the actor can come up against "his own barriers, to the points where in place of a new-found truth he normally substitutes a lie." Creativity in acting comes through rehearsals in which improvisational exercises are faithfully done. The mediocre actor builds his character during rehearsals, Brook said. But the really creative actor comes to the opening night in terror, because during the rehearsals he has only been exploring partial aspects of the character he is playing. Even at the last rehearsal, the creative actor will be willing, if necessary, to "discard the hardened shells of his work" in order to come to a resolution. The creative actor will undergo "the trauma of appearing in front of an audience, naked and unprepared."

When a show goes into a long run, discarding hardened shells and appearing naked and not being prepared before the audience gets to be impossible. This is when the actor must begin to rely on technique. The actor's most difficult job is to be "sincere yet detached." Brook compared the actor's act of creating with that of the painter and the pianist:

> With any of the other arts, however deep one plunges into the act of creating, it is always possible to step away and look at the result. As the painter steps back from his canvas other faculties can spring into play and warn him at once of his excesses. The trained pianist's head is physically less involved than his fingers and so however "carried away" he is by the music, his ear carries its own degree of detachment and objective control. Acting is in many ways unique in its difficulties because the artist has to use the treacherous, changeable and mysterious material of himself as his medium. He is called upon to be completely involved while distanced—detached without detachment. He must be sincere, he must be insincere: he must practice how to be insincere with sincerity, and how to lie truthfully.

Jeff Corey

Film actors also seek training and the company of other actors. During the 1950s, one of the most revered acting teachers in Hollywood was Jeff Corey. Patrick McGilligan, in a biography of actor Jack Nicholson, described Corey as "an actor's actor" who had been blacklisted for left-wing political activities and so began to teach acting. Among his students in the early 1950s were Carol Burnett, Gary Cooper, and James Dean. Corey accepted students by audition and interview. The imaginative and physical exercises Corey created helped the actors for many years. The actors were asked to do a physical task, and then while doing it, they would have to sing a Gershwin song or recite a monologue from an Arthur Miller play. McGilligan said, "This taught students not to complicate a role with 'psychological gyrations,' making the point that a physical lie begets a psychological lie." The students would focus on an art reproduction or antique furniture and then do free associations from their reflections.

Corey would have them take a famous scene from a well-known play and re-do the scene in another time, place, and context. This taught students to deal with the subject matter of scenes obliquely. The screenwriter Robert Towne described Corey's purpose: "The situation he would give would be totally contrary to the text, and it was the task of the actors, through the interpretation of various bits of business they could come up with, to suggest the real situation through lines that had no bearing on the situation." Corey had studied with the Group Theater, with Yiddish actor Jules Dassin, and with Russian-born actor Michael Chekhov. In his classes the young actors did not do film scenes, but they would rehearse classic scenes from literature and the Bible. Corey would advise his students to "make the bizarre choice. Be unpredictable. Go for laughter where someone else would think tears. Interrupt yourself with a sudden, inexplicable rage." Corey said that the actor will have in common with the character at least seventy-five percent, even if the character is Hitler or Peter Pan. The acting comes from the twenty five percent that is different. "Discover yourself in the part. Don't imitate anyone else. Be the head of your own academy," Corey advised the young film actors.

In summary, the actor's creativity is rewarded in the emotional and nonverbal responses of audiences to the skills the actor has been able to use in order to portray human behavior, gestures, personalities. The actor's body, observational powers, memory of emotions, and prior experiences all enter into the creativity that is expressed when the actor acts.

Psychological and Biographical Studies of Actors

Unlike visual artists, actors—for all the value we accrue to them by paying a few of them their huge salaries and by writing about their loves and lives in many popular magazines and gossip columns—have attracted little scientific curiosity as to their personality characteristics. A few psychometric studies do exist, however. In the Myers-Briggs Type Indicator technical *Manual*, a sample of sixty-two actors was found to be among the top five professions that preferred ENFJ (Extroversion, Intuition, Feeling, and Judgment). Also showing this configuration were clergy, home economists, priests and monks, and health teachers, as well as writers, artists, entertainers, and agents.

The ENFJ personality is thought to combine intuition with extroversion; they are change agents; they have broad interests, and like new relationships and new patterns. FJ's prefer to use feeling in the behavior they outwardly show, and, as would be necessary for actors, they are very observant, especially about the needs of people. They are expressive leaders who "spend energy in making people happy and in bringing harmony into relationships." The bibliography in the *Manual* showed that the only study of actors, though, was of theater majors in a college, in an unpublished study presented at a regional conference.

Using the Myers-Briggs Type Indicator, Buchanan and Bandy conducted two studies of psychodramatists. The researchers administered the MBTI to thirty-seven prospective psychodramatists, and the ten successful psychodrama applicants were found to be ENFP (extroverted, intuitive, feeling, and perceiving); they were innovative people who were not conservative. In a study of 170 certified psychodramatists, nine out of ten certified psychodramatists were intuitive (N) types, and only one fourth of psychodramatists were extroverts. The psychodramatists were more like experiential psychologists and least like psychoanalytic therapists. The authors suggested that creativity and spontaneity are essential to psychodrama.

The biographies studied by Goertzel, Goertzel, and Goertzel numbered many actors, but several of these biographies do not in fact reveal much of the inner substance of their subjects but instead are mere puffery, a list of famous people met, a catalog of performances with little introspection about the art of those performances.

Why does society have such an ambiguous attitude toward the profession of acting? On one hand the famous actor is venerated and paid millions of dollars to do a blockbuster action film or to play a cartoon character; on the other, the actor is thought to be somewhat frivolous, weird, outside of the norm. The theater crowd at school is often separate from other academic achievers and from social butterflies. This ambiguous attitude has historical foundations; that is, the traveling company who went from town to town was welcomed as a diversion from the everyday, yet was looked at suspiciously as carrying the news of the outside world, and also as having lower morals. We do not remember the names of the characters our favorite actors played in their roles; we remember that the movie or play starred Al Pacino or Tom Cruise, but not the characters they played unless the character's name was Jerry McGuire, the title of the movie.

The actor, the sacred icon—Marilyn Monroe, Brad Pitt—carries a shining weight of awe that could even approach worship: actor as shaman, as muse, as magician, as wizard, as healer. The similarity of the layouts of churches and theaters is also worth noting. The preacher and the actor bear striking likenesses, both in their power of oratory and in their power to mesmerize by the roles they play. This connection of the theater with the divine has existed for centuries, and though this is not the time or place to discuss it at length, we should not leave the topic of the actor without mentioning this strange power of creation of feelings of awe and wonder that actors seem to work within the hearts of the audience. The doppelganger-like phenomena of fandom, fan clubs, and the dark side of such astonishing adoration, the existence of the obsessed stalker so enthralled with the celebrity actor that the actor must meet the public behind bodyguards and live behind iron gates, are also worth pondering. What basic need in the audience does adoration of the actor, the athlete, the rock/popular musician fulfill?

Dancers

Almost every little girl wants to be a dancer at some time in her life. She imagines herself as Isadora Duncan being rebellious and so very artistic, in her bare feet swinging her scarves around, or as Pavlova, Margot Fonteyn, Suzanne Farrell, or Moira Shearer in *The Red Shoes*, dancing a *pas de deux* with Nureyev, Diaghilev, Nijinsky, or Jacques D'Amboise. Or she imagines herself the daughter of Shirley MacLaine in *The Turning Point*, having a romance with Baryshnikov. If her body doesn't meet the ballet standard, she may imagine herself a modern dancer, one of the kids of *The Chorus Line*, or hoofing it with Fred Astaire in an old black and white movie, gliding in a frothy white dress as Ginger Rogers or Cyd Charisse, or as *Flashdance*'s heroine, coming up the hard way from welder to dancer.

The career of the ballet dancer is brief, a flame ignited before adolescence, at the age of eight or nine, and extinguished in her twenties or thirties when, if she has had any success at all, she goes back home to the Midwest and opens a ballet school in her hometown, to teach the hopeful children with the same dreams she had. Of course, there have been exceptions, such as Martha Graham, who didn't dance until she was in her twenties. Modern dancers seem to have longer professional lives than classical ballet dancers. Some continue dancing through their forties and into their fifties.

The creativity of dance is a creativity of the body in motion to the sound of music. Dance is the province not only of the highly trained ballet dancer, but the folk dancer, the tribal dancer, the dancer as ritualist from time immemorial. Whirling dervishes danced themselves into trances of ecstasy. All primitive cultures used dance in religious ceremonies. Dance, movement to music, induces ritualistic behavior and, coupled with substances such as alcohol or peyote, bestows a feeling of well-being and of communion with the other dancers. Ballroom dancing, disco dancing, rock 'n' roll and hip hop dancing, slow dancing, jitterbug, the frug, the twist, the mashed potato, the slam dance, the tango and the waltz have been practiced by people in our culture as a means of entertainment. Dance is an immensely pleasurable form of creativity, both in the watching and in the doing.

It is also painful. Professional dancers are notorious for having injuries, and dance aficionados know the disappointment of coming to a performance and finding a substitute because the featured player was injured. Readers of dance criticism are just as likely as readers of the sports pages to hear litanies of pulled ligaments, twisted shoulders, overworked knees.

The Aesthetics of Dance

What are the aesthetics of dance? H'Doubler said that the dancer uses bodily tension and disciplined movement to communicate meaning. The dancer is always distant from that meaning, removed, using her body as a tool. The dancer, however, must be inspired by emotion and, through concentration on her body, must convey that emotion to the audience. H'Doubler said, "Thus dance may be considered a neural projection of inner thought and feeling into movement, rhythm being the mold through which the creative life flows in giving its meaning form."

Walter Terry, for many years *The New York Times* dance critic, in *Dance in America*, called dance an art of danger in which we as spectators participate vicariously. The aesthetic of dance is kinesthetic, and we "journey with the dancer along the paths of adventure created by the choreographer." The philosopher Susanne Langer, in *Form and Feeling,* called dance a phenomenological art, an art that exists in the moment, that is apprehended in the moment. Dance provides an illusion of force through the skill of the dancer, who uses her body to implicitly provide that force. Even more than the actor, who has voice and speech, the dancer must rely on gesture, extension, and physical being to tell a story. The music is the framework, but the dancer is the frame.

The movement of the dancer has four dimensions or qualities which Maxine Sheets described in *The Phenomenology of Dance*. First is the tension that the body of the dancer shows. Second is the linear quality of the dancer's extensions. Third is the shape or range of the force in the dancer's body, and in the form of the movements the dancer makes upon the stage area. Fourth is what is projected by the dancer. These projections can be abrupt, sustained, or explosive (ballistic). In all of these, what the dancer is conveying is abstract, not real but a simulation of the real, communicated through gesture and subject to the training and perfection of form that the dancer has attained.

The ballet, begun in the sixteenth century, is the most formal form of dance in the Western world. The dancer needs a classic body, a certain shape of neck and curve of the arch of the foot. The dancer must not be too tall or too short, though those limits are being currently stretched. In 1988 Peter Martins defended his use of the short dancer Gen Hogiuchi, who was criticized by dance critic Arlene Croce for being offensively diminutive.

Throughout ballet's history, Russian ballet became the standard for other countries' ballet. In the United States, the New York City Ballet, founded by George Balanchine, preserved the Russian standard, while the American Ballet Theater, under Michel Fokine, began to drift from that standard, according to Agnes de Mille in *America Dances*.

The American Ballet Theater incorporated the techniques of the modern, or Martha Graham, style of dance. De Mille said, "The ballet dancer now on occasion droops and convulses, falls to the floor, spins on a nonvertical or changing spiral axis, beats and jumps off beat." Balanchine, who danced with Diaghilev's company before it closed in the 1920s, was asked by two young Harvard graduates, Lincoln Kirstein and Edward Warburg, to start an American ballet in the Russian style. Balanchine preserved Russian classical ballet but gave it an American flavor. Among his many accomplishments, Balanchine choreographed the works of his fellow Russian, the composer Igor Stravinsky.

While the more avant-garde modern dance draws upon the rigid ballet training of its dancers, it is choreographed to music that is less formal than typical ballet music. Agnes de Mille's use of roping and riding in *Oklahoma* and of fantasy and dream in *Carousel*, Twyla Tharp's variations on Sinatra's music, Pina Bausch's abstractions of dance hall behavior, Pilobolus's athletic and not ascetic geometries of gymnastics done to rock 'n' roll, Mark Morris's explorations of form and space done to the music of the Violent Femmes, Merce Cunningham's silent and still interpretations of John Cage's four minutes of silence—all of these have extended dance from the classical standard, yet all have been created by dancers who began in classical training.

Again, in our consideration of creativity, we come to the word training. Or practice. This is the key element in all considerations of the creative product. The development of expertise is predicated on practice, and there is some evidence that the amount of practice affects the attainment of the practicer. Talent, according to some, is not necessary. The product is shaped by practice. The product of the actor is a role. The product of the dancer is a role. The product of the musician is the performance of a piece. The role, in order to be enacted with perfection, demands that the person enacting be trained.

Dance is an ephemeral art, and many dances have not been written down. The Lee Theodore American Dance Machine Company has as its aim the reconstruction of the dances of the American theater, the dances of such choreographers as Jerome Robbins and Bob Fosse. They go to the people who did the dances originally and ask them to remember what they did; they then write the dances down. Theodore said in Gruen's *People Who Dance* in 1988, "On one number alone, there might be five or six of them, because what happens is that one person will come in and remember the first sixteen bars, and the next person will remember what happened afterwards, and so on, down the line." Of the dances that have been written down, many of the choreographers' notes are indecipherable, or the dance was changed so much in performance that the choreographer's notes are useless. This, to me, illustrates the nonliterary quality of dance, and the lack of interest many dancers have in the written word. Dancers prefer moving over the static drudgery of documentation.

Biographies and Memoirs of Dancers

As with actors, the biographies of dancers are often puff pieces, chronicles of who danced what when and who met whom where, with little insight given as to the process of dance in the dancer's mind. Suzanne Farrell's 1990 autobiography, *Holding On To The Air*, is a notable exception.

Suzanne Farrell

Suzanne Farrell was the premier ballerina for Balanchine's New York City Ballet from the mid-1960s until the mid-1980s. Her work was called by Mark Morris "perpetually astonishing." He said, "I learn things just by watching Suzanne Farrell dance . . . She has a spontaneity that I can't believe; I can't believe she can pull it off all the time. She dances with the speed of thought." Farrell was born and reared in Cincinnati, in a family of women. Her grandmother was divorced, her aunts were divorced, her mother divorced her father. In her 1990 autobiography, Farrell described her life with her two older sisters as that of a daring tomboy who lived in a small four-room house, and who, for play, would walk the beams and pipes of the construction site of a nearby subdivision being built. Like most active girls, Farrell had a childhood of scrapes and bruises, scabs on knees and elbows, but this was the childhood of a girl slated to become one of America's premier ballerinas.

Suzanne and her sisters studied dance at the Cincinnati Conservatory. Her mother was good at getting her daughters scholarships, and so the girls went to school at Ursuline Academy, near the Conservatory, so they could get to their lessons easily. The three girls shared a bedroom, and one of their favorite games was called "Ballet." One would be the Teacher, one would be the Mother, and Suzanne would be the Student.

What she liked about her early ballet lessons were the acrobatics they did for the first fifteen minutes, and the tap dancing for the last fifteen minutes. Farrell said that early on she "loved the way the clicks and the rhythms overtook my body and made it move." The only reading she remembered doing while she was growing up was looking at the picture books of ballet that she found in the Cincinnati Public Library. She also had a girlfriend who was as obsessed about dance as she. The two girls would call each other up on the phone and give each other combinations to do, writing them down in the dark, using flashlights: "Glissade, jeté, glissade, jeté, pirouette . . . and then we'd both put the receiver down and get up and slide, jump, slide, jump, turn before reconvening on the phone to discuss the difficulties and changes necessary."

School was not her favorite activity: "I wasn't stupid, but I had a hard time sitting still in class and was always being reprimanded for fidgeting. Nonphysical concentration was simply boring." Suzanne's talent was apparent early on. She was chosen to be Clara in the *Nutcracker.*

Farrell was discovered in Cincinnati by a Balanchine scout, the ballerina Diana Adams, who had been sent by the New York City Ballet throughout the country after the Ballet received a Ford Foundation grant. Adams spotted

Suzanne, advising her that if she ever got to New York, she should audition. That was enough for Suzanne's mother, and within weeks, in July of 1960, the family moved to New York City. Diana Adams had told Balanchine that Suzanne had one flat foot, injured when a horse had kicked it. During the audition, Balanchine examined the foot, pressing it hard to test for resilience. When Suzanne's foot successfully passed the test, Balanchine arranged a scholarship for her to study with the company. Suzanne also attended two high schools, but her dance schedule at the New York City Ballet was so strenuous and touring so demanding that she never did graduate from high school.

While she credited her mother for the opportunity to go to New York City, Suzanne said that her mother, a nurse, was not a stage mother. She had made lessons available to the girls, but she didn't watch the classes and never stayed outside the room commenting on their progress with the other mothers. Her mother had to work. "She had been lonely as a child, and perhaps she knew that if you have the arts in your life you will never be lonely. I have often been alone, but I have never felt lonely when I was dancing, even dancing by myself." Her absent father never came to the Farrell sisters' recitals. Farrell said, "It mattered to me that he didn't seem to care."

Within two years after the family arrived in New York, Balanchine, then in his sixties, was making ballets for the eighteen-year-old Suzanne, sending her love poems, and treating her as a real ballerina. He had been married several times to several ballerinas and was still married, but the young Suzanne became his latest muse. They would take long walks next to the Seine, talking, when the Ballet played in Paris. By 1964, she had danced sixteen new ballets. This progress was unusual, and she said she "skipped through the natural hierarchy of the profession" because "Balanchine felt there wasn't time." In a 1997 television documentary, Farrell stated that she loved Balanchine and he loved her, but that was not the important thing. What was important was that Balanchine was the foremost choreographer of the land, and he felt that she could do the dances he created better than anyone else.

> He obviously had already chosen to commit himself to me, and he had plans, serious plans, for what he might do with me. But he had already lived a hundred different lives in the ballets he had choreographed before I was even born, and for us to continue forward together I had to pass through his past. And his past, even his loves and personal passions, were in his ballets. All those movements, all those pirouettes, all that music, all those stories and styles, all that

romance, all that beauty and joy and heartbreak, all of that
was who he was. I am convinced that he wanted me to catch
up to him.

Meanwhile, Farrell was also being courted by another dancer in the company,
Paul Meija, and in 1969, when she was twenty-three, they married. Her mother was so upset she stopped speaking to her, and Balanchine was so upset that
he dropped her and her new husband from the New York City Ballet. "I was
now a Balanchine dancer without Balanchine," Farrell said. Occasionally, she
was asked to guest-star with such companies as the National Ballet of Canada,
and finally, she and Paul were asked to join the Ballet of the Twentieth
Century in Brussels, Belgium. The company, more avant-garde than
Balanchine's, did more world touring than the New York City Ballet, and
Farrell got rave reviews.

In 1975, she wrote to Balanchine, asking to dance with him again, and he
took her back—but not Paul. In 1977, the Company performed on the
Corporation for Public Broadcasting "Dance In America" series. Farrell said,
about the filming of her dancing, that the results were not representative of
either her dancing or of the ballets, for the editing and splicing took their toll
and the immediacy of the performance was lost: "Videotape seemed to spread
an even sheen over the nuances of any movement." She said that she would
lock up any filmed performances of hers, if she had her way. "I certainly don't
relish the idea of future generations watching a film and thinking that that is
how I danced, because it is not." This again illustrates the transitory nature of
dance, of choreography, of the creativity that goes into the performance. It
also illustrates that dancers are not as concerned with historical preservation
as they are with the moment's mastery of movement.

Farrell, like many creative people, suffered a deep depression just when
everything seemed to be going well. "I couldn't understand why I was so
depressed at such a wonderful time in my life—I had come back to the company, I was dancing, and Mr. B. was making new ballets." The incidence of
depression in creative people was discussed with reference to writers, but creative people of all types have been prone to depression.

Mikhail Baryshnikov joined the company in 1979, but Farrell didn't work
with him because of the great difference in their heights. Balanchine had suffered heart attacks. Her husband Paul was in Chicago working with one of
Balanchine's five ex-wives, Maria Tallchief, choreographing for the Chicago
City Ballet. Balanchine died in 1983. By 1985, when she was forty, Farrell
had developed a hip problem that prevented her rehearsing for the long hours

necessary. The hip degeneration continued. "I could find no relief. I could hear clicking and grinding inside my hip where the cartilage was completely gone. Bone was gnawing bone, and I was visibly limping." In 1987, a hip operation, a plastic hip, and a reunion with her father after thirty years followed. She performed again in 1988. Her last performance was on November 26, 1989, with Peter Martins. She then retired to teach, at her school in the Adirondacks and as a guest with other ballets.

Farrell's life as a ballet dancer was typical of that of many. The concentration and dedication necessary must come early. The biography of any dancer reads like a medical report, at times, as well as a list of dances performed and people met. But the physical repercussions to the bodies of dancers are always present.

Gelsey Kirkland

Gelsey Kirkland, who followed Suzanne Farrell as a lead ballerina for George Balanchine's New York City Ballet, began in 1969, at the age of 17, to be partnered by such dancers as Peter Martins, Mikhail Baryshnikov, Jacques D'Amboise, and Ivan Nagy. Like Farrell, Kirkland dropped out of high school in order to dance with Balanchine's company. She wrote her autobiography, *Dancing On My Grave*, with the collaboration of her husband, Greg Lawrence, in 1986. In describing the influence of Balanchine's body standards on the development of ballet in America, Kirkland said that Balanchine insisted he see bones:

> I was less than a hundred pounds even then. Mr. B. did not seem to consider beauty a quality that must develop from within the artist; rather, he was concerned with outward signs such as body weight. His emphasis was responsible in part for setting the style that has led to some of the current extremes of American ballet. He did not merely say, "Eat less." He said repeatedly, "Eat nothing."
>
> The physical line of a ballerina seemed to have been ordained. A thin body carried the most definition. A slender figure was supposed to be the prerequisite for movement . . . Mr. B's ideal proportions called for an almost skeletal frame, accentuating the collarbones and length of the neck. Defeminization was the overall result, with the frequent cessation of the menstrual cycle due to malnutrition and physi-

cal abuse. A fulsome pair of breasts seemed the only
attribute with which a ballerina could assert her sexuality.

Kirkland, who herself had silicone implanted in her breasts during her teenage
years, noted that the Balanchine standards have been adopted by nearly every
ballet troupe and school in the United States. Those who refuse to go along
are more likely not to find employment as dancers or teachers. Kirkland said
that a "concentration camp aesthetic" was emphasized, and said that many of
the dancers she knew abused diet pills, went on quack diets, and became
anorexic or bulimic, or both. The death by heart attack of a young anorexic
dancer from Boston in 1997 indicates that the concentration camp aesthetic
might still be operant in the dance world.

Another caution that Kirkland made to dancers was about the dangers of
narcissism that came from staring at oneself in the dance studio mirror. "The
mirror was my nemesis, seductive to the point of addiction," she says of her
early career. In the mirror, she found "a double who exposed all of my flaws
and pointed out all of my physical imperfections," a person incapable of meeting the ideal of bodily beauty:

> As a primary teaching tool for dance, the mirror fosters the
> delusion that beauty is only skin-deep, that truth is found
> only in the plasticity of movement. It seems preferable to
> imitate rather than to create. Imitation can be varied to cre-
> ate the impression of originality. There are endless possibil-
> ities for breaking the human mold into novel patterns. To be
> daring in dance no longer involves risk, virtuosity, and
> strength of conviction. The dancer can win approval for
> steps that require no real decision in creative or composi-
> tional terms.

Kirkland found that when she devalued the mirror and worked without it, she
was able to get past the fascination with her image and to create more original steps and dances. "Classical virtuosity is more than technique, line, proportion, and balance." The spectator and the dancer must come together, holding "a bird with a broken wing," and the bird is healed when the performer
achieves "empathy through movement." This requires of the dancer "the most
demanding kind of inspiration," the inspiration of love felt by both performer
and audience.

Alvin Ailey

I am Alvin Ailey. I am a choreographer. I am a black man whose roots are in the sun and dirt of the south. My roots are in the blues, in the street people whose lives are full of beauty and misery and pain and hope. My roots are also in the Gospel church, the Gospel church of the south where I grew up. Holy blues, paeons to joy, anthems to the human spirit.

Born in Rogers, Texas, in 1931, Alvin Ailey and his mother moved to Los Angeles, California, when he was twelve, but his early experiences in rural southeastern Texas were to be the inspirations for the many ballets Ailey made when he founded the Alvin Ailey American Ballet Theater.

He became inspired to be a dancer after a junior high school field trip to the Ballet Russe de Monte Carlo. He then began taking classes with Lester Horton, founder of one of the first racially integrated dance companies in the U.S. After Horton's death in 1953, Ailey took over as the director of the Lester Horton Dance Theater and began to make his own ballets. In 1954, he and his friend Carmen de Lavallade were invited to New York to dance in the Broadway show "House of Flowers" by Truman Capote. In New York, Ailey studied with Martha Graham, Doris Humphrey, and Charles Weidman and took acting classes with Stella Adler.

In 1958, Ailey founded his own company, the Alvin Ailey American Dance Theater. Ailey wanted to create a company that would honor African-American cultural institutions and heritage. The stunning visual effects and the acrobatic gyrations of the sleek Ailey dancers were a feast to the eyes of critics and audiences. Using gospel music and the vernacular, in 1960, he choreographed "Revelations," which was based on the religious heritage of his youth.

During his company's first decade, Mr. Ailey created approximately 20 new ballets, among them "Hermit Songs" (1961) and "Reflections in D" (1962). These were followed by "The Lark Ascending" (1972), "Love Songs" (1972), "Hidden Rites" (1973), "Night Creature" (1974), "The Mooche" (1975), "Memoria" (1979), "The River" (1981), "Landscape" (1981), "For 'Bird'— With Love" (1984), "Survivors" (1986), "Witness" (1986), and "Opus McShann" (1988).

Although he created some 79 ballets, Mr. Ailey maintained that his company was not a repository for his work exclusively. The Company's varied repertory includes works by dance pioneers as well as by emerging young choreographers. More than 170 works by 63 choreographers have been performed by the Ailey Company.

In 1965, he discovered an extraordinarily talented young dancer named Judith Jamison, whose brilliant dancing and style provided the inspiration for a number of Ailey works, including "Cry," his best known solo. "Cry" was created as a tribute to Mr. Ailey's mother and was dedicated to "all Black women everywhere—especially our mothers." Ailey had a lifelong relationship with his mother that was extremely close, and he dedicated much of his work to her.

In 1969, he founded the Alvin Ailey American Dance Center, the official school of the Ailey Company, and he went on to form the Repertory Ensemble, the second company, in 1974.

Throughout his lifetime, Ailey received notable recognition for his achievements. He was awarded numerous honorary doctoral degrees, including one from Princeton University. In 1976, the NAACP awarded Ailey the Spingarn Medal, and in 1982 he received the United Nations Peace Medal. From the world of dance he received a 1975 Dance Magazine Award, the Capezio Award (1979) and modern dance's most prestigious prize, the Samuel H. Scripps American Festival Award, in 1987. In 1988, he was honored by the Kennedy Center for his extraordinary contribution to American culture and achievement in the performing arts. Ailey died on December 1, 1989.

Anna Kisselgoff of The New York Times wrote, "You didn't need to have known Ailey personally to have been touched by his humanity, enthusiasm and exuberance and his courageous stand for multiracial brotherhood." Judith Jamison, named Artistic Director of the Alvin Ailey American Dance Theater, said, "Mr. Ailey's spiritual and moral support served as a constant inspiration to me as an artist. He was my spiritual walker, my mentor and support. He gave me legs until I could stand on my own, as a dancer and choreographer. I view this appointment as the course to take to continue my vision and to keep Mr. Ailey's legacy alive."

With all his accomplishments, talents, and accolades, Ailey suffered from his own demons. He experienced severe depression and was hospitalized after setting off fire alarms in his building in the middle of the night; he sat across the street on a park bench watching the excitement. He also used and abused cocaine and alcohol. A homosexual, he experimented with promiscuous male prostitutes. Many of his close friends worried about his physical safety. He went to the building where one of his lovers lived and aggressively banged on the door until he was thrown out. He died of AIDS. Dunning, his biographer, quoted many of his dancers and friends as saying he worked on new ballets and on his Alvin Ailey camps for young, black, poor dancers right up until his death.

Physical Repercussions

Dancers' lives are constantly filled with practice. Along with that practice comes an ethic of self-denial. Researchers have found that dancers suffer not only from physical injuries, but from physical maladies, among them eating disorders, trouble with menstrual periods, and wounded self-concepts.

The rigorous demands on the body and the continuous pressures to meet the body standard of ballet often produce eating disorders in young dancers. In one study of forty-five dancers and forty-four nondancers, Braisted, Mellin, Gong, and Irwin found that adolescent ballet dancers exhibited the characteristics of anorexia nervosa significantly more often than did the nondancers. These characteristics were underweight, distorted body image, amenorrhea, and binge eating. The dancers also used frequent strategies to reduce their weight, such as fasting and purging. They also used vitamin C more, and were not prone to eat carbohydrates.

Lowenkopf and Vincent, in a study of fifty-five female student ballet dancers, found that most of them weighed significantly below national norms and had the eating and hyperactivity patterns of people with anorexia nervosa. The girls were obsessed with food and weight. They also experienced delayed menstruation, were likely to be virgins, and did not date. Their unhealthy eating habits were reinforced by the dance world in which they were immersed. Their concern with their dancing ability went along with their rejection of their body images.

Dancers, figure skaters, and swimmers were studied by Brooks-Gunn, Burrow, and Warren. This study confirmed the earlier studies, showing that dancers and skaters were leaner and lighter than swimmers, were more likely to have delayed menarche, and that they had more negative eating habits than swimmers. Suzanne Farrell insisted that Balanchine did not encourage the symptoms of anorexia in his dancers, but Buckle's biography of Balanchine indicated that Balanchine would often speak to his dancers about being light, about being easy to lift, about being thin.

Farrell spoke about the "endless diet," the object of which was not to overcome obesity but "to attain the ideal shape for a dancer." Farrell herself failed to recognize that she was pregnant because she was so used to the irregularity of her menstrual periods. "I was having a miscarriage, but I didn't know it because I didn't know I was pregnant. Like many dancers, I had irregular cycles, and skipping a month or two had never been cause for alarm." Kirkland's comments about her addiction to cocaine resulting from her obsession with weight also resonate.

In a study of 345 adolescent dancers and nondancers, looking at time of maturation, Brooks-Gunn and Warren found that more dancers were late maturers (having menarcheal age after fourteen years). These late maturers weighed less, were leaner, and had higher oral control scores and lower diet scores than the girls who matured on time (eleven-and-a-half to fourteen years). Those dancers who matured on time had higher psychopathology, perfection, and bulimia scores than the late maturers. They also had lower body image scores.

Brooks-Gunn, Warren, and Hamilton surveyed fifty-five adult dancers in four dance companies in the U.S. and Western Europe. They found that 56 percent of these adult dancers had delayed menarche (age 14 or later), and 19 percent of these had not had a menstrual period for the preceding five months. One third of these dancers self-reported that they had had eating difficulties resembling anorexia nervosa or bulimia. The researchers found that amenorrhea and eating problems were related, and that 50 percent of the dancers who reported anorexia nervosa also were not having menstrual periods. The dancers were dieting at the time, and this was found to be significantly related to their amenorrhea.

Eating disorders occur among certain groups of athletes as well. A study by Stoutjesdyk and Jevne indicated that different groups of athletes may be at different risks of eating disorders. Trent Petrie looked at female collegiate gymnasts. He studied 215 gymnasts and classified them as normal/nondisordered eaters, exercisers, bingers, dieter/restricters, subthreshold bulimics, or bulimics. Only one-fifth of the women athletes had normal eating habits; three-fifths had intermediate eating disorders. The wish to lose weight, low self-esteem, and a great desire to meet society's standard of female attractiveness were the reasons for the eating disorders. However, in 1994 Taub and Blinde published a study about eating disorders and weight control in adolescent female athletes and performance squad members. They found that these girls did not have any more eating disorders than other girls, but that about seven to ten percent of all teenage girls may begin the habit of disordered eating.

Besides these eating and menstrual disorders, dancers and athletes are also prone to permanent physical injury. Common dance conditions, according to Arnheim, include ingrown toenails and other great toe injuries from being en pointe, stress, compression, and friction injuries, calluses, metatarsal arch and other foot injuries. Strains, sprains, dislocations, and fractures are also prevalent.

Personality Studies of Dancers and Athletes

Dancers' personalities are a little different from those of visual artists, creative writers, musicians, scientists, and actors. They are more similar to athletes than any other creative people, except for their tendency to have low self-esteem.

That the presence of eating disorders in such a large number of dancers would indicate a low self-concept was confirmed in a study by Bakker. Two groups of young dancers, aged eleven to twelve and fifteen to sixteen, were compared with control groups; the results showed that though the leisure activities of the dancers and nondancers differed only slightly, the dancers had less favorable attitudes in physical self-esteem and self-concept, especially in the older group. Dancers were more introverted also.

Gifted and Tolerated

The reason that personality difficulties in athletes may not be as well known as those in writers or actors may have to do with a halo effect. Anderson, Denson, Brewer, and Van Raalte indicated in a study of personality and mood disorders among athletes that their aberrations are often tolerated by the public and by their institutions because they are so talented. If they come to practice late, they are barely chastised. If they get into trouble with the law, fines are paid. The two most common personality disorders among athletes are narcissism, a state of excessive self-admiration, and antisocial personality disorder. In the latter disorder, the athlete has a history of behavior which violates the rights of others. Of the antisocial athlete, the authors described a typical case:

> A male football athlete has been arrested for vandalizing another athlete's car. The incident occurred in a parking lot at a local tavern and seemed connected to an argument over a female. There were several witnesses and an arrest occurred soon after the incident. The athlete had been drinking. This is not the first time the athlete has blown up. He once threw his roommate's tape deck out a fifth floor window because he did not like the rap music. There is also a long history of scrapes with the law such as petty larceny and drug possession while in high school. Hot-tempered incidents in the locker room have occurred and there are hints of continued substance use. Again, as with the narcissist, he is gifted and tolerated . . . At the hearing, the victim

agrees not to press charges if the athlete agrees to pay for all
the damages.

Mood disorders also occur in athletes. It has been estimated that about five to
six percent of athletes suffer from depression, which is similar to that in the
regular population. Depression is diagnosed by one or more of these symptoms: eating irregularities, insomnia or sleeping too much, fatigue and low
energy, low self-esteem, poor concentration, and feelings of hopelessness.
The depression has usually gone on for at least twenty-two months within a
two-year period. Some athletes also display the manic or elated end, acting
wild and crazy, being the life of the party, cajoling their friends into fast driving, picking up fast women, and acting heedlessly. Athletes usually don't
adequately use mental health services because they don't want to admit weakness and want to maintain autonomy. They fear being teased and ridiculed by
teammates.

Androgyny in Athletes

Several studies have shown that male and female athletes at elite levels (on
national teams) are remarkably similar in personality. They have high
achievement motivation, high tolerance for pain, are highly competitive, and
are able to train with great intensity. A study by Anshel and Porter of elite
Australian swimmers indicated that there were more similarities than differences between genders. While the males were more willing to sacrifice their
recreation time to practice, especially after a disappointing performance, the
females also trained extremely hard. Wittig and Schurr said, "Successful
female athletes tend to be more assertive, dominant, self-sufficient, independent, aggressive, and achievement-oriented and to have average to low emotionality." They resemble the average successful male athlete. A study by
Craig Wrisberg and his colleagues used the Bem Sex Role Inventory (BSRI).
Sex role orientations among female athletes showed higher femininity scores
for females who performed in individual sports, and more androgyny in
females who performed in team sports. Male athletes showed no differences
between team and individual sports.

The androgyny may come with some cost. Sex role identity was investigated in female athletes by Diane Wetzig, who indicated that there are similarities in sex-role conflict between female athletes and alcoholic women.
Findings showed female athletes and female alcoholics were similar to each
other and different from controls along dimensions of sex-role conflict.

Female athletes seemed to be more susceptible to alcoholism than other women. Wetzig said, "Some addictive women favor an overtly masculine manner. On the surface they exhibit genetic traits of assertion, independence, and achievement. Under this veneer, however, lie feminine needs for dependency and affiliation." The female athletes she studied (only 30 of them) fell into this category and thus may be more at risk for substance abuse than the regular population. Wetzig said, "The rigors and requirements of competition" pose an additional danger to these females, and "mood altering chemicals initially symbolize the magical key enabling an athlete to be physically and emotionally primed at a moment's notice."

Barron's Study of Dancers

Barron published a study in 1972 of thirty-two dance students at a dance school. Twenty-seven of them planned to dance professionally. They had already experienced years of rigorous professional training, had made the cut so to speak, in being encouraged to continue to study dance and to fulfill their aspirations. They were flexible, spontaneous, and had what Barron called "a lot of steam." They had high standards for themselves and their work, and expected their teachers to set such standards. The most respected teachers were those who had solid knowledge and background in dance, teachers who loved teaching and the dance, teachers who were interested in the students and who interacted with them but who were still very strict, perfectionistic, and demanding.

A good dance class was, likewise, "demanding, arduous, and challenging," leaving the dancer with fatigue, exhilaration, and a sense of accomplishment from having a thorough workout, increasing body strength and skill. Good dance students were those who were self-critical about their dance, students who were able to work hard, long, and with great perfectionistic demands on their abilities. Discipline was a trait that the dance students admired in each other.

When asked why they danced, they answered that dancing gave them a feeling of joy and elation and an uplifting release of emotions. They liked that they could use their bodies for self-expression, and that they had honed their bodies to such responsiveness that they could express complex emotions with small movements. They also liked to the fact that their dancing gave pleasure to others.

Physical factors affected their dance: when they were tired or sick, their dancing was less resonant. The dancers said that their extensions were not as high, their limbs didn't respond to their minds, and they were more prone to injury, with a result that they experienced "an overall loss in creativity, bounce, and eagerness" in their dancing. The experiencing of tension in their outside lives also affected their dance, and they often experienced "deficits in control and concentration." However, several of the dancers said that dancing even when fatigued or under tension created a release of these and a feeling of well-being after the dance class. Barron said that the young dancers were very intrinsically motivated and viewed dance as necessary for their very existence.

Dance students considered dance a form of art that helps society and the dancer to creative expression: "The purpose of art in general and dance in particular was to provide forms for the expression of universal principles of life, oneself, spirituality, that would allow the artist to share his experiences with others, enriching their lives as well as his own."

Gender differences in dancers revealed that the female dancers were open, generous, energetic, and quite excitable, while the male dancers were even more so. Barron said, "He is much like his female counterpart, though more complicated, conflicted, and flamboyant." Male dancers were more "impulsive," more "show-off," and their humor sometimes had a "hostile quality," while their external behavior was "mischievous, rebellious, zany, frank, flirtatious, and pleasure-seeking." They were also good-looking. Both male and female dancers were quite ambitious. They both described themselves as "determined, ambitious, and capable," with a need to succeed.

A study by Zakrajsek and colleagues comparing the learning styles of dancers and physical education majors found that there were no significant differences between the two groups, and that both preferred to learn in concrete ways. There were also no gender differences. The researchers used the Kolb Learning Style Inventory. The females tended to be concrete or dependent learners, needing personalized feedback and preferring to work with others. They were not interested in self-directed learning through printed materials or books. This would seem to indicate that teachers of dance and of physical education should modify their teaching styles to include concrete experiences rather than lecture.

Another study by Predock-Linnell postulated that dancers, musicians, and artists would be alike, in preferring abstract, asymmetrical, and complex designs on the Barron-Welsh Revised Art Scale, and that dancers who studied modern and jazz dance would prefer these more than ballet and flamenco dance majors. Predock-Linnell said, "The creativity measure was disappointing." She found no significant differences among the three artistic groups and the control group, and somewhat disappointedly concluded, "It is likely that even a limited aspect of creativity calls upon unconscious motivations, specialized cognitions and variations in approaches to learning and problem-solving." She also concluded that the Barron-Welsh Art Scale may not have been the proper test to use to try to discover abstract thinking preferences. This again illustrates the difficulty, or perhaps the folly, of using paper and pencil tests to assess creativity.

And that is the problem with assessing the creativity of dancers, athletes, and actors. The results of their training, the training of their talent, into the end result, creativity, is seen in the audience's reaction—the audience being moved, suffering, laughing, oohing and ahing or the critics rejoicing or grousing. When a friend and I saw Dustin Hoffman in *Death of a Salesman*, we left the theater speechless, went to a restaurant speechless, and sat there speechless. Hoffman defined the role for us, for all time, and we were so struck we were unable to discuss how he had moved us. That is the result of the actor's art. When Pavlova performed the Dying Swan, crowds all over the world cheered and cried. When young Tiger Woods won the U.S. Open, the beauty of his performance changed the standards of world class golf. Are actors, athletes, and dancers creators? Of course. Can we find their talent early? Yes.

I jokingly asked some basketball coaches once what paper and pencil test they use to find basketball players for their high school teams. They laughed and said, "Can he run? Can he shoot? Can he dribble? Is he tall?" We should evaluate performers by means that look directly at the tasks they have to do while performing. We should attend performances and do the myriad practical, useful, and time-consuming things that experts have been doing for years in order to determine which of the young actors, athletes, and dancers have potential. The talent can be developed if the possessor of the talent has the drive to do so. Talent development is a partnership between the talented and the field.

Summary

1. Dancers, athletes, and actors are similar to other creative people in that they master complicated tasks in order to do their work.
2. They have kinesthetic and emotional intelligence.

3. The actor's art has been influenced by Stanislavski, The Actors Theater, The Group Theater, The Living Theater, The Theater of Cruelty. All have reacted to what Stanislavski wrote and taught.
4. Actors are observant and use what they have observed in the characters they create.
5. Dancers and athletes show a talent for specific movement from early ages.
6. To study dance and athletics is painful, and a career is often ephemeral.
7. Young and professional dancers and athletes often have suffered from eating disorders and delayed or missed menstrual periods.
8. Dancers and athletes often have permanent physical injuries.
9. Athletes may not receive treatment for problems because their behaviors are tolerated by the public and by the institutions.
10. There are no paper and pencil tests that will identify physical performers.

PART IV

How To Enhance Creativity

It is the middle of October. Katherine and Brad were married in August, and, after the honeymoon, spent at a nature camp in a national park, Katherine has come back to work, a new bride, a teacher of the talented with one year's experience. The year is going well. Katherine feels she has some control over what she is doing; she isn't just reacting. She actually has a long-term curriculum plan. Long-term until Christmas, that is.

One morning Katherine feels nauseous. Luckily, her preparation time is first period and she doesn't have to teach just yet. She barely makes it to the faculty room. Within a few days she knows: she and Brad are to become parents. She begins the healthful diet regime of well-educated, modern, savvy mothers-to-be. She stops all caffeine, all alcohol. She has never smoked, so that is no problem. She takes vitamins and goes to bed early. She and Brad know that their baby is going to be the healthiest, strongest, most intelligent and creative baby of all time, and she knows that a healthy pregnancy is crucial.

With what she had learned during her first year of teaching about the childhoods of creative people, she feels a little confused, for it seems that some of the most creative people had awful childhoods. She and Brad love each other, never fight, have good jobs, and want to be parents. Didn't some of the most creative people have parents who were teachers? But then, maybe she shouldn't work while the baby is young. Maybe she should quit her job. But she loves her job and her kids at school and is getting to be very good at what she does. Maybe Brad should quit his job. Well, the baby will be born in July and she'll have some time before school starts. But what if the baby turns out to be creative? Does she want a creative child? Aren't all children creative? What good is being creative if it requires a childhood that is full of trouble?

Chapter 11

Encouraging Creativity:
Motivation and Schooling

Our schools demand far too little of the best or the worst. And too many bright young people are encouraged to regard their playful fantasies and emotional effusions as "creativity". . . . Marianne Moore meant it when she said, "There are things that are important beyond all this fiddle."

— Howard McCord

My life is what I have done, my scientific work; the one is inseparable from the other. The work is the expression of my inner development, for commitment to the contents of the unconscious forms the man and produces his transformations. My works can be regarded as stations along life's way. All my writings may be considered tasks imposed from within; their source was a fateful compulsion. What I wrote were things that assailed me from within myself.

— Carl Jung

How does one become a creative adult? Can creativity be taught? Do we even want more creative people? Where do creativity and the discipline to practice intersect? What have we learned about how creative adults have become creative? Is it the place of the schools to encourage creativity? What happens when we stifle creativity? Can we stifle creativity? What is the place of trauma in the enhancement of creativity?

In reading the many biographies and accounts of the childhoods of creative people to research this book, I have been awed and dismayed. Often, the childhoods of creative people had sad elements; some of these creative people experienced literal orphanhood, while others had clearly dysfunctional families. This makes it difficult to write a chapter on how to enhance creativity. While writing this book, I have shared the process with my students, as each week they ask me whom I've been reading about this week, and what their childhoods were like. I have begun joking that when I get to the last chapters, about teaching and parenting for creativity, I will give just a few words of advice and be done with it. For teachers, these words are the following: Try to be the teacher that the creative child will remember as encouraging, not as discouraging. For parents, these words—only partially tongue-in-cheek—might be: To enhance your child's creativity, get divorced, or die.

The jokes fade, but the questions remain. Does family trauma automatically yield creative genius? Do not all the biographical reports point to this? Or is Alice Miller right, that creative people experience trauma in their childhoods, but they also have some warm person to be close to, while destructive persons experience trauma in their childhoods without that warm person being there? Of course, nowadays, it is the fashion to come from a dysfunctional family. Everyone is codependent, addicted, messed up. There is a whole industry based on psychological healing from childhood trauma. We can all blame our mothers and fathers for our problems. If the ideal family ever did exist, no one today came from one, if the television talk shows are to be believed. Then why isn't everyone creative?

Many creative people have little or nothing good to say about their families or their schools, and many creative people certainly have had family lives with early trauma, including moving often, the death of a parent, sickness, the absence of a parent through divorce or substance abuse, childhood abuse and neglect. You name it, creative people have experienced it during their childhoods.

What Creative Writers Said about Their Schooling

A few years ago I did a survey of published poets and novelists who worked in the old National Endowment for the Arts Poets in the Schools program. These were writers listed in *A Directory of American Poets & Writers*, meeting the criteria for listing. To be eligible, a writer must have accumulated twelve points of credits based on previous publications. For example, a published novel is worth twelve points, as is a published chapbook or book of poetry. A short story in a journal is worth four points, and a published poem is worth one point. Most of these authors are still writing, publishing novels, poetry, essays, and criticism. Most still chose to list themselves in the 1997 poets' and writers' directory.

Here is a sampling of what twenty-five contemporary American writers had to say about their own childhoods and school experiences in answer to the question "How did your own experiences as a child in school help or hinder your creativity?"

Writer 1: I was given responsibility and allowed to fail, but I was also allowed to see myself grow and was given recognition. I was also given the sense that there are forces working through us that help us grow and do worthwhile work, and I have ever since believed in these forces.

Writer 2: I was lucky enough to have teachers who told me to get started, praised what I did, and encouraged me to continue. They also insisted I learn much of what is my craft, the skill of using the tools and rules of the trade. My family also, being creative and artistic, kept me encouraged, admonished, and also believing it to be not unusual, but ordinary to do such things well. They were often my best critics.

Writer 3: My artistic life is a negative response to the negativity of this world to my well-being. I think it is therefore very positive in its energy flow. I've never quit being the daydreaming nonconformist I was at eighteen.

Writer 4: Hard to remember—I was always full of "chutzpah." I always loved school even when I had awful teachers, the way Francie, in *A Tree Grows In Brooklyn*, loved the library. You must understand that no creativity can occur in uptight, tense places. Kids must feel good in themselves. That's the first job.

Writer 5: It is tempting to say that they hindered it. But not all. In my day when a quick child was finished before the rest of the class he was asked to do a report or sometimes write a story. What began as busy work sometimes became the best part of any day. But all too often the different answer was crushed, the need to question what seemed too pat was seen as insolence, a novel approach or use of materials was disallowed automatically without a trial. An abiding horror from grade one on was the objective test in which no possible answer was really right, and my desperate need to explain why could not be met. Under the pressure one's creativity soon gets put to figuring out what might have been in the test maker's mind, so one can guess what the test maker expects. The best thing was learning, in high school, to put a textbook in front of me, to look up from time to time with an interested expression as if I were taking notes, while I wrote my stories in class after class and refined them in study hall. Aside from two excellent high school teachers who continually challenged our imaginations and abilities, virtually nothing in my schooling helped much.

Writer 6: We had "dramatics" for thirty minutes each Tuesday, and were required to recite—with prescribed gestures—a poem. God, how dreadful! Art class was a reward if the whole class was good the whole week and if the teacher had a project she liked, and if there were materials (which our parents paid for in September but we never saw except as a handout of one sheet of manila paper at a time), this on Friday afternoon. Music wasn't much more. What helped my creativity was having a place of my own in the attic that even my brothers, even my mother, couldn't invade, and where I could even spill ink or paint (not to mention tears) without being punished.

Writer 7: I had the benefit of encouragement by a fine teacher—fine teachers, I should say—my parents, especially my father; and much luck. Most of what gets done in school and most of what gets encouraged in school does not contribute to creativity. When I feel I'm dealing with my own experiences at something like their true value—however this is brought about by those around me and my environment—I feel capable of doing things. I learned perseverance working in the fields; I learned about persons and nature in those same fields. Having operated a commercial garden and orchard for some thirty years I've had reasons to cultivate the habit of observation and reflection. Schools have helped in that regard, I think.

Writer 8: As a child in a small town school in a high Colorado valley my teachers let me express my feelings for the earth, my horse, and how I hated leaving the ranch to come to town. The influence before that was the limited far-from-town library of three books—The Bible, the poetry of Robert Burns, and *The Diseases of Cattle*. The latter book first made me want to write poetry. I came across the words *hemorrhagic septicemia*. When my father pronounced them for me and told me what they meant I heard the words sing and saw the tragic death of cattle.

Writer 9: totally terrible
depressing
& self-destructive
made me develop a "closet"
personality & a disdain
for mass society at large

Writer 10: I was a bookworm and read for escape; I was also paranoid and persecuted by other kids through fifth grade or so. After that, I eventually went to a school for gifted children that was better socially—I wasn't so weird. High school was an utter waste and that was one of the country's supposedly best school systems. My creativity? Growing up outside New York and having access to Manhattan's cultural life was my salvation. Also sympathetic parents.

Writer 11: Even though teachers encouraged us to draw, and even though some of my own paintings and pastel drawings were given special honor and hung in the hall outside the principal's office, I lost all interest in visual art by the fifth grade. Art projects were too structured (so that teachers wouldn't fail, I imagine). But then too, in those days, imagination wasn't much of a priority.

Writer 12: Since I was an only child and my parents were divorced, I grew up in a fairly lonely environment. I think this fostered my reading and my work habits. Writing is a lonely profession. So, I was prepared.

Writer 13: School must have helped—but who knows, finally, where the lyric impulse comes from? Some aestheticians believe the creative impulse begins with an experience bordering on the traumatic. But certainly my reading—which was intense and wide—helped. Otherwise I might believe that schooling plays a very minor part in kindling the creative fires. But I know many poets who never read a book until their late teens and who were uniformly poor in school.

Writer 14: I had a wonderful language/literature teacher through junior high/high school; sheer encouragement there as far as anything in early life helping or hindering my urge & ability to write; experiences as a child at home, certainly, the far greater factors.

Writer 15: I got F in conduct in junior high. That helped a lot. I had fun in class. My father was pissed. But I don't mean badness, cruelty, hoody behavior. I mean acting up wittily, that glee that shakes up a long school day. My father and I get along fine now, but in those days he must have imagined that I was being mean and foul or something—to get that F. I was being, simply, irreverent and spontaneous. I was finding my own way to like school while the teacher was going over and over stuff. And I know that's elitism. Some of the kids needed all that drill—and I was in the way with my whispering and chortling. But I kept it up. Irrepressible. A pain. Guilt tormented me when I lay awake thinking how much the teachers resented my ways. Next day I'd do it all again. Well, I was, luckily for me, intellectually quick, and they might have had some way of endorsing that. The "quick" kid is often discriminated against by the necessities of disciplined mass education. Something in me was addicted to rebellion in this matter.

Writer 16: I would say that most of my school experiences were godawful. However, I was a very rebellious student, and often learned things of value by default. For example, at thirteen I was subjected to the first "teaching" of Shakespeare (*The Merchant of Venice*). I immediately responded to W.S., and realized that the teaching had nothing to do with the poetry. Accordingly, and with full recognition of what I was doing, I read all of Shakespeare on my own. I did not wish to have it spoiled. One old classics master was an amateur botanist, and he sparked a lifelong interest in me, on walks in the woods which got me out of competitive sports. Probably the most positive of any of my school experiences.

Writer 17: A dual language background and a large dose of ethnicity helped. I was, for the most part, discouraged rather than encouraged by my teachers.

Writer 18: For the most part I was lucky. I ran into several teachers who encouraged me to write as much as I wanted to and rewarded me with kind words. Also my classmates seemed to enjoy my efforts. God bless them all. In college however I was not so lucky. I could not and would not write a standard paper. One idiot actually asked me if I would mind writing a more conventional paper the next time. And I did mind, and that's why I dropped out. I'm getting mad right now just thinking about it—and also this other idiot in teachers college, who took us to visit a classroom—where, by coincidence, this incredible woman was doing a creative writing class. I wrote an essay on whatever it was we were supposed to report from that visit, but I went on to report on the creative writing aspects—and this nut marked me down for going beyond the limits of his assignment. Shame on him. He is the reason I seriously question the creative capacity of anyone who graduates from a teachers college. In fact, my college experience was so bitter, so anti-creative, I have my doubts about anyone who graduates. Period.

Writer 19: I remember school as a struggle to slant my paper in the same direction as the right-handed kids. School generally is carefully constructed to eliminate sensitivity, assertion, intelligence, and guts. The question is, if I didn't get the creative impulse from school, where did it come from? Certainly not from middle-class parents. Not from my genes. I think it came from the fact that I was fat, repressed, left out of the social scene. And when you've got that many strikes, you've got to be creative to survive. Creativity then, was a survival option—and survival is the synonym of public education and of middle class, middle Ohio parents.

Writer 20: I think my experience hindered my creativity in the sense that there was no structured openness. We would write an occasional poem (in rhyme, of course) for a holiday or for some kind of Catholic school competition, but there was no joy or interest in the process of the poem, only a dogged persistence until a certain result was achieved. There were no "arts" taught, no music, and so I think it might be fair to say that creativity was neglected rather than hindered. Real hindrance and destruction did not begin until college where no one made any bones about women's inability to create anything but babies.

Writer 21: I certainly go back to moments of childhood often. I think I give a special place to "creative/epiphany" experiences. I'm not sure any specific "creative projects" were important in their own right. But if you listen and respect someone who fascinates you with the ability to perceive what you can't quite (and I think a creative artist should do this naturally) and offers you an opportunity to pierce the veil of the mysteries, I think this becomes the route to creative experiences of your child's own. Creative experiences are not planned—that's an opposition of concepts.

Writer 22: I was somewhat self-willed. Schools did not hinder or help. They simply functioned. I was the one with the motivation and it was outside of their sphere.

Writer 23: Creativity was a secondary, perhaps even tertiary, priority in my schooling, hence, even though my creative output was exemplary it did not truly flower until college. Curriculum designers need to develop creative tracks in the same way that academic and business tracks are defined, to isolate students with creative talent and to model their studies to develop and refine this talent. This is not to say that the minimally creative student should be ignored; every student should be exposed to creative endeavors and encouraged to foster, if not their own creative output, at least an appreciation and understanding of the arts.

Writer 24: My school experiences were hindered, thwarted, denigrated, ignored by insensitive, dull prejudiced elementary school teachers on the one hand, but freed up, encouraged, praised, and shown off by loving, caring, talented teachers in junior high school on the other.

Writer 25: I didn't get help from school until I was in college. I started to write a lot in Latin, where I was bored silly, and to avoid getting bad citizenship marks, I wrote and kept my mouth shut. It was a great place for "reverie." An hour where no one could interrupt me (except to translate an occasional sentence). College classes were even better because in lectures I wouldn't be called on.

From these comments it can be seen that some writers liked school and others hated it; some were openly rebellious and others were sneakily rebellious. Some hated and others liked college. But they all had a strong reaction to their schooling, and praise for good teachers and encouraging parents. Perhaps the personality traits that Barron and his group found were already taking hold; the independence of judgment, the nonconformity, the challenging of authority, the search for truth, the uncompromising verbal intelligence that saw fools for what they were and called them that. Personal attention from teachers, encouragement, and love for the subject matter being taught—all influenced these writers and led them to praise. Writers are probably not much different from other creative people in their reactions to school, though one would suppose that writers would get better grades, since so much of the school curriculum is verbally oriented.

Motivating Creative Behavior

Should we do nothing special, but just what we are doing now, and then the truly creative ones will emerge, through rebellion? If so, the next generation, our children, should be very creative, for 50 percent of them have been children of divorce, victims of the excesses of us—parents who grew up in the 1950s and 1960s and had children in the 1970s and 1980s.

Strong Emotion as a Motivator

I remember talking with five college-aged people who attended select Eastern colleges. All had parents who had divorced; as youth they had all experienced trauma and the emotional consequences were still clearly evident in their unconventionality. Actually, their dress was conforming, but conforming to current styles of rebelliousness. They wore black and dyed their hair black, green, or red, or had it bleached blond. The young men wore spiked hair and earrings in the proper ear for their sexual preferences. I remember saying, "What will happen when you begin writing your novels?" The pointed statement in reply was, "We are just beginning to deal with our anger."

A few years have passed, and these youth, graduated from their colleges, are settling into careers. They have gravitated towards the arts, publishing, theatre, music. One began as a physics major but switched to music composition, transferring from M.I.T. to a liberal arts school. I have no doubt that emotion played a great part in their career choices as well as in their motivations to be creative. Singer/songwriter Christopher wrote a song about the internal war fought by a sensitive young man.

My War
My old room
was a dirty cold room
many ways to get in
I know every one
To drag us both here.
Someone inside
Is locked there inside.
When we try to ignore him.
Feel him beat against the door.

This is my war
I have fought from every side
I've conquered and I've died
This is my war.
I am the blood on the steel
Chariot and the wheel. Oh.

My old room.
Remember my cold room?
You're dead and gone.
You'll tend to your own
Inside your home
My head of stone
Is a heavy cold stone
Stands between us like a wall
We climb and then we fall
Never really touch at all

This is my war.

With regard to emotion as a motivator, we parents had already parented for creativity, but we didn't even know it. Even so, it remains important when working with children to try to create an atmosphere that permits relatively free expression of emotion within the structures of school and home. But besides this, what are some specific processes or techniques that may be helpful in enhancing the creative process?

Close Your Eyes

In an early article I wrote for *Gifted Child Quarterly*, I detailed the creative process I used as an Arts in Education poet in the schools. It was a rather naive article, but it did describe helping students with the creative process through the use of preparation, imagery, and most important, having them close their eyes. I talked about the incubation phase of the creative process and how to use it in the schools. Guided breathing and imagery are helpful in facilitating a feeling of creativity. I did it a little more directively, though:

> I knew I would have to put them in the mood to write, if they were to produce any inspirations, or random thoughts written down which some teachers call poems. I had some gestalt training when I was a school counselor, and I have found the fantasy work in gestalt helpful to my own writing. This technique combines relaxation and suggestion, in order to facilitate what could be called a "creative response" in the participant.
>
> My objective was to have them explore their teenage desire for privacy, for a place to go where they could be alone and be themselves. I talked to them a little about this need, and I read them a few short poems. I used a soft voice and spoke slowly, and with a smile. One of the characteristics of high school students, especially boys, is that they never have pencils or paper, and must borrow from the girls, thereby having a chance to flirt a little, and so I had made sure, before starting the exercise, that they had pencils and paper, so that they knew they were going to be asked to write.
>
> "What a weirdo," one boy said. "I can't think of anything to write about. I just took this class for an easy English credit."
>
> Undaunted, I asked them to close their eyes, after I felt they were with me, and I asked them to get into their own private spaces, to forget the presence of their friends, to focus on

themselves and on their breathing. I took my time. There were, at first, protests and giggles, but soon they were all quiet and listening to me.

I asked them, after a few moments, to think about their bedrooms at home, to imagine themselves behind a full-length mirror, looking into their bedrooms: "How does your room look right now, empty, with no one there? Pretend you are a stranger, seeing the room for the first time. What details do you see that will tell you who the person who sleeps in this room, really is? It could be the dusty rock collection on top of the dresser, or the dried flowers pinned up on the bulletin board, or the hubcap in the middle of the floor, or the beer can collection on the shelf, or the dirty clothes under the bed." I paced this slowly, and then paused, asking them to focus on these details.

Soon I asked them to open their eyes, and in the same soft voice I asked them to write about their room, to show the reader, by use of specific objects, who the owner of that bedroom really is. I gave them about fifteen minutes, and I suggested that they write at least ten lines. The time limit and space limit also helped to focus them, to give their reverie some structure.

I said that I would collect the poems after they were done with this initial draft, and would read them aloud, so the whole group could share; if they were shy about this, they could make up a *nom de plume*. Adolescents are usually very shy about having their work read; little children clamor for the privilege. Perhaps this speaks to the inculcation, within the schools, of a fear of spontaneous expression, as children grow older.

Then I included in the article some of the poems the recalcitrant teenagers wrote, and concluded:

Perhaps parents and teachers of gifted children should pay more attention to allowing daydreams and reverie into the lives of their children. Who ever heard a parent or teacher say, "Go and think awhile. Go and daydream"? Perhaps we should send them out into the woods to sit under the trees and contemplate. Perhaps we should give some thought to creating conditions and situations conducive to incubation.

When I think about the structured lives children seem to lead, with lessons in music and tutors for math and teams coached and organized by adults, in city leagues with many rules, I wonder when they can play freely and experience creative solitude, away from the watchful eyes of caretakers. In my 1995 book, *A Location in the Upper Peninsula*, I described the rural neighborhood we lived in, Cleveland Location, the woods and bluffs, the lakes we swam in, the rocks we climbed, the long summer days when we would hear the distant calls of someone's mother at suppertime. We would reluctantly awaken from our imaginative play, re-enter to family dinner time grace. We would shake off our world of cowgirls and jungle girls, descend from the high rocky bluff, and join the neighborhood boys for a rousing game of Capture the Flag. That imaginative world of childhood play when we would be literally in another mental place, as I look back on it now, seems necessary in shaping the writer I became many years later. When I close my eyes I can still remember the feeling of freedom.

I wish all children could feel that way in these days of fearful guarding, when we teach kindergartners how to be "street smart," to shout "This is not my mother!" if they are being kidnapped, to roll under a car if they are being abducted. In my research on creativity and creative people for the books and articles I've written and for the speeches I give, adult creativity is often shown to be shaped by free imaginative play during childhood. Many inventors, for example, come from rural backgrounds. Being able to play freely, without the invading eyes of adults, was a gift of our neighborhood to us.

I often assign my students to watch children play. The children who cannot lose themselves in play, but who need to come back to the adults and say, "Watch me run! Watch me throw," the children who are already anxious about being free to roam, who are always conscious of the adults, could be already cut off from the flow necessary for the creative process to kick in. The voices of children at play, shouting and squealing, laughing and arguing, unconscious of adults, need to be heard once again. Sitting on my front porch, I noticed the neighborhood girls playing. Their favorite movement was running. Not once did I see them move from one place to another by walking. They were in their own free world. Close your eyes. Hear the child you once were.

Escaping and Getting the Giggles

When I was the principal of a school in New York City, I would take my little writing group of talented boys and girls to the Metropolitan Museum of Art for our "poets' lunches," and we would walk down Fifth Avenue to the Museum, jotting down details with our newly sharpened pencils as we walked. I remember feeling the bumpy bricks on the Central Park side of the Avenue through the thin soles of my leather shoes. Then we would go to the Museum and settle in a room, picked by one of the kids, and we would each write a poem or two about an object in the room.

Sometimes I invited other writer friends along, sometimes not. But uniformly, by the time we got back to the school, where I had to resume being a principal again, we were all filled with giggles, and a feeling of having escaped to do something secret. When my schedule didn't allow time for visiting the museum, the kids would come to my office and bring their lunches and one of them would tape a sign, "Poets at Work," to my door. While eating our lunches, we would talk, write, giggle. I certainly felt creative then, and I think the kids did, too. We had fun. Those moments with the kids stand out as high points in otherwise pressured, over-scheduled days.

The secret feeling of escape, the free feeling of release from duty, the relaxed feeling of being able to giggle, all contributed to our sense of being creative. We were participating in a safe way of breaking the rules, just for an hour. Teachers and parents can do this with small gestures; I have seen classrooms where children sit on beanbags under work tables during reading—they are quietly escaping momentarily. I have known parents who take each child out alone, without siblings, for their special times together, to fly paper kites or to attend a recital.

Creativity as Spontaneous Adventures

A friend, whose two boys have turned out to be art majors like their mother, said that she encouraged them in their art by springing adventures on them when they were little. On a particularly boring Saturday, when the boys were lolling around on the living room floor watching cartoons, she would announce, "All right, up! It's time to go and have an adventure!" With their sketchbooks, they all would pile into the car and go out to some nearby site to sketch. Then they would stop off at the restaurant with the best ice cream cones in town to have double dips. Her boys grew up loving the impromptu adventures as special opportunities to do art. Of course their home was also filled with art books, art reproductions, and discussions of the latest show at the Toledo Museum. But again, the motivation for doing their art was not as work, but as play.

Perhaps we can extrapolate from these stories four hints for enhancing creativity in children. First, from the cold anger shown by college-aged youth, could be the fact that creative production is motivated by deep emotion. Second, creative production even in a classroom can happen after quiet reverie and closed eyes. Third, children need free time for free imaginative play. Fourth, creative production is escape from the mundane, is special, secret, and delicious.

Intrinsic Motivation for Creativity

Theresa Amabile, a social psychologist, has done some of the major work on motivation for creativity. Six terms used in the field of social psychology are *intrinsic* and *extrinsic motivation; field dependence* and *field independence;* and *inner locus of control* and *outer locus of control*. People who produce the most creative works, according to the work Amabile and her colleagues have done, have intrinsic motivation, are field independent, and have inner loci of control. To have intrinsic motivation is to proceed in the work for love of the work itself, and not for fame or glory. To have field independence is to proceed with confidence and individuality rather than with wanting to be liked and wanting to please. To have an inner locus of control is to do what you do because you need or want to do it, not because someone else has given you an assignment to do it. A person who is field independent sings "Climb Every Mountain." A person who is field dependent sings "Raindrops Keep Falling On My Head."

Amabile's studies have been published throughout the creativity literature, as she and her colleagues try one experiment after another that all seem to show that intrinsic motivation produces the most creative responses, and that extrinsic motivation actually hinders creative responses. Her book, *The Social Psychology of Creativity,* detailed earlier studies, and her book for parents and teachers, *Growing Up Creative,* is about the best book I can recommend for learning how to enhance intrinsic motivation in children.

Amabile said that motivation is an important key to creativity, and she gave suggestions for enhancing motivation towards creative ends. "Intrinsic motivation, too, may be inborn to some extent. But it also depends very heavily on social environment. This motivation to be creative has been so neglected that you might call it creativity's missing link." Amabile came up with a Venn diagram similar to Renzulli's three-ringed definition of giftedness, and said that creativity takes place where these three intersect: domain skills, creative thinking and working skills, and intrinsic motivation.

Domain skills are those that are necessary for functioning in the specific area of creativity; for example, a painter needs to know how to paint, and a composer needs to be able to read music. Creative thinking and working skills are those practical habits we develop as we grow up. Intrinsic motivation is the inner drive necessary for achievement. Beth Hennessey, Amabile's colleague, described in a 1997 article the studies on creativity and the enhancement of intrinsic motivation. They found, with a group of undergraduate college students, that those who didn't expect to be evaluated and judged made more creative art products (collages). The team of researchers also found that young children made more creative art products in a free play situation than in a structured and evaluative one.

They also conducted studies in which they attempted to immunize students against having their creativity be motivated by extrinsic rather than intrinsic rewards. They found that two fifteen-minute videos of teachers discussing with students the joys of learning, the pleasures of doing creative projects, and the inner feeling of satisfaction gained from doing something well did seem to work with eleven-year-olds. Hennessey said, "If experimenters, virtual strangers, were able to affect this much attitudinal and behavioral change . . . think how much more could be done by classroom teachers who build naturalistic discussions about motivation, interest, and playfulness into the school day." Amabile said we should never speak of creativity without putting it in some domain, for example, creativity in science, creativity in writing, creativity in drawing.

Rewards

To enhance intrinsic motivation, parents and teachers need to rethink how they are interacting with children. Under what circumstances do we give rewards? Behavioral psychologists advocated token systems as rewards, but cognitive psychologists said that these were extrinsic and did not produce the joy for learning that is needed for intrinsic motivation. External rewards do not enhance intrinsic motivation. When the child comes home from school with the report card, what is the parent's response? No matter what the grade is, does the parent say, "What did you learn?" or does he say, "Only a B? Why didn't you get an A?" Rewards should be given as rewards for quality of performance, and for trying, and not just because the child completed the chore.

Hamachek, in his basic educational psychology textbook, in discussing extrinsic and intrinsic motivation research, said:

(1) both types of motivation are important in the everyday operations of classroom work; extrinsic motivators get things started when interest is lacking, and intrinsic motivation sustains learning itself, and (2) tangible rewards (gold stars, bonus points, and the like) are important extrinsic motivators, but a teacher's oral or written acknowledgments of a good job or fine effort are more likely to be incorporated in students' own feelings of satisfaction. This has the effect of encouraging the self-perpetuating energy behind intrinsic motivation.

We can extrapolate, as parents and teachers, from the educational psychologists' and social psychologists' work on reward. The most enhancing rewards for creative endeavor are in the pleasure the creator takes in doing the work itself, and in achieving the result, and not from the pay or the prize. Even painters who don't have galleries, musicians who don't have audiences, writers who aren't published, actors who act in community theatre, dancers who dance alone, scientists and mathematicians who spread the table with arcane formulas to solve personally challenging problems, do not stop doing. While some may say that creative people need a killer instinct, and need to be so driven that they would do anything for fame, recognition, or validation, continued creative production derives from less cruel motives. The work itself is intrinsically interesting.

Summary

1. Although the creative adult has often had childhood trauma, there are other ways to enhance creativity in children.
2. Writers had very specific reactions to their schooling, and very specific suggestions for how that schooling could have been improved.
3. Setting a creative tone and valuing creative expression are essential in enhancing creativity.
4. Creating a feeling of escape, of adventure, of play and fun are important in enhancing creativity.
5. Creative expression comes from the need to express emotion and from an inner drive.

Chapter 12

How Parents and Teachers
Can Enhance Creativity in Children

childhood's glut of moments
ticking away like the furnace
just before the blower comes on
                                    —David Citino

Here are twelve suggestions for enhancing creativity in children:

1. Provide a Private Place for Creative Work to be Done.

For Teachers

In a school, where can a child have privacy while doing creative work—writing, drawing, composing, thinking? If you are a teacher of young children, take a look around your room. Mentally re-configure it so that you have a loft or a place where children can go. The days of the early childhood classroom with desks bolted to the floor and lined up in rows is gone. Push the desks together to make tables. Push them together to make a circle so that all the children can see each other at all times. Create a hideout beneath a table or a desk in the back or front of the room. Pitch a tent in the room. Replace the desks with soft chairs and couches. Use your own creativity to imagine a place where good schoolwork can get done and yet there is a place to read, to think, to draw. Use access to this place as a reward.

For Parents

I have done a little informal research on children's private places. "Where do you go when you want to think?" I ask. "Have you ever built yourself a place that is just yours?" Almost all the students have, and when I am doing a writing workshop with them, I ask them to describe this place. As a parent, I remember the places my own children built—beneath the staircases, in the garage, in the living room with blankets and pillows. In fact, in 1979 I published a poem called "Forts," about my children's search for private places away from adults.

> **Forts**
> there's one beneath the basement steps
> carpeted with a crib mattress
> closed off with a worn out bedspread
>
> there's one in the attic
> secret in the junk and jumble
> small hollow under caving boxes
>
> there's one in the garage
> where this week's neighborhood club
> exchanges officers
> "No Grils Allowed"
>
> there's one this rainy Sunday
> hung from the television
> over chair and stool, one quilt's
>
> drooping width to the beanbags
> holes shut with towels
> corners pegged with books
>
> the cat slips in to visit
> reclining brother and sister
> covered inside a warm soft roof
>
> whispering and bickering
> in the world of the marxes
> three stooges

they told me
when I peeked
I'm too big to fit
©1979 Jane Piirto

If parents and teachers keep in mind that a safe, secret place is a necessity for children's creativity to unfold, they will be providing much that is valuable in later life. The writer Graham Greene, by any accounts an imaginative adult, would sneak upstairs to the attic to read alone in a private place. He was reading mysteries and adventures before his family knew he could read. Then, when he would come back downstairs, he would sit patiently while they read him the primer. At age six he already had a private place for creative work to be done. Even for large families living in small spaces, some effort must be made so that the child can have privacy for thinking, dreaming, wishing.

One of my students told a story after reading this precept: She said she would scold her youngest child, who wouldn't keep her room to the immaculate standard of the household. She said the child kept running away to sit and hide on the rock beneath the porch, and the mother had made a vow to close off that space next summer. After reading this, she felt tears rising in her throat. She loosened her immaculate standards, and the house became a home for the child as well as for the mother. "I let her begin being a person who lives there, and not just a hotel resident," my student said.

2. Provide Materials (e.g., Musical Instruments, Sketchbooks).

For Teachers

If the child has talent in a certain area, and the parents have no means to develop that talent, the school has a responsibility to try to do so. School materials should be made available to students when not being used for classes. Does your school room have supplies, and are the children encouraged to be free with the supplies? Teachers are known for their propensity to gather odd pieces and bits of materials and to recycle them for use in the classroom—oatmeal cartons, scraps of cloth, milk bottles, discarded containers—all become part of the teacher's supply closet. I know one teacher who haunts auctions and stays until the end when the leftovers are sold for a dollar. She has gathered many treasures this way, and they find their way to her classroom in craft projects, fantasy play, and even science fairs and invention fairs.

For Parents

Yes, it costs a lot and takes a year or two to pay it off, those time payments for the piano, the trumpet, the saxophone, but do it. No one started to be creative in adulthood without having some thread for that creativity leading back to childhood. My son, who decided to major in visual arts later on in college, had never taken an art course because he was in band, and at his high school, you couldn't be in art if you were in music. This is not uncommon due to the scheduling requirements of high schools.

But he had always had sketchbooks, and he would go to his room and spend hours drawing and sketching. His thirst for the visual arts can be traced to his earliest childhood. When we went to museums, he would remember the paintings in great detail as we discussed them on the way home. His trumpet is on the shelf now, though he says he will never sell it, and his BFA degree provides his living as a professional photographer.

Let your house be the house where the kids hang out. Besides knowing where your children are, the richness your life acquires with a houseful of teenagers cannot be duplicated. Junior high school boys who are creative often get involved in role-playing games such as Dungeons and Dragons. My son's D & D group lasted until their junior year, when social lives with girl-friends typically takes over. They often played at our house, probably because I was a single mother and a little more permissive than some of the other parents. Having a houseful of teenage boys in sleeping bags on the living room floor after playing D & D all night is one of my most pleasant parenting memories. I was happy to make breakfast for them. I even served them in the dining room, where they joked around while devouring stacks of pancakes and tall glasses of orange juice. I also got a short story from the experience, called, of course, "D & D."

However, if as a parent you don't like to have hordes of kids around, don't fake it. Kids can tell. Just remember to provide supplies, private places, and encouragement.

3. Encourage and Display the Child's Creative Work, but Avoid Overly Evaluating It.

For Teachers

Do you as a teacher know what creative talents your students have, and do you praise them for themselves, or are you in the dark? Many a child has stopped singing or drawing because of a teacher's or other students' sarcastic comments. We all know people—and perhaps we are among them—who, in giving a speech or demonstration, say, when illustrating something on the blackboard, "I'm not an artist, but . . ." They make the drawing anyway, and most often we can tell what it is. The self-deprecating statement reflects on some past perceived failure in drawing.

Look back at your childhood in school for a moment. What did a teacher or a peer say to you that made you stop singing, stop drawing, stop writing? Are you that same teacher, making remarks to children? Your remarks will live forever in those children's minds. As a teacher myself, I have to constantly remind myself that any remark I make will be magnified by my students and they will take it into themselves. A colleague told me this story the other day. He wrote on a student's paper that she was very talented in mathematics, and he forgot about the comment. A few years later, she sent him a card, telling him that she was finishing studies for her Ph.D., and that his comment had given her inner permission to go to graduate school. Your words have legs, wings, and immense power. Use them for good.

My graduate and undergraduate students have to do an individual creativity project as a final assignment in the creativity classes I teach. "I'm not creative," my graduate students often say. "I was going to drop the course the first night." One student made a timeline of her project, and for the first step in the project she spent time asking friends and acquaintances, "How am I creative?" She had no view of herself as a creative human being. Who had done that to her? I have another friend who was told he couldn't sing, and so he always mouthed the words. He wanted to sing. Then he told the choir director at our church. The choir director knew that everyone can sing and challenged my friend. It turned out my friend thought he was a baritone, but he was a tenor. He's been in the choir for ten years, and recently started singing in a barbershop chorus. Some teacher had arrested his singing development for thirty years.

For Parents

So what if it doesn't look like a dog? Do you say that to your children when they come to you with their attempts to draw a dog, an automobile, a person? I have a theory that many people stop attempting to draw when they view their work and see it lacks verisimilitude, doesn't look like the object being drawn. The child knows; you don't have to rub it in. Is the refrigerator door an art gallery, covered with your child's work? How about the walls of the child's room? Do you need to have control over your house, and are you such a neatnik that your child's creative work is thrown away with the rest of the trash? Would someone entering your house know that your child lives there? My children and I used to draw portraits of each other. Here is a poem about it:

> **A Profile**
> practicing profiles
> with charcoal
> on drawing pads
>
> my children and I
> buffoons at the hippodrome
> before the chattering TV
>
> doing ballet-to-commercials
> and somersaults
> we are giggle boxes
>
> now it's her turn.
> she hushes me
> sits right-angled
>
> squinting at me
> slowly setting lines
> to my portrait
>
> "Mama you will love this!"
>
> later she shows me coded
> a squat pumpkin
> with clenched teeth

full face front
carol burnett's smile
pigtails with triton ends

"I can't draw curly hair"
philodendron-leaf eyes
a pig's snout

and stars on my crown!

©1979 Jane Piirto

Along the same lines, does your child's practicing of his musical instrument drive you nuts? My sister's violin practice used to do that to me. But she had to practice. That was a rule of the house. She was so rebellious about having to practice both the violin and the piano that our mother finally let her quit the piano after the requisite five years of lessons that were the guideline for us young musicians growing up in our home. Now she says our mother should have made her continue. She has taken up the kantele, and her training in violin has helped her master the chords and strings. Some people say you shouldn't force lessons on your children, but I'm the living grateful example that it didn't hurt me. Although I never had the raw talent or practice obsession to become a professional musician, my piano goes with me whenever I move houses, and the hours of solitary pleasure it provides as I improvise and sing feed my soul. I play well enough for my own pleasure and for that of the people who like to sing old songs behind me.

Among the most musically talented families I know is one where you were invited to hear the latest piano or violin piece when you come to visit. When you would visit Suzanne and John, you asked the children to play for you. And did they play well! John, a college professor, was the one who sat with each child for an hour at night, listening to them play their music lessons. It provided not only quality time for the children with their father, but also a household atmosphere that said that music was important. Their son David quit playing violin in high school, when peer pressure took over and he felt ashamed that his friends would know he played the violin in concerts throughout the area in Massachusetts where they live. His father was hurt but philosophical. "He'll come back to it some day, and he'll never go to a concert and be ignorant about the music being played."

4. Do Your Own Creative Work, and Let the Child See You Doing It.

For Teachers

So what if you're a math teacher? Do your students know you are also a cabinetmaker? A painter? A writer? That you sew, or knit, or design boats? The wee bit of humanizing that such information about you does for you with your students can make a big difference in their feelings of freedom of expression with you. Try it. When I conduct workshops with teachers, I often ask them to write briefly and then to share how they are creative. I ask them what puts them into a state of what Czikszentmihalyi so aptly called *flow*. Many of them say they aren't creative, but when I push them, we find that their creativity is expressed in their hobbies. The cooking, the crafts, the building, the refinishing of furniture, the designing of exercise routines and gardens all emerge in these teachers' descriptions as times when they feel creative.

When I give workshops for teachers, I ask what activities make them lose track of time, what endeavor is so challenging that it entices them, so pleasurable that they can keep going for a long time. Everything from computer games to running comes up, but what inevitably is said is that teaching well also gives them the pleasure of flow. This leads me to think that teaching as a creative activity is undervalued by the curriculum designers who tell teachers they should teach this for fifteen minutes and this for ten minutes.

The postmodern idea that teaching is meandering pleasurably with students in a river of knowledge where the ideas to be pursued arise from the context of the discussion supports the idea of teaching as a creative activity, but the curriculum planners who make teachers hand in detailed behavioral lesson plans and check off detailed task boxes have taken the creativity out of what is essentially an art form, a form of skilled craft raised to the sublime when the teacher is really in there with the kids. Teaching as a creative activity, an art form. What a droll idea!

For Parents

Does your house have a special place where the parents (as well as the children) can do their creative work? The writer Lucia Nevai is author of the 1997 book of short stories, *Normal*. She also won the prestigious Iowa Short Fiction Award in the late 1980s. She lives in a small apartment in New York City and supports herself with a job in media. When she writes, she goes to her room and puts this sign on the door: "Lucia's writing." The message machine on her telephone has this message. "Lucia's writing. She'll get back to you later. Leave a message." She values her own creativity, and her family values creativity also.

This is especially difficult for women to do. Loeb called it the "If I haven't dusted the furniture do I have the right to begin carving?" syndrome. We think that we have to sneak our creative work, not telling anyone that we're doing it. When my children were young, I wrote while the children were outside playing or after they went to bed. I would be all alone in the living room, or in the small office in our home, working on poems, my husband and kids long asleep. It was the only time I had, as a working mother, to be alone, to be private. But everyone knew I was doing it, as the rejection letters and a few acceptances arrived regularly.

Here is a poem I wrote in the early 1970s.

Poetmother
the afternoon is calm
silence time to write
the paper is green
like the summer

the mind floats into itself
like distanced birdsong
with images bright
as the kitchen sink

the polished coffee table
slowly right there
the words twist
from the images

and the fingers
take dictation
fast and willing
then the back door slaps

and his feet
in dirty sneakers tramp
and the voice begins

"Mom where are you?
I can't find anyone to play with
Where's the juice?"
(Mom I want)
(Mom I own you)

"You can't catch me!"
and the front door crashes
and a little girl runs
shrieks laughing

through the twisting words
and out again
the back door slams
on my resentment

a child's voice yells
"Bye Mom!"
I sit up and try again
for stillness

Now I write in the morning. For me, such morning writing time is a joyous luxury. The point is that people must make space and time for their creative work.

5. Set a Creative Tone.

For Teachers

When I was a school principal, I tried administratively to set the school's tone as one of valuing creativity. When the long-awaited, six-months-late first copy of my novel arrived from my publisher one afternoon just before an assembly, I was so thrilled to see it, I jumped up and down and shouted, "Yes! Yes!" As the assembly began, one of the teachers announced to the kids why I was behaving so strangely. Everyone applauded and laughed They recognized that I was a struggling writer as well as a principal.

When I left the school a few years later, one of the kids in a goodbye speech described me as a writer as well as a principal and said he would remember me because I encouraged the kids to write a lot of poems and stories. Besides hiring professional writers to work with the students, through the

Teachers and Writers Collaborative, I myself wrote for them. My Principal's Message in the yearbook was always a story (such written addresses are usually dull reading for the students). For example, I once wrote about the neighborhood characters where I grew up, and exhorted the readers to "read my story, and then write your own about your neighborhood characters." Then I told them about Mrs. Ollikainen, who made rag rugs and dolls out of hollyhocks, and Old Joe, who had a bull that we used to tease; Mr. Nelson, who yelled for his kids all the time; Brandon, who had a mysterious past and incessantly walked downtown; and Bulltop, who drove old cars into the mine pit. Many of the children subsequently did write about their neighborhoods. It seems important to have someone in authority be a model for the risk-taking involved.

Many of the teachers in that school likewise set examples of creativity, and it showed in their rooms. The halls were filled with art work; the bulletin boards were replete with children's efforts. The rooms were filled with learning centers, and every week there was a performance or a class project. Getting detailed behavioral lesson plans from these teachers was almost impossible. They weren't about to say "*The student will* be able to recite the Pledge of Allegiance correctly 75% of the time."

The point I am trying to make is that the *atmosphere* was creative. The teacher's lounge talk was often of movies, plays, books and musical performances, with opinions freely given about the latest pan by the local theater critic. The teachers traveled, too, even on their teachers' salaries, to Europe, Asia, and Africa. Many had never been to Yellowstone Park, but they had been to the Louvre. The teachers were interesting people, interested in creative things, and it showed in their interactive teaching. When you enter a school you can just tell what the atmosphere is. What do the administrators and teachers value? Are there stern signs ordering you to go immediately to the principal's office, but no directions as to how to get there? Are there institutional lockers and gray walls? Is the school more nearly like an army barracks than a joyful place where children learn to value their own creativity and humanity?

Just go into any school and see what message is conveyed by the walls, the corridors, the signs, the windows, the children themselves. When I was a central office consultant for regional education offices, I had to go into many schools each day. This is where I learned this lesson about tone. The schools I wanted to come back to were the ones which conveyed a welcome, even to central office administrators used to schools, but especially to children and their scared parents (for parents are often afraid to come to school). One school I remember well. There was an actual waiting room near the entrance, with couches, lamps, magazines, and bulletin boards of children's work. When parents came, they chatted with each other, shared the gossip of the day, and felt as if they, too, had a place in the school their children attended.

6. Value the Creative Work of Others.

For Teachers

Yes, I know you live in some small rural town, miles from any *real* cultural life. I grew up there too. So why, in my home town of Ishpeming, Michigan, is there a project that has preserved the local history, the accomplishments and experiences of the whole community? And why has that research been done by seventh graders? The Red Dust Project is the yearly effort (since 1975) of students in a small junior high school to collect the stories of the local residents and to publish them in an illustrated book. Every summer when I go there to visit my family, I buy the latest edition.

This project was initiated by a teacher. Teachers are usually the most stable part of a community: administrators leave, parents are only involved in the school while their children are in school, but teachers often stay for twenty, twenty-five, thirty years. One teacher, with the support of her administrator, has taught a generation of children to interview and to write up the stories, with incredible results: the children have had their work presented at the Smithsonian Museum. They have been interviewed themselves for national television. All because a teacher had an idea that junior high school students could do a creative project with the people in this small mining community. Each year a theme is chosen, and students volunteer to participate in the project.

For Parents

Is your house filled with books? Do you subscribe to any magazines? Do your children subscribe to any magazines? Do you visit the public library? Does your child have a library card? When was the last time you went to a museum? A live performance of theatre or music? You say you live in South Dakota and have two radio stations on the dial, both of them country-western? Photographer James Mackay grew up in Pollock, South Dakota, and ran his family's newspaper there for many years. He is among the most creative people I know. His collection of blues albums taught me almost all I know about the blues. My late friend, the poet and novelist Peggy Simpson Curry, grew up miles from any town on a ranch in Wyoming, yet she was one of the least provincial people I knew. As James Thurber said, "The most provincial people I ever met were the ones I met in New York City." When we moved to New York where my daughter attended La Guardia High School for the Performing Arts, one of her friends asked if there were drugstores in Ohio. (Yes, this is a true story!)

Once I was stuck in traffic on my way from my apartment in Brooklyn to my work in Manhattan and was forced to listen to a radio station giving away two tickets to a Broadway show. The winner, a resident of Queens—five miles from Broadway—said it was her first Broadway show. She was forty. Provincialism is a state of mind, not geography.

7. What Is Your Family Mythology?

For Parents

What I like to call your family mythology, or your family script, is important. Finish this sentence. "In our family, we —" "In our family we—value the arts, and talk about art." "In our family we—go to college." "In our family we—read books." "In our family we—go to museums." "In our family we—play on sports teams." When parents ask me how to get their kids to do certain things, I ask them what their family mythology is. In my family I knew I was going to college from kindergarten, even though my parents were children of Finnish immigrants and neither had been to college. In fact, my parents couldn't speak English when they went to kindergarten.

But in our family mythology, we went to college. On my paternal side, eighteen of my first cousins went; only two, both female, did not. My younger sisters and I formed only one of very few families in our mining location who went to college (we called our neighborhoods "locations"). I wrote about this in my book, *A Location in the Upper Peninsula.* In our high school class of 130, a friend and myself are the only ones with Ph.D.s. One of our classmates is a dentist and one has an M.S.W. But those are the only terminal degrees among us, though we represent a lot of bachelor's and master's degrees, more than our parents' generation earned.

What family mythology made all my cousins, my sisters, and me believe we could go to college? I suspect it had to do with our grandmother, educated only in elementary school in Finland. Once when my father wanted to drop out of high school, his father said he would have to work harder then, and put him shoveling manure all day long (they had cows and delivered milk before school). My father said he went back to high school rather than do that, and he graduated. Ten of his eleven brothers and sisters had some education beyond high school, mostly trade education, but there were two teachers, a dentist and a nurse there, too.

The motivation of immigrant families is not new, and my family's story is probably similar to your family's story. The story is still happening. Asian families in particular have succeeded, by and large, in our school structure. One may argue that the increased necessity for both parents to work, as well as the great rise in single-parent families, most of which are headed by over-burdened mothers, preclude this parental involvement. But if parents are aware of their great importance to their children's education, and schools become welcoming places for parents, with planned outreach efforts such as personal telephone calls to share good news, parents might overcome their great fear of school.

For Teachers

If your students don't have a family mythology that encourages cultural activities such as museums, concerts, or books, then your role is crucial. Field trips are a bother, yes, and busy school administrators often discourage efforts to take students to cultural events; but this should be a priority and a necessity, not a burden. Even if there is no encouraging atmosphere for field trips, videos of cultural events can be used. However, students are television-sated, so videos can be both a blessing and a curse. A rule of thumb is that doing is better than passive viewing.

At the very minimum, each student should have a public library card, and each classroom should have a set of encyclopedias. As teachers, you can make sure that this happens. And model for your students that research and learning are part of your life, as well. Here is what one writer I studied said about her favorite teachers:

> My "creative writing" teacher in high school was certifiably senile; I switched out of the class, an honors one, to a regular English class with a teacher who loved grammar. I hated grammar, but I learned there to love learning, precision with words. Other memorable teachers were so only because they loved what they taught; thus I, who cannot draw a straight

line with a ruler, recall the electricity and excitement of geometry class; I have a lot of buried knowledge and continuing fanaticism about Alexander the Great, because of an ex-jockey-turned-history-teacher whose love of that period of history sent me to the most obscure and advanced of resources, gave me a knowledge of library sources that has served me since, and gave me an absolute adoration of the whole process of knowledge: from the atmosphere in libraries to love of books for their new bindings and type as well as for their contents. It was not, I emphasize, WHAT these people taught, but HOW that worked the miracles— and I try to remember that every day I go into a classroom.

Remember what the writer quoted above said about it not being what her teachers taught, but how they taught. It may help to be aware that the school must compensate when the other environmental suns are clouded over.

8. Avoid Emphasizing Sex-role Stereotypes.

For Teachers

Many people who are homosexuals, regardless of gender, seem to have always known this about themselves, though some repress the knowledge. A book about how a talented boy discovered his homosexuality is the cult classic, *Best Little Boy in the World,* by John Reed. The works of the prize-winning fiction writer David Leavitt are also instructive in the description of coming to awareness of one's homosexuality. Whether homosexuals are more creative than other people is not known; it would seem that creative fields are more open to sexual divergence.

The presence of red ribbons on the lapels of entertainment stars at award ceremonies on national and international television is not just a political statement that there should be research on AIDS; it is a personal statement that good friends and colleagues have died, and the wearer is wearing a token in memoriam. This should not be forgotten by jaded television viewers who think that the entertainers are self-promoting. One characteristic of creative people is emotionality and empathy, and every red ribbon probably means a friend has died. The creative fields of the arts, fashion design, and theater have been visited by a great plague in the past fifteen years.

But the point is not that there is a risk of homosexuality in being creative; the point is that following rigid sex-role stereotyping limits creativity. Again, the personality attribute of androgyny should be emphasized here. In order to succeed in the world of visual arts, for example, a female artist needs to be willing to exhibit what are typically called masculine characteristics. The profession of artist demands an extraordinary commitment in terms of willingness to take rejection, to live in poverty, and to be field-independent. Those are typical traits of committed males, but not of committed females, who often choose careers as art educators and not as artists.

Girls' problems come when they try to reconcile the stereotypical paradox of the nurturing, recessive, motherly female with that of the unconventional artist. Boys' problems come when they try to reconcile the stereotypical paradox of the six shootin' muscle-flexing "real" man with that of the sensitive, perceptive, and insightful artist. There is no evidence that creative people are more often homosexual than people in other fields, such as teaching, politics, the military, or athletics. In the field of fashion, however, the recent deaths of homosexual males from AIDS has decimated the industry; on the popular television show *20/20*, reporter John Stosill and Barbara Walters wondered aloud whether the fashion industry attracted homosexuals more than other design fields such as engineering or architecture. The answer is probably yes. A corollary question might be whether athletics attracts more lesbians than other performance or entertainment fields. The answer again may probably be in the affirmative. So what?

For Parents

I'll bet the Marlboro Man and the Sweet Young Thing aren't very creative, for they represent the extremes of masculinity and femininity. If you recall the studies described earlier in this book, creative men and women were more androgynous than noncreative men and women. On a continuum of masculinity-femininity, with the most masculine and most feminine at either end, creative children and adults are more towards the middle. The humorist and screenwriter Nora Ephron, in her essay "Breasts," described her childhood thus: "I did not feel at all like a girl. I was boyish. I was athletic, ambitious, outspoken, competitive, noisy, rambunctious, I had scabs on my knees, and my socks slid down into my loafers and I could throw a football."

The emphasizing of sex-role stereotypes by parents and teachers makes for rigid, rules-filled environments, where boys don't cry and girls don't climb. The rigidity and the rules are what stifle creativity. By the age of five, children are strongly identified with their genders: regardless of the family environment, they understand that boys are firemen and girls are ballerinas. The creative home and school environment softens these expectations, and children can come to understand that girls can be firemen and boys can be ballet dancers.

There is a strong element of homophobia in our society. A teacher once told me that when she noticed one of her talented students was a great actor, she told the parents about their son's talent. The mother said, "We don't want him to act in any more plays. Actors are homosexual." Perhaps she had forgotten John Wayne. A softening of gender role expectations does not lead to homosexuality, for most people are heterosexual. The presence of gays in many creative fields may represent the attitudes of creative people, who seem more tolerant of differences and more accepting of people whose beliefs are freer. Androgyny is the key word. Or to put it another way, creative people seem to have both yin and yang. John Fraas and I did a small study using the High School Personality Questionnaire (HSPQ) that indicated that yes, indeed, high school boys in the arts were more tender-minded and more non-conforming than a comparison group of other boys. Our study supported, in a small way, the research of Barron and others that showed that creative men had traits of sensitivity.

9. Provide Private Lessons and Special Classes.

For Parents

Most schools, unless they are special schools for the arts or sciences, are not going to provide all of what your child needs to truly develop the talents she has, and so you must be the one to do so. This means lessons as well as materials. Even if your child plays in the band, the orchestra, jazz band, or string ensemble, if your school is fortunate enough to have such groups, your child also needs private lessons in order to develop musically. This is usually understood in the field of music and dance, but is less understood in writing, visual arts, and theatre. Few children who have talents and desire to learn get private lessons or tutoring in these fields, and this is a terrible shame.

The Development of Talent Project described by Bloom documented well the sacrifices and provisions that parents went through for their talented children. Parents are the first and most important influences on their children's talent development.

If there are special schools for the arts or sciences in your area, they should be considered. Students who attend these special schools demonstrate potential in the particular domains they are studying. Students are accepted as a result of their concrete performance on tests, auditions, in portfolios and with assessment by professionals. A typical eight-period day at the La Guardia High School in New York City contains three or four periods of intensive study of the art (for example, an instrumental music student studies music theory, has an ensemble period, and then has one or two periods of band or orchestra), as well as four periods of general academic study. Most schools for the arts have similar curricula.

The danger of attending these special schools is that the students may, in developing their special talents, become narrow. The challenge in special schools is to provide young, developing minds with a general education as well as a special, focused one, and young students may regard general education in literature, mathematics, history, geography, and government as boring, irrelevant, and unnecessary.

Teachers in general education at such special schools often must justify and relate to students' lives the material being taught, to motivate students to learn and remember it. Most students at special schools are vocationally minded, so focused on the specific skills they are developing that they would prefer not to have any liberal arts classes at all. Their teachers must be very skillful in educating the whole person, not just the creative person.

The talented adolescents are chosen for these schools on the basis of their creative products, not for the successful completion of paper and pencil tests that measure IQ, academic achievement, or divergent production. While they attend the school, they practice. Talented children who become successful adult professionals study and practice the skills of their field to the point of automaticity. The notion that creativity is separate from what is produced by the adolescent, that it springs from exposure to general exercises in fluency, flexibility, brainstorming, and elaboration, without specific nurturing in the field in which the creativity is exhibited, seems not to have influenced, at this time, the curricula of special schools for talented adolescents. Whether such activities would enhance the adolescents' creativity, or whether such activities are desirable as curricular options, is doubtful.

Actually, the role of parents and specialized teachers in these adolescents' talent development seems more important than whatever structured creativity training they have had. Parents often nurture and direct their children in the fields in which the parents themselves have interest and talent. Begun by the parent, the talented child is then taught by a teacher, who passes on what knowledge he or she can, and then the teacher passes the child to a more masterful teacher. That is the path of creative adult production. In the very depth of their special training, these children are developing automaticity. In their adolescent years, spontaneity in young creatively talented students often gives way to conformity. Residential schools for young artists make special provisions to deny the stereotypes that young artists are interested in drugs, rock 'n' roll, and sex. In an interview, an administrator at the North Carolina School of the Arts said, "Peer pressures with our students are more intense than with other students. We try to create an atmosphere for them where they can pursue academic and artistic pursuits without undue pressure." Parents who don't have proximity to special schools should send their talented students to special summer and Saturday programs.

For Teachers

The value of mentors is often spoken of in the literature for the talented. Researchers such as Simonton and Zuckerman have concluded that a person will not reach eminence in science without apprenticing himself to a mentor scientist, without studying with the right teacher. Kogan also discussed the importance of having the right teacher, who will have access to the right connections.

The classroom teacher and the specialist in talent development education also have a role, and that is to provide the child and the parents with information about suitable mentors. While the relationship between mentor and student or learner is deeply personal and cannot be legislated or mandated, efforts can be made. Schools must also play a part in the development of talent, helping find private teachers and mentors for talented children from families without financial resources. Petitioning local clubs and organizations to pay for lessons for a struggling but talented child can best be done by the school (anonymously, of course). One teacher herself paid for the room and board of one of our students at a summer institute last year. She did it so quietly that I never learned her name, but the child's life was changed by the experience.

The black Caribbean poet, Derek Walcott, Nobel Prize winner and MacArthur Fellow, in an interview in the "Writers at Work" series in the *Paris Review*, told this story about growing up in the Caribbean country of St. Lucia, having the good fortune to come under the influence of the visual artist, Harry Simmons:

Harry taught us. He had paints, he had music in his studio, and he was evidently a good friend of my father's. When he found out that we liked painting, he invited about four or five of us to come up to his studio and sit out on his veranda. He gave us equipment and told us to draw. Now that may seem very ordinary in a city, in another place, but in a very small, poor country like St. Lucia it was extraordinary. He encouraged us to spend our Saturday afternoons painting; he surrounded us with examples of his own painting. Just to let us be there and to have the ambience of his books, his music, his own supervision, and the stillness and dedication that this life meant in that studio was a terrific example. The influence was not so much technical. Of course I picked up a few things from him in terms of technique; how to do a good sky, how to water the paper, how to circle it, how to draw properly and concentrate on it, and all of that. But there were other things apart from the drawing. Mostly, it was the model of the man as a professional artist that was the example.

Harry Simmons might not have had a teacher's certificate, but he was certainly a mentor and a teacher.

10. If Hardship Comes into Your Life, Use It Positively to Teach the Child Expression Through Metaphor.

For Teachers

Try to notice and be sensitive to the situations of the children you teach. Ban the term *broken home* from your vocabulary. Don't be under the impression that a child will not be creative because he is poor or dishevelled. A student of mine, a bilingual Spanish-English teacher, discovered the creativity of a boy living in extreme poverty because he was always reading. She took photographs of him reading in the bus line, in the lunchroom, in the hallways, in math class, on the playground. She then identified him as having potential writing talent by asking him to write stories, which were extraordinary blends of Mexican and Central American mythological characters. She recommended him to the specialists in talent development education in his district, even though his IQ scores did not meet the threshold cutoff.

Release of emotion through the arts is often indirect, thus more therapeutic than therapy itself. There are branches of therapy called music therapy, art therapy, poetry therapy, and dance therapy that recognize the positive effects that the arts can have when a person has experienced trauma or emotional upheaval. The depth psychologists, the archetypal psychologists, the Jungians, speak of the fire within that is turned into an *image*, a thing *out there*. However, the child should also have a right to privacy. Snooping in private journals, asking for detailed explanations of what may seem to be weird artistic endeavors, is against the rules. The expression is itself enough. Remember the life of Christy Brown as shown in the movie, *My Left Foot*? Brown's family refused to let him be institutionalized for his profound handicaps and provided him with materials, company, support, and a neighborhood full of loving friends.

Singer/songwriter and high school teacher F. Christopher Reynolds has created an extracurricular program called Creativity, Inc. He works with selected students in ten areas that combine their personal experience with the creation of image. Many of the suggestions and books on how to enhance creativity focus on the "springtime" of creativity; but the creative person must visit winter as well. Many speakers about creativity celebrate the joy of creativity, using such words as *enhancing, unlocking,* and *tapping,* with images of leaps, flights, openings, growings, and increases. These metaphors are good and useful and necessary. Creativity is also reflection as to what has occurred, and this is felt in a receptive mode—returning what has been received—vs. making brand new things, acting outward, and making things happen. Spring is innovation. Fall is reflection, which is also essential in walking the path of creative development.

Before expressing, one must reflect, take the image inside and nurture it. Creativity enhancement must explore the fall and winter of creativity, which is not a response to a potential to grow, but one that includes loss, depression, and the tragic modes of life. In this way creativity can be permitted to be somber and to sing the blues, drawn inward toward gravity. Creativity and productivity across a lifetime should not only mean optimism and excitement, the idea of constant improvement with no regrets of wrong turns, for creativity also involves the dark side, the introversive, contemplative, intuitive, insightful side, in order to round out the whole picture.

James Hillman, the archetypal psychologist, has said that depression and loss are essential for creativity. He noted that Renaissance thinkers and artist such as Ficino and Michelangelo were "filled with anima: depression, weakness, sickness, complaint, love of different kinds, helplessness." They wrote widely of their moods, and said that they were held back by them. Hillman continued:

> Of course, these men were extremely active: Ficino never stopped his work despite all his complaints about being paralyzed and being unable to do anything anymore. Michelangelo thought he was old when he was forty and then he went on living beyond eighty. The soul builds its endurance, its *stamina,* as Rafael Lopez calls it, through hope-

lessness and depression . . . You live your life in the depression. You work with the depression. It doesn't completely stop
you. It only stops you if you're manic. Depression is worst
when we try to climb out of it, get on top of it.

When the *image* is created, a metaphor, a personal poem, story, song, painting, theater piece, clay sculpture—anything that objectifies the emotion that
is churning, the young creator can begin to have some peace. One of the
teams that visited Kuwait after the Gulf war was a team of art therapists,
who asked Kuwaiti children to draw the horror they had seen, of invading
soldiers breaking down the doors of their homes and raping their mothers.
The therapeutic value of creative work should not be overlooked. Self therapy is one powerful reason for creativity. After all, the word *create* means
to make.

However, the biographer Joan Dash differentiated between ordinary
autotherapeutic creativity and the creativity of very talented people. She said
of Edna St. Vincent Millay, American poet/playwright:

> If Edna Millay had been only a neurotic woman, death-haunt-
> ed, claustrophobic and sexually ambiguous, she might have
> found considerable satisfaction as well as worthwhile therapy
> in whatever art form she took up in her spare time . . . But she
> had also been born with the peculiar genetic equipment that
> can become high talent, perhaps even genius, and in her earli-
> est years had acquired the habit of hard and precise observa-
> tion of the world around her, as well as the discipline that
> leads to transmuting experience into something more than
> therapeutic art. Her fears of death became everyman's fear of
> death, her longing for love and her denial of it became the uni-
> versal cry of the spirit to be part of something greater than the
> single self. Just as the poetry transcended her own individual
> nightmares, so did the poet herself, in the very act of writing,
> push back the cage of self to join humanity at large.

For Parents

This book has described how childhood hardship often leads to creativity.
People ask me, "Aren't there normal creators? Can't a creative person live in
a happy family and have a happy life?" "Well, of course," I answer. Look at

the lives of scientists. Many if not most of them had childhoods with active involvement by both parents, and support for study and for projects. It only makes sense to give children such emotional and intellectual backing.

This question of whether trauma is necessary to creative expression is certainly debatable. One new study has shed some light on this. Barbara Kerr at Arizona State University has been questioning undergraduate and graduate students who call themselves creative and whom she designates as "normal creatives." She is finding that they come from homes rich in books, with lively discussions and lessons in art and music. The parents are themselves creative, and their style of discipline is either authoritative or permissive. The students had a voice in the home and were raised to be independent decision-makers. I myself have noticed that the teachers I teach often parent in this way, and so it may not be out of line to say that teachers make good parents of creative children.

However, if trouble comes into your family, try to make something of it. Writer and storyteller Marie Vogl Gery told of her yearlong residency at a junior high school where the mother of one of the boys she worked with committed suicide. This boy demonstrated talent and expressed his feelings through poetry that didn't specifically refer to the suicide, but that permitted him indirectly to defuse his feelings of sorrow, confusion, and sadness. The creation of an image or metaphor is helpful and even necessary in bringing the hurt outside without having to talk about it. Indeed, "talking therapy" often does not work with young people, who, when asked what is wrong, may not be able to say. However, by the creation of an image, the hurt can be diffused into the metaphorical, and thus healing can begin.

11. Emphasize that Talent is Only a Small Part of Creative Production, and that Discipline and Practice Are Important.

For Teachers

Teachers of the talented especially must realize that such children are often overly praised and rewarded just for possessing the talent. Teachers of visual arts, writing, music, dance, and theatre know what it takes to realize that talent, but often such talented students are often not given special help by the school. They are instead thrown in with far less talented students in art, music, math, and science. This would never happen in athletics, where talented students are permitted to advance according to their abilities, competing with people at their own levels of expertise. Accurate and qualified feedback is important in the development of talent, and the child should have access to people who have some expertise. Thus, mentoring is important.

Talented people often are talented in many dimensions, and it is hard to choose which field to pursue. Art? Music? Acting? Helping talented children to make these choices without closing down options is a challenge. The clue is often found in passion. If a person likes to practice, likes to work at the domain, loses track of time while doing it, thinks of it when not doing it, the answer may be found. If the doing is more play than work, the "gift" is poking towards consciousness.

Another challenge is not to counter-identify. Often the teachers of talented students are almost as jealous and anxious as parents are. When teachers counter-identify, they feel horrible when the student doesn't perform or when the child makes a mistake. They are as narcissistic as the parents described by Alice Miller in *The Drama of the Gifted Child*. This is particularly difficult when the teaching relationship becomes a coaching relationship. Teachers can be temperamental and cruel, pushing hard until the students hate the field. A former swimmer once told me that he would never swim again, never go near a pool, because his college coach demanded that he swim seven hours a day in order to improve his time a few seconds. Swimming will never again be a pleasure for him. Kogan also spoke to this difficulty in describing the idiosyncratic Juilliard teachers; she said that the greatest discovery for a student of music who has spent her life practicing is that of the pleasure of music. Often musicians are so technically oriented that they have difficulty listening to music without analyzing it unduly.

For Parents

Talent is necessary but not sufficient. That is why I have put talent in the domain at the top of my Pyramid of Talent Development and personality attributes as the base, the bottom, the foundation. True realization of creativity comes through hard work, tolerance for ambiguity, preference for complexity, passion, motivation, and discipline. That has been emphasized repeatedly through studies of creative people and their interactions with their domains of creativity. A child gradually realizes that talent comes through habits of hard work. Remember that there are two stages in the development of talent. The first stage is the natural stage, where everything seems to come easily; during the second stage the adolescent learns the formal aspects of the discipline—the talent becomes consciously developed. The world is full of talented people, but fully creative people do a lot of hard work.

Does that mean you should make your child practice the piano? Use your own judgment. The key is to realize that discipline and practice are important. No creative adult in any field got to be successful without first having had many fits and starts and having spent many hours in conscious practice. How many times did Edison try, before he came up with a successful electric light bulb?

12. Allow the Child to be Odd: Avoid Emphasizing Socialization at the Expense of Creative Expression.

For Teachers

The schools often see their major roles as socializing children so they fit into a mold and become acceptable to the society that the schools serve. This is considered to be as important as teaching the children to read and write and figure, for this is what the "real world" demands, say some educators. But creative people are often at odds with the world and are prickly, rebellious, and nonconforming. Often their nonconforming is actually conforming, but conforming to a stereotype similar to how they perceive creative people to behave. Often creative students act out in class, are argumentative, and consciously underachieve; that is, they do well in classes they like but don't care about classes they don't like or see as irrelevant to their futures.

Often creative students stereotype their teachers by age and looks. One summer I was teaching a fiction writer's workshop to a group of specially selected teenagers from throughout the state of Ohio. One of the young women was quite surly as she looked at me in my middle-aged ways, my conservative haircut, my comfy, rumpled clothes. Then I mentioned that one of the guest readers I was going to bring in was a well-known local poet, Nick Muska, who had written a theater piece about Jack Kerouac called *Back to Jack*. The young woman was from Nick's town, Toledo, and knew him from the poetry scene in that city.

"*You* know Nick Muska?" she said incredulously.

"Yes. We've been friends for many years," I said simply.

"But I *love* Nick Muska!" And she brought in her own personal collection of Jack Kerouac's books to show me the very next session. She had thought me too school-teacherish and uncool to be able to teach her anything. She had stereotyped me and was not willing to learn from me until this incident. Then I became her teacher, but not before.

Rimm recommended that such creative students may need therapy. They view themselves as *too* different, *too* creative, *too* cool for any intervention from the schools. However, often their rebelliousness carries over to the therapist's office as well. One teenage creative writer I know said she sat silently and stubbornly when she was sent to a therapist. Another creative child videotaped for a case study by one of my students said that even though her mother made her go to therapy because of her nonconforming behavior, she didn't feel she had benefited because she felt smarter than the therapist. But therapy can also be chosen for the wrong reasons, and the unwarranted intrusion may lead to unwanted results: One of our creative adolescents at a summer institute spent the whole time on psychotropic drugs, falling asleep in her morning classes. Her parents insisted she take the medication because she had begun wearing black clothes and black lipstick, which worried her parents, so they sent her to a therapist who prescribed the drugs.

Perhaps when considering whether a creative child needs therapy, families and the schools should themselves be willing to undergo therapeutic questioning. The selection of the therapist is also quite important. Creative people generally understand creative people, recognize kindred spirits. Sending a creative child to a rigid therapist may not work.

For Parents

So your daughter didn't get to dance the role of Clara and had to settle for being a soldier in *The Nutcracker*. So your son didn't get his brilliant short story accepted for publication by that magazine of children's writing. Is this the end of the world? Is it your child's or your own ego that is hurt? Parental narcissism—that is, parents investing so much of themselves in their children's successes and failures that they lose sight of the purpose of the practice—can be very harmful. In the high-powered world of national children's chess, parents became so involved in their children's chess tournaments that fathers came to blows, and the chess association finally had to ban parents from the chess arenas at the primary levels.

We all know the phenomenon of the Little League parent. This syndrome is found in the creative world as well. Sometimes these parents are called stage mothers. Sylvia Rimm wrote about the necessity for children, especially talented children, to be able to take the second lead in the play, or second chair in the band. She said when children work for their achievements they learn how to fail, and thus appreciate their achievements more.

At the other end of the continuum, some parents either deny that their children have talent, seemingly fearful of what might be the implications for their future development, or they don't see their children's talent as important. Or, like the mother of a talented young actor, who told the teacher never to put him into another play because all actors are weird homosexuals, they fear the child's talent will lead him into paths the parents do not want.

But the need to get along with others is not paramount in creative people. Most creative people weren't president of the club or queen of the prom or the one voted most likely to succeed. Often, they were odd. For many, high school was the most painful time, as the pressures for conformity beckoned. Often, too, high school creative youth will band together in what they call nonconformity but will still dress the same as their other nonconformist friends, listening to the same music, reading the same books, and rebelling together.

I read somewhere, years ago, that the "enfants terribles" of 1970s movie directors, the Spielbergs, Lucases, Bogdonoviches, Coppolas, were not, in high school, the boys that the pretty blond cheerleaders chose for boyfriends, and they spent a lot of time yearning for these ice goddesses. It was only when their creative talents were realized, years later, that they got to make themselves noticed by their high school dream-girls, as Bogdonovich did by casting Cybill Shepherd in *The Last Picture Show.* That is probably why many adult women also love the movie *The Way We Were*, because the odd rebel Streisand got the gorgeous blond hunk Redford.

One of my younger graduate students in Georgia told us that he and his friends in high school proudly called themselves "the band geeks." A reverse snobbery took them over as they looked at the pitiful muscle-bound athletes with their blond babes. "They couldn't even read music," he said. "What pleasure can there be in life if you can't even read music?"

13. Develop a Creative Style: Use Kind Humor and Get Creativity Training.

For Parents and Teachers

Besides enjoying and being frustrated by that child's sense of humor, we as parents and teachers should monitor our own ways of dealing with creative children. Do we enjoy children? Do we laugh with children (or at them, if appropriate)? Do we have fun with children? In other words, is being with creative children the pleasure it can be?

Bryant and Zillman studied the use of humor in classrooms. Elementary school teachers use more humor than junior high teachers. Junior high teachers most frequently use funny comments, funny stories, and jokes, though male junior high teachers told jokes more often. Junior high, high school, and college teachers used hostile and tendentious humor such as ridicule and sarcasm more often than did elementary teachers. In fact, almost half the humor used by these teachers was sarcastic. Humor used in a hostile manner is not what is meant here, but humor used in gentler ways creates a happier, more relaxed class-room, and thus may help students to have positive attitudes towards learning. Ziv has shown that humor contributes to the development of creative thinking, and one can see why, for nonhostile humor creates the feeling of freedom and play that is necessary for creative thinking.

People can be taught to be more creative and less fearful. Project Vanguard in Ohio in the development of creative thinking offered creativity training to elementary and middle-school teachers in two suburban districts. As a result of this creativity training, which consisted of 30 hours for each teacher, participants were able to identify creative children, to utilize open-ended techniques of teaching, and to value the creative thinking of the children they taught.

If school districts are serious about effectively teaching creative thinking, they must provide the necessary backup training. There are many commercial programs available and many trained people who can provide creativity training to school districts. School districts also should provide the rigorous instruction in the fields in which the creativity training can be applied. Many opportunities for teaching students to be more creative exist. Some of these are extracurricular, and some of these are curricular. Few schools offer special classes in how to be more creative, and so the technique and lessons must be integrated and incorporated into the courses as they are taught. Every school has experts who can help the student who is creative in some domain to be nurtured in that domain.

Many people do not believe that the school is the place to work to enhance student creativity, and in fact, they doubt whether any such exercises do really train people to be more creative. I am of mixed opinion on this; on the one hand, doing such exercises can make people aware of what goes into creativity, if the exercises are based on the research about creative people. These would be likened to the drills that athletes practice or the scales that musicians practice or the skills that one seeks to acquire to get automaticity in an area in which one wants to be expert. On the other hand, perhaps such exercises are too abstract to promote transfer.

After all, does practice in risk-taking encourage the risk-taking that creative people must have do in their creative work, as well as in pursuing their careers? Is risk-taking teachable through a creativity enhancement exercise? If one begins to think about this, though, one realizes that the "ropes courses" through which many businesses send their employees to build a sense of trust in each other, also encourage physical risk-taking as a "safe" rehearsal for "dangerous" life. With these caveats in mind, I have compiled a list of possible activities teachers could use to construct educational experiences for their students in hopes they will learn to be more creative. Ultimately, the purpose of such training is to free the inner person through imagery. Colleagues who teach in our program use fingerpainting, storytelling about the ancestors, clay, construction paper to make each person's personal monster, singing, and other means to encourage the students to express themselves through metaphor.

A Typical Creativity Course

My own creativity course utilizes exercises in risk-taking, trust-building, and the cultivation of an attitude of naiveté. The students also try exercises in cultivating self-discipline. They work daily in creativity thoughtlogs. We work with the five *I*s: (1) *Imagery*, including guided imagery and film script visualizing; (2) *Imagination*, including storytelling; (3) *Intuition*, including the intuition probe, psychic intuition, and dreams; (4) *Insight*, including grasping the gestalt, going for the *aha*, and zen sketching; and (5) *Inspiration*, including the visitation of the muse, creativity rituals such as solitude, creating ideal conditions, and using background music. We imitate those creative people who treasure nature and its contents, making naturalist notations and drawings. I have an exercise called "This is the day which the Lord hath made / Let us rejoice and be glad in it." We try meditation, meditating on beauty, on the dark side, on God. We do improvisation with jazz, theater, word rivers, writing practice, creative movement, rhythm and drumming, scat singing, and doodling.

We try to see the humor in everything. We tell jokes. We cultivate all five of our senses and also blend them for a sense of synaesthesia. We vigorously exercise so endorphins will kick in. We try to find our domains of passion by noticing when we go into a state of flow. We explore the joys of good conversation and start a monthly salon at my house. We visit a bookstore, a library, a museum in order to honor the creativity of others. We attend a concert, a play, a movie, a poetry reading or a lecture.

The culmination of the course is an individual creativity project. The students may not use already existing kits or molds, and must avoid the "season curriculum"—Christmas decorations, Halloween pumpkins, or St. Patrick's Day shamrocks. One wrote a poem when we visited the art museum, and it became the lyrics for the first song she composed. Other individual creativity projects have included an autobiographical video ("My creative self"); performance of an original song; performance of an original radio play; design and modeling of an original dress for a sorority formal; a plan for an advertising campaign; a synchronized swimming routine; a grunge rock band audio tape; a photographic exhibit; an exhibit of original art works; a reading of an original short story; an autobiographical multimedia presentation; a translation into English of Chinese, Greek, or Spanish literature; an original dance routine; a new recipe for scones; an original afghan; designs for costumes for a play; a reading of original poetry; a business plan for a new business; a music video; *a capella* singing; an original rock n' roll song; philosophical musings about the meaning of life; and display and demonstration of a particularly creative Thoughtlog. One football player, a defensive back, took all the football game tapes for his entire college career, and spliced them together to show himself in the improvisatory acts of dodging, running, and hitting. Projects are evaluated with a wholistic scoring system, and we are often so moved at the projects that we weep. At the end of the course, most agree that indeed, creativity can be enhanced through direct teaching.

Summary

1. Provide a private place for creative work to be done.
2. Provide materials (e.g. musical instruments, sketchbooks).
3. Encourage and display the child's creative work and avoid overly evaluating it.
4. Do your own creative work and let the child see you.
5. Pay attention to what your family mythology is teaching.
6. Value the creative work of others.
7. Avoid emphasizing sex-role stereotypes.
8. Provide private lessons and special classes.
9. If hardship comes into your life, use the hardship positively, to encourage the child to express him/herself through metaphor.
10. Emphasize that talent is only a small part of creative production and that discipline and practice are important.
11. Allow the child to be odd; avoid emphasizing socialization at the expense of creative expression.
12. Develop a creative style: use kind humor and get creativity training.

APPENDIX A

Creativity Theory

The Need for Theory

The question of what creativity is has many answers. Theories seek to explain what and why. A theory is a framework explaining the relationships among factors that pertain to creativity. Depending on a theoretician's predilection, field of expertise, and sense of self, the answer differs. The impetus for theorizing about creativity may come from a person's thinking about his or her own creativity. There are several basic species of creativity theory. Among them are philosophic theory, psychological theory, psychoanalytic theory, and domain-specific theory.

Those who write psychoanalytic theory are psychoanalysts, and their reason for theorizing about creativity is to probe the psyche of the creative person, looking for the key incidents or events that led to the creative person being as she is. There is also a group of psychoanalysts, therapists, and physicians, who belong to a group called "Creativity And Madness." They meet regularly in various locations such as Vienna, Amsterdam, or New York City, to discuss the lives of creative people who had mental difficulties. I was invited by a psychoanalyst friend to be his guest at one of their meetings at the Plaza Hotel near Central Park, where they discussed Van Gogh, in conjunction with the exhibit at the Metropolitan Museum of Van Gogh's sojourn in Arles.

As stated in Chapter 1, psychological theorists also want to probe the psyche, but to find out what happens in the mind of the person creating (cognitive psychologists) or to make the perfect test for creativity in order to be able to predict who will be creative (psychometrists), and to discover the traits of the creative person and the aspects of the creative process. Humanistic psychologists are not so much interested in a creative product as they are in enhancing the creative potential in every human being. Information processing theorists want to probe the brain of the creative person in order to find out what dendrons flash with what speed so that the creative person's processing can be replicated, perhaps artificially, with computers.

Philosophers are among the most interesting creativity theorists. They want to assess the meaning of creativity, especially as it relates to certain philosophical problems. Philosophers in existentialism explore the meaning of freedom. Philosophers in esthetics explore the meaning of beauty.

The domain-specific theorists, or artist/scientist theorists, want to explain what happens when one is creative, and their accounts are among the most interesting to read. It is when they formulate a theory—that is, when they generalize for all artists, scientists, inventors, or mathematicians—that their accounts get a little questionable.

A look at a basic book, *The Creativity Question* (1976), edited by one of the major psychoanalytic theorists, Alfred Rothenberg, and one of the major philosophic theorists, Carl Hausman, gives a clue about the diversity of theories. Another interesting book that summarizes theories is the psychoanalyst Arieti's (1976) *Creativity: The Magic Synthesis*. Sternberg, who seems to be the editor of editors, edited a 1988 book summarizing creativity theories in cognitive psychology, called *The Nature of Creativity* (1988). Rothenberg took issue with the title of this book in a comment in *The Creativity Research Journal*, saying that the psychologists were falsely implying that they knew the nature of creativity, and that most of the theorists writing in this book were just recycling their old ideas. Mark Runco edited a book on creativity theory, in 1990. He is also editing a new *Encyclopedia of Creativity* (1999). Gardner (1993) and Csikszentmihalyi (1995) have elaborated on earlier theories of creativity in recent best-selling books. The continual visitation by thinkers in the sciences, social sciences, and arts, regarding the concept of creativity illustrates again, the proprietary feelings that creativity incites.

The following list gives a brief summary of some of the major theories and their proponents. Some of these ideas were implicitly stated and not fully developed, and some were explicitly developed as full-blown theories of creativity. I have mentioned merely a few of these thinkers and have summarized their thoughts as if I were writing a movie blurb for *TV Guide*. This is not to give them short shrift, but to provide an overview of the deep morass one surveys when one begins to study creativity.

Many of these thinkers have written, studied, summarized, and agonized over what creativity truly is. They have spent much of their professional life-times thinking about creativity, and their work is appreciated by us novices. You also may have some objections as to which categories I placed people in; for example I placed Hofstadter in the philosophical category, and Huxley into the domain-specific category. These categories are broad outlines.

Philosophic Theorists

Kant (1778): Genius, or creativity, is found in the arts but not in science; there is a necessary interplay of the faculties of imagination and understanding in the production of art.

Bergson (1907): Creativity is the result of intuition when all precedents are absent.

Croce (1909): Creativity in art is the expression of intuitive pre-cognition.

Collingwood (1938): In creative people, imagination is the synthesizing activity that occurs before discursive or relational thought.

Maritain (1953): Human creativity can be traced to the power of the divine, through poetic insight and mystical illumination.

Langer (1957): Creativity is found where the abstract apparition of a form produces a symbolic emotional reaction in the perceiver.

Blanshard (1964): What the creator creates is an end that results from inner necessity. The subconscious is present in invention.

Hausman (1964): Creativity, spontaneous and nonrational, produces true novelty.

Hofstadter (1985): "The crux of creativity is the ability to manufacture variations on a theme."

Psychologists

Galton (1869): Special talent or genius in diverse areas is inherited.

Thorndike (1911): Relevant experience is essential to creative problem-solving.

Wallas (1926): The creative process takes place in four specific phases occurring in a fairly regular sequence including a phase of incubation where creative work occurs outside of consciousness.

Rossman (1931): There are seven steps to the creative process, similar to Wallas's.

Guilford (1950, 1967): Divergent production, an intellectual factor, is present in the creative response; the divergent producer provides alternate solutions to open-ended problems.

Osborn (1953): There are seven stages in the creative process. These evolved into the Creative Problem-Solving Process.

Stein (1953): There are three stages in the creative process.

Rogers (1954): The creative individual has an openness to experience, an internal locus of evaluation and the ability to toy with elements and concepts.

Watson (1958): Creative problem-solving comes because of transfer. Similarly, old problem solutions are generalized to the new solution.

Taylor (1959): Creativity exists at five different levels.

Gordon (1961): Previous theories of creativity were elitist and stressed inspiration and genius. Everyone can be creative. Making metaphors is the creative process.

Vygotsky (1962): Creative imagination is developmental, requiring the collaboration of concept formation.

Mednick (1962): Remote associations are combined to form creations by contiguity, serendipity, and mediation.

Roe (1963): The creative process is separate from the final product. It happens in most people and is not unique to those who produce superior final products

Dabrowski (1964) and **Piechowski** (1989): Creativity is talent in a specific field, exemplified by intense emotional, imaginational, intellectual, sensual, and/or psychomotor overexcitability or intensity.

Wallach and Kogan (1965): Creativity can be differentiated from IQ or g-factor intelligence.

Torrance (1966, 1979): Certain aspects of creativity, divergent thinking in particualr, can be tested.

Barron (1968, 1972, 1994): Creative people have the paradoxical presence of high degrees of ego strength along with psychopathologic qualities. Creativity can only be understood through the metaphor of ecology; it is pervasive and environmentally diverse.

Maslow (1968): Creativity is in everyone, and many of the people who created tangible achievements were not self-actualized. He differentiated *special talent creativeness* from self *actualizing creativeness*.

Bogen and Bogen (1969): Creativity results from the coordinated function of the repropositional mind and the appositional mind. The connecting structure between right and left hemispheres is the seat of creativity.

Skinner (1971): Creativity is a result of natural selection over evolved time.

Gowan (1972): The creative individual develops as a result of certain childhood experiences.

Krippner and Murphy (1973): The capacity for extrasensory perception, telepathy, precognition, clairvoyance, and psychokinesis are very necessary for creativity.

Gruber (1974, 1988): Creativity is an evolving system: key phases of this system are insights, metaphors, the transformation of experience, and organization of purpose.

Getzels and Csikszentmihalyi (1976): Creativity comes about in problem-finding, not in problem-solving.

Renzulli (1978): Creativity is a necessary component of gifted behavior, along with above-average intelligence and task commitment.

MacKinnon (1978): Creative people have certain personality attributes that are different from those of noncreative people.

Willings (1980): Creative people have defensive, productive, adaptive, elaborative, or developmental personalities.

Perkins (1981/1988): Creativity is inevitable invention produced by people with certain personality attitudes using tactics of selection, planning, and abstracting.

Feldman (1982, 1988, 1994): Creativity is the developmental transformation of insight into novelty that makes a product that changes the field.

Amabile (1983): Creative people have certain personality traits such as intrinsic motivation, which can be temporarily affected by external interference.

Tannenbaum (1983): Creativity is necessary for giftedness and is integrated into all five aspects of giftedness.

Brown (1986): Transpersonal psychology helps to understand creativity through exploring higher states of awareness.

Weisberg (1986): This anti-theorist systematically dismantled what he called the "Myths of creativity," stating that creativity is incremental, that is, grounded in the work of those who came before.

Langley and Jones (1988): Creativity involves reasoning by analogy and qualitative mental models.

Schank (1988): The creative person can program him or herself to ask the right questions.

Piirto (1994): Creativity is in the personality, the process, and the product within a domain in interaction with genetic influences and with optimal environmental influences of home, school, community and culture, gender, and chance. Creativity is a basic human instinct to make new.

Sternberg and Lubart (1988/1992): Creativity is derived from an investment of personality attributes, problem definition, insight, flexibility, intrinsic and extrinsic reward, and a certain legislative or executive style.

Gardner (1993): Creativity is the work of a person who habitually solves problems, makes products, or finds new questions in a domain in a way that is at first considered new but that eventually becomes accepted in the culture.

Simonton (1995): Creativity comes about through the chance-configuration theory, which postulates that social factors interact with personality factors to produce genius. Creativity is a form of leadership. The more works a creator produces, the more the chance of influencing the domain, and of assuming leadership in the domain.

Czikszentmihalyi (1995): "Creativity is any act, idea, or product that changes an existing domain, or that transforms an existing domain into a new one." Creativity is the interaction of a person working with the symbols of a domain or field at a certain time in history. Thus it is an internal systems model.

Runco (1997): Productivity is necessary for creativity but not for giftedness.

Psychoanalytic Theorists

Lombroso (1895): Creative genius is related to insanity; he differentiated between ordinary insanity and the insanity associated with genius.

Freud (1908): Fantasy is essential in the production of literary works. Such fantasy is primarily a manifestation of preconscious thoughts and feelings. The Unconscious also has a role in creation.

Jung (1923): Creativity is located in autonomous complexes which unearth the Collective Unconscious. These have a determining effect on consciousness in creation. The Collective Unconscious accounts for an audience's favorable response to a creation. The creative act can never be explained.

Lee (1940): Artistic creation is the result of symbolically compensating for disabilities.

Kris (1952): "Regression in the service of the ego" or ego-controlled regression is the specific means whereby preconscious and unconscious material appear in the creator's consciousness.

Kubie (1958): Preconscious processes produce creations.

Schachtel (1959): Allocentric perception, or openness to the world, is necessary for creativity to take place. This is characteristic of the most mature stage of human perceptual development.

Rank (1960): An artist type is distinct from the neurotic type. He overcomes his fear of death by an act of will directed toward immortality. Male creativity is developed by jealousy of female ability to bear children.

May (1975): Creativity takes courage, in making form from chaos.

Arieti (1976): Creativity is a primitive magic synthesis performed by gifted people.

Rothenberg (1979, 1990): Janusian thinking is involved in creation; this is the capacity to conceive and utilize two or more opposite or contradictory ideas, concepts, or images simultaneously.

Miller (1990): Creative production is a result of childhood trauma where warmth was present.

Jamison (1994). Creative people have more psychopathology, especially manic-depression, than others.

Hillman (1996). Every person possesses a daimon of creativity which influences how life is lived. This daimon is like an acorn, ready to grow under encouraging conditions.

Domain-Specific Theories

Coleridge (1817): An active and constructive imagination is necessary for poetic creativity.

Poe (1846): Logic and deliberately controlled techniques are important in the creative process.

Morgan (1933): Predictability is perhaps not necessary for scientific creation.

Cannon (1945): Creativity is an extraconscious process rather than unconscious, with no necessary determining effect upon consciousness. Hunches are important in certain phases of the scientific approach.

Huxley (1963): The use of psychedelic drugs can enhance creativity.

Koestler (1964): Bicosiation—the combination of two consistent but habitually incompatible frames of reference—is meant to account for creations in all areas: culture, societies, nature, individuals.

Ehrenzweig (1967): The role of the unconscious in artistic creation follows a specific process called "unconscious dedifferentiation."

Findlay and Lumsden (1988): Creativity is evolutionary. Creative products and people have evolved through a mutational process.

APPENDIX B

Focus Questions for Teachers Who use *Understanding Those Who Create*

CHAPTER 1—Creativity and Talent Development

1. Do a small research study. Ask three people for their definitions of creativity. Then ask them whether they think some people have more ability to be creative than other people. Report your findings.

2. Do a small research study. Ask three teachers how they teach students to be more creative. Report your findings.

3. Can creativity be tested? Why or why not?

4. Give four examples of how you would teach divergent production: fluency, flexibility, novelty/originality, or elaboration.

5. Discuss the reasons of **quantity and quality** as reasons for teaching people to be creative.

6. Discuss **nationalism** with relationship to emphasis on creativity enhancement.

7. Can a person be creative without a creative product? Discuss.

8. Can a person be creative without outstanding talent? Discuss.

9. Discuss the notion of freedom with relationship to creativity.

10. In order to be truly creative, must a person have mastered the field in which the creativity is demonstrated? Discuss.

CHAPTER 2—The Creative Process

1. Describe a time when you were inspired to create by love (the Visitation of the Muse).

2. Describe a time when you were in a state of semitrance or flow while creating.

3. Discuss Wallas's steps in the creative process: (1) preparation; (2) incubation; (3) illumination; (4) verification with relation to yours or a friend's creativeness.

4. What do you think Ghiselin meant by "oceanic consciousness" while creating?

5. What is the place of *automaticity* in the creative process?

6. Discuss the aesthetics of a certain field or domain of creativity with which you are familiar. What beauty do the practitioners strive for and appreciate?

7. Interview two people and ask them what rituals they observe while creating. What rituals do you observe while creating, if any?

8. Interview two people and ask them whether they've had illuminations or *Aha!*s in their creativity. What illuminations have you experienced?

9. Discuss your background and experience with right brain and left brain theories of the nature of creativity. Do you think this explanation for creativeness is adequate?

10. Discuss the role of chemical substances (alcohol, drugs, hormones released through exercise) in the creative process.

11. Discuss solitude as opposed to loneliness, and the place of each in the creative process.

12. What connections do you see between spirituality and creativity?

13. Discuss the importance of having an attitude of *naiveté* in doing creative work.

14. Discuss the necessity for *discipline* and *perseverance* in doing creative work.

15. Discuss the role of *intuition* and *insight* in the creative process.

CHAPTERS 3 & 4—Creativity Tests & Significance; Creativity Training, Questionnaires, Checklists

1. Can creativity be tested? Why or why not?

2. Discuss the importance of validity in creativity testing.

3. Discuss reliability and testing for creativity.

4. Discuss your experience of administering standardized tests. Was the administration reliable?

5. Do people fall on a normal curve of creativity? When? How?

6. Critique the Dabrowski Overexcitability Questionnaire (OEQ).

7. Discuss your experience with any of the creativity training packages.

8. Why should all students (not just the academically talented students) receive creativity training?

9. Why should all teachers receive creativity training?

10. Interview three teachers (perhaps in music, literature, theater, athletics) about how they teach students to be more creative.

CHAPTER 5—Visual Artists and Architects

1. Discuss the romantic view of the easel painter/visual artist.

2. Why is spatial intelligence important for the visual artist and architect?

3. Do some research on gender differences in spatial ability. What did you find?

4. Discuss a child you know who has the reputation of being class artist. Do his or her characteristics fit Hurwitz's observations?

5. Why do male visual artists who decide to go into fine arts often have difficulty when they announce their career choice to their families and friends?

6. Why do many women choose to become art educators rather than fine artists?

7. Discuss the concept of *problem-finding* as compared to *problem-solving.*

8. Ruminate on the concept of the loft culture and the visual artist.

9. Discuss your own Myers-Briggs Type Indicator preferences with relationship to those found in studies of visual artists and architects.

10. Interview an architect about his or her career. Note similarities and differences to what the chapter says.

CHAPTER 6—Creative Writers

1. Discuss why people choose creative writing as a profession.

2. What are some differences between writers in different genres? What are some similarities?

3. Look up some information about your favorite novelist. How does this person compare with the research findings in this chapter?

4. Look up some information about your favorite poet. How does this person compare with the research findings in this chapter?

5. Interview a creative writer—nonfiction, fiction, playwright, screenwriter, or poet. Discuss your findings.

6. Look up the writers in your state in the *Directory of American Poets and Fiction Writers*. Make some observations.

7. Look up all the works of a famous writer. Are you surprised at his or her productivity? Discuss the concept of productivity with regard to creativity.

8. Discuss depression with regard to writers. Add information not in the text.

9. Why is humor an aspect of verbal intelligence?

CHAPTER 7—Children with Extraordinary Writing Talent

1. Look up the juvenilia of a writer you admire. Make some comments.

2. Try a writing exercise with your students or with a class. See whether you can recognize a talented writer with the lists given in the chapter.

3. Survey your students or your friends for their reading habits. Make some comments about those whom you discover to be omnivorous readers. Are they writers also?

4. Make some comments about the children's work shown in this chapter.

5. Discuss the concept of overexcitabilities or intensities as it relates to young talented creators.

6. Look up the childhood of a writer you admire. Was there a developmental crisis? Make some comments.

7. Compare your own childhood reading and writing with that of the children here discussed.

8. Take the work of a child writer you know and analyze it using the characteristics listed in the chapter.

CHAPTER 8—Creative Scientists, Mathematicians, Inventors, and Entrepreneurs

1. In considering the patterns in the lives of creative scientists, mathematicians, and inventors, which patterns seem to you to be the most surprising? Explain.

2. Which seem to you to be most expectable? Explain.

3. Interview a scientist, mathematician, inventor, or entrepreneur. Relate the patterns in the chapter to the life of a person in a biography you have read.

4. The aesthetic appreciation of any domain by the person doing work in the domain seems to be its most salient feature. Describe your aesthetic appreciation of science or mathematics.

5. Why are scientists likened to religious people in their mysticism?

6. Describe your own experience as a science or mathematics student in relation to the patterns of creative lives in science.

7. A characteristic of inventors is their propensity to tinker. Why should tinkering lead to inventing?

8. If you were to invent something, what would you invent?

9. If you were to start a business, what business would you start?

10. Discuss gender with regard to science, math, invention, or entrepreneurialism.

CHAPTER 9—Musicians, Composers, and Conductors

1. What is the difference between musical creativity and musical ability?

2. What is the difference between musical intelligence and performing ability?

3. Discuss Copeland's statement that women can't be composers because they have difficulty thinking abstractly.

4. Why is it important in musical development that the family have some history in musical appreciation, performance, or amateur participation?

5. Do you believe that a person can become a musician without family involvement in the development of the talent? Give examples. Explain.

6. Interview a musician, conductor, or composer with regard to the findings in this chapter.

7. Discuss your own musical past and why you stopped playing, if you did.

8. Why are people so picky about their music?

9. Why do people often become arrested in their musical appreciation development with the music that was popular when they were young?

10. List and briefly discuss five ways a person can be creative musically.

11. Look at the childhood of a favorite rock star or popular musician. How is it different and how is it similar to the childhoods of classical musicians?

CHAPTER 10—Physical Performers: Actors, Dancers, and Athletes

1. Why do people forget the name of the character a movie actor played and describe the performance as a "Meryl Streep movie" or a "Robert de Niro movie"? What does this have to do with the actor as shaman?

2. Explain why actors need interpersonal and intrapersonal intelligence.

3. Explain why actors need bodily-kinesthetic intelligence.

4. Look at the biography of a favorite actor (note this means females too); what were his/her formative influences or predictive behaviors?

5. Why have actors historically been "outsiders"?

6. True or false: A dancer must be very thin. Discuss.

7. Dancers and athletes have a tendency to retire with permanent injuries, just as football players do. Discuss injuries from dance or athletics with reference to yourself or someone you know.

8. Why is dance so gender-stereotyped as being more suitable for women and football gender-stereotyped as being more suitable for men?

9. Interview a dancer, actor, or athlete. What were his or her formative influences?

10. How are athletes creative?

CHAPTER 11—Encouraging Creativity

1. What do you think about Alice Miller's statement that creative people experience trauma in their childhoods but they also have some warm person with which to be close?

2. Compare and contrast your school experiences with those of the contemporary American writers discussed in the chapter.

3. Tell a story about how you or someone you know acquired intrinsic motivation to be creative.

4. How is extrinsic motivation also important in creativity?

5. Discuss a time when great emotion helped you to be more creative.

6. Discuss how childhood play shaped the creativity of you or someone you know.

CHAPTER 12—How Parents and Teachers Can Nurture Creativity

1. Discuss three of the items on the list in the chapter with relationship to your own development or with relationship to the development of some-one you know.

2. How do you as a teacher nurture creativity? Do any items on the list apply?

3. How do you as a parent nurture creativity? Do any items on the list apply?

References

Abbs, P. (1989). *A is for aesthetic.* New York: Falmer Press.

Abell, A. (1946). *Talks with the great composers.* Garmisch-Partenkirchen, Germany: G.E. Schroeder-Verlag.

Adler, S. (1970). In T. Cole and H. Chinoy (Eds). (1970). *Actors on acting* (pp. 601-605). New York: Crown.

Aizenstat, S. (1995). Jungian psychology and the world unconscious. In T. Roszak, M.E. Gomes, and A.D. Kanner (Eds.), *Ecopsychology: Restoring the earth and healing the mind* (pp. 92-100). San Francisco, CA: Sierra Club Books.

Albert, R. (1975). Toward a behavioral definition of genius. *American Psychologist, 30*, 140-151.

Allen, J. S. (1992). Educating performers. *The American Scholar, 61* (2), 197-209.

Alter, J. (1984a). A factor analysis of new and standardized instruments to measure the creative potential and high-energy action preference of performing arts students. A preliminary investigation. *Personality and Individual Differences, 5*, 693-699.

Alter, J. (1984b). Creativity profile of university and conservatory dance students. *Journal of Personality Assessment, 48*, 153-158.

Amabile, T. (1989). *Growing up creative: Nurturing a lifetime of creativity.* New York: Crown.

Amabile, T. (1983). *The social psychology of creativity.* New York: Springer-Verlag.

Anderson, M.B., Denson, E.L., Brewer, B.W., and Van Raalte, J.L. (1994). Disorders of personality and mood in athletes: Recognition and referral. *Applied Sport Psychology, 6*, 168-184.

Andreason, N. (1987). Creativity and mental illness: Prevalence rates in writers and their first-degree relatives. *American Journal of Psychiatry, 144*, 1288-1292.

Andreason, N. and Canter, A. (1974). The creative writer: Psychiatric symptoms and family history. *Comprehensive Psychiatry, 15*, 123-31.

Anshel, M.H., and Porter, A. (1996). Self-regulatory characteristics of competitive swimmers as a function of skill level and gender. *Journal of Sport Behavior, 19* (2), 91-110.

Argulewicz, E.N. (1985). Review of the Scales for Rating the Behavioral Characteristics of Superior Students. In [Buros Institute of Mental Measurements]. *The Ninth Mental Measurements Yearbook* (Vol. II, pp. 1311-1312). Lincoln, NE: The University of Nebraska Press.

Arieti, S. (1976). *Creativity: The magic synthesis.* New York: Basic.

Armstrong, T. (1995). *Multiple intelligences in the classroom.* Arlington, VA: Association for Supervision and Curriculum Development.

Arnheim, D. (1975). Dance injuries: Their prevention and care. St. Louis: C.V. Mosby.

Artress, L. (1995). *Walking the sacred path: Rediscovering the labyrinth as a spiritual tool.* New York: Riverhead Books.

Baer, J. (1994). Performance assessments of creativity: Do they have long-term stability? *Roeper Review, 17* (1), 7-11.

Baer, J. (1993/1994). Why you shouldn't trust creativity tests. *Educational Leadership, 51* (4), 80-83.

Baer, J. (1991). Generality of creativity across performance domains. *Creativity Research Journal, 4* (1), 234-243.

Bagley, M., and Hess, K. (1983). 200 ways of using imagery in the classroom. New York: Trillium.

Baird, L. L. (1985). Do grades and tests predict adult accomplishment? *Research in Higher Education, 23* (1), 3-85.

Bakker, F. (1988). Personality differences between young dancers and non-dancers. *Personality and Individual Differences, 9*, 121-131.

Bamberger, J. (1986). Cognitive issues in the development of musically gifted children. In R. Sternberg and J. Davidson (Eds.), *Conceptions of giftedness* (pp. 388-415). New York: Cambridge.

Bariaud, F. (1988). Age differences in children's humor. *Journal of Children in Contemporary Society, 20*, 15-45.

Barron, F. (1968). *Creativity and personal freedom.* New York: Van Nostrand.

Barron, F. (1972). *Artists in the making.* New York: Seminar Press.

Barron, F. (1995). *No rootless flower: An ecology of creativity.* Cresskill, NJ: Hampton Press.

Bates, B. (1987). *The way of the actor.* Boston: Shambhala.

Bateson, M.C. (1989). *Composing a life*. New York: Atlantic Monthly Press.

Belenky, M.F., Clinch, B.M., Goldberger, N.R., and Tarule, J.M. (1986). *Women's ways of knowing*. New York: Basic.

Bell, Q. (1972). *Virginia Woolf: A biography*. New York: Harcourt Brace Jovanovich.

Benbow, C. (1992). Mathematical talent: Its nature and consequences. In N. Colangelo, S. Assouline, and D. Ambroson (Eds.), *Talent development: Proceedings from the 1991 Henry B. And Jocelyn Wallace National Research Symposium on Talent Development* (pp. 99-123). Unionville, NY: Trillium Press.

Benbow, C., and Lubinski, D. (1995). Optimal development of talent: Respond educationally to individual differences in personality. *The Educational Forum, 59* (4), 381-392.

Bergson, H. (1976). The possible and the real. in A. E. Rothenberg, and C. Hausman (Eds.), *The creativity question* (pp. 292-295). Trans. M. Andison. Durham, NC: Duke University Press. (Original translation published 1946.)

Bernstein, D.K. (1986). The development of humor: Implications for assessment and intervention. *Topics in Language Disorders, 6*, 65-71.

Bernstein, J.E. (and Blue, R.). (1990). *Judith Resnik: Challenger astronaut*. New York: Dutton.

Berryman, J. (1950). *Stephen Crane*. New York: William Sloane Associates.

Blanshard, B. (1976). The teleology of the creative act. In A. Rothenberg and C. Hausman, (Eds.), *The creativity question* (pp. 97-103). Durham, NC: Duke University Press. (Original work published 1964).

Block, J., and Kremen, A.M. (1996). IQ and ego-resiliency: Conceptual and empirical connections and separateness. *Journal of Personality and Social Psychology, 70* (2), 349-31.

Bloom, B. (Ed.). (1985). *The development of talent in young people*. New York: Ballantine.

Bloom, B. (1986). The hands and feet of genius. *Educational Leadership, 43*, 70-77.

Blumberg, S. A. and Panos, L. G. (1990). *Edward Teller: Giant of the golden age of physics*. New York: Macmillan.

Bogen, J. and Bogen, G. (1969). The other side of the brain III: The corpus callosum and creativity. *Bulletin of the Los Angeles Neurological Societies, 34.* Los Angeles: Los Angeles Society of Neurology and Psychiatry.

Bold, A. (Ed.). (1982). *Drink to me only: The prose (and cons) of drinking.* London: Robin Clark.

Bookspan, M. and Yodkey, R. (1981). *Andre Previn: A biography.* New York: Doubleday.

Borland, J. (1986). A note on the existence of certain divergent-production abilities. *Journal For The Education of the Gifted, 9* 239-51.

Bowers, N. (1990). The contest racket. *Poets and Writers, 18*, 37-39.

Boyd, J. With Warren, H.G. (1992). *Musicians in tune: Seventy-five contemporary musicians discuss the creative process.* New York: Simon and Schuster.

Braisted, J., Mellin, L., Gong, E., and Irwin, C. (1985). The adolescent ballet dancer: Nutritional practices and characteristics associated with anorexia nervosa. *Journal* of Adolescent Health Care, 6, 376-371.

Brandwein, P. (1955). *The gifted student as future scientist.* New York: Harcourt, Brace, and World.

Brennan, M. (1982). Relationship between creative ability in dance and selected creative attributes. *Perceptual and Motor Skills, 55,* 47-56.

Brennan, M. (1985). Dance creativity tests and the Structure-of-Intellect model. *Journal of Creative Behavior, 19,* 185-190.

Brodsky, M. A. (1993). Successful female corporate managers and entrepreneurs: Similarities and differences. *Group and Organization Management, 18*(3) 366-378.

Brody, L. (1989, Nov.). *Characteristics of extremely mathematically talented females.* Paper presented at National Association for Gifted Children Conference, Cincinnati, Ohio.

Brook, P. (1989). The act of possession. In T. Cole and H.Chinoy (Eds.). (1970). *Actors on acting* (pp. 223-229). NewYork: Crown.

Brooks-Gunn, J., Burrow, C., and Warren, M. (1988). Attitudes toward eating and body weight in different groups of female adolescent athletes. *International Journal of Eating Disorders*, 7, 749-757.

Brooks-Gunn, J., and Warren, M. (1985). The effects of delayed menarche in different contexts: Dance and nondance students. *Journal of Youth and Adolescence, 14*, 285-300.

Brooks-Gunn, J., Warren, M. and Hamilton, L. (1987). The relation of eating problems and amenorrhea in ballet dancers. *Medicine-and-Science-in-Sports-and-Exercise, 19* (1), 41-44.

Brown, F. (1968). Bereavement and lack of a parent in childhood. In E. Miller (Ed.), *Foundations of Child Psychiatry*. Oxford, England: Pergemon.

Brown, K. (1990). *You'd never know it from the way I talk: Lectures.* Ashland, O: Ashland Poetry Press.

Brown, M. (1988, Aug). *Transpersonal psychology: Exploring the frontiers in human resource development.* Paper presented at the Annual Meeting of the American Psychological Association, Atlanta, Georgia.

Bryant, J. and Zillman, D. (1989). Using humor to promote learning in the classroom. In McGhee, P. (Ed.). *Humor and children's development* (pp. 49-78). Binghamton, NY: Haworth Press.

Buchanan, D. and Bandy, C. (1984). Jungian typology of 37 prospective psychodramatists: Myers-Briggs Type Indicator analysis of applicants for psychodrama training. *Psychological Reports, 55,* 599-606.

Buckle, R. (1988). *George Balanchine, ballet master.* New York: Random House.

Bulfinch, T. (1855). *Bulfinch's mythology: The age of fable.* Boston: S.W. Tilton.

Buttsworth, L. M., and Smith, G. A. (1995). Personality of Australian performing musicians by gender and by instrument. *Personality and Individual Differences, 18*(5), 595-603

Cameron, J. (1992). *The artist's way: A spiritual path to higher creativity.* Los Angeles, CA: Jeremy Tarcher.

Campbell, D.T. (1960). Blind variation and selective retention in creative thought as in other knowledge processes. *Psychological Review, 67,* 380-400.

Campbell, J. (1968). *The masks of god: Creative mythology.* New York: Viking.

Campbell, L., Campbell, B., and Dickinson, D. (1992). *Teaching and learning through multiple intelligences.* Stanwood, WA: New Directions for Learning.

Cannon, W. (1945). *The role of hunches. The way of an investigator.* New York: W. W. Norton.

Cattell, R. and Cattell, M.C. (1969). *Handbook for the High School Personality Questionnaire (HSPQ).* Champaign, IL: Institute for Personality and Ability Testing.

Chafe, W. (1987). Humor as a disabling mechanism. *American Behavioral Scientist, 30,* 16-26.

Christopher. (1997). *Released from the past.* Recording on compact disc. Berea, OH: Shirtless Records.

Citino, D. (1990). *The house of memory.* Columbus, OH: Ohio State

University Press.

Clark, R. (1971). *Einstein: The life and times.* New York: World Publishing.

Cohen, L. (1989). A continuum of adaptive creative behaviors. *Creativity Research Journal, 2,* 169-183.

Colangelo, N., Kerr, B., Huesman, R., Hallowell, K., and Gaeth, J. (1992). The development of a scale to identify mechanical inventiveness. *Talent development: Proceedings from the Henry B. and Jocelyn Wallace National Research Symposium on Talent Development* (233-239). Unionville, NY: Trillium Press.

Coleridge, S.T. (1817). *Biographia literaria,* I. London: Rest Fenner.

Coles, R. (1989). *The call of stories: Teaching and the moral imagination.* Boston: Houghton Mifflin.

Collingwood, R. (1976). Consciousness and attention in art. in A. Rothenberg, and C. Hausman, (Eds.), *The creativity question* (pp. 334-343). Durham, NC: Duke University Press. (Original work published 1938).

Cooper, E. (1991). A critique of six measures for assessing creativity. *Journal of Creative Behavior, 25* (3), 194-204.

Cowger, H., and Torrance, E.P. (1982). Further examination of the quality of changes in creative functioning resulting from meditation (Zazen) training. *Creative Child And Adult Quarterly, 7,* 211-217.

Crabbe, A., and Betts, G. (1990). *Creating more creative people II.* Greely, CO: Autonomous Learner Press.

Crews, H. (1987). From *A childhood: The biography of a place.* In D. McCullough (Ed.). American childhoods (pp. 327-344). Boston: Little, Brown.

Croce, A. (1990, Oct. 15). Angel. *The New Yorker,* pp. 124-127.

Croce, B. (1976). Intuition and expression in art. in A.Rothenberg and C. Hausman, (Eds.), *The creativity question* (pp. 327-333). Durham, NC: Duke University Press.(Original work published 1909).

Cross, J.W. (1903). *George Eliot's life as related in her letters and journals.* New York and London: Abbey.

Csikszentmihalyi, M. (1988). Society, culture, and person: systems view of creativity. In R. Sternberg (Ed.), *The nature of creativity* (pp. 325-339). New York: Cambridge.

Csikszentmihalyi, M. (1990). *Flow.* New York: Cambridge.

Csikszentmihalyi, M. (1993). *The evolving self: A psychology for the third millenium.* New York: Harper Collins.

Csikszentmihalyi, M. (1995). *Creativity.* New York: Harpercollins.

Csikszentmihalyi, M., Rathunde, K., and Whalen, C. (1993). *Talented teenagers: The roots of success and failure.* New York: Cambridge University Press.

Dabrowski, K. (1965). *Personality shaping through positive disintegration.* Boston: Little Brown.

Dabrowski, K., and Piechowski, M. M. (1977). *Theory of levels of emotional development.* Oceanside, N.Y.: Dabor.

Dash, J. (1988). *A life of one's own: Three gifted women and the men they married.* New York: Paragon House.

Davidson, J. (1992). Insights about giftedness: The role of problem solving abilities. In N. Colangelo, S. Assouline, and D. Ambroson (Eds.), *Talent Development: Proceedings of the 1991 Henry and Jocelyn Wallace National Research Symposium on Talent Development* (pp. 125-142). Unionville, NY: Trillium Press.

Davis, G. A. (1981). *Creativity is forever.* Cross Plains, WI: Badger Press.

Davis, G.A. (1989). Testing for creative potential. *Contemporary Educational Psychology, 14,* 257-274.

Davis, G.A. and Rimm, S.G. (1980). *Group inventory for finding interests. (II).* Watertown, WI: Educational Assessment Service.

Davis, G.A. and Rimm, S.B. (1982). Group inventory for finding interests (GIFFI) I and II: Instruments for identifying creative potential in the junior and senior high school. *Journal of Creative Behavior, 16,* 50-57.

deBono, E. (1970). *Lateral thinking.* New York: Harper Colophon.

deBono, E. (1978). *CoRT thinking lesson series.* Blanford Forum, Dorset, UK: Direct Education Services.

de Mille, A. (1980). *America dances.* New York: Macmillan.

Dewey, J. (1934). *Art and experience.* New York: Putnam. *Directory of American Poets and Fiction Writers.* (1989-1990). New York: Poets and Writers, Inc.

Dollard, P. (1987). A review of *The Three-Week Trance Diet. Small Press, 4* (4), 25.

Dudek, S., and Hall, W. (1991). Personality consistency: Eminent architects 25 years later. *Creativity Research Journal, 4,* 213-231.

Duke, P., and Turan, K. (1987). *Call me Anna.* New York: Bantam

Dyce, J. A., and O'Connor, B. P. (1994). The personalities of popular musicians. *Psychology of Music, 22*(2) 168-173.

Eberle, B. (1982). *Visual thinking.* Buffalo: D.O.K.

Eccles, J. (1985). Model of students' mathematics enrollment decisions. *Educational Studies in Mathematics, 16,* 311-314.

Eccles, J., and Harold, R.D. (1992). Gender differences in educational and occupational patterns among the gifted. In N. Colangelo, S.G. Assouline, and D. Ambroson (Eds.), *Talent development: Proceedings of the 1991 Henry B. and Jocelyn Wallace National Research Symposium on Talent Development* (2-30). Unionville, NY: Trillium Press.

Edwards, A. (1975). *Judy Garland.* New York: Simon and Schuster.

Edwards, B. (1979). *Drawing on the right side of the brain.* Los Angeles: Tarcher.

Ehrenzweig, A. (1976). Unconscious scanning and dedifferentiation in artistic perception. in A. Rothenberg and C. Hausman, (Eds.), *The creativity question* (pp. 149-152). Durham, NC: Duke University Press. (Original work published 1967).

Einbond, B. (1979). *The coming indoors and other poems.* Tokyo: Charles E. Tuttle.

Els, S. M. (1994). *Into the deep: A writer's look at creativity.* Portsmouth, MA: Heinemann.

Erikson, J. (1988). *Wisdom and the senses: The way of creativity.* New York: W. W. Norton.

Ephron, N. (1983). A few words about breasts. In M. Richler (Ed.), *The best of modern humor* (pp. 467-475). New York: Knopf.

Estés, C. P. (1992). *Women who run with the wolves: Myths and stories of the wild woman archetype.* New York: Ballantine Books.

Estés, C. P. (1991). *The creative fire: Myths and stories about the ycles of creativity.* Jungian Storyteller Series. Audiotapes.

Ewen, D. (1968). *The man with the baton: The story of conductors and their orchestras.* Freeport, NY: Book for Libraries Press.

Fabrizi, M.S. and Pollio, H.B. (1987). Are funny teenagers creative? *Psychological Reports, 61,* 751-761.

Farrell, S. (1990). *Holding on to the air.* New York: Summit.

Feldhusen, J. (1995). Talent development v. gifted education. *The Educational Forum, 59* (4), 34-349.

Feldhusen, J., and Clinkenbeard, P. (1986). Creativity instructional materials: A review of research. *Journal of Creative Behavior, 20,* 176-188.

Feldhusen, J. F., and Treffinger, D. J. (1985). *Creative thinking and problem solving in gifted education.* Dubuque, IA: Kendall/Hunt.

Feldman, D.H. (1982). A developmental framework for research with gifted children. In D. Feldman (Ed.), *New directions for child development: Developmental approaches to* giftedness and creativity, 17, (pp. 31-46).

San Francisco: Jossey-Bass.

Feldman, D.H., with Lynn Goldsmith. (1986). *Nature's gambit: Child prodigies and the development of human potential.* New York: Basic.

Feldman, D.H. (1988). Dreams, insights, and transformations. In R. Sternberg (Ed.), *The nature of creativity* (pp. 271-297). New York: Cambridge.

Feldman, D.H. (1990, November). *Universal to unique: Developmental domains of giftedness.* Paper presented at National Association for Gifted Children Conference, Little Rock, Arkansas.

Feldman, D.H., (1994). *Beyond Universals in Cognitive Development.* Second Edition. Norwood, NJ: Ablex.

Feldman, D.H., Csikszentmihalyi, M., and Gardner, H. (1994). *Changing the world: A framework for the study of creativity.* Westport, CT: Praeger.

Feldman, D.H., and Piirto,J. (1995). Parenting talented children. In M. Bornstein (Ed.), *Handbook of Parenting, I* (285-304). Hillside, NJ: Erlbaum.

Ferucci, P. (1990). *Inevitable grace.* Los Angeles: Tarcher.

Findlay, C. and Lumsden, C. (1988). *The creative mind.* London: Academic Press.

Foley, P. (1986). *The dual role experience of artist mothers.* Unpublished doctoral dissertation. Northwestern University, IL.

Foley, P. (1996). Artist mothers. *Advanced Development 7*, 2-23.

Fitzgibbon, C. (1965). *The life of Dylan Thomas.* Boston: Little, Brown.

Friend, T. (1990, December 9). Rolling Boyle. *New York Times Magazine*, pp. 50, 64-68.

Freud, S. (1976). Creative writers and daydreaming. in A. Rothenberg and C. Hausman, (Eds.), *The creativity question* (pp. 48-52). Durham, NC: Duke University Press. (Original work published 1908.)

Fuller, B. (1981). *Critical path.* New York: St. Martin's.

Fuller, B. (1983). *Grunch of giants.* New York: St. Martin's.

Galton, F. (1976). Genius as inherited. in A. Rothenberg and C.Hausman, (Eds.), *The creativity question* (pp. 42-47). Durham, NC: Duke University Press. (Original work published 1869.)

Gardner, H. (1982). *Art, mind, and brain.* New York: Basic.

Gardner, H. (1983). *Frames of mind.* New York: Basic.

Gardner, H. (1985). *The mind's new science: A history of the cognitive revolution.* New York: Basic.

Gardner, H. (1988). Creative lives and creative works: A synthetic scientific approach. In R. Sternberg (Ed.), *The nature of creativity* (pp. 298-321). New York: Cambridge University Press.

Gardner, H. (1989, December). Learning Chinese style. *Psychology Today*, pp. 54-56.

Gardner, H. (1993). *Creating Minds: An anatomy of creativity seen through the lives of Freud, Einstein, Picasso, Stravinsky, Eliot, Graham, and Gandhi*. New York: Basic Books.

Gardner, H., with the collaboration of Laskin, E. (1995). *Leading Minds: An anatomy of leadership*. New York: Basic Books. Basic Books Paperback with a new introduction, 1996

Gardner, H. (1997). *Extraordinary Minds: Portraits of Exceptional Individuals and an Examination of our Extraordinariness*. New York: Basic Books.

Gardner, J. (1978). *On moral fiction*. New York: Basic.

Garfield, P. (1974). *Creative dreaming*. New York: Ballantine.

Gawain, S. (1978). *Creative visualization*. New York: Bantam.

Getty, J.P. (1976). *The autobiography of J. Paul Getty*. New York: Prentice Hall.

Getzels, J. (1987). Creativity, intelligence, and problem finding: Retrospect and prospect. In S. Isaksen (Ed.), *Frontiers of Creativity Research* (pp. 88-102). Buffalo, NY: Bearly Ltd.

Getzels, J., and Csikszentmihalyi, M. (1976). *The creative vision: A longitudinal study of problem finding in art*. New York: Wiley.

Getzels, J., and Jackson, P. (1962) *Creativity and intelligence: Exporations with gifted students*. New York: Wiley.

Ghiselin, B. (Ed.). (1952). *The creative process*. New York: Mentor.

Gilligan, C. (1990, April). *Invited address*. Paper presented at the meeeting of the American Educational Research Association, Boston, Mass.

Gilligan, C., Lyons, N.P., and Hanmer, T.J. (Eds.). (1990). *Making connections: The relational worlds of adolescent girls at Emma Willard School*. Cambridge, Mass: Harvard University Press.

Glass, P. (1987). *Music by Philip Glass*. New York: Harper and Row.

Gleick, J. (1992). *Genius: The life and science of Richard Feynman*. New York: Vintage.

Glover, J. S., Ronning, R.R., and Reynolds, C. R. (1989). *Handbook of creativity*. New York: Plenum.

Goertzel, V., and Goertzel, M.G. (1962). *Cradles of eminence*. Boston: Little, Brown.

Goertzel, B., and Goertzel, M.G., and Goertzel, T. (1978). *Three hundred emi-

nent personalities: A psychosocial analysis of the famous. San Francisco: Jossey-Bass.

Goldberg, N. (1986). *Writing down the bones.* New York: Quality Paperbacks.

Goleman, D. (1995). *Emotional intelligence.* New York: Bantam.

Gondola, J. (1987). The effects of a single bout of aerobic dancing on selected tests of creativity. *Journal of Social Behavior and Personality, 2,* 275-278.

Gordon, W. (1961). *Synectics: The development of creative capacity.* New York: Harper and Row.

Gough, H.G. (1952). *Adjective Check List.* Palo Alto, CA: Consulting Psychologists Press.

Gough, H.G. (1979). A creative personality scale for the Adjective Check List. *Journal of Personality and Social Psychology, 37,* 1398-1405.

Gough, H.G., and Heilbrun, A.B. (1983). *The Adjective Check List Manual.* Palo Alto, CA: Consulting Psychologists Press.

Gourley, T.J. (1981). Adapting the varsity sports model for non-psychomotor gifted students. *Gifted Child Quarterly, 25,* 164-166.

Gowan, J. (1972). *Development of the creative individual.* San Diego, CA: Robert R. Knapp.

Green, J. (1961). *Diary: 1928-1957.* New York: Carroll and Graf.

Greer, G. (1979). *The obstacle race: The fortunes of women painters and their work.* New York: Farrar Straus Giroux.

Gruber, H. (1982). *Darwin on man.* 2nd ed. Chicago: University of Chicago Press.

Gruber, H. (1982). On the hypothesized relation between giftedness and creativity. In D. Feldman (Ed.). *New directions for child development: Developmental approaches* to giftedness and creativity (pp. 7-29). San Francisco: Jossey-Bass.

Gruber, H., and Davis, S. (1988). Inching our way up Mount Olympus: the evolving-systems approach to creative thinking. In Sternberg, R. (Ed.), *The nature of creativity: Contemporary psychological perspectives* (pp 243-270). New York: Cambridge University Press.

Gruen, J. (1988). *People who dance.* Princeton, NJ: Princeton Book Co.

Guilford, J.P. (1950). Creativity. *American Psychologist, 5,* 444-454.

Guilford, J.P. (1967). *The nature of human intelligence.* New York: McGraw-Hill.

Guilford, J.P. (1970). Traits of creativity. in Vernon, P. E. (Ed.), *Creativity* (p. 167). London Harmondsworth: Penguin.

Guilford, J.P. (1988). Some changes in the Structure-Of-Intellect model. *Educational and Psychological Measurement, 48,* 1-6.

Gulbenkian Report (1978). *The arts in schools.* London: Calouste Gulbenkian Foundation.

Halperin, J. (1986). *The life of Jane Austen.* Baltimore: Johns Hopkins.

Halpin, G. and Halpin, G. (1973). The effect of motivation on creative thinking abilities. *Journal of Creative Behavior, 7,* 51-53.

Hamacheck, D. (1990). *Psyychology in teaching, learning, and growth.* 4th edition. Boston: Allyn and Bacon.

Hanson, S.L. (1996). *Lost talent: Women in the sciences.* Philadelphia, PA: Temple University Press.

Hanson, L., and Hanson, E. (1954). *Noble savage: The life of Paul Gauguin.* New York: Random House.

Harman, W., and Rheingold, H. (1984). *Higher creativity: Liberating the unconscious for breakthrough insights.* New York: Houghton Mifflin.

Haskins, J. (1987). *Black music in America: A history through its people.* New York: Crowell.

Hausman, C. (1976). Creativity and rationality. in A. Rothenberg and C. Hausman, (Eds.), *The creativity question* (pp. 343-351.) Durham, NC: Duke University Press. (Original work published 1964.)

H'Doubler, M. (1968). *Dance: A creative art experience.* Madison, WI: The University of Wisconsin Press.

Heausler, N. and Thompson, B. (1988). Structure of the Torrance Tests of Creative Thinking. *Educational and Psychological Measurement, 48,* 463-468.

Helson, R. (1983). Creative mathematicians. In R. Albert (Ed.), *Genius and eminence: The social psychology of creativity and exceptional achievement* (p. 211-230). London: Pergamon Press.

Hennessey, B.A. (1997). Teaching for creative development: A social psychological approach. In N. Colangelo and G.A.Davis (Eds.), *Handbook of gifted education,* 2nd Ed. (282-291). Needham Hts., MA: Allyn and Bacon.

Hennessey, B. A., and Amabile, T.M. (1988). Storytelling as a means of assessing creativity. *Journal of Creative Behavior, 22,* 235-247.

Hillesum, E. (1985). *An interrupted life: The diaries of Etty Hillesum,* 1941-1943. New York: Washington Square Press.

Hillman, J. (1996). *The soul's code: In search of character and calling.* New York: Random House.

Hocevar, D. (1980). Intelligence, divergent thinking, and creativity. *Intelligence, 4*, 25-40.

Hoerr, T. R. (1996, Nov) Introducing the theory of Multiple Intelligences *NASSP Bulletin, 80* n583 p8-10.

Hofstadter, D. (1985). Metamagical themas. New York: Basic.

Hoge, R.D. (1988). Issues in the definition and measurement of the giftedness construct. *Educational Researcher, 16*, 22.

Hollander, L. (1987). Music, the creative process, and the path of enlightenment. *Roeper Review, 10*, (1) 28-32.

Hornby, R. (1994). *The end of acting: A radical view.* New York: Applause.

Horowitz, F. and Degan, M. (1985). *The gifted and talented: Developmental perspectives.* Washington, D.C.: American Psychological Association.

Howe, M. J., Davidson, J. W., Moore, D. G., and Sloboda, J. A. (1995). Are there early childhood signs of musical ability? *Psychology of Music, 23*(2) 162-176.

Hurwitz, A. (1983). The gifted and talented in art: A guide to program planning. Worcester, Ma: Davis.

Huxley, A. (1963). *The doors of perception.* New York: Harper and Row.

Isaksen, S. (Ed.). (1987). *Frontiers of creativity research: Beyond the basics.* Buffalo, NY: Bearly Limited.

Isaksen, S.G., Puccio, G.J., and Treffinger, D.J. (1993). An ecological approach to creativity research: Profiling for creative problem solving. *Journal of Creative Behavior*, 27(3), 149-170.

Jamison, J. With Kaplan, H. (1993). *Dancing spirit: An autobiography.* New York: Doubleday.

Jamison, K. (1993). *Touched with fire : Manic depressive illness and the artistic temperament.* New York: The Free Press.

Jamison, K. (1995). *An unquiet mind: A memoir of moods and madness.* New York: Vintage Books.

Jamison, K. R. (1995, February). Manic-depressive illness and creativity. *Scientific American*, pp. 62-67.

Jarvie, I. (1981). The rationality of creativity. in D. Dutton and M. Krausz (Eds.), *The concept of creativity in science and art* (pp. 109-128). The Hague: Martinus Mijhoff.

Jenkins-Friedman, R. (1992). Zorba's conundrum: Evaluative aspects of self-concept in talented individuals. *Quest, 3* (1), 1-7.

Jenkins-Friedman, R., and Tollefson, N. (1992). Resiliency in cognition and motivation: Its applicability to giftedness. In N. Colangelo, S. Assouline, and D. Ambroson (Eds.), *Talent development: Proceedings from the 1991 Henry B. And Jocelyn Wallace National Research Symposium on Talent Development* (pp. 325-333). Unionville, NY: Trillium Press.

John-Steiner, V. (1985). *Notebooks of the mind: Explorations of thinking.* New York: Harper and Row.

Jung, C.G. (1976). On the relation of analytical psychology to poetic art. in A. Rothenberg and C. Hausman, (Eds.), *The creativity question* (pp. 120-126.) Durham, NC: Duke University Press. (Original work published 1923.)

Jung, C.G. (1965). *Memories, dreams, reflections.* New York: Vintage.

Kaltsounis, B. and Honeywell, L. (1980). Instruments useful in studying creative behavior and creative talent. Part IV. Non-commercially available instruments. *Journal of Creative Behavior, 5,* 117-126.

Kant, I. (1952). Genius gives the rules. in A. Rothenberg and C. Hausman, (Eds.), *The creativity question* (pp. 37-41). Durham, NC: Duke University Press. (Original work published 1790.)

Karnes, F., Chauvin, J., and Trant, T. (1985). Comparison of personality profiles for intellectually gifted students and students outstanding in the fine and performing arts attending self-contained secondary schools. *Psychology in the Schools, 22,* 122-126.

Kemp, A.E. (1981a). The personality structure of the musician I: Identifying a profile of traits for the performer. *Psychology of Music, 9,* 3-14.

Kemp, A.E. (1981b). The personality structure of the musician II: Identifying a profile of traits for the composer. *Psychology of Music, 9,* 67-75.

Kemp, A.E. (1982a). The personality structure of the musician III: The significance of sex difference. *Psychology of Music, 10,* 48-58.

Kemp, A.E. (1982b). Personality traits of successful music teachers. *Psychology of Music,* Special Issue, 72-73.

Kets de Vries, M. (1996). The anatomy of the entrepreneur: Clinical observations. *Human Relations, 49* (7) 853-883.

Khatena, J. (1978). *The creatively gifted child.* New York: Vantage.

Khatena, J. and Torrance, E.P. (1973). Norms-technical manual: Thinking creatively with sounds and words. Lexington, MA: Personnel Press/Ginn.

Kilpatrick, A. (1996). *Of permanent value: The story of Warren Buffett.* Birmingham, AL: APKE.

Kingon, M. (1990, October 28). How Calvin Trillin changed my life. *New York Times Book Review,* p. 10.

Kirton, M. J. (1989). A theory of cognitive style. In M.J. Kirton (Ed.),

Adaptors and innovators: Styles of creativity and problem solving (pp. 1-36). London: Routledge.

Kizer, C. (1990). A muse. In L. Lyfshin (Ed.), *Lips unsealed* (pp. 26-32). Santa Barbara: Capra.

Klein, E. (1967). *A Comprehensive Etymological Dictionary of The English Language.* New York: Elsevier.

Knapp, R.H. (1962). Stylistic consistency among aesthetic preferences. Journal of *Projective Techniques and Personality Assessment, 16,* 61-65.

Koestler, A. (1964). *The act of creation.* New York: Macmillan.

Kogan, J. (1987). *Nothing but the best: The struggle for perfection at the Juilliard School.* New York: Random House.

Kough, J. (1961). *Practical programs for the gifted.* Chicago: Science Research Associates.

Kozinn, A. (April 11, 1991). Shulamit Ran and the Pulitzer Prize. *New York Times,* p. B4.

Krippner, S. and Murphy, G. (1973). Humanistic psychology and parapsychology. *Journal of Humanistic Psychology, 13,* (4), 2-24.

Kris, E. (1976). On preconscious mental processes. in A. Rothenberg and C. Hausman, (Eds.), The creativity question (pp. 135-142). Durham, NC: Duke University Press. (Original work published 1952.)

Krutetskii, V. (1976). *The psychology of mathematical abilities in schoolchildren.* In J. Wirszup and J. Kirkpatrick, (Eds.), J. Teller (Trans.). Chicago: University of Chicago Press. (Original work published 1968.)

Kubie, L. (1976). Creativity and neurosis. in A. Rothenberg and C. Hausman, (Eds.), *The creativity question* (pp. 143-148). Durham, NC: Duke University Press. (Original work published 1958.)

Langer, S.K. (1953). *Feeling and form.* New York: Charles Scribner's Sons.

Langer, S. K. (1957). *Problems of art.* New York: Charles Scribner's Sons.

Langley, P. and Jones, R. (1988). A computational model of scientific insight. In R. Sternberg (Ed.), *The nature of creativity.* (pp. 177-201). New York: Cambridge University Press.

Langan-Fox, J., and Roth, S. (1995). Achievement motivation and female entrepreneurs. *Journal of Occupational and Organizational Psychology, 68*(3), 209-218.

Lazear, D. (1994). *Multiple intelligence approaches to assesment: Solving the assessment conundrum.* Phoenix, AZ: Zephyr Press.

Lebrecht, N. (1991). *The maestro myth: Great conductors in pursuit of power.* New York: Birch Lane Press.

Lee, H. (1940). A theory concerning free creation in the inventive arts. *Psychiatry, 3.* The William Alanson White Psychiatric Foundation, Inc.

Leonard, L. (1989). *Witness to the fire: Creativity and the evil of addiction.* Boston: Shambhala.

Lewis, C.S. (1955). *Surprised by joy: The shape of my early life.* New York: Harcourt, Brace, Jovanovich.

Lissitz, R., and Willhoft, J. (1985). A methodological study of the Torrance Tests of Creativity. *Journal of Educational Measurement, 22,* 1-11.

Loeb, K. (1975). Our women artist/teachers need our help: On changing language, finding cultural heritage, and building self image. *Art Education, 18,* 10.

Lombroso, C. (1895). The man of genius. London: Charles Scribner's Sons. Lowenkopf, E., and Vincent, L. (1982). The student ballet dancer and anorexia. *Hillside Journal of Clinical Psychiatry, 5,* 53-64.

Lozanov, G. (1978). *Suggestology and outlines of suggestopedia* (psychic studies). New York: Gordon and Breach.

Lysy, K.Z., and Piechowski, M.M. (1983). Personal growth: An empirical study using Jungian and Dabrowskian measures. *Genetic Psychology Monographs, 108,* 267-320.

MacKinnon, D. (1962). The nature and nurture of creative talent. *American Psychologist 17,* 484-95.

MacKinnon, D. (1978). *In search of human effectiveness: Identifying and developing creativity.* Buffalo, NY: Bearly Limited.

McAleer, N. (1989, April). On creativity: The roots of inspiration. *Omni,* p.42.

McConnell, J.V. (1982). *Understanding human behavior,* 6th Edition. New York: Harcourt.

McDonough, P. and McDonough, B. (1987). A survey of American colleges and universities on the conducting of formal courses in creativity. *Journal of Creative Behavior, 21,* 271-282.

McDonnell, D. and LeCapitaine, J. (1985). *The Effects of Group Creativity Training On Teachers' Empathy And Interactions With Students.* ERIC ED294858.

McGhee, P. (1988). The contribution of humor to children's social development. *Journal of Children in Contemporary Society, 20,* 119-134.

McGilligan, P. (1994). *Jack's life: A biography of Jack Nicholson.* New York: W.W. Norton.

Madigan, C., and Elwood, A. (1984). *Brainstorms and thunderbolts: How creative genius works.* New York: Macmillan.

Malina, J. (1983). In K. Malpede (Ed.), *Women in theatre* (pp.196-217). New York: Limelight.

Manes, S., and Andrews, P. (1993). *Gates: How Microsoft's mogul reinventeed an industry—and made himself the richest man in America.* New York: Doubleday.

Maritain, J. (1953). *Creative intuition in art and poetry.* Trustees of the National Gallery of Art, Washington, D.C. The A.W. Mellon Lectures in the Fine Arts. Bollingen series XXXV. Princeton, NJ: Princeton University Press.

Martindale, C. (1972). Father absence, psychopathology, and poetic eminence. *Psychological Reports, 31,* 843-84.

Maslow, A. (1968). *Creativity in self-actualizing people. Toward a psychology of being.* New York: Van Nostrand Reinhold Company.

Maslow, A. (1973). *The farther reaches of human nature.* London: Harmondsworth.

Mathieu, W.A. (1994). *The musical life: Reflections on what it is.* Boston, MA: Shambhala.

May, R. (1975). *The courage to create.* New York: Bantam.

Mednick, S. (1962). The associative basis of the creative process. *Psychological Review,* 220-232. Washington, D.C.: American Psychological Association.

Meeker, M. (1973). *Divergent production sourcebook.* Vida, OR: SOI Institute.

Meeker, M.N., and Meeker, R. (1975). *Structure of Intellect Learning Abilities Test—Examiner's manual.* El Segundo, CA: SOI Institute.

Mellow, J.R. (1974). *Charmed circle: Gertrude Stein and company.* New York: Praeger.

Miklus, S. (1989, April). Forum. *Omni,* p. 16.

Miles, B. (1989). *Ginsberg.* New York: Simon and Schuster.

Miller, A. (1987). *Timebends.* New York: Harper and Row.

Miller, A. (1990). *The untouched key: Tracing childhood trauma in creativity and destructiveness.* New York: Doubleday.

Miller, A. (1981). *Drama of the gifted child.* New York: Doubleday.

Miller, L. K. (1994) The "Savant Syndrome:" Exceptional Skill and Mental Retardation. In N. Colangelo, S.G. Assouline and D.L. Ambroson (Eds.) *Talent Development, Volume II: Proceedings from the 1993 Henry B. and Jocelyn Wallace National Research Symposium on Talent Development.*

Dayton: Ohio Psychology Press, pp. 215-238.

Miner, J. B. (1997). The expanded horizon for achieving entrepreneurial success. *Organizational Dynamics, 25*(3), 54-67.

Monson, K. (1983). *Alma Mahler: Musto genius.* Boston: Houghton Mifflin.

Morgan, C. (1933). *The emergence of novelty.* London: Williams and Norgate.

Morgan, D.L., Morgan, R.K., and Toth, J.M. (1992). Variation and selection: The evolutionary analogy and the convergence of cognitive and behavioral psychology. *The Behavior Analyst, 15*, 129-138.

Morrison, M., and Dungan, R. (1992). *The identification of creative thinking ability: A multifactored approach.* Columbus, OH: Ohio Department of Education, Gifted Education Research and Demonstration Project.

Morse, D. and Khatena, J. (1989). The relationship of creativity and life accomplishments. *Journal of Creative Behavior, 23*, 23-30.

Moustakas, C. (1967). *Creativity and conformity.* New York: Van Nostrand.

Murphy, E. (1991). *The developing child.* Palo Alto, CA: Consulting Psychologists Press.

Myers, I.B., and McCaulley, M.H. (1985). *Manual: A guide to the* development and use of the Myers-Briggs Type Indicator. Palo Alto, CA: Consulting Psychologists Press.

Myers, S. A. (1983). The Wilson-Barber Inventory of Childhood Memories and Imaginings: Children's form and norms for 1337 children and adolescents. *Journal of Mental Imagery, 7* (3) 83-94.

Nachmanovitch, S. (1990). *Free play: improvisation in life and art.* Los Angeles: Tarcher.

Navarre, J. Piirto (1978). *A study of creativity in poets.* Paper presented at National Association for Gifted Childlren Conference, Houston, Texas.

Navarre, J. Piirto (1979). Incubation as fostering the creative process. *Gifted Child Quarterly, 23,* 792-800.

Nietzsche, F. (1979). *Ecce homo.,* tr. R.J. Hollingdale. London: Harmondsworth.

Nixon, L. (1996). A comparative study of Charles Darwin and Therese of Lisieux. *Advanced Development, 7*, 81-100.

Noller, R.B., Parnes, S.J. and Biondi, A.M. (1976). *Creative actionbook.* New York: Scribners.

Nowell, E. (1960). *Thomas Wolfe: A biography.* New York: Doubleday and Co.

Oates, J.C. (1988). *(Woman) writer: Occasions and opportunities.* New York: Dutton.

O'Connell-Ross, P. (1993). *National Excellence: A case for developing America's talent*. U.S. Office of Education. Washington, D.C.

Olivier, L. (1967). In Burton, H. (Ed.), Great acting (pp. 23-32). New York: Hill and Wang. Reprinted in T. Cole and H. Chinoy (Eds.). (1970). Actors on acting (pp. 410-417). New York: Crown.

Osborn, A. F. (1963). Applied imagination. New York: Scribners.

Ostrander, S. (1979). Superlearning. New York: Delacourte.

Ornstein, R.E. (1993). *The roots of the self*. San Francisco, CA: Harper San Francisco.

Owens, H.M., and Hogan, J.D. (1983). Development of humor in children: a study of incongruity, resolution and operational thinking. Psychological Reports, 53, 477-478.

Oxford English Dictionary, 2nd Ed. (1989). Oxford: Clarendon Press.

Parloff, M.B., Datta, L., Kleiman, M., and Handlon, J.H. (1968). Personality characteristics which differentiate creative male adolescents and adults. Journal of Personality 36 (4), 528-552. Parnes, S. (1967). Creative behavior guidebook. New York: Scribners.

Parnes, S. (1981). The magic of your mind. Buffalo, NY: Creative Education Foundation.

Parnes, S. (1987). The Creative Studies Project. In S. Isaksen (Ed.), Frontiers Of Creativity Research: Beyond The Basics (pp. 156-188). Buffalo: Bearly.

Passarro, V. (May 19, 1991). Dangerous Don DeLillo. The New York Times Magazine, 34-38, 76.

Pendarvis, E., Howley, C., and Howley, A. (1990). *The abilities of gifted children*. Boston: Allyn and Bacon.

Perkins, D. (1981). *The mind's best work*. Boston: Harvard University Press.

Perkins, D. (1988). The possibility of invention. In R. Sternberg (Ed.), *The nature of creativity* (pp. 362-386). New York: Cambridge.

Petrie, T.A. (1993). Disordered eating in female collegiate gymnasts: Prevalence and personality/attitudinal correlates. *Journal of Sport and Exercise Psychology, 15*(4) 424-436

Pfeiffer, J.E. (1982). *The creative explosion: An inquiry into the origins of art and religion*. New York: Harper and Row.

Piechowski, M.M. (1975). A theoretical and empirical approach to the study of development. *Genetic Psychology Monographs, 92*, 231-297.

Piechowski, M.M. (1978). Self-actualization as a developmental structure: A profile of Antoine de Saint-Exupery. *Genetic Psychology Monographs,*

97, 181-242.

Piechowski, M.M. (1979). Developmental potential: In N. Colangelo and R. Zaffer (Eds.), *New voices in counseling the gifted* (pp. 25-57). Dubuque, IA: Kendall-Hunt.

Piechowski, M.M. (1990). Emotional development and emotional giftedness. In N. Colangelo and G.A. Davis (Eds.), *Handbook of gifted education*, (pp. 195-207). Needham Hts., MA: Allyn and Bacon.

Piechowski, M.M. (1997). Emotional giftedness: The measure of intrapersonal intelligence. In N. Colangelo and G.A. Davis (Eds.), *Handbook of gifted education*, 2nd Ed. (pp. 36-381). Needham Hts., MA: Allyn and Bacon.

Piechowski, M.M., and Tyska, C.A. (1982). Self-actualization profile of Eleanor Roosevelt, a presumed nontranscender. *Genetic Psychology Monographs, 105*, 95-153.

Piechowski, M.M., and Cunningham, K. (1985a). Patterns of overexcitability in a group of artists. *Journal Of Creative Behavior, 19*, 3. 153-174.

Piechowski, M.M., Silverman, L., and Falk, F. (1985b). Comparison of intellectually and artistically gifted on five dimensions of mental functioning. *Perceptual and Motor Skills, 60,* 539-549.

Piirto, J. (1985). *The three-week trance diet.* Columbus, OH: Carpenter Press.

Piirto, J. (1987). *The existence of writing prodigy.* Paper presented at the National Association for Gifted Children Conference, New Orleans.

Piirto, J. (1989a). Does writing prodigy exist? *Creativity Research Journal, 2,* 134-35.

Piirto, J. (1989b, May/June). Linguistic prodigy: Does it exist? *Gifted Children Monthly,* pp. 1-2.

Piirto, J. (1990). Profiles of creative adolescents. *Understanding Our Gifted, 2,* 1.

Piirto, J. (1990, March). Creative adolescents at a Governor's Institute. Paper presented at the Ohio Association For Gifted Children Conference, Columbus.

Piirto, J. (1991a). Encouraging creativity in adolescents. In J. Genshaft and M. Bireley (Eds.). *Understanding the gifted adolescent* (pp. 104-122). New York: Teachers College Press.

Piirto, J. (1991b). Why are there so few? (Creative women: visual artists, mathematicians, musicians). *Roeper Review, 13* (3), 142-147.

Piirto, J. (1992). The existence of writing prodigy: Children with extraordinary writing talent. In N. Colangelo, S.G. Assouline, and D. Ambroson

(Eds.), *Talent development: Proceedings of the 1991 Henry B. and Jocelyn Wallace National Research Symposium on Talent Development* (387-388). Unionville, NY: Trillium Press.

Piirto, J. (1994a). *Talented children and adults: Their development and education.* New York: Macmillan.

Piirto, J. (1994b). A few thoughts about actors. *Spotlight: Newsletter of the Visual and Performing Arts Division of the National Association for Gifted Children, 4* (1), 2-5.

Piirto, J. (1995a). Deeper and broader: The Pyramid of Talent Development in the context of the giftedness construct. *Educational Forum, 59* (4), 363-371.

Piirto, J. (1995b). *A location in the Upper Peninsula: Poems, stories, essays.* New Brighton, MN: Sampo Publishing.

Piirto, J. (1995c). *Themes in the lives of female creative writers at midlife.* Invited paper presented at the 1995 Henry B. And Jocelyn Wallace National Research Symposim on Talent Development. Iowa City, Iowa.

Piirto, J. (1996). Why does a writer write? Because. *Advanced Development, 7* (39-59).

Piirto, J. (1997a). *Between the memory and the experience.* 2nd. Ashland, OH: Sisu Press.

Piirto, J. (1997b). A survey of psychological studies in creativity. In A. Fishkin and B. Cramond (Eds.), *Investigating creativity in youth: Research and methods*, pp. 27-48.. Cresskill, NJ: Hampton Press.

Piirto, J. (Ed.) (1997c). *Five studies on talented adolescents.* Ashland University: Ashland, OH.

Piirto, J., and Fraas, J. (1995). Androgyny in the personalities of talented teenagers. *Journal of Secondary Gifted Education,* (2), 93-102.

Plato. The republic. In R. Ulrich (Ed.). (1954). *Three thousand years of educational wisdom: Selections from great documents* (pp. 31-62), Trans. P. Shorey. Cambridge: Harvard Univ. Press.

Plimpton. G. (Ed.). (1988). *Writers at work.* 8th series. New York: Penguin.

Plimpton, G. (Ed.). (1989). *Women writers at work.* New York: Penguin.

Poe, E. (1846, April.) The philosophy of composition. *Graham's Magazine of Literature and Art,28,* 4., pp. 163-64.

Polkow, D. (1988). Solti speaks: A rare and candid conversation with the Maestro (Part I). *Journal of the Conductors' Guild, 9* (1), 2-15.

Predock-Linnell, J. (1987). Comparison of Barron-Welsh Art Scales of artists and nonartists and between dancers of two training styles. *Perceptual and*

Motor Skills, 65, 729-730.

Project Vanguard: A manual for the identification of creatively gifted students. (1991). Ohio Department of Special Education.

Radford, J. (1990). *Child prodigies and exceptional early achievers.* New York: Macmillan/ The Free Press.

Random House Dictionary of the English Language. 2nd Ed. (1988). New York: Random House.

Rank, O. (1960). *Art and artist.* New York: Knopf.

Razik, T. (1970). Psychometric measurement of creativity. In P. Vernon (Ed.), *Creativity* (pp. 147-156). Harmondsworth: Penguin.

Redgrave, M. (1946). The Stanislavsky myth. *New Theatre. 3,* 16-18. Reprinted in T. Cole and H. Chinoy (Eds.), (1970). *Actors on acting* (pp. 403-408). New York: Crown.

Reed, H. (1985). *Getting help from your dreams.* Virginia Beach, VA: Inner Vision.

Reese, W. (1980). *Dictionary of philosophy and religion: Eastern and western thought.* New Jersey: Humanities Press.

Renzulli, J. (1978). What Makes Giftedness? Re-examining a definition. *Phi Delta Kappan, 60,* 180-184, 261.

Renzulli, J., Smith, L.H., White, A.J., Callahan, C.M., and Hartman, R.K. (1976). *Scales for Rating the Behavioral Characteristics of Superior Students.* Mansfield Center, CT: Creative Learning Press.

Renzulli, J. and Westberg, K. (1990, November) *The 1990 revision of the Scales For Rating the Behavioral Characteristics of Superior Students.* Paper presented at National Association for Gifted Children Conference, Little Rock, Arkansas.

Reynierse, J. H (1997). An MBTI model of entrepreneurism and bureaucracy: The psychological types of business entrepreneurs compared to business managers and executives. *Journal of Psychological Type, l 40,* 3-19.

Reynolds, F.C. (1997). *Reifying creativity during the adolescent passage.* Paper presented at Ashland University Ohio Summer Institute. July 13, 1997.

Reynolds, F.C. (1990). Mentoring artistic adolescents through expressive therapy. *Clearing House, 64,* 83-86.

Rico, G. (1983). *Writing the natural way: Using right brain techniques to release your expressive powers.* Los Angeles: Jeremy Tarcher.

Rico, G. (1991). *Pain and possibility: Writing your way through personal crisis.* Los Angeles: Jeremy Tarcher.

Rimm, S.B. (1986). *Underachievement syndrome: Causes and cures.* Watertown, WI: Apple Publishing Co.

Rimm, S. (1990, November). Identifying creativity: The characteristics approach. Paper presented at National Association for Gifted Children Conference, Little Rock, Arkansas.

Robinson, R. (1989). Georgia O'Keeffe: A Life. New York: Harper and Row.

Robinson, S., and Ritz, D. (1989). *Smokey: Inside my life.* New York: McGraw Hill.

Roe, A. (1952). The making of a scientist. New York: Dodd, Mead.

Roe, A. (1963). Psychological approaches to creativity in the sciences. in Coler, M. and Hughes, H. (1963). Essays on creativity in the sciences. New York: New York University Press.

Roe, A. (1975). Painters and painting. In C. Taylor and J. Getzels (Eds.), Perspectives in creativity (pp. 157-172). Chicago: Aldine.

Roedell, W., Jackson, N., and Robinson, H. (1980). Gifted young children. New York: Teachers College Press.

Rogers, C. (1954). Toward a theory of creativity. *ETC: A review of general semantics, 11,* 250-258. New York: International Society of General Semantics.

Root-Bernstein, R.S. (1987). Tools of thought: Designing an integrated curriculum for lifelong learners. *Roeper Review, 10* (1), 17-21.

Rosen, C.L. (1985). Review of Creative Activity Packet. In [Buros Institute of Mental Measurements] *The Ninth Mental Measurements Yearbook* (Vol. I, pp. 411-412). Lincoln, NE: The University of Nebraska Press.

Rosenthal, A., DeMers, S.T., Stilwell, W., Graybeal, S., and]Zins, J. (1983). Comparison of interrater reliability on the Torrance Tests of Creative Thinking for gifted and nongifted students. *Psychology in the Schools, 20,* 35-40.

Rosner, S., and Abt, L. (Eds.). (1970). *The creative experience.* New York: Grossman.

Rossman, J. (1931). *The psychology of the inventor: A study of the patentee.* Washington, DC: The Inventors Publishing Company.

Rothenberg, A. (1979). *The emerging goddess: The creative process in art, science, and other fields.* Chicago: University of Chicago Press.

Rothenberg, A. (1990). *Creativity and madness.* Baltimore, MD: Johns Hopkins University Press.

Rothenberg, A., and Hausman, C. (1976). *The creativity question.* Durham, NC: Duke University Press.

Rothenberg, A. and Hausman, C. (1988). A comment on *The nature of creativity*. *Creativity Research Journal, 1*, 123-124.

Rudolf, M. (1987). The conductor's dilemma: The hazards of being judged. *Journal of the Conductors' Guild, 8 (4)*, 98-106.

Rugg, H. (1963). *Imagination*. New York: Harper and Row.

Runco, M. (1986). Maximal performance on divergent thinking tests by gifted, talented, and nongifted children. *Psychology In The Schools, 23*, 308-315.

Runco, M. (1987). The generality of creative performance in gifted and nongifted children. *Gifted Child Quarterly, 31*, 121-125.

Runco, M. (Ed.) (1990a). *Divergent production*. Norwood, NJ: Ablex.

Runco, M. (Ed.) (1990b). *Theories of creativity*. Norwood, NJ: Ablex.

Runco, M. (Ed.) (1994). Ed.). *Problem finding, problem solving and creativity*. Norwood, NJ: Ablex.

Runco, M. (1997). Is every child gifted? *Roeper Review, 19* (4), 220-224.

Runco, M. and Albert, R. (1986). The threshold theory regarding creativity and intelligence: An empirical test with gifted and nongifted children. *The Creative Child And Adult Quarterly, 11*, 212-218.

Samples, B. (1976). *The metaphoric mind*. Reading, Mass: Addison-Wesley.

Santayana, G. (1896). *The sense of beauty: Being the outline of aesthetic theory*. New York: Dover Publications.

Sarton, M. (1973). *Journal of a solitude*. New York: W. W. Norton.

Sartre, J. (1947). *Existentialism*, tr. Bernard Frechtman. New York: The Philosophical Library.

Schactel, E. (1959). *On the development of affect, perception, attention, and memory*. New York: Basic Books, Inc.

Schank, R. (1988). *The creative attitude*. New York: Macmillan.

Schechner, R. (1993). *The future of ritual: Writings on culture and performance*. New York: Routledge.

Schechner, R. (1985). *Between theater and anthropology*. Philadelphia, PA: University of Pennsylvania Press.

Schickel, R. (1986). *Intimate strangers: The culture of celebrity*. New York: Fromm.

Schorer, M. (1961). *Sinclair Lewis*. New York: Random House.

Scribner, C. (1990, Dec. 9). 'I, who knew nothing, was in charge.' New York Times Book Review, pp. 1, 39.

Sears, P.S. (1979). The Terman studies of genius, 1922-1972. In A.H. Passow (Ed.), *The gifted and the talented: Their education and development* (pp. 75-96). The Seventy-eighth yearbook of the National Society For The

Study Of Education. Chicago: University of Chicago Press.

Sears, R. (1977). Sources of life satisfactions of the Terman gifted men. *American Psychologist, 32*, 119-128.

Schneiderman, L. (1988). *The literary mind: Portraits in pain and creativity.* New York: Insight.

Seifert, C.M., Meyer, D.E., Davidson, N., Patalano, A.L., and Yaniv, I. (1995). Demystification of cognitive insight: Opportunistic assimilation and the prepared-mind perspective. In R. Sternberg and J. Davidson (Eds.), *The nature of insight* (pp. 65-124). Cambridge, MA: The MIT Press.

Shallcross, D.J. (1985). *Teaching creative behavior: How to evoke creativity in children of all ages.* Buffalo, NY: Bearly Ltd.

Sheets, M. (1966). *The phenomenology of dance.* Madison, WI: University of Wisconsin Press.

Shekerjian, D. (1990). *Uncommon genius. New York:* Viking.

Sherry, Norman. (1989). *The life of Graham Greene, I.* New York: Viking.

Shone, R. (1984). *Creative visualization.* New York: Thorstons.

Silverman, L.K. (Ed.). (1993). *Counseling the gifted and talented.* Denver, CO: Love Publishing.

Simon, C. (1994, April 3) "Diagnosing the Muse: Science struggles to find a link between creativity and madness." *The Boston Globe,* Sunday, city edition.: Magazine, p. 10.

Simonton, D.K. (1975). Age and literary creativity: A cross-cultural and transhistorical survey. *Journal of Cross-Cultural Psychology, 6*, 259-277.

Simonton, D.K. (1984) *Genius, creativity, and leadership.* Cambridge, Mass. Harvard University Press.

Simonton, D.K. (1986). Biographical typicality, eminence and achievement styles. *Journal Of Creative Behavior, 20,* (1), 17-18.

Simonton, D.K. (1988). *Scentific genius: A psychology of science.* New York: Cambridge University Press.

Simonton, D.K. (1992). The child parents the adult: On getting genius from giftedness. Invited Paper. In N. Colangelo, S.G. Assouline, and D. Ambroson (Eds.), *Talent development: Proceedings of the 1991 Henry B. and Jocelyn Wallace National Research Symposium on Talent Development* (278-297). Unionville, NY: Trillium Press.

Simonton, D.K. (1995). *Greatness: Who makes history and why.* New York: The Guilford Press.

Simpson, E. (1982). *Poets in their youth.* New York: Random House.

Simpson, L. (1972). *North of Jamaica.* New York: Harper and Row.

Skinner, B.F. (1971). *Beyond freedom and dignity.* New York: Knopf.

Sloane, K.D., and Sosniak, L.A. (1985). The development of accomplished sculptors. In B. Bloom (Ed.), *Developing talent in young people* (pp. 90-138). New York: Ballantine.

Sloboda, J. A., Davidson, J. W., Howe, M. A., and Moore, D.G. (1996). The role of practice in the development of performing musicians. *British Journal of Psychology, 87*(2), 287-309

Solomon, D. (March 31, 1991). Elizabeth Murray: Celebrating paint. *New York Times Magazine*, p. 20-25, 40, 46.

Sosniak, L. (1985). Learning to be a concert pianist. In B.Bloom (Ed.), *Developing talent in young people* (pp. 19-66). New York: Ballantine.

Spearman, C. (1927). *The abilities of man.* New York: Macmillan.

Spoto, Donald. (1985). *The Kindness of strangers: The life of Tennessee Williams.* Boston: Little, Brown.

Stanislavsky, S. (1935/1964). *An actor prepares.* New York: Routledge.

Stanley, J. and Benbow, C. (1986). Youths who reason exceptionally well mathematically. In R. Sternberg and J. Davidson (Eds.), *Conceptions of giftedness* (pp. 361-387). New York: Cambridge University Press.

Stanton, D. (1991). An interview with John Irving. *Poets and Writers, 19* (3), 15-21.

Stearns, D. P. (1993). Interview with Salonen. *Stereo Review, 5*, 61.

Stein, M. (1953). Creativity and culture. *Journal of Psychology, 36*: 311-322.

Stein, M. (1986). *Gifted, talented, and creative young people: A guide to theory, teaching, and research.* New York: Garland Reference Company.

Stimpson, D. V., Narayanan, S., and Shanthakumar, D.K. (1993). Attitudinal characteristics of male and female entrepreneurs in the United States and India. *Psychological Studies, 38*(2) 64-68.

Sternberg, R. (Ed.). (1988a). *The nature of creativity.* New York: Cambridge.

Sternberg, R. (1988b). *The triarchic mind: A new theory of human intelligence.* New York: Viking.

Sternberg, R. (1985). *Beyond IQ: A triarchic theory of human intelligence.* New York: Cambridge University Press.

Sternberg, R. and Davidson, J. (Eds.). (1986). *Conceptions of giftednesss.* New York: Cambridge.

Sternberg, R. and Davidson, J. (Eds.) (1995). *The nature of insight.* Cambridge, MA: The MIT Press.

Sternberg, R., and Lubart, T. (1991). An investment theory of creativity and its development. *Human Development, 34*, 1-31.

Sternberg, R.J., and Lubart, T.I. (1992). Creative giftedness. In N. Colangelo, S.G. Assouline, and D.L. Ambroson (Eds.), *Talent development: Proceedings from the 1991 Henry B. and Jocelyn Wallace National Research Symposium on Talent Development* (pp. 66-88). Unionville, NY: Trillium Press.

Stone, I. (Ed.). (1937). *Dear Theo*. New York: Doubleday.

Stoutjesdyk, D., and Jevne, R. (1993). Eating disorders among high performance athletes. *Journal of Youth and Adolescence, 22* (3) 271-82.

Stravinsky, I. (1990). On conductors and conducting. *Journal of the Conductors' Guild, 11* (1 and 2), 9-18.

Storr, A. (1988). *Solitude: A return to the self*. New York: The Free Press.

Subotnik, R.F., and Arnold, K. (1996). Success and sacrifice: The costs of talent fulfilmment for women in science. In Arnold, K.D., Subotnik, R.F., and Noble, K. D. (Eds.), *Remarkable women: Perspectives on female talent development* (pp. 263-280). Cresskill, NJ: Hampton Press, Inc.

Subotnik, R. and Steiner, C.L. (1994). Adult manifestations of adolescent talent in science: A longitudinal study of 1983 Westinghouse Science Talent Search winners. In R.F. Subotnik and K.D. Arnold (Eds.), *Beyond Terman: Contemporary longitudinal studies of giftedness and talent* (pp. 52-76). Norwood, NJ: Ablex.

Subotnik, R.F., Duschl, R.A., and Selmon, E.H. (1993). Retention and attrition of science talent: A longitudinal study of Westinghouse Science Talent Search winners. *International Journal of Science Education, 15*, 61-72.

Sulloway, F. (1996). *Born to rebel: Birth order, family dynamics, and creative lives*. New York: Pantheon Books.

Suzuki, S. (1983). *Nurtured by love: The classic approach to talent education*. Smithtown, NY: Exposition Press.

Swafford, J. (1996). *Charles Ives: A life with music*. New York: W.W. Norton.

Tannenbaum, A. (1983). *Gifted children: Psychological and educational perspectives*. New York: Macmillan.

Tannenbaum, A. (1986). The enrichment matrix model. In J. Renzulli and S. Reis (Eds.), *Systems and models for the gifted and talented* (pp. 391-428), Watertown, Conn: Creative Learning Press.

Tardif, T.Z., and Sternberg, R.J. (1988). What do we know about creativity? In R.J. Sternberg (Ed.), *The nature of creativity: Contemporary psycho-*

logical perspectives. New York: Cambridge University Press.

Taub, D.E. and Blinde, E. M. (1994). Disordered eating and weight control among adolescent female athletes and performance squad members. *Journal of Adolescent Research, 9* (4) 483-97.

Taylor, C.W. (1969). The highest talent potentials of man. *Gifted Child Quarterly, 13,* 9-30.

Taylor, D.B. (1990, October 17). Asian-American test scores: They deserve a closer look. *Education Week*, p. 22.

Taylor, I. (1959). The nature of the creative process. In P.Smith (Ed.), *Creativity: An examination of the creative process* (pp. 51-82.) New York: Hastings House.

Terman, L., and Oden, M. (1947). *The gifted child grows up: Twenty five years follow up of a superior group. Genetic Studies of Genius, IV.* Stanford, CA: Stanford University Press.

Terry, W. (1971). *Dance in America*. New York: Harper and Row.

Tomlinson-Keasy, C., and Little, T. (1990). Predicting educational attainment, occupational achievement, intellectual skill, and personal adjustment among gifted men and women. *Journal of Educational Psychology, 82* (1), 442-455.

Torrance, E.P. (1966). *Torrance tests of creative thinking: Norms-technical manual*. Princeton, NJ: Personnel Press.

Torrance, E.P. (1974). *Torrance tests of creative thinking: Norms and technical manual.* Lexington, MA: Personnel Press/Ginn-Xerox.

Torrance, E.P. (1979). *The search for satori and creativity*. Buffalo, NY: Bearly Limited.

Torrance, E.P. (1987a). Teaching for creativity. In S. Isaksen, (Ed.), *Frontiers of creativity research: Beyond the basics* (pp. 190-215). Buffalo, NY.: Bearly Limited.

Torrance, E.P. (1987b). Recent trends in teaching children and adults to teach creatively. In Isaksen, S. (Ed.), *Frontiers of creativity research: Beyond the basics* (pp. 204-215). Buffalo, NY: Bearly Limited.

Torrance, E.P., Bruch, C., and Torrance, J.P. (1978). Interscholastic futuristic problem solving. *Journal of Creative Behavior, 10*, 117-125.

Torrance, E.P., and Goff, K. (1989). A quiet revolution. *Journal of Creative Behavior, 23*, 112-18.

Torrance, E.P., and Myers, R.E. (1970). *Creative learning and teaching*. New York: Dodd-Mead.

Torrance, E.P., and Safter, H.T. (1989). The long range predictive validity of the Just Suppose Test. *Journal of Creative Behavior, 23*, 219-223.

Treffinger, D. (1987). Research on creativity assessment. In S. Isaksen (Ed.), *Frontiers of creativity research: Beyond the basics* (pp. 103-119). Buffalo, NY: Bearly.

Wagar, J. (1991). *Conductors in conversation: Fifteen contemporary conductors discuss their lives and profession.* Boston, MA: G.K. Hill.

Updike, J. (1989). *Self-consciousness: Memoirs.* New York: Knopf.

Van Gogh, V. (1937). *Dear Theo.* I. Stone (Ed.). New York: Doubleday.

Vernon, P.E. (1986). Creativity. In R.Harré and R. Lamb (Eds.), *The Dictionary of Developmental and Educational Psychology* (pp. 44-46). Cambridge, MA: The MIT Press.

Vidal, G. (1996). *Palimpsest: A memoir.* New York: Random House.

Vygotsky, L. (1962). *Thought and language.* Boston: MIT Press.

Wakefield, D. (1988). *Returning: A spiritual journey.* New York: Doubleday.

Wakefield, D. (1995). *New York in the 50's.* New York: Houghton Mifflin.

Wakefield, J.F. (1991). The outlook for creativity tests. *Journal of Creative Behavior, 25* (3), 184-193.

Wallach, M. (1971). *The creativity-intelligence distinction.* New York, NY: General Learning Press.

Wallach, M. and Kogan, N. (1965). Modes of thinking in young children: A study of the creativity-intelligence distinction. New York: Holt, Rinehart, and Winston, Inc.

Wallas, G. (1926). The art of thought. New York: Harcourt Brace Jovanovich.

Watson, J. (1958). Behaviorism. Chicago: University of Chicago Press.

Weiner, J. (1990). The next one hundred years: Shaping the fate of our living earth. New York: Bantam.

Weisberg, R. (1986). *Creativity: Genius and other myths.* New York: W. H. Freeman.

Weisskopf, V. (1990). *The joy of insight: Passions of a physicist.* New York: Basic Books.

Weisskopf-Joelson, E., and Eliseo, T. (1961). An experimental study of the effectiveness of brainstorming. *Journal of Applied Psychology, 45*, 45-49.

Welsh, G.S. (1975). *Creativity and intelligence: A personality approach.* Chapel Hill, NC: Institute for Research in Social Science.

Wertheimer, M. (1959). *Productive thinking.* New York: Harper and Row.

Wetzig, Diane L. (1990). Sex-role conflict in female athletes: A possible marker for alcoholism. *Journal of Alcohol and Drug Education, 35* (3)45-53.

Williams, F. (1970). *Classroom ideas for encouraging thinking and feeling.* Buffalo, NY: DOK.

Willings, D. (1980). *The creatively gifted.* Cambridge: Woodhead-Faulkner.

Winchester, I. (1985). *Creation and creativity in art and science.* Interchange, 16, 76.

Winner, E. (1996). *Gifted children.* New York: Basic Books.

Wittig, A.F., and Shurr, K.T. (1994). Psychological characteristics of women volleyball players: Relationships with injuries, rehabilitation, and team success. *Personality and Social Psychology Bulletin, 20* (3), 322-330.

Wolff, T. (1989). *This boy's life: A memoir.* New York: Atlantic Monthly Press.

Woolf, V. (1954). *A writer's diary.* New York: Harcourt Brace Jovanovich.

Wright, F.L. (1932/1977). *An autobiography.* New York: Horizon Press.

Wrisberg, Craig A.; And Others (1988). Sex role orientations of male and female collegiate athletes from selected individual and team sports. *Sex Roles: A Journal of Research, 19* (1-2), 81-90.

Wubbenhorst, T.M. (1994). Personality characteristics of music educators and performers. Special Issue: Assessment in music. *Psychology of Music, 22*(1) 63-74.

Zakrajsek, D.B., Johnson, R.I., and Walker, D.B. (1984). Comparison of learning styles between physical education and dance majors. *Perceptual and Motor Skills, 58,* 583-588.

Zarnegar, Z., Hocevar, D., and Michael, W. (1988). Components of original thinking in gifted children. *Educational and Psychological Measurement, 48,* 5-16.

Zimmerman, B.J., Bandura, A., and Martinez-Pons, M. (1992). Self-motivation for academic attainment: The role of self-efficacy beliefs and personal goal setting. American *Educational Research Journal, 29* (3), 329-339.

Ziv, A. (1976). Facilitating effects of humor on creativity. *Journal of Educational Psychology, 68,* 318-322.

Ziv, A. (1988). Using humor to develop creative thinking. *Journal of Children in Contemporary Society, 20,* 99-116.

Zuckerman, H. (1977). *The scientific elite.* New York: Free Press.

Index

A

A is for Aesthetic (Abbs), 293
Abbs, R., 293
Abell, A., 45
Abercrombie, J., 292
abstract art, 27
Abt, L., 294
acorn theory, 69
acting
    actors on, 313–318
    predictive behaviors, 305–312
active memory, 304
actors on acting, 313–318
Actors on Acting (Brook), 316
Adams, D., 324–325
Adjective Check List, 109
The Adjective Check List Manual (Gough and Heilbrun), 110
Adler, S., 41, 314
administering tests, reliability, 94
African Americans influence on contemporary music, 286
Agassiz, A., 215
aha!s, 53–54
Ailey, A., 329–330
Aizenstat, S., 66
Albert, R.A., 91
Albert, R.S., 19
alcoholism, writers and, 190
Allen, D., 187
Allen, J.S., 34, 304
Allen, P., 257
alternative high schools, 28–29
Alvin Ailey American Dance Theater, 329
Amabile, T.M., 6, 19, 117–119, 354
American Ballet Theater, 322
American Childhoods, 220
American Dances (de Mille), 322
American Heritage Dictionary of the American Language, 7
analyzing ability, Guilford on, 10
Anderson, M., 287, 333
Andre Previn (Bookspan and Yodkey), 290

Andreason, N., 197–198
Andrews, P., 257
androgyny, athletes, 334–335
Anshel, M.H., 334
architects, 162–170. *See also specific architects*
Argulewicz, E.N., 114
Armstrong, L., 287
Armstrong, T., 117
Arnheim, D., 332
Arnold, K., 237
The Art of Thought (Wallas), 46
art students, characteristics, 138–140
artists
    differences according to specialty, 142
    successful, high achieving, 142–143
Artists in the Making (Barron), 149
The Artist's Way (Cameron), 126
Artress, L., 58
Assouline, S., 247
asynchrony, 20
athletes
    androgyny, 334–335
    personality studies, 333–337
athletics, creative imagery and, 64–65
attitude of playfulness, improvisation, 70
Austen, J., 218
Autobiography (Wright), 166
automaticity, 47

B

Bacharach, B., 282
Baer, J., 117, 118
Bagley, M., 126
Baird, L.L., 37
Bakker, F., 333
Balanchine, G., 45, 322, 325
Ballet of the Twentieth Century, 326
Bamberger, J., 47, 216, 266, 282
Bandy, C., 319
Barron, F., 112, 139, 148, 149–152, 152, 163, 165, 166, 176, 182–183, 186, 335–337
Barron-Welsh Revised Art Scale, 336, 337
Bartok, B., 285
Baryshnikov, M., 326

Bates, B., 307–308
Bateson, M.C., 67
beat poets, 191–193
beauty in creator's field, 47–48
Beck, J., 314
Beckett, S., 185
Beethoven, L., 282, 283
Bell, Q., 219
Bellow, S., 176
Bem Sex Roles Inventory (BSRI), 270, 334
Bement, A., 147
Benbow, C., 22, 247
Bergson, H., 67
Berio, L., 273
Bernstein, L., 274
Berryman, J., 190, 191, 217
Betts, G., 126
biographical studies, 186–189
    actors, 318–320
    dancers, 323–332
    musical talent, 282–283
birth order, 239
Black Music in America (Haskins), 286
Blomstedt, H., 275
Bloom, B., 22, 47, 148, 215, 230–231, 277, 373
Bloom's Taxonomy of Educational Objectives, 119
Blumberg, Panos, 228
Bly, R., 25, 187
Bockris, V., 152
Bohr, N., 230
Bold, A., 57
Bolden, B., 287
Bond, V., 275
Bookspan, M., 290
Borges, J.L., 185
Borland, J., 87
Borofsky, J., 141
Boyd, J., 272, 280, 292, 299
Boyle, T.C., 178, 187
Brahms, J., 45
brainstorming, 6
Brainstorms & Thunderbolts: How Creative Genius Works (Madigan and Elwood), 53
Braisted, J., 331
Brando, M., 308–309, 312
Brandwein, P., 231, 241
Braque, G., 161
Bread Loaf Writer's Conference, 179
Brewer, B.W., 333
broadsides, 182
Brodsky, J., 255
Brody, L., 22, 226
Brontë family, 220
Bronx High School of Science, 28–29
Brook, P., 315–317
Brooks-Gunn, J., 331, 332

Brown, J., 288
Brown, K., 198, 315
Browning, E.B., 45
Bryant, J., 383
Buchanan, D., 319
Buddhism, 62
Buffalo Creativity Studies program, 123
Buffett, W., 256–260
Burrow, C., 331
Burrow, W., 331
Buttsworth, L.M., 270
Byrd, Admiral, 59

C

California Achievement Test, 91, 111
California Psychological Inventory (CPI), 164, 227
Calliope, 44
Cameron, J., 126
Campbell, B., 117
Campbell, J., 9, 19
Carver, G.W., 177
Carver, R., 173
Casals, P., 282
Castaneda, C., 56
Cattell, R., 113, 227
Cattell High School Personality Questionnaire (HSPQ), 111–113, 269
Cattell, M., 113
Cezanne, P., 135
Chafe, W., 201
chance or luck, 40
Changing the World (Feldman), 17
chapbooks, 181
Charles, R., 288
Chauvin, J., 111
Cheever, J., 185, 198
Chekhov, A., 177
chemical substances, creative process and, 56–57
Chesebrough, G., 54
Chicago, J., 45, 155
Child Prodigies and Exceptional Early Achievers (Radford), 204
A Childhood (Crews), 220
children. See also creativity in children
    writers as, 187, 217–224
    with writing talent, 214–216
Chinoy, H., 312
church, 240–241
Citino, D., 173
City Lights, 193
Clark, R., 228, 241
Clio, 44
cognitive aspect, Pyramid of Talent Development, 37
cognitive psychology, 20
cognitive science, 73
    creative process as, 70–71

Cohen, L., 67
Colangelo, N., 247, 250–252
Cold War, 28
Cole, N., 288
Cole, T., 312
Coleridge, S.T., 46, 172
college courses, creativity training, 121
Collins, P., 292
Comet, C., 274
The Coming Indoors and Other Poems (Einbond), 206
community and culture, 39
composers. *See also specific composers*
    personalities, 271
    women, 294–295
Composers Guild of Great Britain, 271
Composing A Life (Bateson), 67
concentration of life, 51–52
concurrent validity, creativity tests, 91–93
conductors. *See specific conductors*
Conroy, F., 180
content/construct validity, 88–89
Copland, A., 294
Corey, J., 317–318
coRT Lateral Thinking, 126
Counseling Readiness Scale (CRS), 110
Cowger, H., 65
Cox, J., 235
Crabbe, A., 126
Cramond, B., 87
Crane, S., 217–218
Creating Minds (Gardner), 20, 160
Creating More Creative People (Crabbe and Betts), 126
creative, American usage, 8
Creative Action Book (Noller), 122
creative behavior, motivating, 348–354
"creative education," 7
The Creative Experience (Rosner and Abt), 294
creative giftedness, 13
creative imagery, athletics and, 64–65
The Creative Mind (Findlay and Lumsden), 73
Creative Mythology (Campbell), 9
creative potential, 84
Creative Problem Solving (CPS), 74–75, 122, 124
Creative Problem-Solving Institute, 5
creative process, 43–76
    chemical substances and, 56–57
    as cognitive science, 70–71
    common descriptions, 46–54
    right/left brain and, 55–56
    traditional theories, 44–45
The Creative Process (Ghiselin), 46
"creative sales policy," 7
creative thinking, 84
Creative Vision (Getzels and Csikszentmihalyi), 44–45, 138
creative writers, 171–202, 203–224
    deviance and, 183–185

creativity
    equity and, 28–29
    future and, 29–30
    giftedness and, 13–14
    as human freedom, 30–31
    improvisation and, 290–294
    minority participation and, 29
    nationalism and, 28
    natural, 41–42
    origin of word, 6–7
    as process of life, 65–70
    psychological research on, 15–25
    psychology and, 9–12
    quality, 26–27
    quantity, 25–26
    terminology, 6–8
    without mastery, 33–34
    without product, 31–34
Creativity: Flow and the Psychology of Discovery and Invention (Csikszentmihalyi), 18, 20, 49
"Creativity and Culture" (Stein), 7
Creativity and Madness (Rothenberg), 184
Creativity and Personal Freedom (Barron), 150
creativity course, 385–386
creativity exercises, Goldberg's, 126
creativity in children
    avoid stereotypes, 371–373
    creative adults, 364–366
    display work, 361–363
    enhancing, 357–359
    family mythology, 369–371
    materials for, 359–360
    private lessons and special classes, 373–376
    set creative tone, 366–368
    value creative work of others, 368–369
creativity studies project, 122–123
creativity testing, 81–100
    significant results studies, 96–99
    validity, 88–93
creativity tests
    concurrent validity, 91–93
    predictive validity, 90–91
creativity training, 119–130
    college courses, 121
    as differentiation for talented, 128–129
    in schools, 124–128
Crews, H., 220–221
criterion validity, 90
Critical Path (Fuller), 244
Cross, J.W., 217
Crutchfield, 152
crystallizing experience, 41
Csikszentmihalyi, M., 17–18, 20, 40, 44, 52, 88, 138–140, 142, 144, 146–148, 177, 178, 192, 216, 237, 242, 364
    on flow, 49

D

Dabrowski, K., 22, 23–25, 68, 102–103, 215
Dabrowski Overexitability Questionnaire (OEQ), 103, 189
daimon, 40, 41
Damarin, 113–114
dance
    aesthetics, 321–323
    physical effects, 331–332
    without mastery, 33
Dance in America (Terry), 321
dancers, 320–323. See also specific dancers
    biographies and memoirs, 323–332
    personality studies, 333–337
Dancing On My Grave (Kirkland), 327
Darkness Visible: A Memoir of Madness (Styron), 194
Darwin, C., 173, 236
    Gruber on, 232–235
Darwin On Man (Gruber), 67, 232
Dash, J., 378
Davidson, J., 248
Davies, D.R., 273
Davis, G.A., 89, 91, 99, 116, 117, 126
Davis, M., 288
de Bono, E., 5, 126
de Mestral, G., 54
de Mille, A., 322
de St. Exupery, A., 68
de Vries, K., 255
Dear Theo (Stone), 136, 154
degree of complexity, Guilford on, 11
DeLillo, D., 181
Denson, E.L., 333
depression and writers, 194–200
The Descent of Man (Darwin), 234
The Developing Child (Murphy), 109
Developing Talent in Young People (Bloom), 47, 215, 277
development of talent in music domain, 277–282
Development of Talent Research Project, 277, 373
developmental levels and overexcitabilities, 23–25
developmental potential, 108
developmental psychology, 15
developmental research, 266–267
deviance and creative writers, 183–185
Dewey, J., 46
The Dictionary of Developmental and Educational Psychology, 7
Diddley, B., 288
The Dinner Party (Chicago), 155
Directory of American Poets and Fiction Writers, 174
Directory of American Poets and Writers, 342
discovery proposition, 72–73
divergent production, 87
    as factor of intellect, 10–11

Divergent Production of Figural Units, 97
Divergent Production of Semantic Units, 97
Divergent Production (Runco), 93
divergent production testing, 124
divergent production training, 119–121
divorce, writers and, 188
Doctorow, E.L., 199
domains, Gardner's, 20–21
The Doors of Perception (Huxley), 56
Drabble, M., 194
The Drama Of The Gifted Child (Miller), 159, 380
Drawing on the Right Side of the Brain (Edwards), 55, 126
Drink To Me Only (Bold), 57
Dudek, S., 166
Duke, P., 307
Dungan, R., 118
Dutoit, C., 274, 275
Dyce, J.A., 271

E

East is East (Boyle), 178
Eastman School of Music, 266
eating disorders, dancers, 332
Eban, A., 241
Eberle, R., 125
ecopsychology, 65–70
Edison, T., 236
Educational Forum, 35
educational psychology, 22
Edwards, B., 55, 126
Einbond, B., 206
Einstein, A., 46, 177, 228–229, 236
elaboration, 121
Eliot, G., 217
Ellington, D., 287
Ellison, 7
Els, S.M, 123
Elwood, A., 53
The Emerging Goddess (Rothenberg), 184
emotion as motivator, 348–350
emotional aspect, Pyramid of Talent Development, 36–37
emotional development theory, 68
Emotional Intelligence (Goleman), 63
emotional overexcitability, 102
ENFJ personality, 153, 319
ENFP personality, 153
entrepreneurs, 252–260
environmental suns, Pyramid of Talent Development, 38–40
Ephron, N., 372
equity, creativity and, 28–29
Erato, 44
ERIC Clearinghouse, 7
Erikson, E., 184

Erikson, J., 18
Erskine, P., 292
Escher, M.C., 177
Estés, C.P., 57
Europe, J.R., 287
Euterpe, 44
evaluation, Guilford on, 11
Ewen, D., 275
expert witness proposition, 71
Extraordinary Minds (Gardner), 21

F

factor of intellect, divergent production as, 10–11
families, talent in, 146
family and educational factors, 238–242
Farrell, S., 27, 323–326, 331
Faulkner, W., 185
Feldhusen, J., 35, 124
Feldman, D., 13, 16–18, 41, 53, 69, 134, 146, 204–205, 242
Ferlinghetti, L., 193
Ferrucci, P., 52
Feynman, R., 230, 232, 248, 249
First Earth Run, 66
Fischl, E., 45
Fitzgibbon, C., 219
Fleetwood, M., 272
flexibility, 6, 120
   Guilford on, 10
flow, 49–52
fluency, 6, 120
   Guilford on, 10
Foley, P., 149, 155–156, 193, 299
folk and popular musicians, 285–290
Form and Feeling (Langer), 321
Fraas, J., 373
Frames of Mind (Gardner), 20, 136, 173
Franklin, A., 288
Free Play (Nachmanovitch), 70, 293
Freedom To Write Committee, 182
Freud, S., 8, 183, 236
Fuller, B., 53, 243–244
Funk and Wagnalls Standard Dictionary, International Edition, 7
future, creativity and, 29–30
Future Problem Solving, 6, 30, 125

G

Gablik, S., 141
Galileo, 177
Gallagher, T., 173
Galton, F., 35, 216, 236
Gardner, H., 13, 17, 20–21, 35, 68, 70, 87, 136, 149, 173, 226, 227, 242, 264, 302
   Picasso study, 160–162
Gardner, J., 181, 200

Gardner Multiple Intelligence (MI) theory, 117
Garland, J., 307
Garrett, G., 176
Gates, B., 256–260
Gauguin, P., 135
Gawain, S., 64
Gell-Mann, M., 248
gender, 38
   differences, talent and, 40
genes, 36
Genius, Creativity, and Leadership (Simonton), 231, 235, 283
George Eliot's Life as Related in Her Letters and Journals (Cross), 217
Gershon, D., 66
Gery, M.V., 379
gestalt psychology, 61
Getty, J.P., 256–260
Getzels, J., 11, 20, 44, 52, 138–140, 142, 144, 145, 146, 147, 148, 177, 178, 192
Ghiselin, B., 46–48, 50, 51, 52, 141
Gide, A., 215
GIFFI I and II, 116
GIFT, 116
gifted, defined, 69
giftedness
   creativity and, 13–14
   definitions, 12–15
Gilligan, C., 25
Ginsberg, A., 191, 198, 216
Ginsberg (Miles), 191
Glass, P., 281
Gleick, J., 249
Goertzels studies, 145, 149, 154–155, 186–189, 235, 319
Goethe, J., 53
Goldberg's creativity exercises, 126
Goleman, D., 35, 63
Gondola, J., 65
Gong, E., 331
Gordon, M., 188
Gordon Intermediate Measures of Music Audition (IMMA), 266
Gordon Primary Measures of Music Audition (PMMA), 266
Gordon's synectics, 125
Gough, H., 109, 110, 152
Graffman, G., 291
Graham, M., 321
Greatness: Who Makes History and Why (Simonton), 19, 235
Green, J., 50, 52
Greene, G., 222–224, 359
Greer, G., 155
Grooms, R., 141
Group Theater, 314

Growing Up Creative (Amabile), 354
Gruber, H., 67, 173, 242
  on Darwin, 16, 232–235
Gruen, J., 323
Grunch of Giants (Fuller), 244
Guare, J., 40
Guernica (Picasso), 159
Guilford, J.P., 7, 35, 87, 119, 122
    Structure of Intellect theory, 10–11
Gulbekian Foundation, 264

H

Hall, D., 172–173
Hall, W.B., 166
Halperin, J., 218
Hamachek, D., 355
Hamilton, L., 332
Handy, W.C., 287
Hanson, S., 237
hard work, need for, 51
Harman, W., 66
Haskins, J., 286
H'Doubler, M., 321
Heausler, N., 96
Heilbrun, A.B., 110
Hellman, L., 185
Helson, R., 152, 244–246
Hennessey, B., 117–119, 355
Hereditary Genius (Galton), 216
Hersey, J., 48, 49
Hess, K., 126
High School and Beyond (HSB) data, 237
Hillman, J., 40–41, 69, 377
historiometry, 19, 67, 235–238
Hocevar, D., 101
Hockney, D., 45
Hoerr, T.R., 20
Hoffman, D., 312, 337
Hoffman, H., 143
Hoge, R., 1
Holding On To The Air (Farrell), 323
Holiday, B., 287
Hollander, L., 266–267
home environment, 38
Homer, 44
homospatial process, 184
Hong, E., 91, 101
Horn, P., 292–293
Horn, R., 299
Howe, M., 264
"Howl" (Ginsberg), 191
human freedom, creativity as, 30–31
Human Potential Movement, 65
humanistic psychology, 22–23, 61
humor, 200–201
Hunter High School, 28–29

Hurwitz, A., 137–138
Huxley, A., 56, 177

I

I Really Should Be Practicing (Graffman), 291
Ice-T, 288
Iliad (Homer), 44
illuminations, 53–54
imagery, 61
imaginary playmates, 107
imaginational overexcitability, 102
improvisation
    attitude of playfulness, 70
    creativity and, 290–294
In Search of Human Effectiveness (MacKinnon), 250
Industrial Revolution, 135
Inevitable Grace (Ferrucci), 52
INFJ personality, 153
INFP personality, 153, 186
The Inner Game of Tennis, 64
Institute for Personality Assessment and Research
    (IPAR), 152, 163, 176, 227, 244
intellectual overexcitability, 102
intelligence
    musicians, 276
    scientists and mathematicians, 230–232
Interpersonal Circumplex questionnaire, 271
Intimate Strangers (Schickel), 312
Into the Deep: A Writer's Look at Creativity (Els), 123
intrinsic motivation, 354–356
invention competions, 126
Invention Conventions, 6
inventors, 250–252
IQ tests, 28
Irving, J., 50, 187
Irwin, B., 309
Irwin, C., 331
Isaksen, S., 74, 75, 87, 123, 124
Ives, C., 293
Ivory soap, 54

J

Jackson, M., 288
Jackson, N., 215
Jackson, P., 11
James, A., 236
Jamison, J., 330
Jamison, K., 185, 196
Janov's Primal Therapy, 54
janusian process, 184
Jarrell, R., 190
Jarvie, I.C., 25
Jevne, R., 332
John-Steiner, V., 228
Jones, Q., 288
Joplin, S., 287

Journal Of A Solitude (Sarton), 60
The Joy of Insight (Weisskopf), 226
Julliard School, 283–285
Jung, C., 40, 59, 164

K

Kanter, P., 285
Karnes, F., 111, 117
Kasdan, L., 180
Kazmarov, M., 71
Keaton, B., 309
Keen, S., 25
Kemp, A.E., 269, 276
Kerouac, J., 56
Kerr, B., 247, 379
Khatena, J., 91, 92
The Kindness of Strangers (Spoto), 220
King, B.B., 287
King, S., 179
Kirkland, G., 327–328
Kirton Adaptation-Innovation Inventory (KAI), 74
Kisselgoff, A., 330
Kizer, C., 44
Klee, P., 141, 177
Klug, L., 229
Kogan, J., 11–12, 283–285, 380
Kolb Learning Style Inventory, 336
Kosinski, J., 198
Kough, J., 305
Krasner, L., 143
Kris, E., 183
Krutetskii, V., 226, 232

L

La Guardia High School for the Performing Arts, 28, 374
Langan-Fox, J., 255
Langer, S., 321
Lawrence, G., 327
Lazear, D., 117
Leading Minds (Gardner), 21
Lebrecht, N., 273, 275
LeCapitaine, J., 129
Lee Theodore American Dance Machine Company, 323
Leonard, L., 57
Lewis, C.S., 60, 221–222
Lewis, S., 218
The Life of Dylan Thomas (Fitzgibbon), 219
The Life of Graham Greene (Sherry), 222
The Life of Jane Austen (Halperin), 218
Lissitz, R., 94
The Literary Mind (Schneiderman), 185
Little, T., 237
Living in the Light (Gawain), 64
Living Theater, 314–315
A Location in the Upper Peninsula (Piirto), 352, 369

Loeb, K., 365
logical-mathematical intelligence, 226
Longitudinal Study of American Youth (LSAY), 237
Lost Talent: Women in the Sciences (Hanson), 237
Lowell, R., 190, 191
Lowenkopf, E., 331
Lubart, T., 21
luck and other social factors for success, 145–148
Lysy, K.Z., 108

M

Mackay, J., 368
MacKinnon, D., 152, 163, 176, 228, 250–252
Macleish, A., 172–173
Madame Sousatzka, 279
Madigan, C., 53
The Maestro Myth (Lebrecht), 273
Magritte, R., 45, 141–142
Mahler, A., 294–295
Mailer, N., 50
The Making Of An Artist (Barron), 148
Malina, J., 314–315
Malpede, K., 315
Mandelbaum, H., 181
Manes, S., 257
Manet, E., 135
Mann, H., 46
Mapplethorpe, R., 26, 45
marginality, 241
Marland Report, 13–14
Marsalis, W., 289
Marsalis brothers, 288
Maslow, A., 22, 60, 61, 236
massive concentration, 48
mastery, creativity without, 33–34
mathematicians, 225–261
    studies of, 244–249
mathematicians, intelligence, 230–232
Mauceri, J.B., 180
McAleer, N., 58
McCaulley, M., 108, 153, 186, 270
McDonnell, D., 129
McDonough, B., 121
McDonough, P., 121
McGilligan, P., 317–318
McMurtry, L., 182
Mead, M., 25, 177
meditation, 62–64
Meeker, M., 35, 87, 97, 125
Meija, P., 326
Mellin, L., 331
Melpomene, 44
Melville, H., 7
mental illness, writers and, 190
mental leap proposition, 72
Mental Measurements Yearbook (MMY), 83, 113

Method acting, 309, 311, 312
Michelangelo, 177
Miles, B., 191–192
Milgram, R., 91, 101
Millay, E.S.V., 177, 378
Miller, A., 149, 159–160, 185, 187, 239, 309, 342, 380
The Mind's Best Work (Perkins), 71–73
The Mind's New Science (Gardner), 70
Miner, J., 255
Minnesota Multiphasic Psychological Inventory
   (MMPI), 111, 150
minority participation, creativity and, 29
Miro, J., 141
Moby Dick (Melville), 7
Moore, T., 25
Morgan, C., 17
Morrison, M., 118
Morrison, T., 179
Morse, D., 91
Morton, J.R., 287
motivating creative behavior, 348–354
motivator, emotion as, 348–350
Mrs. Dalloway (Woolf), 50
Multiple Intelligences (MI) schools, 21, 266
Murphy, E., 109
Murray, E., 148
muses, 45
Muses, visitation, 44–45
Music by Philip Glass (Glass), 281
music career, 267–268
Music of the Spheres, 44
Musicians in Tune (Boyd), 280, 292
Muska, N., 381
Myers, I., 108, 153, 186
Myers-Briggs Type Indicator (MBTI), 39, 74, 108–109,
   111, 148, 152–154, 270
   entrepreneurs and managers, 253–254
   writers and, 186
Mythology (Bulfinch), 44

N

Nabokov, V., 185
Nachmanovitch, S., 70, 293
Naifeh, S., 162
National Academy of Design, 143
National Center for Educational Statistics, 237
National Educational Longitudinal Study (NELS), 237
National Endowment for the Arts, 27, 138
*National Excellence: A Case for Developing America's
   Talent* (U.S.O.E.R.I), 14
nationalism, creativity and, 28
natural creativity, 41–42
natural highs, 58
The Nature of Human Intelligence (Guilford), 10
The Nature of Insight (Sternberg and Davidson), 248
Nature's Gambit (Feldman), 204

Nevai, L., 364
New Age Movement, 61
New Criticism, 190
New York City Ballet, 322
Nicholson, J., 307
Nietzsche, F., 185
Nixon, L., 102
No Rootless Flower (Barron), 176
Noller, R., 122
normal curve assumption, 98–99
Notebooks of the Mind (John-Steiner), 228
notebooks proposition, 71–72
*Nothing But The Best: The Struggle For Perfection At
   The Julliard School* (Kogan), 283
novelty, 8
   Guilford on, 10
Nowell, E., 219
Nurtured By Love (Suzuki), 265

O

Oates, J.C., 172, 173, 179, 194
The Obstacle Race (Greer), 155
obvious connections, 53
oceanic consciousness, 46–47
O'Connor, F., 185, 271
O'Connor, S., 288
O'Donnell, R., 201
Odyssey of the Mind (OM) competitions, 6, 120, 125
Office of Special Services, 176
O'Hara, F., 188
O'Keefe, G., 147
Olivier, L., 312, 313
Olsen, T., 194
On Moral Fiction (Gardner), 181
On The Road (Kerouac), 56
organic unconsciousness, 48
Origin of Species (Darwin), 233, 234
originality, 121
originative, 8
Orwell, G., 51
Osborn, A.F., 74, 122, 123
overexcitabilities, developmental levels and, 23–25
Overexcitability Questionnaire, 102–108
   qualitative assessment, 108
Oxford English Dictionary, 7

P

Pantuhoff, I., 143
Paris Review, 48
Parker, C., 288
Parloff, M., 227
Parnes, S., 74, 122
Passaro, V., 181
PEN, 182
Pendergrass, T., 288
People Who Dance (Gruen), 323

performance assessment, 117–119
performers, 302–305
Perkins, D., 71–73, 74, 88
Perls, F., 61
personalities, 36
    artists, 140–142
    dancers and athletes, 333–337
    musicians, 268–276
personality and behavioral checklists, 113–117
personality questionnaires, 101–113
Petrie, T., 332
The Phenomenology of Dance (Sheets), 322
philosophic overtones, 8–9
physical effects, dancing, 331–332
physical performers, 301–338
Picasso, P., 159–162
Piechowski, M.M., 23, 38, 68, 102, 108
Piirto Piiramid, 38
Pinter, H., 185
Pipher, M., 25
Planck, M., 177
Plath, S., 193
Plato, 40
Plimpton, G., 199
Poets In Their Youth (Simpson), 189
Poincaré, 46
Polkow, D., 272
Pollock, J., 148, 162
Polyhymnia, 44
popular musicians, folk and, 285–290
Porter, A., 334
Porter, K.A., 172
Powell, C., 39
precocity, 137
    creativity indicator, 31–32
predictive behaviors, 38
    acting, 305–312
    children with writing talent, 214–216
    of creative performance, 22
    for musical talent, 264–268
    science and mathematics, 227–238
    for visual arts talent, 136–138
predictive validity, creativity tests, 90–91
Predock-Linnell, J., 336
preferences, 154
Prepared-Mind perspective, 249
Presley, E., 27
Previn, A., 290–291
PRIDE Checklist, 116
Primary Integration, 23
problem-finding
    artists, 144–145
    visual artists and, 138–148
process of life, creativity as, 65–70
Project Vanguard, 127, 384
prose talent, 209–214

proximity, 145
Psychoanalytic Explorations in Art (Kris), 183
psychoanalytic overtones, 8–9
psychological research on creativity, 15–25
    actors, 318–320
    developmental psychology, 15
    Gruber's Darwin study, 16
psychology, creativity and, 9–12
The Psychology of Mathematical Abilities in
    Schoolchildren (Krutetskii), 226
Psychology of Writers (Piirto), 174
psychometric artifact, 91
psychometric psychology, 25
psychomotor overexcitability, 102
Puccio, G., 74, 75, 123
Pyramid of Talent Development, 35–42
    cognitive aspect, 37
    emotional aspect, 36–37
    environmental suns, 38–40
    talent in domains, 37–38

Q

qualitative assessment, Overexitability Questionnaire,
    108

R

Radford, J., 204, 220
Rainey, M., 287
Raitt, B., 285
Ran, S., 295
The Random House Dictionary of the English Language,
    204
The Random House Dictionary of the English Language,
    Unabridged Edition, 8
Rathunde, K., 20, 216, 237
Red Dust Project, 368
Redgrave, M., 313
reflections on death, 53–54
Reis, S., 127
reliability, 93–96
    administering tests, 94
    scoring, 94–96
religious overtones, 8–9
Renzulli, J., 13, 127, 306
Renzulli-Hartman Creativity Scale, 113, 114–115, 116
reorganization or redefinition of existing ideas, Guilford
    on, 10
Resnik, J., 232
restlessness, 47
rewards, 355
Reynierse, J., 253–255
Reynolds, F.C., 69, 70, 377
Reynold's Creativity, Inc., 127
Rheingold, H., 66
Richards, K., 152
Rico, G., 55–56, 126

right/left brain, creative process and, 55–56
Rimm, S., 116, 117, 381
rituals, importance, 53
Roberson-Saunders, P., 253
Robert, S., 188
Robinson, R., 215
Robinson, S., 288, 289–290
Rockefeller Foundation, 176
Roe, A., 148–149, 225, 235
Roedell, W., 215
Roethke, T., 190
Rogers, C., 61
Roosevelt, E., 68, 287
Root-Bernstein, R.S., 177
Rorschach, 54
Rosen, C.L., 114
Rosner, S., 294
Roszak, T., 66, 67
Roth, S., 255
Rothenberg, A., 183–184
Rudolf, M., 273
Runco, M., 31, 91, 93, 94, 108, 124, 145
Rushdie, S., 182

S

Safdie, M., 164
Saint-Saens, C., 177
Salinger, J.D., 180
Salonen, E., 274, 275, 276
Samples's metaphorization, 125
Sanders, S., 188
Sarte, 30
Sarton, M., 60
Satanic Verses (Rushdie), 182
Sayles, J., 180
Scales for Rating the Behavioral Characteristics of
    Superior Students (SRBCSS), 113, 114, 116, 306
SCAMPER, 125
Schechner, R., 303
Schickel, R., 308, 312
Schneiderman, L., 185
schools, 38, 39
    creativity training in, 124–128
    influence, 241
    writers on, 342–348
Schwartz, D., 190, 191
science and mathematics, predictive behaviors, 227–238
Scientific Genius (Simonton), 235
scientists. *See also specific scientists*
    intelligence, 230–232
scoring reliability, 94–96
Scribner, C., Jr., 193
sculptors, 156–158
Seashore Measures, 266
Seifert, C., 248
self-actualized (SA) creativeness, 22

Self-Consciousness (Updike), 221
Sendak, M., 141
sensual overexcitability, 102
Seven Spheres, 44
Sexton, A., 193
The Shadow Man (Gordon), 188
Shah Jehan, Mumtaz Mahal, 54
Shallcross, D., 124
Shankar, R., 280–281
Sheets, M., 322
Shelley, M., 51, 53, 181
Sherman, C., 27
Sherry, N., 222
Shorer, M., 218
Shrude, M., 295–299
shyness, 271–272
Sibelius, 285
significant results studies, creativity testing, 96–99
Simmons, H., 375–376
Simon, R.S., 153
Simonton, D.K., 19, 145, 159, 172, 190, 230–231,
    235–238, 238, 241, 242, 283–285, 375
Simpson, E., 189–190
Simpson, L., 51
Sinclair Lewis (Shorer), 218
Singer, I., 53
Sir Wilfred's Seven Flights, 218
Six Degrees of Separation (Guare), 40
16 Personality Factors Inventory (16PF), 111, 227, 269,
    270
Sloane, K.D., 148, 156
Sloboda, G.A., 284
Smith, G.A., 270
Smokey (Robinson), 289
social psychology, 18–19
The Social Psychology of Creativity (Amabile), 354
Socrates, 40
SOI Test of Creative Thinking, 97
solitude, need for, 58–60
Solitude (Storr), 59
Solomon, D., 148
Solti, G., 272, 275
Solugub, 215
Sondheim, S., 177
Sosniak, L., 148, 156, 277–280
soul, 41
The Soul's Code (Hillman), 69
spatial intelligence, 136, 250
Spoto, D., 220
Stafford, J., 190
standardized tests, 266
Stanford Binet, 91
Stanislavski, C., 309, 311, 312, 313
Stanley, J., 22, 247
Stathairn, D., 180
Steiglitz, A., 147

Stein, M.L., 7
Stephen Crane (Berryman), 217
Sternberg, R.J., 13, 21, 35, 87, 136, 248
Still, W.G., 287, 289
Stone, I., 136, 154
Storr, A., 59, 67
Stoutjesdyk, D., 332
Stowe, H.B., 53
Straub, G., 66
Stravinsky, I., 27, 274
Strickland, K., 292
Structure of Intellect Creativity Test (SOI), 87
Structure of Intellect theory, Guilford, 10–11
Study for Mathematically Precocious Youth (SMPY),
    22, 247–249
Stuyvesant High School, 28–29
Styron, W., 180, 194–195, 199
Subotnik, R.F., 22, 237, 240
Sulloway, F., 145, 239, 272
sun of chance, 39, 175
sun of gender, 39, 175
sun of home, 38, 174
sun of school, 38, 175
sun or community and culture, 38, 174
Surprised by Joy (Lewis), 221–222
Suzuki Method, 265
Swafford, J., 293
synaesthesia process, 184
synectics, 125
Synectics, Inc., 129
synthesizing ability, Guilford, 10
Szilard, L., 229

T

Taj Mahal, 54
Talbot, 74
talent
    domains, 37–38
    existence and development, 34–35
    families, 146
    gender differences, 40
    multipotentiality, 40–41
talented, defined, 69
Talented Teens, 20, 216
Talmey, M., 229
Tannenbaum, A., 230–231, 242
Taub, D.E., 332
Taylor, C., 7
Taylor's talents unlimited, 125
Teachers and Writers Collaborative, 208
Tel-Aviv Creativity Test, 91
Teller, E., 228–229
Tennyson, A.L., 54
Terman, L., 35, 231
Terman Concept Mastery Test, 177, 245, 250
Terpsichore, 44

Terry, W., 321
Tesla, 53
testing for creativity, 87–88
Thalia, 44
Theater of Cruelty, 316
Their Ancient Glittering Eyes (Hall), 172
Thematic Apperception Test (TAT), 149
Theodore, L., 323
This Boy's Life (Wolff), 189
Thomas, D., 219
Thomas Wolfe (Nowell), 219
Thompson, B., 96
threshold of intelligence, 11
threshold theory, 91
Through the Flower (Chicago), 155
Timebends (Miller), 187
To The Lighthouse (Woolf), 195
Tomlinson-Keasy, C., 237
Torrance, E.P., 12, 65, 90, 92, 96, 125, 127
Torrance Tests of Creative Thinking (TTCT), 12, 65, 87,
    96, 114
*Touched With Fire: Manic-Depressive Illness and the
    Artistic Temperament* (Jamison), 196
Tough Poise on the 16 Personality Factors Inventory (16
    PF), 39
Towne, R., 318
trancelike state, 48
transfer, 98
transformation, 121
transpersonal psychology, 24, 65–70
Traver, R., 182
Treffinger, D., 74, 87, 89, 123, 124
The Triarchic Mind (Sternberg), 21
triarchies, Sternberg's, 21
triggers and flashes, 53
200 Ways of Using Imagery in the Classroom (Bagley
    and Hess), 126

U

UCONN Confratute, 127
Unilevel Disintegration, 23
University of Chicago Studies, 11–12, 22
The Untouched Key (Miller), 159, 185
Updike, J., 173, 221–222
Urania, 44
U.S. Office of Educational Research and Improvement
    (U.S.O.E.R.I.), 14
*Using Right Brain Techniques to Release Your
    Expressive Powers* (Rico), 55

V

validity, creativity testing, 88–93
Van Gogh, V., 27, 32, 136, 154, 243
Van Raalte, J.L., 333
Vaseline petroleum jelly, 54
Vaughn, S., 287

Velcro, 54
Venn diagram, 19
Vernon, P.E., 7–8
Vidal, G., 50
Vincent, L., 331
Virginia Woolf (Bell), 219
visions and voices, 53
visititation of muses, 44–45
visual artists, 20. *See also specific artists*
    architects and, 135–170
    problem-finding and, 138–148
    without mastery, 33–34
visual arts talent, predictive behaviors, 136–138
visualization, 61
vocation or call, 41
Voice of the Earth (Roszak), 67
Von Karmann, T., 229
Von Neumann, J., 229

W

Wagar, J., 273
Wakefield, D., 63
Waksman, S., 53–54
Walcott, D., 375
Wallace, A., 233
Wallach, M., 11–12
Wallas, G., 46, 249
Warhol, A., 27, 148
Warren, M., 331, 332
The Way of the Actor (Bates), 307
Wechsler Adult Intelligence Scale (WAIS), 246
Weiner, J., 228
Weisberg, R., 58
Weisskopf, V., 226, 230, 243
Westinghouse Science Talent Search, 240
Wetzig, D., 334–335
Whalen, S., 20, 216, 237
Widening Horizons in Creativity (Taylor and Ellison), 7
Wigner, E., 229
will and organic form, 50–51
Willhoft, J., 94
Williams, F., 125
Williams, T., 185, 220
Williams, W.C., 176, 177
Williams Creativity Assessment Packet (CAP), 113–114
Wilson, E., 73
Witness To The Fire: Creativity And The Evil of Addiction (Leonard), 57
Wittgenstein, L., 30
Wittig, A.F., 334
Wolfe, T., 219
Wolfe, V., 219
Wolff, D., 187
Wolff, T., 189
(Woman) Writer (Oates), 172, 194
women

composers, 294–295
    midcentury writers, 193–194
Women Who Run With The Wolves (Estés), 57
Wonder, S., 288
Wood, S., 62
Woods, T., 215
Woolf, V., 50, 59, 60, 194, 195
Wright, F.L., 53, 166–170
Wrisberg, C., 334
writers. *See also specific writers*
    as children, 217–224
    depression and, 194–200
    on schooling, 342–348
Writer's Diary (Woolf), 59, 194
Writing the Natural Way (Rico), 126
Wubbenhorst, T.M., 270
Wyeth, A., 45

Y

Yalow, R., 237
Yodkey, R., 290
Young Authors Conventions, 6

Z

Zakrajsek, D.B., 336
Zeitgeist, 242–244
Zuckerman, H., 375

About the Author

JANE PIIRTO is Trustees' Professor in the College of Education and is the Director of Talent Development Education at Ashland University, in Ashland, Ohio. She is a native of the Upper Peninsula of Michigan and has her undergraduate degree in English and theater from Northern Michigan University. She has an M.A. in English from Kent State University, an M.Ed. in counseling from South Dakota State University, a Ph.D. in educational administration from Bowling Green State University. She has been a high school teacher, a counselor, a college instructor of humanities, a coordinator of programs for the talented, principal of the Hunter College Elementary School, and an artist in the schools in Michigan, South Dakota, Ohio, and New York City. She has served as a consultant and speaker in Europe, the Near East, Southern Asia, South America, and throughout the United States. She has over a hundred publications of poems, short stories, scholarly articles, and eight books, including an award-winning novel and a co-authored book in Finnish. The first edition of this book has been translated into Chinese. She has received two Individual Artist Fellowships—one in fiction and one in poetry—from the Ohio Arts Council, and a grant from the Fulbright-Hays Foundation. She has two grown children and a granddaughter.